The Identity Trap

ALSO BY YASCHA MOUNK

The Great Experiment

The People vs. Democracy

The Age of Responsibility

Stranger in My Own Country

The Identity Trap

A STORY OF IDEAS AND
POWER IN OUR TIME

YASCHA MOUNK

PENGUIN PRESS NEW YORK 2023

PENGUIN PRESS
An imprint of Penguin Random House LLC
penguinrandomhouse.com

LIBRARY OF CONGRESS CATALOGING-IN-PUBLICATION DATA
Names: Mounk, Yascha, 1982– author.
Title: The identity trap: a story of ideas and power in our time / Yascha Mounk.
Description: New York: Penguin Press, 2023. | Includes bibliographical references and index. |
Identifiers: LCCN 2023024750 (print) | LCCN 2023024751 (ebook) |
ISBN 9780593493182 (hardcover) | ISBN 9780593493199 (ebook)
Subjects: LCSH: Identity politics—United States. |
Identity (Psychology)—United States. | Social justice—United States.
Classification: LCC HM753 .M68 2023 (print) | LCC HM753 (ebook) |
DDC 305—dc23/eng/20230613
LC record available at https://lccn.loc.gov/2023024750
LC ebook record available at https://lccn.loc.gov/2023024751

Printed in the United States of America
1st Printing

Book design by Daniel Lagin

To Ala.

Contents

Introduction: The Lure and the Trap   1

PART I

The Origins of the Identity Synthesis

1. Postwar Paris and the Trial of Truth   27

2. The End of Empire and the Embrace of "Strategic Essentialism"   39

3. The Rejection of the Civil Rights Movement
   and the Rise of Critical Race Theory   49

4. The Identity Synthesis   63

PART II

The Victory of the Identity Synthesis

5. The Identity Synthesis Goes Mainstream   83

6. The Short March Through the Institutions   97

7. Dissent Discouraged   113

PART III

The Flaws of the Identity Synthesis

8. How to Understand Each Other   133

9. The Joys of Mutual Influence   147

10. Speak Freely   161

11. The Case for Integration   183

12. The Path to Equality   205

13. On Structural Racism, Gender, and Meritocracy   225

PART IV

In Defense of Universalism

14. A Response to the Identity Synthesis   241

15. A Brief Case for the Liberal Alternative   253

Conclusion: How to Escape the Identity Trap   265

Appendix: Why the Identity Synthesis Isn't Marxist   287

Acknowledgments   291

Notes   295

Index   385

The Identity Trap

Introduction

THE LURE AND THE TRAP

I n the late summer of 2020, Kila Posey asked the principal of Mary Lin Elementary School, in the wealthy suburbs of Atlanta, whether she could request a specific teacher for her seven-year-old daughter. "No worries," the principal responded at first. "Just send me the teacher's name." But when Posey emailed her request, the principal kept suggesting that a different teacher would be a better fit. Eventually, Posey, who is Black, demanded to know why her daughter couldn't have her first choice. "Well," the principal admitted, "that's not the Black class."

The story sounds depressingly familiar. It evokes the long and brutal history of segregation, conjuring up visions of white parents who are horrified at the prospect of their children having classmates who are Black. But there is a perverse twist: the principal, Sharyn Briscoe, is herself Black. As Posey told the *Atlanta Black Star*, she was left in "disbelief that I was having this conversation in 2020 with a person that looks just like me—a Black woman. It's segregating classrooms. You cannot segregate classrooms. You can't do it."

The events at Mary Lin Elementary School, it turns out, are not the continuation of an old and familiar story; they are part of a new ideological trend. In a growing number of schools all across America, educators who believe themselves to be fighting for racial justice are separating children from each other on the basis of their skin color.

Some public schools have started segregating particular subjects. Evanston Township High School, in the suburbs of Chicago, now offers calculus classes reserved for students who "identify as Black." Many more are embracing race-segregated "affinity groups." A school district in Wellesley, Massachusetts, for example, recently hosted a "Healing Space for Asian and Asian American Students." As an emailed invitation emphasized, "This is a safe space for our Asian/Asian-American and Students of Color, *not* for students who identify only as White."

The Fourteenth Amendment and the Supreme Court's landmark ruling in *Brown v. Board of Education* establish narrow limits on the extent to which state institutions can discriminate between citizens on the basis of their skin color. As a result, the adoption of racially segregated classrooms and safe spaces at public schools has inspired legal challenges and even a federal investigation. But what happened in Atlanta, Evanston, and Wellesley has long since become common practice in private schools, which are subject to less stringent restrictions.

At some of America's most elite schools, from Boston to Los Angeles, teachers now routinely divide students into different groups based on their race or ethnicity. In many cases, such groups are effectively mandatory. In some, students are so young that their teachers need to tell them which group to join. At Gordon, a storied private school in Rhode Island, teachers start to divide children into affinity groups—which meet every week and are divided by race—in kindergarten. "A play-based curriculum that explicitly affirms racial identity," wrote Julie Parsons, a longtime teacher at Gordon, which was recently honored for its efforts at diversity, equity, and inclusion by the National Association of Independent Schools, is especially important "for the youngest learners."

Dalton, a prestigious school on New York's Upper East Side that educates the children of the city's elite, has gone out of its way to explain the pedagogical goals that animate such practices. According to statements and outside resources hosted on Dalton's website, antiracist institutions must help their students achieve the right racial identity. A conversation between experts convened by a prominent organization that has worked closely with the school and is fittingly called EmbraceRace points out that when students are young, "even a person of color or Black person might say: I don't see myself as a racial being. I'm just human." The task of a good education is to change that attitude: "We are racial beings." And the first step toward that goal is to reject the "color-blind idea" that our commonalities are more important than our differences.

Of late, some schools have even started to encourage their white students to define themselves in racial terms. Bank Street School for Children, on New York's Upper West Side, for example, is one of the most renowned early education institutions in the country. Proud to be at the vanguard of progressive pedagogy, it serves both as a K–8 school and as a training college that educates hundreds of future teachers every year. Recently, Bank Street has started dividing its students into a "Kids of Color Affinity Group" and an (all-white) "Advocacy Group." The goal of the white group, a slide from the school explains, is to "raise awareness of the prevalence of Whiteness and privilege," encouraging students to "own" their "European ancestry."

It is this new approach to pedagogy that inspired Sharyn Briscoe, the principal of Mary Lin Elementary School, to create a "Black class." Briscoe grew up in the suburbs of Philadelphia, attending a predominantly white private school in which she often felt isolated. When she earned a degree in education at Spelman College, she imbibed a new set of ideas that was meant to save children from the fate she herself had suffered. As Beverly Daniel Tatum, a renowned education scholar and former president of Spelman, asks in a highly influential book, "If a young person has found a niche among a circle of White friends, is it really necessary to establish a Black peer group?" Answering in the affirmative, Tatum recommends that schools ensure that all students make friends within their own racial group "by separating the Black students" for at least some portion of every week.

Kila Posey strongly disagrees with this idea. An educator herself, she believes that "putting my daughters in a class with a whole bunch of people who look like them isn't necessarily going to give them community." Picking and choosing which classmates her two daughters should make friends with on the basis of their skin color, she told Briscoe in one of their first encounters, "is not your job."

When I interviewed Posey about her multiyear battle with Atlanta's school district, she spoke with great composure, recalling facts and figures with the precision of somebody who has become consumed by a righteous cause. Only when I asked her to describe what hopes she harbors for her daughters' futures did her voice betray her emotions. "For my girls, the sky is the limit. They can do and be whatever they want," she said with a suppressed tremor in her voice. After her daughters watched Kamala Harris's inauguration as vice president of the United States, they grew determined to follow in her footsteps. But whatever they might ultimately choose to do, Posey insisted, "they're going to be at the table. And they need to be able to get along with everybody."

The profound disagreement between Kila Posey and Sharyn Briscoe is just one small skirmish in a much larger battle of ideas. In the place of universalism, parts of the American mainstream are quickly adopting a form of progressive separatism. Schools and universities, foundations and some corporations seem to believe that they should actively encourage people to conceive of themselves as "racial beings." Increasingly, they are also applying the same framework to other forms of identity, encouraging people to think of their gender, their cultural origin, or their sexual orientation as their defining attribute. And of late, many institutions have taken yet another step: they have concluded that it is their duty to make how they treat people depend on the groups to which they belong—even when it comes to such existential decisions as whom to prioritize for lifesaving drugs.

THE STAKES ARE HIGH

In late December 2021, a doctor in New York City wrote an urgent prescription for a patient who had just tested positive for COVID. It was for a new drug, called Paxlovid, that promised to decimate the likelihood of dying from the disease. Before filling the prescription, the pharmacist sent back a question. What, she inquired, is the patient's race? The doctor was flabbergasted. "In my 30 years of being a physician," he said, "I have never been asked that question when I have prescribed any treatment."

By the fall of the second year of the pandemic, vaccines were widely available. High-quality treatment options were being shipped to hospitals and doctors' offices for the first time. The end of the pandemic finally seemed in sight. Just then, the rapid spread of the Omicron variant led to a perilous surge in infections. Doctors faced stark choices about how to allocate scarce resources: Who should get priority for new lifesaving drugs like Paxlovid and antibody treatments like Sotrovimab until they could be produced in sufficiently great numbers for all patients to gain access?

Long-standing principles about triage suggested that medical authorities should pursue a simple goal in formulating their answer: saving the greatest possible number of lives. During the pandemic, most countries outside the United States duly followed some version of this maxim. Hoping to channel drugs to the patients they were most likely to save, public health officials looked to factors like advanced age or the presence of preexisting conditions that are known to make COVID much more deadly. But for the past decade, some influential doctors, activists, and experts have been pushing to make triage decisions on the basis of a different consideration: racial equity.

There are good reasons for doctors to take disparities between different demographic groups seriously. A host of studies has shown that historically marginalized communities, like African Americans in the United States and some groups of British Asians in the United Kingdom, have worse health outcomes. But instead of remedying those underlying injustices by ensuring that all patients receive the same quality of care irrespective of their race, large parts of the medical profession have concluded that they should explicitly set out to treat members of different ethnic groups differently.

In an influential series of articles, two prominent physicians at Brigham and Women's, one of the world's leading hospitals, described how they are putting this idea into practice. Bram Wispelwey and Michelle Morse demonstrated that nonwhite patients had, in the past, been discriminated against when decisions were made about whom to admit to the hospital's overstretched cardiology unit. But rather than making up for these injustices by taking the necessary measures to ensure that the hospital would treat white and Black patients equally in the future, their "implementation measure to achieve equity" consisted of "a preferential admission option for Black and Latinx heart failure patients."

Some leading academics have even suggested that we should prioritize racial equity over the imperative to save patients' lives. As Lori Bruce, the associate director of the Center for Bioethics at Yale University, recently argued in the *Journal of Medical Ethics*, protocols for whom to prioritize when medical goods are scarce "should be assessed by a broader lens than merely the simplistic measure of the number of lives saved." Instead, physicians should try to lessen disparities between different demographic groups by implementing "a racially equitable triage protocol," paying special attention to such questions as whether "families will remember being denied treatment or being included."

These ideas and practices help to explain how officials approached key decisions during the pandemic. When public health authorities in the United States were tasked with figuring out whom to prioritize for scarce COVID treatments, they too rejected "race-neutral" frameworks that would only take risk factors like age or preexisting conditions into account. The State of New York, for example, committed itself to adopting medical policies that would advance "racial equity and social justice" in 2021, explicitly noting that this would "not mean simply treating everyone equally." Guided by these goals, the New York State Department of Health suggested that doctors could prescribe scarce drugs like Paxlovid to members of ethnic minority groups even if they were under the age of sixty-five and did not suffer from preexisting conditions. Otherwise identical New Yorkers who are white, the guidelines made clear, should not be considered a priority.

The guidelines adopted by the State of New York are part of a wider trend. Earlier in 2021, when vaccines were first being rolled out, Vermont encouraged young, nonwhite patients without preexisting conditions to get shots before allowing otherwise identical white patients to do so. And even though its own models showed that such a course of action would likely result in a higher number of deaths, the Centers for Disease Control (CDC) urged states to give essential workers access to the vaccine ahead of the elderly on the grounds that older Americans are disproportionately white. When a lawsuit tried to put an end to such practices, two dozen prominent institutions, including the American Public Health Association, the American College of Physicians, and the American Medical Association, filed an amicus brief defending them.

The new paradigm also applies far afield from race or medicine. State institutions have started to embrace a similar turn away from neutral rules that aim to treat all citizens equally irrespective of the identity groups to which they belong in a wide variety of contexts. They now explicitly make the receipt of a number of key government benefits depend on such factors as gender and sexual orientation as well as race.

When the federal government made emergency funds available to small businesses that were in danger of going bankrupt because of revenue loss caused by the pandemic, for example, it explicitly favored those owned by women over those owned by men. Meanwhile, the City of San Francisco recently announced a basic income scheme that would provide low-income residents with $1,200 a month. The only catch is that eligibility for the program is restricted to members of one group: those who identify as trans.

Concerns about the role that identity now plays in countries from the United Kingdom to the United States are often ridiculed as an unhealthy obsession with culture war battles on social media. There is an element of truth to this. Twitter and Facebook really do serve up their daily dose of outrage to an increasingly polarized public. And some people who have engaged in deeply reprehensible behavior really do pretend to be the victims of a "cancel mob." But the fact that some of the complaints about these recent transformations are insincere does not make the underlying phenomenon any less real.

A new way of thinking about identity has gained tremendous influence in Canada, Great Britain, and the United States. Fundamental assumptions about justice, the value of equality, and the significance of identity have changed in deeply consequential ways. And while it would be premature to conclude that this ideology has won a full victory, it already shapes the actions of mainstream institutions from the Associated Press to the Massachusetts Institute of Technology, from the American Civil

Liberties Union to the Coca-Cola Company, and from Britain's National Health Service to Canada's National Arts Centre. What is at stake is no more or less than the basic rules, principles, and background assumptions that will structure our societies in the coming decades. Instead of pretending that these changes are irrelevant or imaginary, we need to analyze and assess them in a serious manner.

THE IDENTITY SYNTHESIS

The roots of the new ideology that is changing the key rules and norms of mainstream institutions lie in the transformation of the core commitments of many self-described progressives. The left has historically been characterized by its universalist aspirations. To be on the left was to insist that human beings are not defined by their religion or their skin color, by their upbringing or their sexual orientation. A key goal of politics was to create a world in which we collectively realize that the things we share across identity lines are more important than the things that divide us, allowing us to overcome the many forms of oppression that have marked the cruel history of humanity. But over the past six decades, the left's thinking on identity has—for reasons that are in many ways understandable—undergone a profound change.

In the 1960s and 1970s, a growing number of leftists argued that a theoretical commitment to universalism all too often existed alongside serious discrimination on racial or religious grounds. They also pointed out that many left-wing movements had long been inhospitable to ethnic and sexual minorities. As awareness and understanding of the historical oppression of various identity groups grew, some parts of the left came to embrace the idea that the solution must lie in encouraging new forms of activism and group pride. If some people have suffered serious disadvantages because they were gay or Black, then it made sense to encourage gay or Black individuals to identify with these marginalized groups—and fight for their collective liberation.

Over time, this perceived strategic imperative to double down on identity has morphed into new ideas about the end goals for which the left should strive. Big parts of the progressive movement started to dismiss as naive kitsch the aspiration for a more harmonious future in which "little black boys and girls will be holding hands with little white boys and girls," as Martin Luther King Jr. put it at the climax of his most famous speech. In its stead, they increasingly embraced a vision of the future in which society would forever be profoundly defined by its division into distinct identity groups. If we are to ensure that each ethnic, religious, or sexual community enjoys a proportionate share of income and wealth, they argued, both private actors and public institutions must make the way they treat people depend on the groups to which they belong. A new ideology was born.

Ten years ago, newspaper articles that discussed the rise of this new ideology often talked about "identity politics." As recently as five years ago, many of the people who embraced it would proudly describe themselves as "woke." But the use of both terms has since become deeply polarizing. Nowadays, anybody who talks about identity politics or describes an activist as woke is liable to be perceived as an old man yelling at the clouds. No generally accepted term has so far come to take the place of these earlier labels.

That is a problem. It is hard to have a productive debate about an ideology when you can't even agree on what to call it. So it would be helpful to settle on a name that is acceptable both to its supporters and to its critics. I have a suggestion. This body of ideas draws on a broad variety of intellectual traditions and is centrally concerned with the role that identity categories like race, gender, and sexual orientation play in the world. So I will, for the most part, refer to it as the "identity synthesis."

The identity synthesis is concerned with many different kinds of groups, including (but not limited to) those based on race, gender, religion, sexual orientation, and disability. It is the product of a rich set of intellectual influences, including postmodernism, postcolonialism, and critical race theory. It can be pressed into the service of diverse political causes from a radical rejection of capitalism to a tacit alliance with corporate America.

All of that makes it tempting to assume that the identity synthesis lacks coherence, or even to dismiss the whole thing as a vague cultural "vibe" that will eventually dissipate. Indeed, virtually everything that has been written about this topic so far falls into one of two camps. Either it uncritically celebrates the core ideas of the identity synthesis as a necessary tonic to the injustices of the world, or it summarily dismisses them as a fad that need not be taken seriously from an intellectual point of view. But on closer examination, the ideology that dare not speak its name turns out to have a nature that is all too real. It is time to dissect it in a serious manner. And to do that, we must first understand why it has proven so appealing.

THE LURE

Many advocates of the identity synthesis are driven by a noble ambition: to remedy the serious injustices that continue to characterize every country in the world, including the United States. These injustices are undoubtedly real. Members of marginalized groups have historically suffered terrible forms of discrimination. Even today, women suffer serious disadvantages in the workplace. People with disabilities are sometimes mocked and often marginalized. Ethnic minorities face open vitriol or subtle forms of exclusion. Violent hatred of homosexuals and trans people persists.

Groups that suffered the most extreme injustices in the past are especially likely to continue suffering from the most intractable disadvantages today. The situation of Black Americans has significantly improved over the course of the past half century. Explicit restrictions on their ability to vote or to use public facilities, to start businesses or to marry someone of a different race, have been abolished. A large Black middle class has formed, and African Americans are now represented in the highest echelons of every field of endeavor. But the shadow of the past has not yet lifted. On average, Black Americans continue to earn less and to own much less than white Americans. They are more likely to attend an underfunded school, to live in a deeply disadvantaged neighborhood, to spend time behind bars, and to become the victim of murders and police shootings. The promise of full equality has proved elusive.

Even highly successful members of historically marginalized groups are sometimes made to feel like outsiders. Schools and universities, corporations and civic associations have become vastly more inclusive over the course of the past few decades. But members of groups that continue to be underrepresented in prestigious organizations like Ivy League universities or the executive floors of Fortune 500 companies often have good reason to feel that exclusion has merely morphed into more subtle forms. They field backhanded compliments from older colleagues or face structural obstacles, like unpaid internships, that make it harder for first-generation college students to break into influential fields from politics to the arts.

It is possible to recognize these injustices and fight against them without subscribing to the identity synthesis. Anybody who knows that their country does not live up to universalist ideals like tolerance and nondiscrimination should advocate for the cultural changes and the political reforms that are needed to fix these shortcomings. Pointing out that members of minority groups are at times treated unfairly and suggesting ways to address such injustices does not in itself make anyone "woke," in any sense of the word.

But even though social movements and legislative reforms can help to address real injustices, they rarely do so as quickly or as comprehensively as hoped. Democratic politics, the sociologist Max Weber famously wrote, is the "strong and slow boring of hard boards." And so some of those who are rightfully exercised by the persistence of injustice conclude that we need a much more radical break with the status quo.

The appeal of the identity synthesis stems from promising just that. It claims to lay the conceptual groundwork for remaking the world by overcoming the reverence for long-standing principles that supposedly constrains our ability to achieve true equality. It seeks to do so by moving beyond—or outright discarding—the traditional rules and norms of democracies like Canada, the United Kingdom, and the United States.

Advocates of the identity synthesis reject universal values and neutral rules like free speech and equal opportunity as mere distractions that aim to occlude and perpetuate the marginalization of minority groups. Trying to make progress toward a more just society by redoubling efforts to live up to such ideals, its advocates claim, is a fool's errand. That is why they insist on making forms of group identity much more central, both to our understanding of the world and to our sense of how to act within it.

The first step in overcoming the supposed shortcomings of a universalist outlook, they argue, is to recognize that we can only understand the world by seeing it first and foremost through the prism of identity categories like race, gender, and sexual orientation. In this view, even situations that seemingly have nothing to do with identity, like a run-of-the-mill dispute between two friends, need to be analyzed through the lens of the relative social power each of them enjoys by virtue of the respective identity groups to which they belong. Because of this focus on identity as a way of interpreting social reality, parts of the left are now more likely to invoke new concepts like "microaggressions" and "implicit bias" than they are to invoke older concepts like social class.

In a second step, the rejection of universal values and neutral rules also implies a very different set of views about how to fix persistent injustices. Because neutral rules like nondiscrimination laws are supposedly insufficient to make a difference, the advocates of the identity synthesis insist that we need social norms and public policies that explicitly make how the state treats its citizens—and how we all treat each other—depend on the identity group to which they belong. If we are to overcome the long legacy of discrimination, they claim, it is imperative that members of marginalized groups be treated with special consideration.

The identity synthesis calls attention to real injustices. It gives people who feel marginalized or mistreated a language in which to express their experiences. And it affords its followers the sense of being part of a grand historical movement that will make the world a better place. All of this helps to explain why it is so alluring, especially to the young and idealistic.

But sadly, the identity synthesis will ultimately prove counterproductive. Despite the good intentions of its proponents, it undermines progress toward genuine equality between members of different groups. In the process, it also subverts other goals we all have reasons to care about, like the stability of diverse democracies. Despite its allure, the identity synthesis turns out to be a trap.

THE TRAP

It would be a mistake to dismiss the identity synthesis as incoherent, much less to vilify those who advocate for it as immoral. The new focus on categories of group identity like race, gender, and sexual orientation is motivated by disappointment and anger at the persistence of real injustices. Most of the people who embrace it genuinely aspire to make the world a better place.

And yet I have grown convinced that the identity synthesis will prove deeply counterproductive. The reasons for its rise may be understandable, the motives of its advocates impeccable. But even the best of people can inadvertently do real damage—and the actual influence of this new ideology is likely to make us stray from, not guide us toward, the kind of society to which we all have reason to aspire.

As social psychologists have demonstrated again and again, drawing lines between different groups seems to come naturally to members of our species. We are capable of great courage and altruism when called upon to assist members of our own group, but also of terrifying disregard and cruelty when confronted with people whom we think of as members of another group. Any decent ideology must have an account of how to attenuate the ill effects of such conflicts. One key problem with the identity synthesis is that it fails to do so.

While humans will always retain a tendency to draw distinctions between "us" and "them," the criteria for who is included in the in-group, and how members of the out-group are treated, are deeply dependent on context. When I encounter somebody who stems from a different ethnic group, was born into a different religious community, and lives in a different part of the country, I can think of her as having nothing in common with me. But I can also recognize that we are compatriots, agree on important political ideals, and share the fact of our humanity. Only if most people choose the latter path will diverse societies be able to sustain enough solidarity to treat all of their members with respect and consideration.

Far-right ideologies are so dangerous because they discourage people from widening their circle of sympathy in this manner. Placing specific ethnic or cultural identities on a pedestal, they encourage their followers to value their group over the rights of outsiders or the claims of universal human solidarity. My concern about the identity synthesis is that, in its own way, it too makes it harder for people to broaden their allegiances beyond a particular identity in a way that can sustain stability, solidarity, and social justice.

Pedagogical approaches like the fashionable exhortation to "embrace race" encourage young people to define themselves in terms of the distinct racial, religious, and sexual groups into which they are born. Meanwhile, public policies like the "race-sensitive" protocols for medical triage give citizens a strong incentive to fight for the collective interests of their own groups. Taken together, these kinds of norms and policies are likely to create a society composed of warring tribes rather than cooperating compatriots, with each group engaged in a zero-sum competition with every other group.

The identity synthesis is a political trap, making it harder to sustain diverse societies whose citizens trust and respect each other. It is also a personal trap, one that makes misleading promises about how to gain the sense of belonging and social recognition that most humans naturally seek. In a society composed of rigid ethnic, gender, and sexual communities, the pressure for people to define themselves by virtue of the identity group to which they supposedly belong will be enormous. But the promise of recognition will prove illusory for a great number of people.

A society that encourages all of us to see the world through the ever-present prism of identity will make it especially hard for people who don't neatly fit into one ethnic or cultural group to develop a sense of belonging. The rapidly growing number of mixed-race people in the United States, the United Kingdom, and many other democracies, for example, may find that none of the communities from which they descend consider them "real" or "authentic" members.

Others will chafe under the expectations of such a society because they do not wish to make their membership in some group they did not choose so central to their self-conception. They might, for example, define themselves in terms of their individual tastes and temperaments, their artistic predilections, or their sense of moral duty toward all humanity. People with a wide variety of personal beliefs and religious convictions are likely to feel alienated in a society that most prizes a form of self-conscious identification with some group into which they were born.

Others still are going to take up the call to conceive of themselves, first and foremost, as members of some ethnic, gender, or sexual group with great enthusiasm, hoping that this will allow them to be recognized and appreciated for who they truly are. But since all of us are much more than the matrix of our particular group identities, many are likely to find themselves disappointed. For a culture that thinks of people primarily in relation to some collective is incapable of seeing and affirming its members in all of their glorious individuality. It is surely necessary for a society to communicate respect for all of its members, irrespective of their race or origin, for them to feel a sense of belonging and social recognition. But it does not follow that most people will succeed in gaining such a sense of belonging and social recognition by making their membership in these kinds of identity groups central to their personal sense of self.

The identity synthesis has come to exert tremendous influence over a stunningly short span of time. As a result, the most common criticisms of it center on its excesses. Many people are enraged by an increasingly censorious culture that stifles our ability to have serious debates about urgent social and cultural issues. Accusations on social media are shared by millions of people before anybody has the time to ascertain their veracity. Especially when people run afoul of the "right" way of talking about group identities—including gender, disability, and sexual orientation as well as race—they can find themselves shamed or fired with little regard to whether their actions were terrible or trivial, deliberate or inadvertent. And though the stories that garner attention from major media outlets usually involve celebrities, most victims are ordinary people who never set out to court controversy.

I share these worries. But at the most fundamental level, my concern about the identity synthesis is not about the ways in which it has "gone too far." Rather, it is that the identity synthesis is, even at its best, likely to lead to a society that fundamentally violates my most fundamental values and my most ardent aspirations for the future. The lure that attracts so many people to the identity synthesis is a desire to overcome persistent injustices and create a society of genuine equals. But the likely outcome of implementing this ideology is a society in which an unremitting emphasis on our differences pits rigid identity groups against each other in a zero-sum battle for resources and recognition—a society in which all of us are, whether we want to or not, forced to define ourselves by the groups into which we happen to be born. That's what makes the identity synthesis a trap.

A trap has three key attributes. It usually contains some kind of lure. It is usually capable of ensnaring people even if they are smart or noble. And it usually subverts the goals of those who get caught up in it, making it impossible for them to accomplish what they set out to do.

The new ideas about identity share all three attributes. They are so alluring because they promise to fight injustice. They ensnare smart people who are full of good intentions. And yet they are likely to make the world a worse place—both for members of historically dominant and for members of historically marginalized groups.

WHY THE IDENTITY TRAP IS WORTH WORRYING (AND WRITING) ABOUT

The most striking political development of the past decade has been the rise of the illiberal right. As I chronicled in my last two books, *The People vs. Democracy* and *The Great Experiment*, right-wing parties that once paid allegiance to basic rules and norms of constitutional democracies have gradually embraced a form of authoritarian populism that presents an acute danger to the survival of our political system. Today, dangerous demagogues continue to pose an existential threat to democracies from India to Hungary and the United States.

Why, then, should anybody care about the spread of a well-meaning ideology, like the identity synthesis, that has as its stated goal the fight against injustices that are all too real? Doesn't the subject of this book pale in comparison to the urgency of fighting demagogues like Narendra Modi and Donald Trump? And might warnings about the dangers of the identity trap not give succor to those who pose a much greater threat, especially because many of them already exploit fears about "woke activists"? These are important questions, and I thought about them seriously before embarking on this project. And yet four reasons convinced me of the urgency of writing *The Identity Trap*.

For a long time, the rise of the far right was widely overlooked. But since 2016, it has come to stand at the very center of public discourse across Western democracies. Over the past decade, there has been a deluge of scholarly and journalistic work about every aspect of right-wing populism. I myself have devoted a radio documentary, two books, a dozen academic articles and policy reports, about a hundred episodes of my podcast, and well over a thousand op-eds, reported articles, keynote speeches, and television interviews to the topic. Though far from defeated, the phenomenon is, by now, reasonably well understood. The identity synthesis, by contrast, remains oddly unexplored territory. There is a lot of shouting about it on social media and cable news. But so far, there is surprisingly little work that tells the story of its rise, explains the reasons for its appeal, and seriously assesses the effect it is having on the world. The aspiration to change that was my first impetus to write this book.

Second, the issues raised by the debate over the identity synthesis matter in and of themselves. It makes a big difference whether the prevailing intellectual framework for understanding the world sheds light or sows confusion. It is important how children who belong to one identity group are taught to perceive those who belong to other identity groups. And it is hardly trivial whether, in the middle of a once-in-a-century pandemic, the state prioritizes adherence to the strictures of a new and untested ideology over the saving of lives.

Third, the identity synthesis is likely to prove counterproductive to many of the causes about which its advocates have good reason to care. An atmosphere of misplaced reverence for the core claims of this new ideology makes it hard for well-meaning critics to point out instances when its suggested solutions cause real damage—whether directly, because the policies it encourages are liable to worsen the fate of the most disadvantaged, or indirectly, because the confrontational framing it encourages makes it hard to sustain public support for policies that actually do improve people's lives.

And finally, right-wing populism and the identity trap feed on each other. The widespread horror at the election of Donald Trump accelerated the takeover of the identity synthesis in many elite institutions. But demagogues thrive when societies are deeply polarized and decision makers are out of touch with the views of average citizens. While the advocates of the identity synthesis often point to serious problems that do urgently need to be remedied, the principles they champion and the solutions they offer are likely to drive more voters into the arms of extremists.

Both the demagogues who have won a lot of political power over the past decade and the advocates of the identity synthesis who have gained a lot of cultural power are going for an all-out victory. But it is unlikely that far-right populists will ever wrest control of universities, major foundations, or movie studios. And it is equally unlikely that fervent proponents of the identity synthesis will win a majority in parliament or be elected to the White House. And so the growing dominance of the identity synthesis in the cultural institutions of developed democracies is likely to go hand in hand with the growing strength of dangerous demagogues in electoral politics.

Right-wing populists and the advocates of the identity synthesis see each other as mortal enemies. In truth, each is the yin to the other's yang. The best way to beat one is to oppose the other—and that's why everyone who cares about the survival of free societies should vow to fight both.

THE GREAT ESCAPE

Once you are caught in a trap, it becomes difficult to get out. Thankfully, the identity trap has not yet snapped shut. While the ideas and the assumptions of the identity synthesis have started to influence mainstream institutions, many people remain deeply skeptical of them. There is enough time to make an escape. My goal in this book is to explain the nature of the identity trap, to set out why it is so urgent for us to make that escape, and to show how we can do so.

In the first part of the book, I tell the curious story of how a set of seemingly disparate ideas came to form a new ideology that by around 2010 would prove highly influential in leading universities. Many critics of so-called wokeness have argued that it is a form of "cultural Marxism." But the true history of the identity synthesis turns out to be more surprising. It features the rejection of grand narratives, including both liberalism and Marxism, by postmodern thinkers such as Michel Foucault; an embrace of the need for intellectuals to speak on behalf of oppressed groups by adopting a form of "strategic essentialism" by postcolonial thinkers such as Gayatri Chakravorty Spivak; and the rejection of the key values of the civil rights movement, including the goal of racial integration, by critical race theorists such as Derrick Bell.

In 2010, the identity synthesis held significant sway in universities but had no more than marginal importance in mainstream culture. By 2020, it had reshaped some of the most powerful institutions in the country. In part II, I tell the story of how a seemingly niche academic theory could gain so much influence over the course of a single decade. The growth of social media inspired the rise of a popularized version of the identity synthesis that transformed the ideas of serious thinkers into simplistic memes and slogans. The incentives created by new forms of distribution turned legacy media outlets into loudspeakers for this new ideology. College graduates deeply steeped in its ideals spread the identity synthesis to some of the world's most powerful institutions as part of a "short march through the institutions." And finally, the election of Donald Trump supercharged well-founded concerns about threats to minority groups, making it seem disloyal for progressives to criticize any ideas associated with the left and rendering criticisms of the identity synthesis taboo in many milieus.

As the popularized form of the identity synthesis conquered the mainstream, its proponents have begun to push for radical changes in key areas of public life. They argue that members of different identity groups can never fully understand each other. They are suspicious when members of one group are inspired by the culture of another group, decrying such instances as a harmful form of "cultural appropriation." They are deeply skeptical of long-standing principles such as free speech, insinuating that those who defend its importance must be motivated by a desire to denigrate minority groups. They embrace a form of progressive separatism, favoring the creation of social spaces in which members of different communities remain apart from each other. And they champion public policies that explicitly make the way the state treats people depend on categories of group identity like race, gender, and sexual orientation. In part III, I argue that these applications of the identity synthesis are likely to prove counterproductive, eroding the values that make possible a society in which all people can live in free pursuit of their best selves. Subjecting each of these claims to careful philosophical analysis, I argue that there are better ways to deal with the concerns that motivate them.

Many advocates of the identity synthesis feel righteous anger at genuine injustices. But their central precepts amount to a radical attack on the long-standing principles that animate democracies around the world. Thankfully, there is a principled alternative. In part IV, I make the case for the core principles of philosophical liberalism. Those of us who believe in universal values and neutral rules can formulate a trenchant critique of historical oppression and persistent injustice in our own terms. In fact, our convictions have, over the course of the past fifty years, already helped to bring about enormous progress. They now animate the core institutions of societies that, for all of their persistent flaws, do a better job at avoiding sectarian violence and extreme cruelty than any other in history. The key to an aspirational politics that can actually build a better world lies in living up to, not in abandoning, universal values and neutral rules.

The fight over the future of the identity synthesis will be one of the defining intellectual struggles of the coming decades. Thankfully, individuals and organizations that have understood the dangers it poses can make a real difference in pushing back against it. In the conclusion, I assess the likely future of the identity trap and show how principled opponents of the ideology can stand up to it without risking their own careers and reputations.

Naturally, I hope that you will read this book in its entirety. Taken together, its component parts explain both the nature of the identity trap and how to escape it. But I also recognize that you may be more interested in some parts than in others. To those who want to understand the intellectual history of the identity synthesis, part I will be of greatest interest. To those who want to understand the political, sociological, and technological reasons that led this ideology to escape campus and conquer the mainstream, part II will be of greatest interest. To those who want to understand why the ways in which these ideas have been applied to topics from free speech to cultural appropriation are likely to prove counterproductive, part III will be of greatest interest. And to those who are searching for a coherent alternative to the identity trap, part IV can serve as a guide.

There are good reasons why the identity trap has proven so alluring. The right response to the rise of this new ideology is neither to dismiss it wholesale nor to adopt its key premises without serious reflection. It is to subject the identity synthesis to a serious critique—one that is open to taking its most useful contributions on board, but ultimately insists on striving for a more ambitious and optimistic vision of the future.

PART I

The Origins of the Identity Synthesis

All four of my grandparents were sent to prison for their communist beliefs during the 1920s or 1930s. All four decided to stay in Central Europe after most of their family members were murdered in the Holocaust because they were convinced that new, leftist governments would make the world a better place—managing to overcome the prejudices and tribal hatreds that had, during their lifetimes, twice set the world aflame.

By the time I was growing up, in the 1980s and 1990s, their political views had fundamentally changed. They had belatedly come to recognize the cruelty of Soviet communism. Instead of the revolutionary Marxism of their youth, they were now committed to a reformist creed of social democracy that attempted to humanize capitalism by admixing a strong welfare state to it.

But one commitment remained unwavering through those tragic and turbulent decades. As in their youth, they believed that the historical mission of the left consisted in expanding the circle of human sympathy across the boundaries of family, tribe, religion, and ethnicity. To be on the left was to believe that humans matter equally irrespective of the group to which they belong; that we should aim for forms of political solidarity that transcend group identities rooted in race or religion; and that we can make common cause in pursuit of universal ideals like justice and equality.

That is the universalist leftism with which I was raised. It is the universalist leftism that, despite my disagreement with the communist views my grandparents held when they were young, continues to inspire me. But it is no longer the dominant strain of leftism today.

Instead, it has, over the past five decades, become a mark of many left-wing movements that they reject the existence of objective truth or the hope for a more harmonious society that once inspired them; that they proudly embrace the call of ethnicity and religion where they were once skeptical of the destructive force that such group identities might have in the world; and even that they reject the very possibility that people from different countries and cultures could ever truly come to understand each other.

In part I, I set out to discover the story behind this remarkable transformation. Why did the left jettison its universalism? And how did it come to embrace a new form of tribalism that seems diametrically opposed to its historical core? Along the way, I try to debunk some of the most sensationalist claims that are now being made about the nature of the left's identitarian turn—such as the idea that it is simply a form of "cultural Marxism"—and to provide the groundwork for a more profound critique of it.

Chapter 1

POSTWAR PARIS AND
THE TRIAL OF TRUTH

The end of World War II left Europe in a precarious state. It was far from clear whether formerly fascist countries like Italy and Germany would succeed in building stable democracies. The Soviet Union was imposing communist satellite regimes on most nations in Central and Eastern Europe. Weakened colonial powers from Belgium to Great Britain were waging brutal battles to keep control of their overseas dominions. The future looked highly uncertain.

Amid that sense of chaos, the leading intellectuals of the period fell back on a faith that had long inspired the left. They believed that capitalism was irrevocably doomed; that parliamentary democracy was but a smoke screen that distracts the people from the oppression they suffer; that the proletariat would eventually fulfill its historical mission of staging violent revolutions; and that the rightful goal of every politically responsible writer was to hasten the advent of communism. As Tony Judt summarized the intellectual currents of those years in his magisterial history of postwar Europe, "When it came to changing the world there was still only one grand theory purporting to relate an interpretation of the world to an all-embracing project of change; only one Master Narrative offering to make sense of everything while leaving open a place for human initiative: the political project of Marxism."

The appeal of that master narrative was felt especially strongly in France. *La Grande Nation* had suffered grievously under Nazi occupation. Much of the country's political leadership had collaborated with the Third Reich. And though a relatively low-ranking army officer by the name of Charles de Gaulle had managed to turn himself into the leader of Free France by an act of sheer will, eventually saving the country's honor in the eyes of the world, he could not rescue the legitimacy of its establishment in the minds of its intellectuals. To them, the ethos on which the country should build after its liberation was that of the heroic resistance movement, which had counted many communists among its ranks.

Virtually all of the leading French intellectuals of the late 1940s and the 1950s, from Simone de Beauvoir to Louis Althusser, had strong communist sympathies. Jean-Paul Sartre, the most famous and the most influential, was an especially fervent foot soldier. Marxism, he avowed in 1960, was "the unsurpassable philosophy of our time."

But a small cohort of French philosophers and social scientists soon began to have serious doubts. As the turmoil of the postwar years died down, it became increasingly obvious that the promised revolutions had, once again, failed to materialize in Western Europe. With every passing year, the faith that scientific Marxism had invested in the supposedly inevitable process by which capitalism would founder on its internal contradictions looked increasingly anachronistic.

The violent oppression with which the leaders of the Soviet Union safeguarded their power, both within the country and throughout its neighboring nations, was also becoming difficult to ignore. Three years after the death of Joseph Stalin, in 1953, his successor revealed the extent to which purges had decimated the party's ranks in a shocking speech. "Of the 139 members and candidates of the Central Committee who were elected at the 17th Congress," which had taken place in 1934, Nikita Khrushchev announced, "98 persons, i.e. 70 percent, were arrested and shot." When leaked transcripts of the speech were published in Western newspapers, tens of thousands of members abandoned communist parties from France to the United States.

In the heart of Paris, a small band of intellectuals started to wonder where they had gone wrong. Why, even as others finally woke up to the failings of the Soviet Union, were so many of their friends and colleagues continuing to be unquestioningly loyal to the Kremlin? And how could they themselves have been committed to the intoxicating promise of a violent revolution for so long?

The answer that a rising generation of intellectuals like Michel Foucault and Jean-François Lyotard came up with over the course of the following decades went far beyond a distrust of orthodox Marxism; it rejected the hold that all "grand narratives" have over the human imagination. The true lesson of gulags and show trials, they claimed, was to distrust any ideology that offered a sweeping account of what makes the world tick and how to improve it. They set out to critique any set of ideas which assumed that there are universal truths; that some values are objectively superior to others; or that we can make genuine progress toward building a better society.

THE FALSE PROMISE OF PROGRESS

Michel Foucault was a deeply unhappy child. Born into a well-to-do home in the city of Poitiers in 1926, he was too young to fight the Nazis but too old to remain ignorant about the horrors of war. At home, he struggled to come to terms with his homosexuality and clashed with his stern father, who expected his son to follow family tradition by becoming a doctor. At school, he was lonely, suffering "in fierce and lofty isolation." One of the few surviving photographs from his teenage years shows his classmates at the Collège Saint-Stanislas, the strict Catholic school his father sent him to in hopes that it would teach him discipline: "The students pose against a rock face in two comradely ranks, above which, his body twisted as if recoiling from the camera, his gaze inquisitorially querulous beneath pent brows, utterly alone and strange, stands the future author of *Madness and Civilization*."

Foucault's years at university were equally miserable. He enrolled in Henri IV, a famed preparatory school, and was duly admitted to the École Normale Supérieure, France's most prestigious institute of higher learning.

He began to spend his evenings exploring the gay sex scene in Paris but seemed to have few other social contacts. Unpopular among his peers, he once chased a classmate down the hall of his dorm with a dagger, and repeatedly attempted suicide.

Intellectually, Foucault was at first shaped by the fashionable grand narratives of the time. When he studied with Jean Hyppolite, a follower of Georg Wilhelm Friedrich Hegel, he imbibed the idea that history should be understood as the progressive realization of freedom in the world. And when he went on to study with Althusser, who espoused an orthodox reading of Marx's work and passionately defended the Soviet Union against its critics, he embraced the hope that the proletariat was finally about to stage a worldwide revolution. In 1950, Foucault joined the French Communist Party, which was unquestioningly loyal to Joseph Stalin.

Unlike many of his contemporaries, Foucault quickly chafed at the intellectual orthodoxy required to remain in good standing with his comrades. When Soviet papers blamed an imaginary plot of Jewish doctors for Stalin's illness in 1953, inspiring a vile anti-Semitic campaign both in the Soviet Union and in the French Communist Party, Foucault found that he could no longer toe the line. "Over anyone who pretended to be on the left," he would later complain, the party "laid down the law. One was either for or against; an ally or an adversary." Henceforth, he would be an adversary.

Foucault remained a committed leftist until his death. Many of the stances he embraced in his later life—from a petition to abolish the age of consent to complimentary comments about Ayatollah Khomeini, the Supreme Leader of the Islamic Republic of Iran—are horrifying. But the nature of his activism was always more idiosyncratic than that of his contemporaries. Unlike most of them, for example, he enthusiastically supported opposition movements within the Eastern bloc, including the independent trade union that fatally wounded Poland's communist regime in the 1980s.

This combination of a deep commitment to leftist ideals and an abiding mistrust of power in all its guises also constitutes the core of Foucault's work, which started to come into its own over the course of the 1960s. In

Madness and Civilization, his first influential book, Foucault started to question conventional narratives of moral and scientific progress. According to standard accounts of psychiatry, the history of medicine is one of steady advance toward greater scientific understanding and a more humane treatment of the mentally ill. But Foucault, who had been both a patient and later a kind of practitioner in the mental health wards of French hospitals, distrusted this master narrative and its promise of moral progress.

Notions of who is healthy and who is mentally ill, Foucault argued, are not determined by some objective standard of sanity; rather, deviant behaviors come to be considered a form of madness when they disrupt the smooth functioning of the social order. The real point of mental institutions, he suggested, was not to heal; it was to exclude those labeled aberrant. The appearance of scientific progress was an illusion.

Foucault's treatment of the second big topic he studied, the criminal justice system, follows a similar logic. The way past societies punished criminals looks extremely cruel from the vantage point of the late twentieth century. In some of the most vivid passages of *Discipline and Punish*, Foucault described the public and often gory ways in which criminals had once been tortured, tarred and feathered, even beheaded in front of festive crowds. This makes modern practices, which are characterized by the incarceration of the convicted rather than their physical punishment, seem much more humane. But Foucault, as ever, distrusted the appearance of progress. The purpose of the modern criminal justice system, he argued, is "to punish less, perhaps; but certainly to punish better."

Foucault illustrated this by discussing designs for a model penitentiary in the form of a panopticon developed by the utilitarian philosopher Jeremy Bentham. In such a prison, a guard would sit in a tower at the center of a large hall, with the cells of prisoners arranged in a full circle around him. Though he would never be able to observe all prisoners at once, he might be peeking into the cell of any of them at any one time. Never sure whether they are being observed, the prisoners would start to regulate their own behavior in an act of anticipatory obedience. This act of self-imposed discipline, to Foucault, captures the true purpose of the modern criminal justice system.

Foucault's interpretation of the panopticon also came to serve as his metaphor for the functioning of many other institutions, from schools to corporations. The primary aim of modern societies, he argued, is to ensure that as many citizens as possible follow their norms. They achieve that goal by creating conditions that force the socially deviant to self-discipline. The purpose of the modern state, Foucault argued, is "to permit an internal, articulated and detailed control—to render visible those who are inside it." Like the panopticon, the state seeks "to transform individuals: to act on those it shelters, to provide a hold on their conduct, to carry the effects of power right to them."

Foucault completed his attack on conventional narratives of progress when he turned his attention to his third big topic: sex. According to standard accounts of the history of sexuality, European societies have long made strenuous efforts to repress anything connected to sex. Especially in the Victorian era, indulging in forms of sexual deviance, even just talking about sex, was taboo. This implied a solution that was widely championed in Foucault's own circles at the time: If the institutions of bourgeois society had long repressed the sexual desires of their members, progress would consist in breaking down taboos, eschewing bourgeois sexual norms, and practicing free love. It was, many of Foucault's friends and comrades believed, high time for a "sexual liberation."

According to Foucault, this narrative is all wrong. Far from being reluctant to talk about sex, Victorian scientists were obsessed with cataloging what they considered deviant forms of sexuality, creating many of the identity labels that still structure contemporary thinking about the topic. While there had always been gay sex, for example, the idea of a "homosexual" as a deviant defined by a stable set of predispositions is, Foucault argued, distinctively modern. "Pleasure," Foucault once insisted at a conference, "is something that passes from one individual to another; it is not the secretion of identity."

Foucault's rejection of the idea that the Victorians were uniquely prudish about sex also made him skeptical of calls for sexual liberation in his own day. The idea that practicing our sexuality more freely might lead to our liberation, he wrote, presupposed the existence of a "real self" that was being oppressed by conventional morality. But there is no such thing. Rather, the way we think about and experience sexuality has always depended on prevailing "discourses"—the way in which dominant norms and concepts structure a society at a particular point in time—and will always continue to do so. By challenging such discourses, we might be able to subvert the oppressive powers of a particular moment. But this will only lead us to conceptualize sexuality in new ways, which are likely to prove just as constraining.

In an attempt to justify this conclusion, which disappointed and even enraged many of his followers at the time, Foucault gave a definition of the nature of power that was to prove deeply influential. Classic philosophers such as John Locke, he argued, tended to understand power as a tool that the state can wield to ensure that citizens follow its rules. Radical philosophers thought of it as a system of domination that systematically subjugated a particular category of people, such as the proletariat in Marxist thought or women in feminist thought. But as Foucault now came to conceive of it, power is much more fluid and variegated. Because real power lies in the identity labels we use to make sense of the world and the normative assumptions enshrined in the discourses that structure our society, it is "produced from one moment to the next, at every point. . . . Power is everywhere not because it embraces everything, but because it comes from everywhere."

The consequence of this conception of power was a radical skepticism about the perfectibility of the social world. People, Foucault believed, would always chafe against the form that power takes at their particular historical juncture: "Where there is power, there is resistance." But this resistance itself will, if it should prove successful, immediately come to exercise a power of its own. Because resistance "is never in a position of exteriority in relation to power . . . there is no single locus of great Refusal." Even the most noble struggle against present-day oppression, Foucault was warning his readers, would contain within itself the seed for new and equally constraining forms of future oppression.

THE REJECTION OF IDENTITY

Foucault never intended to found a rigid intellectual school or set out a concrete political program. But as his influence continued to grow over the course of the 1970s and 1980s, first in France and then in North America, those who read his work took away two fundamental lessons.

The first was to turn Foucault's distrust of progress into a kind of intellectual manifesto. The modern era, Jean-François Lyotard argued in *The Postmodern Condition*, was defined by the grand narratives of history—from the progress toward reason and rationality promised by the Enlightenment to the inevitable momentum toward socialist revolution proclaimed by Marxism. By contrast, the intellectual predicament of the second half of the twentieth century should be characterized by the gradual recognition of the falsity of such grand narratives. "Simplifying to the extreme," Lyotard wrote in a line that was to prove highly influential, "I define *postmodern* as incredulity towards metanarratives."

For many people who read Foucault and Lyotard, this incredulity toward metanarratives soon came to extend to the most basic building blocks with which we make sense of the world. Metanarratives give people a sense of the broader moral or political goals they should be aiming to realize. The scientific method—itself a metanarrative that must be distrusted, according to Lyotard—gives people a sense of the objective criteria by which they can assess the truth or the falsity of a statement. Those who come to believe that both are based on a big mistake are forced to reject the most fundamental assumptions that ground our practices and institutions, from the veracity of scientific findings to the value of democracy.

The second lesson was a fundamental skepticism about identity categories. Foucault argued that labels like "mental illness" and "homosexuality" are tools of power rather than descriptions of reality. As the years went by, postmodern thinkers seized on this idea to develop an ever more radical skepticism about the ability of anyone to make claims on behalf of a group defined by some common identity.

In an influential exchange, Michel Foucault and another famous French philosopher, Gilles Deleuze, argued that leftist intellectuals had for a long time considered it their task to speak on behalf of oppressed social groups. Marxists had always claimed to represent the proletariat. Feminists had always claimed to fight on behalf of women. But in the age of postmodernism, Deleuze now concluded, "representation no longer exists."

Foucault agreed. Intellectuals who have understood their own limitations would refuse to speak on behalf of the downtrodden. But thankfully, "the masses no longer need [the intellectual] to gain knowledge." It was time to let people speak for themselves.

A REFUSAL OF POLITICS

On the evening of October 22, 1971, with Richard Nixon in power in the United States and a bloody war still raging in Vietnam, two left-wing luminaries met at the Eindhoven University of Technology in the Netherlands for a hotly anticipated debate.

The first debater, an American, looked rather conventional; wearing a gray suit, a dark tie, and large horn-rimmed glasses, he might have been a CEO on his way to testify in Congress. Asked about the kind of society we should be aiming for, Noam Chomsky offered a hopeful vision for the future rooted in a progressive account of what it is to be human. "The need for creative work [and] creative inquiry," he argued, is a fundamental part of human nature. The task of political activists is to allow human beings to realize their nature by "trying to overcome the elements of repression and oppression and destruction and coercion" that characterize contemporary societies. The best way to accomplish that would be to build "a federated, decentralized system of free associations," also known as a form of anarcho-syndicalism.

Chomsky's antagonist visibly came from a different world. His head shaved bald, he wore a light beige turtleneck that went on to inspire the trademark outfit of Steve Jobs. Michel Foucault at first responded to Chomsky's propositions with deceptive modesty: "I admit to not being able to define, nor for even stronger reasons to propose, an ideal social model for our society." Then he went on the attack. Any attempt to "define the profile and the blueprint of a future society without having properly criticized all the relationships of political violence that characterize our society," he argued, "risks letting them reconstitute themselves—even if we are aiming for such supposedly noble and pure ideals as anarcho-syndicalism."

Instead of embracing ambitious political goals that risk turning into yet another wrongheaded metanarrative, Foucault concluded, we should limit our aspirations: "In a society like ours, the true political task is to criticize the game of the seemingly most neutral and independent institutions; to criticize and attack them in such a manner that political violence, which they exercise in obscurity, is unmasked."

Chomsky was visibly disconcerted by Foucault's refusal to embrace a concrete political program. The radical skepticism with which this self-described left-wing militant dismissed the possibility of progress has troubled him ever since. When I interviewed him in the fall of 2021, half a century after their famous debate, Chomsky remained astonished by Foucault and the wider postmodernist position he represents: "I had never met such an amoral—not immoral, amoral—person in my life."

To most audience members in Eindhoven, it must have seemed likely that Chomsky would prove more politically influential. After all, he was the only one of the left-wing luminaries onstage to offer a clear framework for political action. How wrong they would have been. For despite Foucault's refusal to propose a better model for society, it was his rejection of universal truth, his skepticism about the possibility of progress, and his warnings about the power of oppressive discourses that ended up inspiring an ideology that has gone on to transform the left and gain unexpected influence in the mainstream: the identity synthesis.

KEY TAKEAWAYS

- To understand the rise of the identity synthesis, we must go back to its original impetus in the Paris of the 1950s and 1960s.
- Key "postmodern" theorists like Michel Foucault were steeped in communist ideas. But the core of their philosophy consisted of a rejection of all "grand narratives," including Marxism.
- The rejection of grand narratives led postmodern theorists to grow deeply

skeptical of claims to both objective truth and universal values. It even led them to reject stable identity categories, like "woman" or "proletarian."

- Foucault argued against the widespread notion that democratic societies have become more humane in their treatment of criminals, the mentally ill, or sexual minorities. In reality, he believed, societies have merely found more sophisticated ways of controlling the behavior of the aberrant.

- Philosophers have traditionally assumed that formal institutions like states wield power from the top down. But Foucault argued that modern societies exercise social control in a more subtle way. He argued that it is informal "discourses" which determine what people can do or think. This called into question whether a rebellion against existing power relations could ever set people free.

Chapter 2

THE END OF EMPIRE
AND THE EMBRACE OF
"STRATEGIC ESSENTIALISM"

For centuries, a few countries in Europe controlled more than four-fifths of the world's landmass and nearly one-third of its population. On the eve of World War II, the United Kingdom still ruled half a billion people from Sudan in Africa to Burma in Asia. Even smaller European nations controlled vast territories, imposing their power with ruthless cruelty.

Then these empires collapsed over the course of a few short decades. Weakened by World War II, Europe's colonial powers could no longer muster the resources to impose their will on the world. For the first time in centuries, the sun set on the British Empire.

For most of their lives, scholars and intellectuals from the newly liberated parts of the world had focused their energy on fighting for independence. Now they faced a new set of daunting tasks. They needed to create a cohesive national identity in countries riven with long-standing religious or ethnic rivalries. They needed to agree on the economic and political institutions that would govern them. And they needed to accomplish all of that while discarding the vestiges of a Western intellectual tradition they regarded as a foreign imposition.

This process of self-reinvention was all the more challenging because a great number of leaders from formerly colonized countries had been educated in Western schools and universities. Intellectuals in North Africa had usually attended French-speaking lycées run from Paris (Frantz Fanon) and studied at institutions like the Sorbonne (Habib Bourguiba) or the École Normale Supérieure (Assia Djebar). Intellectuals on the Indian subcontinent or the Anglophone parts of sub-Saharan Africa had usually attended schools modeled on the British education system and gone on to study at Cambridge (Jawaharlal Nehru), Oxford (Indira Gandhi), the University of London (Jomo Kenyatta), or the Inns of Court (Mahatma Gandhi and Mohammed Ali Jinnah). Making a clean break from the colonizing powers that had brutally exploited their nations was no easy feat for a generation of leaders that had itself been deeply shaped by their ideas.

Many postcolonial leaders sought a solution to their predicament in the founding texts of long-standing ideologies. Some wanted to base their new societies on the liberal nationalist tradition to which newly independent countries in Europe had turned over the course of the nineteenth and early twentieth centuries. Many more looked for inspiration in the revolutionary promises of Marxism or sought an alliance with the avowedly anti-imperialist Soviet Union. But this too presented them with serious difficulties. For some of the leading exponents of both liberalism and socialism had made excuses for, or even justified, the colonial enterprise. Both ideologies were also built on a moral universalism that, according to key postcolonial intellectuals, did not pay sufficient attention to the cultural specificities of the world beyond the West. As Fanon concluded, "Underdeveloped countries ought to do their utmost to find their own particular values and methods." But how?

For a cohort of postcolonial thinkers who rose to prominence in the 1970s and 1980s, a big part of the answer came from an unlikely place: they turned to the ideas that were fashionable on the Rue des Écoles and the Boulevard Saint-Michel in Paris. The postmodernist ethos of Foucault and other French theorists, they came to believe, could help them dismantle the "discourses" and "grand narratives" that had justified the brutal colonization of their countries, laying the groundwork for a more authentic self-understanding. But to make these ideas useful for their purposes, they first needed to render them capable of directing concrete political action.

FIGHT THE POWER (OF WORDS)

When Hilda and Wadie Said welcomed their first child into the world in November 1935, they sought to give him an aspirational name befitting the scion of a prosperous merchant family. As Protestants living in Mandatory Palestine, which effectively remained under British rule, they naturally looked to London for inspiration. And so they decided that their son would, like the Prince of Wales, be called Edward.

Edward VIII duly ascended to the throne in January 1936, when his faraway Palestinian namesake was less than three months old. But his reign proved to be brief and unhappy. By the end of the year, he was forced to abdicate because of his determination to marry Wallis Simpson, an American divorcée. Disgraced, he lived the rest of his life in exile.

The strange origin of Edward Said's name proved to be prophetic of his ambivalent relationship with the West. Like so many other postcolonial thinkers, he was the product of Western schools and Western aspirations. As a child, he attended St. George's in Jerusalem and Victoria College in Alexandria, following a British curriculum and developing a taste for classical music. Expelled from Victoria in his teenage years for being a troublemaker, he was sent off to Northfield Mount Hermon, a strict New England boarding school founded by an evangelical preacher. Excelling academically, he earned admission to Princeton, where he wrote a senior thesis on André Gide and Graham Greene, before going on to pursue his PhD in English literature at Harvard.

"My whole education," Said would later recall, "was Anglocentric, so much so that I knew a great deal more about British and even Indian history and geography (required subjects) than I did about the history and geography of the Arab world." Even as a young man, he remained the "creature of an American and even a kind of upper-class WASP education." Nothing seemed to indicate that he was about to transform himself into one of the most famous critics of Western political power. "When students protesting the war in Vietnam disrupted a class of his," a left-wing critic has archly pointed out, "he called campus security."

But then the frustrations and humiliations Said encountered as a

Palestinian American with an ambiguous identity began to accumulate. He recalled being forbidden to speak Arabic as a student at Victoria College. He chafed at the representation of the Middle East in many of the classic texts of the Western canon he was asked to teach as a young faculty member at Columbia University. And he started to feel that most of his colleagues and acquaintances in New York did not adequately appreciate the justice of the Palestinian cause.

For the first time in his life, Said now devoted as much energy to politics as to his academic advancement or his turbulent romantic life. He frequently visited Jordan, forging close connections with Palestinian political leaders including Yasser Arafat. On a sabbatical in Lebanon, he read voraciously in Arabic history and literature. Drawing on his newfound interest in the Middle East, he gradually assembled the ideas that would, upon the publication of *Orientalism*, in 1978, transform him from an obscure professor to a famous public intellectual.

Combining his deep knowledge of the Western canon with an embrace of postmodern methods, Said argued that long-standing "Occidental" representations of the "Orient" were responsible for real harm. Explicitly recognizing his debt to "Michel Foucault's notion of a discourse," he claimed that the way in which Western writers had described the East was a key precondition for wielding power over it: "Without examining Orientalism as a discourse one cannot possibly understand the enormously systematic discipline by which European culture was able to manage—and even produce—the Orient politically, sociologically, militarily, ideologically, scientifically, and imaginatively."

Since antiquity, Said claimed, Western thinkers have tried to make sense of a hugely variegated set of countries in the Middle East, the Indian subcontinent, and the Far East by referring to them under the simplifying category of the "Orient." With the rise of modern academia and its Departments of Oriental Studies, this scholarly tradition has come to claim for itself a kind of scientific neutrality. But "the general liberal consensus that 'true' knowledge is fundamentally non-political obscures the highly if obscurely organized political circumstances obtaining when knowledge is produced." The point of studying Western representations of Eastern cultures was to reveal "that political imperialism governs an entire field of study, imagination, and scholarly institutions."

Western representations of the "East," Said argued, have a concrete political impact. John Stuart Mill's and Karl Marx's reductionist view of the Orient once tempted these thinkers to embrace grand narratives that seemingly justified the temporary need for colonialism. Since then, a newer set of ideas about the "Arab mind" has helped to motivate American interventions in the Middle East. The core purpose of *Orientalism* was to free its readers from the pernicious power still held by these discourses.

PUTTING THE POLITICS BACK IN

Orientalism was an enormous success. It has sold hundreds of thousands of copies since its first publication, been cited almost eighty thousand times, and influenced academics in fields from literary studies to anthropology, launching Said as one of the most famous and fashionable public intellectuals in (ironically) the Western world. But while in the pages of *Orientalism* Said makes clear that his deepest intellectual debt is to Foucault, he turned on postmodernism in the years after its publication.

During the 1980s, postmodernism quickly gained popularity in American academia, with French theorists and their disciples coming to dominate literature departments around the country. But the style of "theory" they popularized was highly self-referential and deeply obscure to outsiders. Over time, Said grew increasingly concerned about the "institutionalization and professionalization of literary studies," complaining that his colleagues were fleeing politics to play obscure word games (or, as he put it, "retreat into a labyrinth of 'textuality'").

For Said, the famous debate between Foucault and Chomsky perfectly encapsulated these shortcomings. The task of a critic, he now came to believe, was to "commit himself to descriptions of power and oppression with some intention of alleviating human suffering, pain, or betrayed hope." Chomsky, with his clear account of human nature and his explicit embrace of a theory for what kind of society to aim for, was able to rise to the occasion. Foucault, in Said's disappointed judgment, was not. Because he embraced the "vastly simplified view" that "power is everywhere," Foucault came to see the powerful as morally equivalent to the powerless and thought that any future society was bound to be just as oppressive as the present one. In the end, Said complained, Foucault's account of power merely served to "justify political quietism."

This critique prepared the ground for a more politically engaged adaptation of postmodernism. For many of *Orientalism*'s readers, it seemed clear that the goal of cultural analysis should be to help the oppressed. Said's distinction between the Occident and the Orient implied a clear distribution of moral roles. There was an oppressor (the Occident) and a victim (the Orient). The goal was to change the dominant discourse in such a way as to help the oppressed resist the oppressor. This was, in other words, a form of discourse analysis for explicitly political ends.

The rapidly growing number of postcolonial scholars who were being hired in humanities departments across American universities quickly embraced this political style of discourse analysis. Soon after, researchers who were primarily concerned with topics like gender, the media, or the experiences of immigrants and ethnic minorities also made it their own. And so the new form of discourse critique quickly became a dominant mode of inquiry in academic disciplines from sociology to media studies.

THE EMBRACE OF STRATEGIC ESSENTIALISM

Said and his followers took the first step toward putting postmodernism to work in the service of the oppressed by giving discourse analysis a more explicitly political edge. But postcolonial thinkers who wanted to turn these ideas into a weapon that the "wretched of the earth" could wield against their oppressors still faced a serious obstacle. For when thinkers like Foucault attacked grand narratives, they had not only rejected the idea of universalist values or scientific truths; they had also argued that it is dangerous to refer to people by virtue of the identity groups to which they belong. Labels like "women," "proletarians," or the "masses of the Third World," they argued, are essentializing distortions that will succeed only in perpetuating oppression.

Many postcolonial scholars were especially aghast when Foucault, in his exchange with Deleuze, argued that the oppressed do not need intellectuals to speak on their behalf. As the Indian literary scholar Gayatri Chakravorty Spivak responded, philosophers such as Foucault and Deleuze could take their own social standing for granted. As a result, they did not realize that the people with whom she was most concerned had fewer resources and enjoyed less social recognition than the kinds of male white workers who could, in the estimation of Parisian intellectuals, speak for themselves. In countries like India, she concluded in her most famous article, the subaltern cannot speak.

This presented Spivak with a serious dilemma. Born in Calcutta in 1942, she was educated at St. John's Diocesan Girls' School and Presidency College before moving to the United States for a doctoral degree at Cornell University. As a young scholar, she was deeply attracted to postmodern authors including Foucault and made a name for herself by writing the introduction to the first English edition of Jacques Derrida's *On Grammatology*, another seminal work in the tradition. Her commitment to the postmodern project of dismantling dominant discourses ran deep, and she recognized that this necessitated a radical skepticism about basic conceptual categories, including those of identity. And yet she also felt that her own experiences of marginalization as an Indian woman gave her a moral responsibility to speak on behalf of the groups to which she belonged. How to square that circle?

In an interview with an Australian feminist, Spivak offered an answer that was to gain tremendous influence over the coming years. The role and the situation of intellectuals in Asia, she argued, was very different from that in Europe. Whereas French intellectuals could choose to "abdicate" their responsibilities, scholars like Spivak did not enjoy the same luxury. The key to doing better, she argued, was to embrace identity markers that could prove useful in practice even if they might be suspect in theory. "I think we have to choose again strategically," she suggested, "not universal discourse but essentialist discourse. . . . I must say I am an essentialist from time to time."

Spivak's interlocutor seemed surprised and perhaps a little confused by this proposition. How, she asked, is it possible to use essentialist concepts without becoming committed to them? "My search is not a search for coherence," Spivak replied. In theoretical terms, she admitted, "it's absolutely on target to take a stand against the discourses of essentialism. . . . But *strategically* we cannot."

To clear up the confusion, Spivak gave a concrete example. On theoretical grounds, she admitted, it might be wrong to say that women are defined by having a clitoris. But because "the other side [defines] us genitally," it made sense, for practical purposes, to make the fact of having a clitoris the basis for a common self-definition as women: "You pick up the universal that will give you the power to fight against the other side." Though doing so involves giving up on one's "theoretical purity," it's a price worth paying to avoid becoming unwittingly complicit in the West's "narratives of exploitation."

These few cryptic remarks quickly took on a life of their own. Faced with the problem of how to speak on behalf of the "oppressed," scholars from a large number of disciplines followed in Spivak's footsteps. They continued to wield the tools of postmodernism to cast doubt on any claims invoking scientific objectivity or universal principles. At the same time, they insisted that they can speak on behalf of groups of oppressed people by invoking the tactical need for what they came to call "strategic essentialism." This attempt to square the circle is still apparent today when activists preface their remarks by acknowledging that race (or gender or ability status) "is a social construct," before going on to make surprisingly essentializing claims about what "Black and brown people" (or women or the disabled) believe.

Over time, the intellectual concession suggested by Spivak turned into a kind of political rallying cry. If people are oppressed on the basis of some characteristic they share, whether it be their gender or the color of their skin, there are two possible responses. One is to fight to dismantle the category so that society no longer distributes duties and rewards on the basis of whether somebody is a woman or happens to be Black. The other is to organize political action around this marker of group identity. If some people experience discrimination because they are thought to belong to some category, the idea goes, they have reason to band together to fight against that injustice—and the more strongly they identify with being a woman or being Black, the more likely they are to succeed. That is the course of action that Spivak's tentative embrace of strategic essentialism has, over the years, inspired in big parts of the left.

KEY TAKEAWAYS

- Postcolonial scholars like Edward Said and Gayatri Chakravorty Spivak sought to speak to the challenges facing former colonies from Asia to Africa without embracing the long-standing Western traditions they distrusted. Postmodernism, with its attack on supposedly universal truths, provided them with a key tool for doing so.

- Edward Said built on the kind of "discourse analysis" pioneered by Michel Foucault to critique Western narratives about the "Orient." His aim was to uncover the ways in which a set of supposedly objective claims about Asia and Africa served as a justification for colonial domination.

- Said and other postcolonial scholars eventually grew dissatisfied with the apolitical nature of postmodernism. They resolved to put discourse analysis to explicitly political use by trying to reshape dominant discourses in ways that would help the oppressed. This soon came to serve as a model for an avowedly political form of discourse analysis in other academic fields.

- Postmodern theorists were also deeply skeptical of the validity of seemingly neutral identity categories, such as "women" or "the oppressed." In response, Spivak advocated the embrace of "strategic essentialism." She recommended that activists should, insofar as this might prove politically useful, encourage people to organize on the basis of their group identities.

Chapter 3

THE REJECTION OF THE CIVIL RIGHTS MOVEMENT AND THE RISE OF CRITICAL RACE THEORY

For the first centuries of the American republic, its noble ideals extended to only some of its residents. Native Americans were driven off their land, forced onto reservations, or killed outright. Black Americans were kept in captivity, torn from their families, and forced to work for the profit of their masters. Even after they won their freedom, official laws and informal customs explicitly restricted their rights and movements, excluding them from full political participation and maintaining a brutal system of segregation in the country's South.

As late as the 1950s, African Americans remained excluded from basic public facilities like schools and businesses in vast swaths of the country. Literacy tests, poll taxes, and the threat of naked violence kept them disenfranchised. Interracial marriage was widely abhorred. In 1963, the U.S. Congress contained only five African American legislators. Then the civil rights movement changed the face of America.

Under intense pressure from activists, American institutions put an end to official forms of discrimination. The Supreme Court ruled that it was unconstitutional to maintain "separate but equal" schools for white and Black children. Congress passed new laws banning employment discrimination on the basis of race and ending practices like literacy tests that were designed to disenfranchise Black voters. A number of carefully choreographed boycotts and sit-ins desegregated public facilities from buses in Alabama to lunch counters in North Carolina.

At the height of the civil rights era, many Americans came to hope that these changes would guarantee the equal treatment of African Americans. Once the new laws were implemented, residential segregation would fade; economic and educational differences between ethnic groups dwindle; opportunities enjoyed by children born to white and Black families equalize. In "I Have a Dream," Martin Luther King Jr. hoped for nothing less than to transform "the jangling discords of our nation into a beautiful symphony of brotherhood."

In some ways, the progress the country has made as a result of the civil rights era really is remarkable. Today, Jim Crow is a thing of the past. African Americans have won election to high office in southern states from Georgia to Virginia. Virtually all Americans support the idea of interracial marriage. In 2023, the U.S. Congress contains sixty-two African Americans. To deny that the United States has made genuine progress toward equality is to insult the memory of the millions who suffered open and explicit restrictions on their freedom to go where they wish or marry whom they love. And yet it is impossible to understand the present intellectual moment without taking seriously the reasons why a cohort of Black scholars and intellectuals came to feel bitterly disappointed. For, measured against the exalted hopes of the civil rights era, America really did—and does—fall painfully short.

In the early 1970s, neighborhoods that had once been entirely white saw Black families move in. But because of "white flight" many quickly became almost entirely Black. Traditionally white public schools finally admitted Black students. But because many white parents responded by taking their children out of these schools, yet another generation of Black pupils languished in segregated classrooms.

Even today, the situation remains ambivalent. Black Americans have made real economic and educational progress since the 1960s, but on average they continue to have less income and much less wealth than white Americans. The number of ethnic minorities in the top ranks of the most prestigious American institutions has grown significantly, but the groups that have historically been at the apex of American society continue to be overrepresented in their ranks. Colleges and corporations have become much more inclusive, but they can still feel cold and alienating to people who are the first in their families to gain access to them. Meanwhile, some predominantly Black neighborhoods continue to suffer from compounded poverty and insecurity; a large number of African Americans remain incarcerated; police shootings are disproportionately likely to kill Black men; and social media has given hate speech a much bigger platform. Nobody would mistake today's America for the "beautiful symphony of brotherhood" of which Martin Luther King dared to dream.

As the noble aspirations of the civil rights movement gave way to these disheartening realities, a generation of young legal scholars such as Derrick Bell and Kimberlé Crenshaw set out to understand what had gone wrong. Why, they began to ask themselves over the course of the 1970s and 1980s, were all those intoxicating victories in courtrooms and legislatures translating into so little progress on the ground? And what did that suggest about the ability of deeply flawed countries, like the United States, to make political progress on the basis of universal values and neutral rules? The answers they devised proved highly influential in the rarefied world of legal academia—and eventually they even helped to shape the core tenets of the new ideology that is now in the ascendant in powerful institutions across the country.

DERRICK BELL'S CASE AGAINST DESEGREGATION

After he graduated from law school in 1957, a young Black law student was able to secure a brief audience with his idol: William H. Hastie, a pioneering civil rights lawyer and the first African American judge to sit on a federal court in the history of the United States. Nervously, the young man told Hastie that he wanted to follow in his footsteps: he too wanted to use the law to fight for equality and dismantle the legacy of Jim Crow.

Hastie looked at his visitor with a benevolent expression. He even called his ambition "praiseworthy." But as it happens, he went on, the young man had been "born fifteen years too late." With landmark civil rights cases like *Brown v. Board of Education*, which provided a legal imperative to desegregate schools, already on the books, the only tasks that were left involved some "mopping up."

The brief encounter with Hastie left that young man, who went by the name of Derrick Bell, deeply disappointed. It also helped to shape his intellectual trajectory. While Bell continued to have grudging admiration for older civil rights lawyers like Hastie, he started to suspect that they had fundamentally misunderstood the nature of the law—and the likely future of America.

Bell was born into a working-class family in Pittsburgh on November 6, 1930. The eldest of four children, he was an overachiever from the start. He excelled in school, finished college at Duquesne University, and served as a U.S. Air Force officer, deploying to Korea for one year. When he gained admission to the Law School of the University of Pittsburgh, he was the only Black student in his class.

Even after Hastie gave him the polite brush-off, Bell remained determined to use the law as a tool for social change. After graduating from law school, he joined the civil rights division of the Department of Justice. Then Bell's bosses called him in for a meeting. It had recently come to their attention that he was a member of the National Association for the Advancement of Colored People (NAACP), the most influential organization advocating for the interests of African Americans. This, they worried, might create the appearance of a conflict of interest. To keep his job, he would have to resign his membership. Bell was soft-spoken and unfailingly polite. But he was also uncompromising and more than willing to forgo advancement on a point of principle. Ignoring the advice of friends, he quit his government position and went to work for the NAACP.

In his role as an attorney for the NAACP's Legal Defense and Educational Fund, Bell's mission was to ensure that the major judicial victories of the civil rights era would actually be implemented. Much of his work focused on integrating schools. In city after city, local authorities used a mix of subterfuge and brute force to stop Black children from enrolling in historically white schools. In case after case, Bell sued those authorities to make *Brown v. Board* a reality. All in all, he helped oversee three hundred cases desegregating schools and small businesses.

At first, Bell found his work exhilarating. He was finally fulfilling his ambition of making a real difference by practicing the law. But the longer he stayed in the job, the more he grew disappointed. Often, it took so long for his lawsuits to wind their way through the courts that the young boys and girls he represented had graduated by the time the school they had hoped to attend was integrated. Even then, true progress could prove illusory. As Black schools were dissolved, many teachers who had taught at them for years or decades lost their jobs. And as white schools were integrated, many parents sent their kids to private schools or moved out of the neighborhood. In the end, some of the newly "integrated" schools were still predominantly Black and still suffered from a serious lack of resources; to add insult to injury, they were now staffed by white teachers who often treated their Black students with condescension or outright hostility.

Slowly, a new resolve grew within Bell: he needed to quit frontline legal work and figure out what he really thought about the promise and the peril of the civil rights movement. He swapped his career as an active litigator for a teaching job at the University of Southern California, then quickly won an even more prestigious position as a faculty member at Harvard University. By the time his first major scholarly article appeared, in 1976, he had come to reject some of the most basic assumptions underpinning his earlier work as a litigator, and even grown deeply skeptical about the civil rights movement as a whole.

Drawing on his own experiences, Bell observed that many civil rights attorneys litigating cases over public schools in the American South were guided by an ideological commitment to desegregation. But the Black clients on whose behalf they were working often had different goals. They wanted their children to have access to a quality education, irrespective of the composition of the student body. At times, this even made them oppose efforts at desegregation outright. As a coalition of Black community groups wrote in a letter to a Boston district court that Bell used as the epigraph for his article,

Any steps to achieve desegregation must be reviewed in light of the black community's interest in improved pupil performance as the primary characteristic of educational equity. . . . We think it neither necessary nor proper to endure the dislocations of desegregation without reasonable assurances that our children will instructionally profit.

Bell's article was written in the sober, even painstaking, tone typical of contributions to American law reviews, with lengthy citations to relevant cases often taking up the bulk of each page. But anybody who read it must have recognized that his conclusion was a political bombshell. Drawing on a line of argument that (as Bell himself acknowledged) had originally been advanced by racist opponents of desegregation, he warned that civil rights lawyers were trying to "serve two masters" at the same time. Caught in a conflict between their clients' wishes and their own ideals, they were wrongly prioritizing what they themselves thought was right.

"Having convinced themselves that *Brown* stands for desegregation and not education," Bell complained, "the established civil rights organizations steadfastly refuse to recognize reverses in the school desegregation campaign—reverses which, to some extent, have been precipitated by their rigidity." It was time for civil rights lawyers to listen to their Black clients. And that, according to Bell, also meant becoming more open to legal remedies that would create schools that were separate yet truly equal.

Many of Bell's progressive colleagues regarded this conclusion as sacrilege. But he was undeterred. In his mind, casting doubts on the merit of desegregation was only the opening salvo in a much wider campaign to question the logic and the values of the civil rights movement.

THE (SUPPOSED) PERMANENCE OF RACISM

The great hopes of the civil rights era were founded on an interpretation of American history that, from the writings of Frederick Douglass to the sermons of Martin Luther King Jr. and eventually the speeches of Barack Obama, constitutes an important strain of African American thought. In this view, the ideals of the American founding have, from the start, been hypocritical. Though the Declaration of Independence proclaimed that "all men are created equal," millions of Black Americans were being held in chains. The best remedy to this hypocrisy was not to reject those principles, however, but to demand that all people, including African Americans, come to enjoy their benefits. Though "America has defaulted on [the] promissory note" contained in the Constitution, King famously said, African Americans should remain determined to "cash this check."

King's underlying hope that the arc of the moral universe, though it may be long, will eventually bend toward justice is of course exactly what Michel Foucault would have called a "grand narrative." As such, it is open to all the familiar criticisms of grand narratives that postmodern theorists had developed over the course of the 1950s and 1960s. So it is hardly surprising that Bell, when he became determined to mount an all-out attack on the cautiously optimistic view of American history shared by men like Hastie and King, drew on the postmodern ideas that were then becoming prominent in law schools as well as the postcolonial use of discourse critique as a political tool that was being pioneered in literature departments.

During the 1970s, left-leaning scholars began drawing on the work of Foucault and other postmodernists to attack what they considered grand narratives about the law, such as the idea that the decisions of judges are generally guided by legal precedents or abstract principles. According to adherents of the growing field of critical legal studies, neither broad principles like those enshrined in the Constitution nor particular legal precedents set by earlier rulings were sufficiently determinative to force judges to rule in a specific way. In reality, the decisions of judges were more likely to reflect whim, personal preference, or material self-interest than objective legal standards.

Inspired by these so-called crits, but disappointed that they did not seem to have a strong interest in racial justice, Bell applied a similar set of postmodern critiques to questions of race. The standard, idealistic explanation for the apparent progress of the civil rights era, he now argued, was hopelessly naive. Far from being driven by a gradual process of moral enlightenment or mandated by the principles enshrined in the U.S.

Constitution, the most storied court cases of the civil rights era had, all along, been driven by the racial self-interest of whites.

According to Bell, the real reason why judges sought to integrate public schools, for example, was that segregation came to hamper the interest of white Americans. *Brown v. Board*, he argued, came to be in the interest of white Americans for three main reasons. It helped to ensure that African Americans would be willing to fight for their country in any future armed conflict. It allowed the American South to "transition from a rural, plantation society to the sunbelt with all its potential and profit." And it served America's geopolitical interest during the cold war. With the Soviet Union seizing on racial oppression within the United States in its propaganda, Bell suggested, the major court decisions of the civil rights era were desperately needed "to provide immediate credibility to America's struggle with Communist countries to win the hearts and minds of emerging third world peoples."

This pessimistic interpretation of the landmark court decisions of the civil rights era led Bell to a stark prediction: "The interests of blacks in achieving racial equality will be accommodated only when it converges with the interests of whites." From this perspective, periods of historical progress come to seem like a kind of illusion: "Even those Herculean efforts we hail as successful will produce no more than temporary 'peaks of progress,' short-lived victories that slide into irrelevance as racial patterns adapt in ways that maintain white dominance."

Bell also distrusted the idea that the racial attitudes of most Americans had improved over the course of the civil rights era. "Racism," he contended, is not "a holdover from slavery that the nation both wants to cure and is capable of curing." Rather, it is "an integral, permanent, and indestructible component of this society."

Bell's thinking proved highly influential both for its pessimistic predictions and for what, echoing Spivak's call for strategic essentialism, it implied about public policy. To a generation of prominent scholars, he bequeathed a defiant pessimism about the nature and the future of America. As Bell put the point, "We Shall Overcome," with its idealistic hope that "the truth shall make us free," had become the "theme song of the civil rights movement." But its hope in a more racially tolerant America was fundamentally misguided. While "contemporary color barriers are less visible" than they had been before the civil rights movement, he wrote in the early 1990s, they are "neither less real nor less oppressive."

Bell's skepticism about the ability of the civil rights movement to achieve real progress also had a key implication for politics, one that would eventually come to exert an unexpected influence on American public policy over the course of the 2010s. According to Bell, the kinds of neutral remedies, like desegregation, that had been implemented during the civil rights era would never suffice to overcome the legacy of slavery. Because judges could always reinterpret precedent in keeping with their racial self-interest, it was high time for a "review and replacement of the now defunct racial equality ideology." To win any kind of durable progress, it would take explicit group rights that favor the historically marginalized, such as the policies and practices that, in an effort to achieve "racial equity," explicitly make the treatment citizens receive from state institutions depend on the color of their skin.

THE INVENTION OF INTERSECTIONALITY

While he was a faculty member at Harvard Law School in the 1970s, Bell expressed many of these ideas in the form of a course called "Race, Racism, and American Law," which quickly attracted a significant following. When he accepted an offer to become dean of the Law School at the University of Oregon in 1980, none of the existing faculty members were qualified to take over from him. Instead of finding a replacement, Harvard hired a veteran lawyer to teach a more traditional course on civil rights litigation.

Many students who had been influenced by Bell found this unacceptable. Under the leadership of an outspoken first-year named Kimberlé Crenshaw, they staged a series of protests that were breathlessly covered in the national press. They also flew in a series of academics to teach an unaccredited, student-run course on race in the tradition of Bell's scholarship.

In the years that followed, those young academics—including Bell, Crenshaw, Richard Delgado, and Mari Matsuda—forged closer ties while attending panels and conferences organized by scholars in the postmodernist tradition of critical legal studies. Increasingly frustrated by their colleagues' lack of interest in questions of race, they were ready to strike out on their own by the end of the decade. When Crenshaw helped to organize a summer workshop at the University of Wisconsin–Madison in 1989, she called it "Critical Race Theory" without much deliberation, and the name stuck. A new movement was officially inaugurated.

Crenshaw played a key organizational role in the rise of critical race theory; she also contributed one of its most influential concepts. Even as a student, Crenshaw had been struck by the ways in which different forms of oppression reinforce each other. When she arrived at Harvard, an acquaintance who had just become the first Black member of a prestigious all-male social club asked her and a friend to visit him on its premises. When they arrived at the club, he apologetically asked Crenshaw to enter through the back; the male guest, though also Black, was free to walk in through the front door. "That provided a lens for me for how we as a community often . . . don't have the same vigilance for intolerance of injustice when it comes to gender," she later recounted in an interview.

In Crenshaw's most influential paper, which she published in 1989, she coined a term for the way in which different forms of discrimination can reinforce each other: "intersectionality." She also gave a compelling example. New legislation introduced during the civil rights era allowed Americans to sue their employers for discrimination if they experienced significant disadvantages based on "protected characteristics" like race, gender, and national origin. During the 1970s and 1980s, many women and many African Americans made use of these provisions to protect themselves from discriminatory practices. But as Crenshaw demonstrated, the law as it was interpreted at the time did not provide adequate protection to people who suffered disadvantages because of a combination of protected characteristics.

In one case, for example, five Black women invoked Title VII of the Civil Rights Act of 1964 to argue that the seniority-based hiring system used by General Motors was discriminatory. They were able to show that General Motors fired all of the Black women the company employed during a recession because they had not accrued enough seniority—something they could not have done before because General Motors had, until a few years earlier, refused to hire Black women. But despite strong evidence, the judge refused to offer them relief because the "plaintiffs have failed to cite any decisions which have stated that black women are a special class to be protected from discrimination."

According to the judge's logic, the plaintiffs would need to prove that General Motors discriminated against its employees on the basis of a protected characteristic that was explicitly listed in the law, such as that of being Black *or* that of being a woman. Because the company had treated both Black men and white women fairly, the special burden suffered by Black women was not legally relevant. But as Crenshaw persuasively argued, this created a legal blind spot. "Under this view, Black women are protected only to the extent that their experiences coincide with those of either [white women or Black men]. Where their experiences are distinct, Black women can expect little protection as long as approaches . . . which completely obscure problems of intersectionality prevail."

INTERSECTIONALITY TAKES ON A LIFE OF ITS OWN

As Crenshaw described the term in her early articles on the topic, "intersectionality" was an intuitively plausible concept. It was also somewhat familiar: social scientists had long thought about the ways in which the presence of two causal factors could have effects that went far beyond a mere addition of each individual effect. What Crenshaw had done was to demonstrate that existing legal practices in areas like antidiscrimination law failed to adequately take such "interaction effects" into account. But as critical race theory became more influential in the following decades, and the once-obscure academic term coined by Crenshaw morphed into an unlikely rallying cry for a new generation of activists, its meaning became increasingly broad and amorphous.

At about the same time as Crenshaw was writing about intersectionality, feminist scholars like Donna Haraway were starting to emphasize the way in which each person's experiences depend on their particular constellation of identities. As another feminist scholar summarized her core argument, "The perception of any situation is always a matter of an embodied, located subject and their geographically and historically specific perspective, a perspective constantly being structured and restructured by the current conditions."

This idea became a central component of critical race theory. According to Bell, for example, "a neutral perspective does not, and cannot, exist." Charles Lawrence, another influential legal theorist, goes even further: "We must learn to trust our own senses, feelings, and experiences and give them authority, even (or especially) in the face of dominant accounts of social reality that claim universality."

It is obviously plausible that members of marginalized groups are more likely to have direct experience with certain forms of injustice, such as police brutality. But in the work of some scholars, the idea of "situated knowledge" went much further. To them, the fact that each person exists at the intersection of different identities came to imply that outsiders could, even if they carefully listened to their stories, never truly come to understand, say, a homosexual Latino or a Black woman. In some of its uses, intersectionality thus came to stand for a belief in the profound incommensurability of human experience.

Another common invocation of intersectionality is rooted in its emphasis on the way in which different forms of victimization can reinforce each other. As Crenshaw had experienced when she sought to pay her friend a visit at his social club, successfully overcoming one form of oppression (such as the policy that had once barred African Americans from membership in the club) does not necessarily entail overcoming other relevant forms of oppression (such as the policy that still required women to enter the club through the back door).

This intersectional analysis of the structure of injustice easily lends itself to an intersectional account of the political action that is needed to make the world a better place. To be intersectional, according to this reading, was to recognize that anybody who is truly committed to the eradication of one form of injustice, like gender discrimination, must also be committed to the eradication of other forms of injustice, like racial or religious discrimination.

As the language of intersectionality became popular in activist circles, this tempted some activists to place a very high entry barrier on anybody who wants to participate in a political movement. If somebody wants to join a feminist movement committed to intersectionality, these activists now also expect that person to agree with a set of specific positions about such varied topics as the nature of race discrimination, the injustices suffered by disabled people, and the conflict in Palestine.

In 1996, the journalist Larissa MacFarquhar wrote one of the first profiles of the scholars who had founded critical race theory. After interviewing Derrick Bell, Kimberlé Crenshaw, and other leading figures in the movement, she summarized their key precepts in a series of slogans: "law is subjective," "neutrality is political," "words are actions," and "racism is permanent."

This brief list of slogans obviously can't do justice to the breadth or the subtlety of the work carried out by a school of scholars that was to grow in influence with astounding rapidity. But it captures something important about the key role that critical race theory played in bringing together disparate intellectual traditions, from postmodernism to postcolonialism, and preparing the ground for the identity synthesis.

Scholars such as Bell and Crenshaw were promiscuous in the inspirations they sought but hyper-focused on the topic to which they applied those ideas. In the process, they were able to transform loosely connected ideas into a closely intertwined set of propositions about the nature of racial discrimination in contemporary America. This was to prove highly influential. Soon, scholars working in other fields focused on a particular identity marker—from gender to disability, and from Latino to Asian American studies—came to emulate the key intellectual moves pioneered by the founders of critical race theory.

KEY TAKEAWAYS

- The civil rights movement transformed the United States by abolishing most of the formal ways in which laws and institutions discriminated against African Americans. But beginning in the late 1960s, a young set of activists came to be bitterly disappointed that triumphant legal victories did not translate into similarly radical changes in conditions on the ground.

- Some legal academics started to blame the basic moral framework of the civil rights movement, with its emphasis on universalism, for these disappointments. Derrick Bell, the biggest influence on the new movement of critical race theory, concluded that civil rights lawyers erred in making desegregation the principal aim of school reform.

- Bell and other theorists within the tradition of critical race theory also denied that universal moral principles could help to bring about genuine political progress. On closer inspection, they argued, the apparent progress of the civil rights era turned out to be a function of the racial self-interest of whites. They saw American racism as a permanent condition that might shift its nature but would never attenuate.

- Kimberlé Crenshaw called attention to the way in which different forms of disadvantage can compound. The concept of "intersectionality" captured how existing discrimination law failed to recognize that the challenges faced by Black women cannot be reduced to a sum of the challenges faced by white women and Black men.

- The concept of intersectionality soon took on a life of its own, becoming a shorthand for two related yet distinct ideas. According to advocates of this broader sense of intersectionality, members of different identity groups can never fully understand each other's experiences. And because different forms of oppression reinforce each other, any effective form of activism against a particular injustice also needs to fight all other forms of identity-based oppression.

Chapter 4

THE IDENTITY SYNTHESIS

In the space of a few years, the Berlin Wall fell, the Soviet Union dissolved, newly autonomous nations in Central and Eastern Europe ditched communism, and China liberalized its economy. The few remaining countries that were communist in a meaningful sense, like North Korea, came to look like horrific relics of the past rather than bright models for the future.

The geopolitical transformation ushered in by the events of 1989 soon brought about an intellectual shift that was, in its own way, just as momentous. For a century and a half, the heart of the left's political aspirations could be encapsulated in the hope that the workers of the world would unite. Even during the latter half of the twentieth century, an emphasis on class struggle remained the default ideology of leftist critics of Western democracy. Now, for the first time since the Russian Revolution, they could no longer take their cue from a state whose legitimacy was premised on the promise of class struggle. At first gradually and then suddenly, the center of gravity on the left swung from class and economics to culture and identity.

Ever since the 1960s, the left had started to devote growing attention to questions of identity. Over the course of three or four decades, feminism and antiracism, gay rights and trans liberation, came to stake their place as integral parts of left-wing political discourse. Once subordinate to questions of class, social movements devoted to gender, race, and sexual orientation had won an equal seat at the table by the late 1980s. So when the vocabulary and the ideology of class struggle fell out of fashion after the fall of the Soviet Union, the cultural left was poised for a takeover.

On campus, the ascendancy of the cultural left transformed many traditional academic disciplines. Scholars in the humanities, from literature to classics, started to pay more attention to the way in which the experiences of ordinary people were shaped by their identities. A new generation of historians interested in various forms of social identity, for example, shifted the discipline's focus from the sphere of high politics (which traditional historians had been most interested in) or questions of class (which Marxist historians had been most interested in) to the lives and contributions of members of marginalized groups. Sociologists, meanwhile, became less interested in grand theories about the nature of society and more focused on empirical research about the disadvantages suffered by ethnic and sexual minorities in the United States.

This shift in academic culture was accelerated by the foundation of new departments and academic centers that were explicitly focused on questions of social identity. As American universities started to admit a much more diverse set of students, and social movements focused on race, gender, or sexual orientation gained in prominence, activists demanded a devoted home for the questions about which they were most passionate. Over the course of a few decades, most major research universities in North America founded academic units with such names as African American studies, gender studies, queer studies, disability studies, Latino studies, and Asian American studies.

It is important not to overstate the extent of consensus within, or between, these emerging disciplines. Many Departments of African American Studies, for example, remain split between faculty members who defend a philosophically liberal vision for the United States, like Harvard University's Henry Louis Gates Jr., and those who prefer a more identitarian vision, like Boston University's Ibram X. Kendi. But despite these important areas of difference, the dominant set of views in these disciplines did come to cohere in key ways. In all of them, the prevalent paradigm was deeply shaped by the triple influence of postmodernism, postcolonialism, and critical race theory.

THE MAIN THEMES OF THE IDENTITY SYNTHESIS

Intellectual life on American campuses has, over the course of the past half century, been fundamentally reshaped by the ascendancy of the "identity synthesis." Inspired by postmodernism, postcolonialism, and critical race theory, a new generation of scholars succeeded in welding a diverse set of influences into one coherent ideology.

Despite the real variation within and between different academic departments, this synthesis is characterized by a widespread adherence to seven fundamental propositions: a deep skepticism about objective truth inspired by Michel Foucault; the use of a form of discourse analysis for explicitly political ends inspired by Edward Said; an embrace of essentialist categories of identity inspired by Gayatri Chakravorty Spivak; a proud pessimism about the state of Western societies as well as a preference for public policies that explicitly make how someone is treated depend on the group to which they belong, both inspired by Derrick Bell; and an embrace of an intersectional logic for political activism as well as a deep-seated skepticism about the ability of members of different identity groups to understand each other, both associated with Kimberlé Crenshaw.

1. Skepticism About Objective Truth

All forms of scientific inquiry are (or should be) built on radical skepticism. Even scholarly traditions that believe in the possibility of approximating objective truth have long recognized that humans are never free from bias. Their cognitive limitations, even their crude self-interest, have a nasty habit of intruding on their belief systems. But these traditions also insist that the mechanisms of serious scholarly inquiry and public debate can help to combat such shortcomings. Insofar as academic debates are genuinely open to people of different beliefs as well as backgrounds, and scientists remain free to question the received wisdom, we can collectively make progress toward genuine knowledge. That is the goal of scientific research.

Most adherents of the "identity synthesis" reject this hope. For them, the way in which our ascriptive identities influence our perception of the world goes deeper than such "positivists" are willing to recognize. Building on the skepticism about "grand narratives" and the focus on the dangerous power of "discourses" championed by postmodern theorists like Michel Foucault, they claim that there is no objective truth, just an infinite series of viewpoints. Those who pretend otherwise aren't struggling, as best they can, to understand the world; they are concealing the way in which they exercise power over the oppressed and marginalized.

This thoroughgoing skepticism about the utility of even trying to approximate objective truth has deeply shaped the views of scholars working on questions of race. Mari Matsuda, a longtime law professor at UCLA, emphasizes that critical race theory "expresses skepticism toward dominant legal claims of neutrality, objectivity, color blindness, and meritocracy." This supposedly provides the grounds for a rejection of any set of political institutions, including liberal democracy, that claim to be founded on universal values. According to Richard Delgado, an influential law professor who used to teach at the University of Alabama, for example, "Liberal democracy and racial subordination go hand in hand."

A similar set of views is expressed by scholars who work in other intellectual traditions within the identity synthesis, from postcolonialism to Latino studies. According to Chela Sandoval, for example, the core of "decolonial theory" consists of the "disavowal of Western rationality."

2. Discourse Analysis for Political Ends

Many scholars who are immersed in the identity synthesis are deeply interested in the way that dominant "narratives" and "discourses" structure our society. Inspired by Edward Said's work in *Orientalism*, they hope to put the tools of "discourse analysis" to explicitly political use. Their ambition is nothing less than to change the world by redescribing it.

Over time, such uses of discourse analysis for political ends have increasingly come to focus on phenomena that scholars might, in previous generations, have considered too trivial to deserve attention. In Departments of Media Studies and Comparative Literature, researchers now analyze pieces of everyday culture from sitcoms to TikTok clips. Their goal is both to critique their subtle biases and to have a concrete political impact. By changing how we frame social and cultural issues, they argue, we can help the marginalized resist their oppressors.

This has had a major influence on the way in which activists engage in politics. In virtually every developed democracy, activists now expend enormous efforts on changing the way in which ordinary people speak. In the United States, for example, activists have successfully championed new identity labels like "people of color" and "BIPOC." Prominent institutions such as Stanford have even published long lists with terms, ranging from "guru" to "sanity check," that affiliates of the university should avoid using because they could inadvertently perpetuate discrimination or commit "cultural appropriation" (a newly popular term that describes a broad class of circumstances in which members of one culture use or co-opt elements of the culture of another group in supposedly objectionable ways).

In other countries, the belief in the political power of verbal redescription has even led to calls to change fundamental aspects of a language's grammar. In Germany, for example, activists have long militated against the language's traditional use of the generic masculine to refer to groups of people comprising both men and women (for example, by replacing *Studenten* with *Studierende*). More recently, they have even begun to insist on using a so-called gender star in writing—as well as a short pause, to be deployed before the ending of every gendered noun, in verbal communication—to render ordinary language more inclusive of people who are nonbinary.

3. Doubling Down on Identity

Trained in postmodern skepticism about seemingly neutral values and concepts, many adherents of the identity synthesis like to emphasize that key aspects of the world are "socially constructed." When somebody claims that some influential concept, like private property or the nation-state, isn't "natural," they emphasize that it was created by human norms and conventions. It could, they usually imply, just as easily be changed. On the theoretical level, adherents of the identity synthesis also believe that this is true of markers of group identity, like race, gender, and sexual orientation. As many sociology professors tell their first-year students—and quite a few Instagram influencers like to inform their followers—"race is a social construct."

This creates a serious dilemma for adherents of the identity synthesis. After all, most of them also believe that the best hope for overcoming historical injustices consists in raising the consciousness of members of marginalized groups so that they can fight for their collective interests. How can they both emphasize that race and gender are social constructs and encourage people to identify as, say, Black or transgender? To answer this question, many adherents of the identity synthesis have taken to invoking Spivak's concept of "strategic essentialism." While it is important to bear in mind the theoretical fact that identity groups are socially constructed, for practical purposes the strategic imperative to encourage the formation of identity groups that can become a locus for resistance against domination must take precedence.

Over time, practice won out over theory, and the emphasis shifted from the idea that these concepts are socially constructed to the prescription that they should, to all intents and purposes, be treated as an objectively given fact. This explains how some of the same writers can both emphasize that race is a social construct and talk about the inherent qualities possessed by "people of color" or "Black and brown people."

The embrace of strategic essentialism also helps to make sense of the evolution in the feminist treatment of gender. In their early work in the late 1980s and early 1990s, the feminist scholar Judith Butler, a professor at the University of California, Berkeley, emphasized that gender norms are socially constructed, and encouraged readers to disrupt them in a playful manner. Today, by contrast, many adherents of the identity synthesis talk about gender in a more naturalistic fashion. When they write about babies being "assigned a sex at birth" and suggest that children must discover their "internal sense of gender identity," they often imply that the latter is an inborn and even natural trait.

4. Proud Pessimism

Writers and orators from Frederick Douglass to Martin Luther King Jr. and Barack Obama were up-front in their criticisms of America's shortcomings. But they also insisted that the country's founding principles could, if only they were fully put into practice, guide America toward a better future. The rejection of this hard-won optimism is a key theme of the identity synthesis. For a new generation of scholars, any apparent progress is liable to prove either illusory or short-lived. Racism, as Derrick Bell has repeatedly insisted, is a permanent condition that might shape-shift but has, so far, shown no real sign of attenuating.

Perhaps unsurprisingly given the nature of American history, the most prominent public exponents of this fatalistic position continue to focus on questions of race. African American intellectuals who insisted on the possibility of progress have always exchanged rhetorical fire with antagonists who did not believe that America could improve without revolutionary change. Today, that more pessimistic tradition, which is most powerfully associated with Malcolm X, is being carried forward by widely celebrated writers such as Ta-Nehisi Coates and Ibram X. Kendi.

But this proud pessimism is by no means limited to the topic of race. Increasingly, advocates of the identity synthesis are also applying it to the experiences of other identity groups, from women to people living with disabilities. Academics and activist organizations focused on the rights of sexual minorities have, despite recent changes like the legalization of same-sex marriage, repeatedly claimed that any appearance of progress is an illusion, for example. As Larry Kramer, a prominent gay rights advocate, argued in *The New York Times* in 2018, "For gays, the worst is yet to come."

5. Identity-Sensitive Legislation

Most advocates of the identity synthesis believe that their skepticism about past progress also has important implications for what to do going forward. Because there have, according to them, been no meaningful improvements in recent times, they naturally suspect that the core features of the current political system will continue to make genuine progress impossible in the future. Indeed, many adherents of the identity synthesis believe that any set of institutions or arrangements that does not explicitly distinguish between people on the basis of their ascriptive identities will merely serve to oppress marginalized minorities. To achieve true "equity," it is, in this view, necessary to jettison the aspiration that governments should treat citizens the same irrespective of the ethnic or sexual groups to which they belong.

In this view, any principles and rules that fail to distinguish between the historically dominant and the historically dominated are inherently suspect. Instead of holding on to the universalist aspirations of movements like the struggle for civil rights, governments should explicitly start to treat citizens differently depending on the group of which they are a part. As Richard Delgado and Jean Stefancic write, "Only aggressive, color-conscious efforts to change the way things are will do much to ameliorate misery."

For a long time, it looked as though such a radical break with established practices was unlikely to win many adherents outside campus. But gradually, calls for state institutions to make how they treat people depend on the groups to which they belong began to influence the mainstream. They were increasingly voiced by activists, endorsed by major grant-making foundations, and even championed by presidential candidates in primary elections. By the time Joe Biden was preparing to take on his new responsibilities as the forty-sixth president of the United States, the incoming administration repeatedly touted its commitment to bringing about "equity" through "race-conscious" and "race-sensitive" public policies. Both at the federal and at the state levels, some such policies have quickly been implemented. From government guidelines giving nonwhite patients priority for scarce COVID drugs to basic income programs reserved for trans people, government institutions have started to adopt schemes that explicitly distinguish between citizens on the basis of their membership in particular identity groups.

6. The Imperative of Intersectionality

As originally conceived by Crenshaw, the concept of intersectionality had comparatively modest goals. It aimed to ensure that the law could deliver justice for people who suffered discrimination because they exhibited two disfavored characteristics at once. (As Crenshaw demonstrated, the challenges faced by Black women did not necessarily boil down to a simple sum of the challenges faced by white women and those faced by Black men.) But the term Crenshaw coined quickly evolved beyond recognition.

When scholars and activists use the term "intersectionality" today, they usually think of it as a kind of logic of political organizing. Drawing on Crenshaw, they emphasize that different forms of oppression reinforce each other. They then draw the inference that effective action against one form of oppression requires effective action against all. As a result, intersectionality is now often taken to imply that activist movements should require their members to sign up to a very broad catalog of causes and positions—with the necessary stance on each being determined by the group that is most directly affected.

This interpretation of intersectionality has had a big impact on the nature of progressive political organizing. It has led to a broadening in the mission of many activist groups, which now feel a need to take a stance on important political issues even when these lie well outside the area on which they have traditionally focused. It has led to frequent demands for intellectual deference, in which organizations that represent a particular identity group claim a special authority to determine what stances other progressive organizations should embrace regarding the topics that touch upon their interests. And it has also raised the price of admission to many progressive organizations, requiring would-be activists who agree with the adherents of the identity synthesis on one issue to accept the orthodox views on all other issues to become—or remain—members in good standing.

7. Standpoint Theory

The idea of intersectionality is also at times used to refer to a concept whose roots lie in feminist scholarship about the way in which the male-dominated enterprise of science has historically distorted our understanding of the world. As feminists have rightly pointed out, the marginalization of women has allowed many false beliefs about such important topics as female anatomy or the prevalence of sexual harassment to persist. But over time, some scholars took this claim one step further: they now started to argue that there were key insights about the social world—and even the policies that would be needed to fix injustices—that members of marginalized groups would never be able to communicate to members of dominant groups. "Feminist objectivity," Donna Haraway wrote in an early and highly influential text in the tradition that came to be known as standpoint epistemology, "means quite simply situated knowledges."

Some advocates of the identity synthesis have even come to believe that the important role that subjective experience plays in generating insights about the social world implies that members of different identity groups can never fully understand each other. As Patricia Hill Collins, a distinguished university professor emerita at the University of Maryland, has argued, "Differences in power constrain our ability to connect with one another even when we think we are engaged in dialogue across differences." In this popularized form, standpoint theory goes far beyond an exhortation to ensure that people from different backgrounds are involved in scientific research or political decision-making; it stipulates that there are some important insights that members of one group will never be able to communicate to outsiders.

Over time, this thought has increasingly been translated into the even simpler form in which it is now often repeated in activist spaces. In this way, the legitimate impetus for standpoint epistemology came to be the kernel for the idea that I have "my truth"—one that you have no right to question or critique on the basis of supposedly objective facts, especially if you do not belong to the same marginalized identity group.

CAREFUL WHAT YOU WISH FOR

It was a cold and windy night. An old man was searching for firewood in the forest. He picked up stick after stick, heaving each onto his hunched back. When he was finally ready to return home to his hut, he nearly buckled under the weight. "I can't bear this life any longer," he mumbled under his breath. "May death come and take me."

As soon as he had finished uttering these words, the old man sensed an eerie presence. "What do you want, old man?" the Angel of Death asked. "I heard you call me." The old man desperately searched for words. "Please," he finally said, "would you kindly help me lift this load of sticks onto my shoulder?"

If Michel Foucault had not passed away from AIDS in 1984, at the premature age of fifty-seven, he might still be alive today. And although it is impossible to know what he would think about the way in which the left has transformed since his death, I have found myself wondering whether he might not identify with the famous fable about the old man and death. For the story of Foucault's influence on the identity synthesis is about as good an instance of "careful what you wish for" as intellectual history has on offer.

Much of Foucault's work was inspired by a nightmare. He distrusted simplistic narratives of good and evil. He rejected the idea that anybody could be defined by virtue of the group to which they belong. He was deeply worried about the way in which prevailing discourses exerted power over every single member of society. And he hated the way in which exemplary punishments for aberrations from a social norm could induce people to become their own taskmasters, striving as best they can to discipline their own thoughts and actions.

In the decades since Foucault's death, his work has proven to have an astonishing staying power. Some of the ways in which it has helped to form the "identity synthesis," such as his skepticism about universal truth, would look recognizable to him. But in other important respects, Foucault would, I believe, have pushed back against the ideology his work inspired. He would have recognized that the attempt to reshape existing discourses for political ends, though conceived as an act of liberation, was likely to create new forms of repression. And he would have abhorred the ways in which big social media platforms like Twitter and Facebook have transformed public debate into a modern-day panopticon, with every misstep subject to draconian punishment and all users trying to follow an amorphous set of rules about what they can or cannot say in an act of anticipatory obedience.

If he really did feel regret about the way in which his ideas took on a life of their own, Foucault would hardly be alone. All of the thinkers whose work has influenced the identity synthesis would likely rejoice in some of the ways the left has transformed over the past half century. But to a remarkable extent, nearly all of them have also, at one point or another, expressed serious reservations about the impact that their own ideas went on to have.

In the years before his premature death of leukemia, in 2003, Edward Said became very critical of the way in which the identity synthesis was starting to transform intellectual life in the United States. Identity, he said at one point, is "as boring a subject as one can imagine." Though some leftists had seemingly started to believe that people who belong to a group that has historically been victimized have some form of privileged access to moral virtue, "victimhood, alas, does not guarantee or necessarily enable an enhanced sense of humanity."

The idea that it would serve progress for members of different ethnic and cultural groups to be more defined by their differences than by their commonalities struck Said as particularly perverse. The trend of supposedly progressive institutions "focusing principally on *our own* separateness, our own ethnic identity, culture, and traditions" wrongly suggested that members of marginalized groups were somehow "unable to share in the general riches of human culture"; in the description of the literary critic Adam Shatz, this struck Said as a kind of "apartheid pedagogy." In the end, Said therefore embraced a form of universalism that stood in direct conflict with some of the core tenets of the identity synthesis: "Marginality and homelessness are not, in my opinion, to be gloried in; they are to be brought to an end, so that more, and not fewer, people can enjoy the benefits of what has for centuries been denied the victims of race, class, or gender."

Spivak was, if anything, even more direct in her complaints about the way in which her own work had helped to shape a new culture on campus. In one interview, she emphasized her admiration for the "political use of humor" that African Americans have long deployed in their fight against oppression. That kind of "robust autocritical humor," she remarked, is often missing in the "university identity wallahs" of today.

Observing how often scholars and activists invoked her notion of strategic essentialism to make confident proclamations about the views and the preferences of ill-defined groups, Spivak even came to rue the term she herself had coined. The idea of strategic essentialism, she lamented, "simply became the union ticket for essentialism. As to what is meant by strategy, no one wondered about that. So, as a phrase, I have given up on it."

Crenshaw has been less critical of the form the identity synthesis now takes. But she too has mixed feelings about the way in which her most influential contribution, the idea of "intersectionality," has evolved since she coined it. As she told Jane Coaston in a 2019 interview for *Vox*, she has on occasion had an "out-of-body experience" when journalists or activists talk about intersectionality. "Sometimes I've read things that say, 'Intersectionality, blah, blah, blah,' and then I'd wonder, 'Oh, I wonder whose intersectionality that is,' and then I'd see me cited, and I was like, 'I've never written that. I've never said that. That is just not how I think about intersectionality.'"

KEY TAKEAWAYS

- Since the 1960s, parts of the American left paid growing attention to social issues connected to oppression on the basis of race, gender, and sexuality. When the Soviet Union collapsed in the early 1990s, the left could no longer look to a powerful country committed to class struggle. It became increasingly focused on questions of culture and identity.

- In the last decades of the twentieth century, this new emphasis started to transform intellectual life on campus. It led to a renewed focus on the experiences of marginalized groups in both the humanities and the social sciences. This transformation was further accelerated by the rise of a new set of academic centers and departments devoted to studying questions of identity, such as gender studies, media studies, African American studies, Latino studies, and disability studies.

- Gradually, the triple influence of postmodernism, postcolonialism, and critical race theory gave rise to an "identity synthesis." This new ideology was defined by seven major themes: a rejection of the existence of objective truth; the use of a form of discourse analysis for explicitly political ends; an embrace of strategic essentialism; a deep pessimism about the possibility of overcoming racism or other forms of bigotry; a preference for public policies that explicitly distinguish between citizens on the basis of the group to which they belong; an embrace of intersectionality as a strategy for political organizing; and a deep skepticism about the ability of members of different groups to communicate with each other.

- The identity synthesis was inspired by major thinkers including Michel Foucault, Edward Said, Gayatri Chakravorty Spivak, Derrick Bell, and Kimberlé Crenshaw. But ironically, many of these thinkers have expressed serious misgivings about the way in which their work has transformed the left.

PART II

The Victory of the Identity Synthesis

Over the course of a few decades, the identity synthesis transformed intellectual life on American campuses. But even to its most passionate proponents, it looked unlikely that these ideas might also come to transform large swaths of American society.

When Kimberlé Crenshaw published an article celebrating the twentieth anniversary of critical race theory, she sounded pessimistic about its prospects outside of campus. She allowed herself a little joy about Barack Obama's recent election as the first Black president of the United States. Then she quickly went on to warn that his ascent was likely to make the public less receptive to the core ideas of critical race theory: "Broad segments of the population seemed to believe that with Barack Obama now in the White House, the chapter on race could at last be closed."

This is in part because, according to Crenshaw, Obama himself came close to denying the role of race in American society. Obama's famous campaign speech on race, for example, acknowledged "racial injury" but ultimately advocated "that we rise above it to address 'universal' interests." This, Crenshaw maintained, put Obama "at odds with key elements of CRT." As a result, Crenshaw lamented, "critiques of racism are losing ground."

Crenshaw need not have worried. Over the course of the 2010s, the American view of identity took a dizzying turn. In the span of a decade, ideas that had once seemed unlikely to escape the ivory tower transmuted into a popular ideology with real influence in the mainstream. At the beginning of the decade, terms like "white privilege" and "structural racism" were barely recognizable outside rarefied intellectual circles. Activist organizations like the American Civil Liberties Union (ACLU) doggedly defended universal principles like free speech. Political campaigns by Democratic candidates avoided calling for welfare programs that would explicitly be reserved for particular ethnic or sexual communities.

Over the course of the following decade, America underwent an astonishing transformation. By 2020, *The New York Times* and *The Washington Post* regularly invoked key concepts associated with the identity synthesis, including both "white privilege" and "structural racism." The ACLU had abandoned parts of its historical mission, refusing to assist defendants whose speech it deemed too offensive. Popularizers of the identity synthesis like Robin DiAngelo and Ibram X. Kendi had become bestselling authors and were making frequent appearances on prime-time television. In the 2016 and 2020 presidential campaigns, Democratic candidates embraced the language of the identity synthesis and promised a slew of policies that would make the receipt of state assistance conditional on the group to which a would-be beneficiary belongs.

As I show in the next three chapters, these remarkable changes in the self-understanding of large segments of the American elite were a product of broader political, sociological, and technological forces. The rise of social media prompted young people to focus on their ethnic, sexual, and gender identities, even empowering them to create new labels by which to identify. Legacy media outlets had a strong incentive to embrace a popularized version of the identity synthesis because of their growing reliance on going viral on Twitter and Facebook, radically transforming the kind of content they published. Students steeped in the identity synthesis at elite universities rose through the ranks of corporations, nonprofit organizations, and congressional offices in a "short march through the institutions," lastingly changing their mode of operation. In a final step, the rise of a genuine threat in the form of Donald Trump increased the pressure to conform within many left-leaning institutions, making it easier for a minority of ideological hard-liners to impose their views on everybody else.

Chapter 5

THE IDENTITY SYNTHESIS
GOES MAINSTREAM

n the spring of 2014, I taught a first-year seminar called "Democracy in the Digital Age" at Harvard University. My students came from every state in the country and many parts of the world. They were planning on majoring in every subject from history to physics. But they also had a few things in common: they were smart, ambitious, unfailingly polite, and deeply convinced that the internet would make the world a better place.

It is now difficult to remember to what extent the conviction that the internet and social media were forces for good had been nurtured by virtually everything my students read as they went through middle and high schools. This positive view first took shape in the late 1990s, when a few writers made a name for themselves as internet evangelists. Thomas Friedman's *The Lexus and the Olive Tree*, published in 1999, is a classic of the genre. "A three-minute call ... between New York and London cost $300 in 1930. Today it is almost free through the Internet," Friedman pointed out. Because technologies like internet telephony reduced the cost of communicating with far-flung people, encouraging them to get to know each other and exchange ideas, they would "weave the world together."

The early boosters of the internet assumed that the radically reduced cost of communication would result in people being more likely to connect across traditional boundaries. Friedman's elderly mother could play bridge with people in France. Democracy activists in Chad could connect with those in Croatia. Along the way, people who previously had little contact with each other might discover that they have a lot in common, uniting in pursuit of shared causes. Costless communication would usher in an age of dialogue, tolerance, and grassroots resistance to dictatorial regimes.

In the years since I first taught that course on democracy and the internet, many of the hopes my students harbored a decade ago have been dashed. The idea that social media would lead people to bridge long-standing divides looks naive in the wake of the rise of polarization and the ascent of far-right populists, the bloody failure of the Arab Spring, and the consolidation of increasingly repressive regimes in Russia and China. Given the freedom to communicate with anybody in the world, most people have chosen to talk to those who already belong to the same identity group.

The internet was supposed to create a world in which distinctions of group identity mattered less than ever before. Instead, it has created a world of proliferating and often competing identities, in which an ever larger number of people passionately define themselves by their membership in ethnic, gender, or sexual groups. The real story about the impact of social media over the course of the 2010s is about how it influenced the way our societies function—in both good ways and bad—by transforming how millions of people conceive of themselves, hugely increasing our collective focus on "identity" in all its forms. And as it happens, that is also a key part in the fascinating story of how the identity synthesis could escape campus and enter the mainstream.

HOW A FORGOTTEN PLATFORM HELPED TO BIRTH A NEW POLITICAL CULTURE

Pundits and political scientists who study the effects of social media tend to focus on Twitter and Facebook, or perhaps on Instagram and TikTok. All of these platforms played a key role in forging a new internet culture. But when the history of the way in which new technologies transformed Western culture in the second decade of the twenty-first century is written some fifty or a hundred years from now, one important and highly illustrative chapter will be about a comparatively small "microblogging platform" that has, since its heyday, virtually vanished from public consciousness: Tumblr.

Founded in 2007 by David Karp, the service allowed its mostly anonymous users to produce or curate just about every type of content, from written posts to visual memes and short videos. Features that were still relatively novel at the time, like topic tags and the ability to repost content with the click of a button, made it easy for them to find those who shared their interests and convictions, no matter how niche. The service grew very quickly, at one point hosting more than 500 million blogs, and was bought by Yahoo for $1.1 billion in 2013.

Because of its architecture, Tumblr quickly became a place for its predominantly teenage users to experiment with new identities. At first, many of these identities were rooted in fandom for some musician or television show. (Sherlock Holmes and *Doctor Who* commanded especially large followings.) Then Tumblr became a place for young people to explore their gender and sexual orientation. Soon, the unrivaled ability to find and build community also took on a darker side: in the early 2010s, some of the service's most popular posters began to offer "thinspiration" to their anorexic followers.

The culture of Tumblr encouraged users to start identifying as members of some identity group, whether that identity was chosen or ascriptive, and whether it reflected a preexisting social reality or expressed a kind of aspiration. As Katherine Dee, a culture writer who has interviewed more than a hundred early users of Tumblr about the role it played in their lives, notes, "Tumblr became a place for people to fantasize and build upon ideas about real identities. . . . Most of the people involved had little lived experience *as* these identities." As this culture came into its own, Tumblr developed wondrously protean properties: a heartfelt manifesto or even a casual joke could become the kernel of an entirely new identity. Tumblr was where new ways of describing one's own sexual orientation (like "demisexual"), new ways of referring to one's ethnic identity (like "Latinx"), and new ways of thinking about one's gender (like "libragender") first reached a large audience.

At the same time, this chaotic and sprawling confederation of identity-based communities also began to develop an overarching culture. And because so much of the platform was organized around distinct communities rooted in various forms of ethnic, sexual, and gender identity, that culture came to be dominated by a set of political precepts drawn from the identity synthesis. "Tumblr was the first place many white people . . . encountered ideas about race and privilege," one enthusiastic profile of the site in the *Pacific Standard* pointed out in 2018. "For many teenagers at the beginning of the decade, no matter their specific interests, their pages included posts about feminism, anti-racism, and social justice."

According to Kenny Lu, one of the avid Tumblr users quoted in the profile, users like him "wanted to educate ourselves; we saw it as a platform to be more woke." Dee has come to a strikingly similar conclusion. "For every strange (or even just unfamiliar) proclamation about identity" that has in recent years come to be passionately debated in American culture and politics, Dee notes, "there's a Tumblr post from the early 2010s introducing the concept."

Being a product of social media rather than the seminar room, the ideology that took shape on Tumblr fell far short of the sophistication that characterizes the work of scholars from Foucault to Said to Crenshaw. Nor was it ever monolithic; at times it could feel like a chaotic jumble consisting of thousands of contradictory thoughts, suggestions, and propositions that were as diverse as the communities within which they spread. And yet the core themes of Tumblr ideology were both surprisingly cohesive and readily recognizable to anybody who has studied the recent intellectual history of the left: they were a popularized—or, if you will, memefied—version of the identity synthesis.

Two core themes that have roots in the identity synthesis came to be especially important on Tumblr: standpoint epistemology and intersectionality. Philosophers of race and gender have thought carefully about the ways in which someone's identity might shape their perception of the world, allowing them more direct access to some forms of knowledge and making it harder for them to access other forms of knowledge. On Tumblr, memes and blog posts turned this intuitive insight into a much more extreme position: it quickly became an article of faith that members of dominant groups, like whites or heterosexuals, could not in any meaningful way understand the experiences of members of disadvantaged groups, like "people of color" or sexual minorities. As a result, it became very fraught to criticize any position for which a member of a disadvantaged group could claim special authority derived from their "lived experience"—even when there was little evidence that most members of that group agreed with the person making the claim on their behalf.

The oft-repeated demand for "intersectionality" turned out to do even more work in holding together the different strands of Tumblr's ideology. As coined by Crenshaw, the concept of intersectionality merely called attention to the fact that some people might suffer disadvantages because of an interplay between different elements of their identity. But as shared and celebrated on Tumblr, intersectionality became an all-purpose operating system for online activism. It allowed each group to define a correct set of views in its area of presumed competence while demanding unquestioning fealty to that new orthodoxy from everyone else. As calls for intersectionality became commonplace, anybody who advocated for one cause without signing on to other fashionable causes became open to severe criticism for failing to live up to its demands. "If your feminism isn't intersectional," one slogan that became a frequent refrain on the platform in those years intoned, "it is bullshit."

The result was a powerful mechanism for keeping people in line. As various users jockeyed to claim the mantle of legitimate spokesperson for their respective identity groups, the nature of the orthodoxy that held sway on Tumblr continually evolved. But if anybody violated the intersectional consensus that held sway at that particular moment in time, they could quickly draw the ire of big parts of the community. In this respect, too, Tumblr proved to be at the vanguard of the internet: it was one of the first online spaces in which users regularly experienced a sudden and dramatic fall from grace on the basis of some minor violation of ever-shifting community norms.

NEW MEDIA PLATFORMS
EMBRACE TUMBLR IDEOLOGY

What began on Tumblr did not stay on Tumblr. As social media platforms like Reddit, Twitter, Instagram, and (later) TikTok became more important as places for young people to construct their identities and express their politics, many of the memes and themes that were taking shape on Tumblr also adapted to these different environments. Nor was the influence of Tumblr ideology restricted to social media. Soon, the popularized form of the identity synthesis also came to shape the content of a growing number of upstart publications—and even that of legacy newspapers and magazines.

At about the same time as the microblogging platform was growing in prominence, another venture was enjoying a meteoric rise. In 2010, Chris Lavergne, a dropout from Hampshire College who was convinced that it was an important endeavor to "catalog every thought," founded a website that published a glut of virtually unedited—and frequently extremely navel-gazing—articles from unpaid contributors. "Our philosophy is that quality is a very subjective thing," one Thought Catalog employee explained. "We're like, 'This is your thought, so it's quality to us.'" By 2014, the website had exploded in visibility, becoming one of the fifty most visited in the United States.

Because of the near absence of editorial standards, the articles on Thought Catalog ran the gamut from far left to far right. But the website's impact would prove especially significant in one respect: it helped to repackage the memes that were growing popular on Tumblr in the written form. Some of the most viral articles that appeared on the site in the early 2010s had titles like "18 Things White People Seem Not to Understand (Because, White Privilege)."

When such articles proved popular, new blogs and online magazines that were springing up all over the internet quickly emulated their tone and content. Publications like *Jezebel*, *xoJane*, *Rookie Mag*, and the *Daily Dot* became key in promulgating a popularized form of the identity synthesis. Even more established publications, like *Salon*, started to follow suit. Tumblr ideology had reached an important milestone: its offshoots were now so visible and influential that even relative "normies" like me were starting to stumble across them.

Since coming to the United States for graduate school, I had often encountered the basic ingredients of the identity synthesis at conferences or in the pages of academic journals. Erudite academics would talk about intersectionality or cultural appropriation, standpoint epistemology and white privilege. I found some of these ideas to be genuinely interesting. Others seemed patently abstruse. But, as with so many ideas that are put forward in the oft-impenetrable language of academia, I assumed that most of them would fail to have a big influence on the world outside campus.

Then I came across everydayfeminism.com, a website that expressed a simplistic version of these new ideas and idioms in a highly accessible form. The concepts I had first encountered in stuffy academic settings were now being packaged into easily understandable—and readily shareable—slogans. This, I quickly realized, was something genuinely new: a way of interpreting the world through a narrow focus on identity and lived experience that might appeal to a mass audience.

The articles that adorned the home page of everdayfeminism.com in March 2015 give a sense of the worldview that was starting to congeal. Its headlines read, "4 Thoughts for Your Yoga Teacher Who Thinks Appropriation Is Fun," "People of Color Can't Cure Your Racism, but Here Are 5 Things You Can Do Instead," and "You Call It Professionalism; I Call It Oppression in a Three-Piece Suit." Once I discovered the website, I couldn't stop looking at it. Over the next months, I read articles with titles like "6 Ways to Respond to Sexist Microaggressions in Everyday Conversations," "White Privilege, Explained in One Simple Comic," and "So You're a 'Breasts Man'? Here Are 3 Reasons That Could Be Sexist."

By the middle of the decade, the identity synthesis had come a long way. Born as a set of sophisticated, if rightly controversial, academic ideas, it had—by the power of memes and viral articles—been transformed into a series of slogans that were capable of appealing to a mass audience. The popularized form of the identity synthesis had taken shape. But for the time being, its influence remained limited to social media platforms and upstart websites.

This was to change as Twitter and especially Facebook grew much more important as distribution channels for more respectable publications. As mainstream news outlets from *Newsweek* to *The New York Times* started to chase clicks, and recognized that first-person articles were especially likely to go viral on social media, they quickly changed the kind of content they published. This transformation could be told through the story of any number of newspapers and magazines. But it was especially striking in the case of a new publication that was founded with the noble ambition of explaining the world to its audience in dispassionate terms yet went on to become a key player in the popularization of the identity synthesis: *Vox*.

THE TRANSFORMATION OF THE MAINSTREAM

In April 2014, Ezra Klein, Matthew Yglesias, and Melissa Bell launched *Vox*, a new digital magazine with a big ambition: to change the nature of journalism. Too much of America's political media, Klein argued at the time, focuses on the wrong kinds of things. It relentlessly covers minor events inside the Beltway and obsesses about horse-race coverage of political elections. But it fails at a more basic and fundamental task: to explain what is happening and why it matters. *Vox*, the site's founders promised, would improve the country's political discourse by engaging in fair-minded and evenhanded "explainer journalism."

In many ways, the venture proved an enormous success. *Vox* quickly established itself as a major player in the ecosystem of progressive political media. The site attracted a large and loyal readership, reaching nearly 100 million website visits per quarter by 2015. But the experiment also fell short of its founders' expectations in some interesting and illuminating ways.

With political polarization in America rapidly increasing, the site's audience ended up being much more ideologically monochrome than anticipated. As those readers clamored for content that did not challenge their values, the attempt at explaining the news through a nonpartisan lens became less important. Many viral articles on the website dispensed with the ambition of being a form of explanatory journalism altogether; card stacks, a much-heralded feature of the site's early days that focused on providing relevant context and background information for news stories, were soon discontinued, in part because they did not perform well on social media networks like Twitter and Facebook.

Instead, *Vox* in June 2015 launched a "first person" vertical that encouraged submissions from people writing about their own experiences, usually about forms of disadvantage or discrimination they had experienced because of the identity group to which they belong. In the following months and years, the website underwent a remarkable transformation. First-person articles about an author's "lived experiences" came to stand at the center of a publication that had once promised to explain the world to its readers in a tone verging on the technocratic.

This change of format went hand in hand with a change of values. In the hands of young writers who were fresh out of college and spent a lot of time on social media, these first-person stories usually served to express the core tenets of the popularized form of the identity synthesis. They often combined an account of an injustice the author had suffered due to their identity with a call for a remedy that would help to "dismantle" some aspect of racism, sexism, white supremacy, or heteronormativity. The moderate liberalism associated with the website's founders gradually made way for the proudly progressive ideology that was dominant among its younger staffers.

At the end of the decade, most of the website's founders left a publication that had in many ways become an awkward fit for them. In the summer of 2020, Yglesias signed an open letter, published in *Harper's* magazine, that criticized the increasingly illiberal norms that held sway in many elite institutions across America. A number of *Vox* employees attacked him for signing the declaration; in a widely shared open letter, Emily VanDerWerff, a transgender staff writer, implied that his willingness to be associated with other signatories, like J. K. Rowling, made her "feel less safe" in her workplace. Four months later, Yglesias left *Vox* to start his own newsletter on Substack; by the end of the year, Klein followed suit, finding a new home at *The New York Times*.

There are many reasons for *Vox*'s striking transformation. But one especially important mechanism has to do with the way in which social media created new distribution channels for journalistic content. When *Vox* was founded, most article views came from direct visits to its website. This meant that articles had to appeal to a large share of the publication's regular readers to reach a lot of eyeballs. But as social media continued to grow in importance, the way most articles find their readers began to change—not only at *Vox*, but across the industry. By the second half of the decade, the most important distribution mechanisms were Twitter and especially Facebook. And that fundamentally changed what kind of content gained traction. For an article to be widely read, it no longer needed to entice a high percentage of a publication's regular readership to click on a headline; it needed to reach a few people who would share it within social networks whose members were, themselves, likely to reshare it.

What kinds of articles were likely to be shared and reshared on Facebook and Twitter? Some appealed to fervent ideological communities that had a strong commitment to a particular issue, like people who favor the legalization of marijuana. Others were excellent at playing on readers' emotions, often because they vilified an ideological out-group. But because social media users tend to "follow" or "friend" those who are similar to them, especially on dimensions like cultural background and sexual orientation, a large percentage of the most successful articles spoke directly to the interests and experiences of particular identity groups. Ever since Facebook and Twitter became the main distribution mechanisms for digital content, articles on the experiences of Korean Americans or the prejudices faced by bisexuals became much more likely to go viral—changing both what major news platforms published and what kind of content the general public consumed.

As Yglesias observes in a recent article, some of the most important media trends of the mid-2010s were "a direct consequence of Facebook's influence over journalism. . . . Objectively speaking, hard-core identity politics and simplistic socialism performed incredibly well on Facebook during this period." This gave seasoned journalists an incentive to cultivate an interest in these topics and allowed younger writers who were true believers in the identity synthesis to outcompete their colleagues. "So you ended up with this whole cohort of discourse structured around 'Is Bernie Sanders perfect in every way or is it problematic to vote for a white man' as the only possible lens for examining American politics."

These commercial incentives led to a remarkable explosion in first-person content at major news outlets over the course of the last ten years. They also help to explain the growing emphasis on other journalistic content that, executives at media ventures believed, was especially likely to appeal to members of particular identity groups. And as legacy media outlets came under increased pressure to adapt to the changing times—turning themselves into digital-first publications that came to be just as obsessed with clicks and likes as many of their less storied competitors—these changes soon inspired a broader transformation of America's public sphere.

THE GREAT AWOKENING

The story of how the dynamics of social media transformed public discourse starts, at the beginning of the decade, with the rise in prominence of seemingly niche platforms like Tumblr and Thought Catalog. It culminates, at the end of the decade, in seismic changes at the most influential media outlets, from the BBC to NPR and MSNBC.

Anyone who compares a copy of *The New York Times* or *The Guardian* in 2010 with a copy of those same newspapers in 2020 would be struck by the difference in their tone and content. One small indication of this transformation lies in some of the articles and op-eds that would have been considered too extreme to see the light of day a decade earlier. "Can My Children Be Friends with White People?" one article in *The New York Times*, by an African American law professor, asked in November 2017. The conclusion he came to seemed to rule out the possibility of any genuine trust between members of different ethnic groups: "I will teach my boys to have profound doubts that friendship with white people is possible."

Another important difference lies in how mainstream newspapers framed everyday stories. Clear quantitative evidence backs up the speed and extent of this change in the content of the most prestigious newspapers in the English-speaking world. The share of *New York Times* articles using the term "racist," for example, increased by an astonishing 700 percent in the eight years between 2011 and 2019, according to an analysis by Zach Goldberg, a doctoral student in political science at Georgia State University. Over the same time period, uses of the word "racist" in *The Washington Post* increased even more quickly, by 1,000 percent.*

But the key change was not even in how often mainstream media outlets talked about racism; it was that the way they did so increasingly incorporated the ideas and the vocabulary of the identity synthesis. Both in *The Washington Post* and in *The New York Times*, the share of articles invoking "systemic racism," "structural racism," or "institutional racism" increased by tenfold between 2013 and 2019. The share of articles associating the word "white" with the idea of "racial privilege" grew at an even more rapid pace: their incidence increased twelve-fold in *The New York Times* and fifteen-fold in *The Washington Post*.

Goldberg draws an unambiguous conclusion. Over the course of Obama's presidency, key concepts of the identity synthesis, like microaggression and white privilege, "went from being obscure fragments of academic jargon to commonplace journalistic language," he writes. "Along with the new language came ideas and beliefs animating a new moral-political framework to apply to public life and American society."

These rapid changes in the way the most prestigious media outlets described the world were to have an enormous influence on a small yet highly influential segment of American society. As Goldberg demonstrates, the rapid uptick in the focus on race and racial inequality in *The Washington Post* and *The New York Times* was followed—not preceded—by a significant increase in progressive views about race, such as the number of people who favor "race-conscious" public policies, in the electorate. And because the audience of mainstream news outlets is disproportionately white and educated, attitudes about race changed much more drastically among this

---

* It's tempting to think that the growing attention to racism was simply driven by political events, from videos capturing police killings of unarmed Black men to the infamous Unite the Right rally in Charlottesville, Virginia. But Goldberg shows that exponential growth in the use of terms like "racist" began at the beginning of the 2010s, before the popular contestation over the 2014 police shooting of Michael Brown in Ferguson, Missouri, and Donald Trump's 2015 entry into American politics.

comparatively "privileged" group of Americans than they did in the population at large.

This led to some strange ironies. In the so-called feeling thermometer, for example, social scientists have long asked respondents about the general impression they have of members of a particular ethnic or religious group. Until recently, white liberals were more likely to have positive feelings toward white people than toward African Americans. By 2016, this had changed: white liberals were now more likely to say they had negative feelings toward white people—a group that presumably included their parents and other close relatives—than did Black Americans.

In 2019, Matthew Yglesias coined a new term for the massive sociopolitical changes that a key segment of the American public was undergoing: "The Great Awokening." As he put it, "White liberals have moved so far to the left on questions of race and racism that they are now, on these issues, to the left of even the typical Black voter."

The popularization of the identity synthesis played a key role in the events of the past decade. It is only when a complex academic theory was translated into memes and blog posts that it became ready for prime time. And it is only when that memefied version of the identity synthesis migrated from social media platforms and upstart blogs into the pages of *The Guardian*, *The Washington Post*, and *The New York Times* that it could start to influence the mainstream.

But though this part of the story is deeply important in setting the cultural background for the events of the past decade, it is missing a key element. For even when prestigious media outlets started to give a big platform to these ideas, they swayed only a comparatively small segment of the public. Most people of all colors and creeds continued to disagree with the idea that white and Black people cannot be friends and rejected the suggestion that public policies should explicitly distinguish between people on account of the identity group to which they belong. And yet some of the core ideas and ideals of the identity synthesis quickly came to have tremendous influence over powerful institutions. Why?

To answer this question, we need to trace a second, parallel development. The popularized version of the identity synthesis became so influential in part because a new generation of employees entered the workforce and fought to enshrine the ideas they had imbibed in universities and on social media as the operating system of major institutions. It is their "short march through the institutions" to which we turn next.

KEY TAKEAWAYS

- The rise of social media fundamentally transformed the role that group identity plays in the lives of young people. Making it far easier for them to experiment with new labels with which to describe themselves, it encouraged the emergence of a popularized version of the identity synthesis, which originated on social media platforms such as Tumblr and found its written form in publications such as Thought Catalog.

- Social media became more important as a distribution mechanism for both new media ventures and legacy publications, putting a premium on content that would appeal to particular identity groups. As a result, the main themes and concepts of the identity synthesis quickly spread to prestigious outlets including *Vox* and *The New York Times*.

- By the end of the decade, these concepts had helped to reframe the views of a large segment of the American population. This shift in views was most pronounced among white and highly educated Americans.

Chapter 6

THE SHORT MARCH
THROUGH THE INSTITUTIONS

At the height of its influence in the 1960s, the student movement debated a key strategic question. Should it compete for the vote in democratic elections? Should it focus on peaceful protests and other forms of "extra-parliamentary" resistance? Or should it stage a violent revolution? What proved to be one of the most influential strategies was proposed by Rudi Dutschke, a German student leader whose following only grew after a far-right fanatic shot him in the head in the streets of Berlin.

Revolutionaries, Dutschke argued in 1967, should try to subvert the political system by means of a "long march through the institutions." In Dutschke's original formulation, the purpose of this infiltration was to subvert and sabotage. But by 1972, when the German American philosopher Herbert Marcuse picked up on these ideas in his highly influential *Counterrevolution and Revolt*, the strategy had come to encompass more subtle avenues of influence. When "working against the established institutions while working within them," Marcuse counseled, activists should be "doing the job" by learning "how to program and read computers, how to teach at all levels of education, how to use the mass media, [and] how to organize production."

Many of the people who, consciously or unconsciously, embarked on this "long march" ended up being co-opted by the institutions they sought to transform before they had a chance to exert significant power. And yet historians and sociologists have invoked the long march through the institutions to explain many of the social and cultural changes that came about as members of the student movement entered workplaces, C-suites, and parliaments over the course of the 1970s, 1980s, and 1990s. Even as most of them lost revolutionary zeal and embarked on much more conventional lives than they had once envisaged, their collective influence transformed the culture of countries from Germany to France to the United States.

The lasting influence of the long march is owed to the strength of its underlying mechanism. When college students are deeply steeped in a new and radical ideology, they are uniquely well placed to have an outsized impact on the world outside the ivory tower. For as these students join mainstream institutions, they have a lot of opportunities to advocate for change and even to rise to positions of power. And this is especially likely to be the case when those who buy into the new ideology are concentrated within elite universities from which a country's most influential institutions recruit a disproportionate number of their employees.

Another such march through the institutions is an important part of the explanation for what has happened in Canada, the United States, and (to a lesser extent) the United Kingdom over the course of the past decade. What I call the "short march through the institutions" provides a key part of the explanation for how the identity synthesis went from an ideology that was influential in some corners of campus in 2010 to one that had a firm grip over some of the world's most powerful foundations and corporations by 2020.

To be clear, the great majority of those who participated in the short march through the institutions did not see their actions as part of some grand strategy. They probably did not even know who Rudi Dutschke was. They didn't have to. They simply left their universities deeply steeped in the core tenets of the "identity synthesis" and imbibed its popularized version on social media. Following their ambitions, they took jobs in prestigious newspapers and well-endowed foundations, in giant corporations and powerful government offices. As their presence within these institutions took on critical mass, they were able to transform the norms, rules, and assumptions that govern them.

One reason why the march through the institutions could be so short is that it took place against the background of the wider cultural and technological changes I discussed in the last chapter. In the past, unhappy employees might have grumbled to each other or privately taken their grievances to their bosses; now they increasingly took to social media, blasting their own organizations in Twitter threads or Instagram posts that quickly went viral and boosted their professional profile. In the past, news of such fights would usually remain limited to insiders, leaving the reputation of companies and the funding opportunities for nonprofits intact; now mainstream media outlets are quick to give a big platform to stories about identity and accusations of bigotry, whether serious and well founded or trivial and ill-sourced. In short, the arrival of a new cohort of junior employees deeply steeped in the identity synthesis had such an outsized impact on some of the most important institutions in America in part because the wider technological and ideological transformations of the past decade gave their bosses good reasons to fear them.

THE TRAINING GROUND

The short march started on campus. In the span of a few decades, enrollment in departments dominated by scholars who embrace the identity synthesis, such as gender studies and media studies, increased manifold. Over the same time period, the influence of postmodernism, postcolonialism, and critical race theory also grew in more traditional humanities and social sciences departments. By 2010, the advocates of the identity synthesis were teaching hundreds of thousands of students around the country every year. Even students studying science, business, or engineering were now likely to learn about these ideas when fulfilling course requirements outside their major field.

Students were even more likely to encounter a version of the identity synthesis outside the classroom. From 1976 to 2011, the number of students at American universities nearly doubled. The growth in the size of the faculty failed to keep pace, with the number of professors increasing by just 76 percent. But the size of nonteaching staff skyrocketed over the same time period, with the number of administrators on American campuses growing by 139 percent and the number of other professional employees, such as student affairs officers and mental health counselors, growing by a staggering 366 percent. Professors had once comfortably outnumbered other administrative and professional employees at American universities; by the end of the 2010s, they were in the minority.

Both the duties and the political views of these administrators are, of course, variable. But a significant share is actively promoting the identity synthesis. The Office of Student Affairs at Sarah Lawrence, for example, has offered seminars on such topics as "Understanding White Privilege" and "Stay Healthy, Stay Woke." Meanwhile, administrators at the University of California have instructed students to refrain from using "offensive" phrases like "melting pot" or "there is only one race, the human race." A growing number of universities even empowers administrators to intervene when students use "microaggressions" in conversation with each other, encouraging students to report infractions to an anonymous hotline.

The influence of the identity synthesis is especially pronounced at America's most prestigious institutions. Top research universities took the lead in the establishment of new academic disciplines centered on the study of some form of identity. They were more likely to hire young scholars deemed to be at the cutting edge of their disciplines. And they have much more lavish budgets to pay an army of administrators to propagate the core theses of the identity synthesis, compelling students to participate in an ever-growing number of trainings and orientations. (Yale, for example, now employs more administrators than it enrolls undergraduates.)

All of this made the most elite institutions in the country more likely to have a political monoculture on campus. The political composition of faculty and university staff is one indication of this. At American colleges, incoming students are twice as likely to say that they are liberal as to say that they are conservative. Faculty are even more likely to lean left than their students: professors are six times more likely to say that they are liberal than to say that they are conservative. Administrators have a still clearer political slant: they are twelve times more likely to call themselves liberal than they are to call themselves conservative.

Surveys asking who is liberal—a vague designation often used in American political discourse to indicate that someone is left-wing—can be useful in demonstrating how strongly universities lean to the left. But they are too vague to capture the nature of the views that now predominate on campus. In particular, they fail to capture the distinction between professors who are both liberal in the political sense and liberal in the philosophical sense (like me) and those (unlike me) who both lean left politically and reject basic precepts of philosophical liberalism.

Polls asking about specific propositions that violate philosophically liberal principles like academic freedom can help to disambiguate between these positions. And those paint a worrying picture. According to one study sampling twenty thousand students across the nation, for example, one in three now "believe that it is acceptable to block an entrance and try to prevent others from entering a room to hear a speaker." That share is even higher among those who attend one of the ten most elite schools in the country, with half championing such illiberal tactics.

As the students of these elite institutions left campus and started to pursue their careers, they had a large influence on every facet of American life. But they were especially successful in transforming institutions that recruit a large share of their staff from elite universities, give employees significant power at a comparatively early stage of their careers, and are especially sensitive to employee demands or criticisms on social media. Tech start-ups and media companies, congressional offices and top professional firms, all fulfill these criteria. But arguably, it is major nongovernmental organizations and grant-making foundations that best fit this description. And as the rapid transformation of the ACLU demonstrates, it is these nonprofits that proved especially responsive when a new generation of college graduates steeped in the identity synthesis knocked on their doors.

THE IDENTITY SYNTHESIS TAKES OVER NONPROFITS

In the fall of 1977, the National Socialist Party of America applied for a permit to hold a rally in the city of Skokie, a heavily Jewish town that was home to a large number of Holocaust survivors. When the city imposed onerous conditions that were evidently designed to stop the protest from taking place, Francis Joseph Collin, the party's leader, filed a seminal lawsuit with the help of an unlikely ally: the ACLU, a nonprofit that had for decades fought for the civil liberties of pacifists, communists, and anti-segregationists.

David Goldberger, a progressive Jew who served as the lead lawyer on *National Socialist Party of America v. Village of Skokie*, took the case to defend a key constitutional right. He knew that carving out exceptions to the First Amendment, which guarantees free speech and free assembly, would make life difficult for some noxious organizations he despised. But he recognized that it would also make it more difficult for people he admired, like strident critics of racism or government overreach, to find a hearing. "The constitutional guarantees of freedom of speech and press would be meaningless if the government could pick and choose the persons to whom they apply," Goldberger explained.

The ACLU won its case. For the next four decades, its principled defense of the right to free speech defined its image in the public imagination. Even today, the organization continues to trumpet this proud part of its history on its website, claiming that the *Skokie* case has "come to represent our unwavering commitment to principle." But over the course of the past decade, the organization has quietly started to abandon those commitments. "Once a bastion of free speech and high-minded ideals," the feminist legal scholar Lara Bazelon recently concluded in *The Atlantic*, "the ACLU has become in many respects a caricature of its former self."

The ACLU's transformation is, in part, rooted in a strong case of mission creep. Young employees who have joined the organization over the past decade want it to fight for a broad range of leftist values, not just those that are directly connected to its historical mission of defending civil liberties. They are backed up by an army of small donors who became members of the ACLU in the months after Donald Trump was elected in the hope that it would pursue all kinds of progressive priorities. As a result, the ACLU now habitually takes public stances on a hodgepodge of issues—some worthwhile, others less so—that are at best tenuously connected to its historical mission.

In the past decade, the ACLU has called for the federal government to provide broadband access to all and for student debt to be canceled, for police departments to be defunded and for universities to build dorms reserved for Black or Hispanic students. The justification for these policies is often couched in the language of the identity synthesis. "People without broadband access," one recent ACLU publication emphasized, "are disproportionately Black, Latinx, Indigenous, rural, or low-income."

These new areas of advocacy have come at the expense of the ACLU's traditional strengths. Since 2016, the organization's "annual budget has grown threefold and its lawyer staff has doubled," according to a recent report in *The New York Times*. Even so, "only four of its attorneys specialize in free-speech issues, a number that has not changed in a decade."

The ACLU has also become much more hesitant to stand up for the rights of rightly unpopular clients. In August 2017, it helped to litigate a case regarding the infamous Unite the Right rally, which attracted a broad cross section of far-right extremists and white supremacists, successfully opposing attempts by the City of Charlottesville to move it to a less central location. After the protest descended into deadly violence, many younger staffers blamed the ACLU, arguing that it should abandon its commitment to an expansive definition of free speech rights.

Hundreds of staffers published an open letter that argued that the ACLU's "rigid stance" on free speech undermines its "broader mission." Waldo Jaquith, a board member of the ACLU in Virginia, implied that the organization had become "a fig leaf for Nazis" in a Twitter thread that quickly went viral. When Claire Guthrie Gastañaga, the state director of the local ACLU affiliate, tried to explain the organization's long-standing principles at an event at William & Mary, students—holding signs that read, ACLU, FREE SPEECH FOR WHO? and THE OPPRESSED ARE NOT IMPRESSED—shouted her down before she had a chance to speak.

At first, the ACLU stood firm. Even as a spokeswoman for the national organization acknowledged that it "was concerned about donors turning away," she insisted that it would stick by its longtime policies. But it didn't take long for the tune to change. Within ten months of the rally in Charlottesville, a committee composed of senior staff members laid out new criteria for the ACLU's lawyers to consider before agreeing to defend an organization's First Amendment rights. When deciding what cases to litigate, they should consider factors such as "the structural and power inequalities in the community in which the speech will occur." In the view of some past leaders of the ACLU, this change of policy sounded the death knell for its long-standing commitment to defending the speech rights of all people, irrespective of their views or their identity.

Once it became clear that the ACLU was willing to bend to the preferences of its younger staffers and the wishes of its progressive donors, other changes quickly followed. Since Charlottesville, the organization has increasingly taken up causes that stand in direct conflict to its historical mission. When Abigail Shrier argued that some forms of "social contagion" may be helping to drive a surge in teenage girls experiencing gender dysphoria in a controversial book, one senior ACLU staffer called for it to be banned. "Stopping the circulation of this book and these ideas is 100% a hill I will die on," Chase Strangio, a deputy director at the ACLU's LGBT & HIV Project, wrote on Twitter. And when the Department of Education sought to amend the rules governing sexual misconduct investigations on college campuses, allowing universities to grant the accused basic due process rights like access to the evidence that is being used against them, the ACLU tweeted that this "promotes an unfair process, inappropriately favoring the accused." (As critics pointed out, the organization has a long tradition of defending extensive due process rights for all suspects, including those accused of other heinous crimes such as murder or terrorism.)

Goldberger, the lawyer who argued the *Skokie* case, is unsparing in his assessment of the new ACLU. It now seems "more important for ACLU staff to identify with clients and progressive causes than to stand on principle," he recently lamented. "Liberals are leaving the First Amendment behind." Some of the senior staff members who remain at the organization share his assessment that the wider ideological transformation of America's progressive elite and the influx of young staffers steeped in the identity synthesis are to blame for the ACLU's transformation. Sensing that many job applicants are opposed to the organization's historical mission, one older staffer has started to mention landmark cases like *Skokie* in interviews, asking them "if they are comfortable with that history." Tellingly, he asked *The New York Times* "not to be named because of the fear of inflaming colleagues."

The ACLU is not alone. Over the past decade, many other nonprofit organizations have transformed for some of the same reasons and in some of the same ways. Under pressure from young staffers deeply steeped in the identity synthesis, wary of viral posts on social media and the mainstream media attention they might attract, and fearful of losing favor with their donors, they too have embraced a ragbag of progressive causes—or given up on key elements of their historical missions.

As staffers throughout the philanthropic sector advocated for an embrace of "intersectionality," many organizations came to broaden their missions in ways that diluted their core identities. Influenced by the idea that all forms of oppression are connected, young staffers at institutions that have historically focused on a clearly circumscribed issue area have demanded that they become vocal on all kinds of progressive causes. As a result, the distinction between different advocacy groups has become increasingly fluid, and the ideological price of admission to all of them increasingly steep.

The Sierra Club, for example, is an environmentalist group that has historically seen it as its mission to "promote the responsible use of the earth's ecosystems and resources." But the organization now issues statements on a bewildering range of different topics, from demanding that the Biden administration "tear down the wall" on America's southern border to joining calls to "defund the police."

The ideological transformation of the nonprofit sector is unlikely to be reversed anytime soon. For, driven by the same generational and ideological trends, major grant-making foundations that serve as the key financial backers for a whole range of activist groups, think tanks, and arts organizations have increasingly embraced the core tenets of the identity synthesis.

As the leaders of institutions from the Ford Foundation to the MacArthur Foundation came under pressure from their own staff, they threw their support behind increasingly radical causes, and explicitly started to prefer grantees "who are Black or brown."

As an investigation by *The Economist* concluded in 2021, "Philanthropy is veering left." Deep-pocketed foundations are increasingly pursuing equity, "defined not as equal opportunity, but rather as equal outcomes." This shift in the ideological assumptions of the country's biggest foundations has led to a massive influx of funding into organizations that campaign for ideas and issues inspired by the identity synthesis. According to Candid, an organization that compiles information about nonprofits, for example, philanthropies handed out or promised a total of about $28 billion in "racial equity funding" from 2011 to 2021.

Much of this money supports admirable work against racism and other forms of discrimination. But some of it also goes to organizations that promote educational policies that split students into different ethnic groups or advocate for state institutions to adopt race-sensitive policies; to controversial activists who have channeled donor dollars into lavish lifestyles and purchased giant villas that appear to have gone to predominantly personal uses; or to extreme political causes, like abolishing police departments.

Over the course of the past decade, major grant-making foundations and key activist groups alike have undergone an enormous change, embracing the core tenets of the identity synthesis and weakening their commitment to philosophically liberal principles. It is perhaps unsurprising that the nonprofit sector, with its explicit commitment to making the world a better place, proved especially receptive to young staffers who demanded that it embrace ever more radical ideas. More surprisingly, some of the same mechanisms also turned out to transform other areas of American life—including the corporate sector.

THE IDENTITY SYNTHESIS ENTERS THE C-SUITE

If there is one iconic company that does business with a huge cross section of customers in America and around the world, giving it a strong incentive not to take fringe political positions with which many people are likely to disagree, it is Coca-Cola. This makes it all the more remarkable that the company has, over the course of the past decade, become vastly more outspoken on political issues.

In 2020, Coca-Cola announced plans for a radical change in the company's internal culture. "To help foster conversation and promote understanding as part of our holistic Racial Equity plan," Coca-Cola announced in 2020, "we are launching an immersive diversity, equity and inclusion employee enrichment platform." Of course, it is heartening to see companies aim to recruit a diverse workforce, take a strong stance against racism, and encourage their employees to get along. But the programs and commitments embraced by Coca-Cola are rooted not in universal ideals of tolerance and genuine inclusivity but in the concepts and convictions of the identity synthesis.

"Confronting Racism," one of the trainings that Coca-Cola offered to its employees through the company's training portal, for example, features a slide telling employees to "try to be less white." For anybody who might be confused about what this exhortation might entail, or how they can possibly accomplish it, the training helpfully elaborates that being less white is to be "less oppressive," "less arrogant," "less certain," "less defensive," and "less ignorant." In an accompanying video, the bestselling author Robin DiAngelo—who is herself white—explained that becoming less white would take considerable commitment: it is "a lifelong process."

Asked how Coca-Cola decided to attach its iconic logo to such inflammatory content, a company spokesperson insisted that the course was part of a broader training program designed by LinkedIn and used by many major corporations. But that only helps to show how commonplace such content has now become across corporate America. In fact, the presence of DiAngelo—who first rose to prominence as a facilitator of diversity, equity, and inclusion workshops and has worked with dozens of major corporations, including Amazon, Facebook, Goldman Sachs, American Express, and CVS—is telling.

Since their widespread adoption in the 1960s, the nature of diversity trainings at American companies has radically changed. Long focused on teaching the importance of mutual respect and the benefits of a diverse workplace, they have of late shifted to inculcating DiAngelo's core conviction that even well-meaning employees are inescapably sexist or racist. Assessing the changes that such trainings had undergone over the previous decade in January 2020, Raafi-Karim Alidina, a human resources consultant specializing in diversity, equity, and inclusion, rejoiced in the rapid spread of the core elements of the identity synthesis. "The term 'psychological safety' was only used in academic journals in 2010," he writes by way of example; "now, C-suite executives discuss its importance."

So why did the nature of diversity trainings change so drastically over the course of a decade? And how did corporations, which have long been reluctant to take controversial positions, start to give a major platform to the popularized forms of the identity synthesis? The answer is, once more, connected to the short march through the institutions.

Tech companies like Google and Amazon, consulting firms like McKinsey and the Boston Consulting Group, and investment banks like J.P. Morgan and Goldman Sachs recruit a disproportionate number of their students from elite institutions. (Google, for example, recruits the biggest number of its employees from Stanford and Berkeley. At McKinsey, graduates from Ivy League universities like Harvard are especially well represented. Goldman Sachs branches out a little bit further: it also hires a lot from New York University and the London School of Economics.) Given the way in which America's top universities had changed over the preceding decades, the crop of young employees who joined these companies was therefore especially likely to be immersed in the identity synthesis.

Once these young recruits donned their freshly bought suits (or T-shirts) and arrived in the glitzy new world of conference rooms in Midtown Manhattan (or sprawling campuses in Silicon Valley), many got on with the business of making money and earning promotions. But a significant share started to engage in what social scientists have termed "insider activism." Whether they suffered from serious injustices like sexual harassment or less serious ones like perceived microaggressions, they used a combination of internal channels of dissent and external threats of bad publicity from Twitter or *The New York Times* to push their employers to change their ways.

Among social scientists who study the business world, there is a remarkable consensus that this form of activism rapidly increased over the course of the 2010s. According to one report, for example, "The voice of the workforce will insist on being heard as never before. If traditional, internal communication channels fail to meet their needs, external means of raising concerns will fill the gap." Indeed, according to a survey of four hundred C-suite executives at major corporations around the world conducted in 2019, "81% of companies anticipate a rise in employee activism in the future."

The prediction came true faster than anticipated. As Mae McDonnell, an associate professor of management at Wharton, found the following year, "In the first half of 2015, there were six instances of employee activism in tech firms reported in mainstream media. In the first half of 2020, there were 60." As I know from numerous conversations with top corporate leaders, senior executives grew deeply concerned about this kind of internal pressure. As one survey respondent summarized the theme, "All it takes is one particularly vocal, particularly difficult individual to raise concerns through social media and whether or not there's any basis to it, often you can't defend yourself publicly."

Once some top firms and companies agreed to meet key demands of such insider activists, most of the others in the same industry quickly followed suit. This process of "isomorphic diffusion"—the tendency of similar organizations to emulate each other—was, in part, driven by the competition for top talent and the desire to keep up with the Joneses. In industries that rely on hiring the best graduates from prestigious universities, no employer felt that they could refuse their would-be recruits what a competitor was offering. Insider activists, Apoorva Ghosh, a sociologist at Emory University, writes, often "highlight the adoption of similar policies and practices by peer corporations, and question these employers directly: 'Don't we want to become as good as [our peers]?'" And because no corporation wants to be out of step with the leaders of its industry, even less prestigious workplaces soon adopted some of the same changes.

The rapid spread of new norms and practices also had a legal dimension. When companies are sued for sexual harassment or racial discrimination, courts often seek to determine whether they have taken sufficient steps to protect their employees. A key part of this analysis turns on whether they have instituted the kinds of practices and offered the kinds of training programs that are typical among their peers. So when a few companies adopted new norms and practices, their competitors acquired a compelling legal incentive to follow suit—whether or not the evidence shows that they are effective in achieving their purported goals.

In the past, top managers might have resisted the demands of junior employees if they considered them expensive, ineffectual, or potentially controversial. But in the last decade, a mixture of insider activism, competition with peers, pressure from social media, and legal risk has given them strong reason to override such qualms. Gabriel Rossman, a professor of sociology at UCLA, illustrates this point with a compelling thought experiment:

> Suppose that you're a manager who reads the academic literature, sees that the heavy-handed self-criticism styles of sexual-harassment or racial-diversity training are somewhere between useless and counterproductive, and proposes canceling next year's training. Legal is going to complain that this will look bad if you face a wrongful-dismissal suit anytime soon.... Many employees will complain that they expect the firm to express their values, which includes holding seminars featuring "privilege walks" to reaffirm the firm's commitment to ending white supremacy and other forms of domination. These stakeholders will point to the fact that all your leading rivals in the industry hold such seminars; it is a "best practice."

What, Rossman asks, would you do? Probably, he suggests, the same as the managers of America's biggest and most prestigious corporations, from Google to Coca-Cola: keep mum about any concerns you might privately harbor about the way that everyone is doing things, hire fashionable diversity trainers even though you think they are unlikely to do any good, sign off on fringe demands by employees, and move on to the next item on your agenda.

KEY TAKEAWAYS

- The student activists of the 1960s transformed the culture of many countries through a "long march through the institutions." As they entered workplaces in business, entertainment, and politics, they gradually changed prevailing norms and practices. Though they did not consciously set out to emulate that strategy, a new crop of students deeply steeped in the identity synthesis both at college and on social media completed a similar "short march through the institutions" over the course of the 2010s.

- Pressure from young employees was especially effective in transforming foundations and nonprofits pledged to making the world a better place. Activist organizations like the ACLU became less likely to fight for liberal values, like free speech, when these clashed with other progressive priorities. Similar changes at major grant-making foundations ensured that the identity synthesis lastingly increased its influence throughout the nonprofit world.

- Even major corporations, like Coca-Cola, became more likely to embrace key aspects of the identity synthesis and to train their employees in concepts like white privilege. The short march through the institutions started in tech companies and professional firms that recruit from elite universities, compete for top talent, and are highly averse to negative publicity. Other major corporations quickly followed suit due to employee activism and legal incentives to emulate the actions of their peers.

Chapter 7

DISSENT DISCOURAGED

What a thousand political scientists and campaign strategists had declared impossible came to pass on November 8, 2016. In a close-run election, Donald J. Trump beat Hillary Rodham Clinton to become the forty-fifth president of the United States. Trump's supporters reveled in the shock they had delivered to a political establishment they held in contempt. But just as many Americans were scared about what Trump might do to the country and the most vulnerable people within it.

The reasons for concern were real. During his campaign, Trump promised to ban Muslims from entering the United States. He implied that cops should rough up criminal suspects when arresting them. He called for his adversary to be locked up. He hesitated to distance himself from extremist supporters like David Duke. He called into doubt whether he would accept an electoral defeat.

Many fears turned into reality. In the first months of his presidency, Trump barred millions of people with links to one of seven Muslim countries from entering the United States. He banned transgender people from serving in the military. He fired the director of the FBI under dubious circumstances. And when he did lose his bid for reelection, four years later, he refused to concede, inspiring a mob to storm the Capitol.

At first, the threat posed by Trump provoked a huge outpouring of protest. On the day after his inauguration, half a million people converged on Washington, D.C., for a "women's march"; millions more took to the streets in cities across the United States. When the White House's executive order on immigration was published one week later, stranding scores of travelers from Muslim countries, thousands of Americans spontaneously converged on airports around the country.

Americans also infused organizations that opposed Trump with fresh energy. Activist groups like the ACLU and the NAACP took in millions in small-donor donations, significantly growing their financial resources. Indivisible, a grassroots movement whose progressive founders explicitly sought to emulate the Tea Party, mobilized its members to oppose the confirmation of Trump's nominees. Across the country, thousands of citizens who had never held political office decided to run for their city council, their state legislature, even for Congress.

In the first weeks and months after Trump's victory, activists harbored the hope that all of these efforts would somehow force him from office. Perhaps "faithless electors" in the Electoral College would conspire to save the republic from its president-elect. Perhaps imminent revelations about his connections to the Kremlin would persuade the leaders of the Republican Party to make him resign. Perhaps Robert Mueller, the special counsel appointed to investigate Russian interference in the 2016 election, would bring criminal charges against Trump. Perhaps Congress would succeed in impeaching the president. Encouraged by breathless predictions on cable news, a large segment of the American population came to believe that somehow, sometime, perhaps by some as yet unimagined avenue, all of this massive popular foment would translate into Trump's removal.

But the promised salvation did not come to pass. The Electoral College duly elected Trump. The "pee tape" never materialized. Mueller did not indict the president. A (first) attempt to impeach the president was defeated by a (largely) party line vote. No deus ex machina popped up to make Trump disappear.

Many of Trump's opponents dealt with that disappointment in the way participants of mass movements tend to do when the initial period of excitement wanes. They returned their attention to their jobs, their kids, and their hobbies. Progressive organizations never repeated the small-donor funding haul they enjoyed in November 2016. Attendance at protests started to dwindle. The last women's march before the pandemic, held in January 2020, drew a tiny fraction—about a fortieth—of its original crowd.

But as the high hopes of the "resistance" movement were dashed, some of its members reacted very differently: instead of continuing to protest or tuning out politics, they redirected their anger toward the inside. Left-leaning institutions from universities to foundations to arts organizations were consumed by internal strife. Campaigns to fire or shun "problematic" people for a whole gamut of offenses, some serious and some trivial, some real and some imagined, took up enormous energy. In some milieus, the popularized version of the identity synthesis hardened into an orthodoxy, with dissent discouraged in an increasingly heavy-handed manner. For much of the Trump era, big segments of progressive America seemed to be directing more anger at aberrant members of their own tribe than at their nominal enemy in the White House.

AN IDENTITY ORTHODOXY DESCENDS
ON PROGRESSIVE INSTITUTIONS

When the mass protests of late 2016 started to die down, and the various schemes to force the newly elected president to resign from office ran aground, a debilitating sense of powerlessness set in. As leftist activists recognized that there was little they could do to protect themselves against a president who—for perfectly rational reasons—made them afraid, some of them redirected their focus to those things that did remain under their control. "Maybe I can't end racism by myself, but I can get my manager fired, or I can get so and so removed, or I can hold somebody accountable," one veteran of the progressive movement who worked as the executive director of a major leftist organization during this period explained. "People found power where they could, and often that's where you work, sometimes where you live, or where you study, but someplace close to home."

That is a big part of the reason why, from 2016 to 2020, some of the most intense energy on the left was devoted to getting rid of anybody who supposedly threatened to pollute the moral purity of their community. Professors working at the nation's universities and liberal arts colleges; poets, painters, and photographers affiliated with its major arts institutions; even employees at the country's progressive organizations could do frustratingly little to defend their nation against Donald Trump. What they could do was to identify some person who, deliberately or inadvertently, in reality or in their imagination, flouted the new political certitudes to which the country's most progressive communities had committed themselves.

This helps to explain the extraordinary upswell of attempts to fire or ostracize people for alleged violations of community norms. Donald McNeil, the first print journalist at a major American newspaper to warn the country about the threat posed by COVID, was pushed out of *The New York Times* for reportedly repeating the n-word when inquiring about the context in which somebody else had used it. David Shor, a data journalist at a progressive campaign organization, lost his position after he shared a paper by a prominent African American political science professor discussing the adverse consequences of violent protests. Emmanuel Cafferty, an apolitical electrician with roots in Latin America, was fired from a San Diego utility company after activists on Twitter misinterpreted a hand gesture he made while driving his truck as a white power symbol.

By the end of the 2010s, a constricting orthodoxy had descended—not just on famous institutions whose dustups might be covered in the paper of record, but on countless schools, associations, and corporations all around the country. Anybody who offended the political sensibility of their peers was liable to be portrayed as a sexist, a racist, or a secret sympathizer with Donald Trump. And because anybody who was guilty of such political sins would pollute the purity of the community, a small but powerful contingent of activists appointed themselves the caped heroes whose calling it was to ensure that swift and decisive action would punish perceived traitors, grifters, and saboteurs.

As the leftist journalist Ryan Grim has chronicled in *The Intercept*, progressive institutions proved especially vulnerable to this self-destructive dynamic. "It's hard to find a Washington-based progressive organization that hasn't been in tumult, or isn't currently in tumult," Grim wrote in June 2022. "The Sierra Club, Demos, the American Civil Liberties Union, Color of Change, the Movement for Black Lives, Human Rights Campaign, Time's Up, the Sunrise Movement, and many other organizations have seen wrenching and debilitating turmoil in the past couple years." (A lot of movement insiders, such as the head of the Working Families Party, have since come forward to agree with Grim's assessment.)

The executive director of a major progressive organization who quit in frustration at this hothouse atmosphere explained the toll this took. "So much energy has been devoted to the internal strife and internal bullshit that it's had a real impact on the ability for groups to deliver," he told Grim. "My last nine months, I was spending 90 to 95 percent of my time on internal strife." Another institutional leader who has not yet thrown in the towel sounded even more despondent. "We used to want to make the world a better place," he said. "Now we just make our organizations more miserable to work at."

There is something peculiar about all of this. During the Trump years, there were many urgent and valuable causes to which progressive activists and organizations could have devoted their attention. And yet they became consumed with internal struggles. Why did this happen? Or, to quote the anthropologist Roy D'Andrade: "Isn't it odd that the true enemy of society turns out to be that guy in the office down the hall?" The answer to these questions requires a brief detour into the science of group psychology. For it is rooted in what makes groups tick, how dissenters can help to keep them sane, and when the pressure to conform becomes so strong that extremists gain the power to impose their views on everybody else.

PEER PRESSURE AND
THE RADICALIZATION OF GROUPS

In the spring of 1915, a little boy in central Poland celebrated Passover with his family. As is the custom, his grandmother poured out an extra glass of wine, explaining that it was an offering for the prophet Elijah. "Will he really take a sip?" the seven-year-old asked in amazement. "Oh, yes," his uncle told him. "You just watch when the time comes."

The little boy watched the glass closely. A natural skeptic, he could not imagine such a wonder taking place right in front of his eyes. But when his cousin shouted that the wine in the glass was draining, the little boy agreed: there really did seem to be a little less wine in the cup!

A few years after that memorable Passover dinner, the little boy, who goes by the name of Solomon Asch, immigrated to the United States. He taught himself English by reading the novels of Charles Dickens, made his way to City College, in New York, and became a professor of psychology at Swarthmore. Shocked by the cruelty of World War II, he became obsessed with understanding why members of groups so often go along with extreme beliefs or immoral actions. Unable to find an answer in the existing literature, he kept coming back to what he himself had experienced as a young boy. Just how suggestible, he wondered, are human beings?

To answer this question, Asch recruited college students for a deceptively simple study. He showed them two cards. One card had a single line on it. The second card had three lines on it. Then he asked them to choose which of the three lines on the second card was equal in length to the line on the first card. It was an easy task, and the students mastered it with aplomb. Nearly all of them gave the right answer.

But then Asch added a twist to the experiment. He now placed the subjects of his study in groups that mostly consisted of paid actors. For the first few rounds, both the uninitiated college students and the paid actors gave the obviously correct answer. But in the third round, all of the actors gave the wrong response. What would the real test subjects do? Would they trust their own eyes—or, like Solomon when he was a little boy, prove susceptible to suggestion?

The results were astonishing. Three out of four college students went along with the obviously wrong answer at least some of the time. Perhaps they really came to believe the wrong answer. Or perhaps they lied so they wouldn't stand out among their peers. Either way, they were frighteningly prone to conformity with a group that was obviously making a mistake. Asch's findings, which have been replicated by psychologists in a large number of different contexts, illustrate how whole groups can come to embrace wrong, extreme, or even dangerous ideas. If a few influential members of a group loudly proclaim some belief, the other members might feel pressured into professing their agreement with it—even if most of them secretly harbor well-founded concerns.

In the experiments conducted by Asch, the stakes were seemingly low. But over the following decades, researchers interested in the effects of group conformity in areas from law to business drew on his central insight to demonstrate that similar effects can also lead to seemingly irrational behaviors in contexts where the stakes are high. Take, as an example, a group of people who have to decide how much damage a company should have to pay because its negligence resulted in a small child being injured. In the experiment, each member of the group privately recorded what sum they deemed appropriate, with suggestions ranging from $500,000 to $2 million. What sum did they agree on after they had a chance to discuss the issue as a group? The intuitive answer is that the group would strike some kind of compromise. Given the range of initial estimates, it might set damages at, say, $1.5 million. But the intuitive answer turns out to be wrong. In most cases, groups deliberating on damages in such a situation awarded a much higher penalty—as high as $5 million or $10 million.

Experiments that asked groups to deliberate about more classic questions of public policy, from abortion to gun rights, suggested the same takeaway. When groups of people who largely agree on an answer to some pressing moral or political question debate the issue together, they don't tend to moderate or split the difference; on the contrary, they tend to egg each other on. In a surprising number of cases, they come to a conclusion that is more radical than that initially embraced by any individual member of the group. This is what the eminent Harvard behavioral economist Cass Sunstein has termed "the law of group polarization": after groups of like-minded people have a chance to deliberate about some question of morality or politics, the conclusions they come to are more radical than the beliefs of their individual members.

Group polarization need not be bad. Sometimes, it takes deliberation with like-minded people to recognize that the radical answer is the right one. (Perhaps we would, for example, all be safer if companies always had to pay enormous damages for their negligence.) But given that consensus on a radical position within a group is often based on peer pressure, and can fly in the face of clear and objective evidence, it is especially important for groups to have some built-in mechanism to stop them from going off the rails.

That is why researchers have, of late, focused on the extremely important role that dissenters play in moderating the effects of the law of group polarization. "Internal criticism and dissent are vital for social groups' success," the psychologists Levi Adelman and Nilanjana Dasgupta point out in a recent paper. "They prevent group members from insulating themselves against viewpoints that could be crucial to group decision-making. They also prevent groupthink, the process by which members of a group overemphasize similar opinions and shut down dissenters."

Much of the time, this works surprisingly well. Many groups are tolerant of internal dissent. They recognize the importance of open discussion, and may even reward critics who dare to speak their mind. This is especially true when those who speak up are perceived as loyal members of the group who are keen to make it better rather than as outsiders who don't share its goals. But often is not always. And research also suggests that there are times when healthy norms that encourage dissent and keep group polarization in check give way to enormous peer pressure and "reputational cascades" that entrench the views of a small minority—even when most members of the group secretly disagree with them.

So can we predict when the pressure to conform becomes so crushing that anyone who dares to dissent is vilified and those who are left in the group feel an even stronger need to go along with the views of its loudest members? The answer appears to be yes. Over the past two decades, researchers have found compelling evidence that there is a particular set of circumstances that makes it much more likely for a group to become less tolerant of dissent, and for internal critics to suffer such high reputational penalties that most choose to fall silent.

The pressure to conform, social psychologists have found, becomes much bigger when a group is in the middle of a conflict that involves high moral stakes, making its members feel that they are under threat. Whereas internal critics are normally seen as sincere, anybody who dares to disagree with the views or actions endorsed by the leaders of the group under such circumstances is liable to be accused of moral deviance—and to come under the suspicion of being a saboteur.

"Intergroup conflict increases enforcement of within-group norms and [is] correlated with intolerance toward critical ingroup members," Adelman and Dasgupta summarize the state of the literature. "Thus, when threat to the ingroup is salient, group members may become less open to criticisms of their group and respond negatively even to ingroup critics." Under such conditions of threat, "criticism from ingroup members may be perceived as an act of betrayal and attributed to the critic's malevolent motives." At times, these dynamics prove so powerful that it is no longer necessary to dissent consciously or explicitly to incur the wrath of the group; anybody who is seen as violating the norms of the group, however tentatively or inadvertently, becomes a target.

A sense of powerlessness is a big part of the reason for the fading tolerance toward dissenters under conditions of perceived threat. When the real target of your wrath is beyond your grasp, and the moral stakes of the moment are high, the inability to do anything useful becomes intensely frustrating. Some people who are desperate to do something—anything—to keep the threat at bay then start to direct their anger at those who are under their control.

This can help to explain what happened to parts of the progressive movement during Trump's presidency. The guy down the hall may not really be the biggest enemy of society. But he often turns out to be the biggest enemy over whom you have some modicum of control. So when activists came to feel that they did not have the tools to protect the country against the threat emanating from the White House, a small but consequential portion of them grew intolerant of internal dissent—and directed much of their anger at anybody who dared to violate the unwritten norms of the identity synthesis.

THE INTELLECTUAL ENFORCERS
OF THE IDENTITY ORTHODOXY

At first, these trends emerged more or less organically. As the risk grew that any open form of dissent with the popularized version of the identity synthesis would be seen as "running interference for Trump," more and more members of progressive institutions who disagreed with the prevailing consensus chose to stay silent. And as more members of progressive institutions chose to stay silent, the cost for anyone who still insisted on speaking up grew. A vicious cycle had emerged. But soon, a pair of bestselling books went one step further, giving this new identity orthodoxy a kind of intellectual superstructure, which sanctified intolerance of disagreement as a necessary part of the resistance against bigotry in all its forms.

Two assertions became especially effective enforcers of the new identity orthodoxy, and neither would be surprising to anybody who has read the psychological literature on how groups vilify dissenters under conditions of perceived threat. The first claimed that there are only two sides in the fight between racists and antiracists, making anybody who refuses to join the (supposedly) antiracist side a racist—a very effective way of portraying those who are not in full conformity with the new norms of the community as moral deviants. The second insisted that any form of resistance to this orthodoxy must be motivated by a self-serving refusal to acknowledge one's own complicity with racism—a very effective way to portray all dissenters as having nefarious intentions.

In the first decade of the twenty-first century, much of the American left had rightly resisted George W. Bush's Manichaean claim that "either you are with us, or you are with the terrorists." But now a strikingly similar sentiment came to be shared as a meme, incorporated in countless diversity trainings, and even plastered on corporate websites. Every act, person, institution, and public policy, Ibram X. Kendi argued in a bestselling 2019 book, is either racist or antiracist; there is no such thing as a neutral act:

> In writing *How to Be an Antiracist*, I've had one singular goal. If I could somehow shape the world, what I would hope would come out

of this book is very simply we would eradicate the term "not racist" from the American vocabulary. And then it would force people to recognize that they're either what? Racist or anti-racist.

Now, it is perfectly plausible to maintain that all human beings have a moral duty to oppose racism; I myself strongly agree with that claim. But the way Kendi defined his key terms, including the nature of "antiracism," made his theory much more radical than might at first be obvious. For, according to Kendi, the sole criterion of whether a particular act, person, institution, or public policy is "racist" or "antiracist" is whether it helps to increase or decrease the gap in income (or wealth or some other desirable metric) between white and Black people. As a result, he has declared that an extraordinary array of entities that, in his assessment, do not reduce such racial disparities are racist—from capitalism to the SATs, and from the filibuster to the U.S. Constitution.

Nor did Kendi hesitate to make clear how he regarded the moral status of anybody who failed to embrace this antiracist program, as he understands it. According to Kendi, anyone who claims that they are "not racist" is effectively siding with segregationists, eugenicists, and slave traders: "Americans who self-identify as not racist—whether they're conservatives, moderates, liberals, radicals, progressives—they don't realize . . . that we are connecting ourselves to a history of slave traders who self-identified as not racist."

The second belief played an even bigger role in discouraging disagreement with the new orthodoxy. Professing that no white person is capable of overcoming the racist patterns of thought and action that they are taught from an early age, Robin DiAngelo—the diversity trainer whose course has been used to train employees of Coca-Cola and many other major corporations—proudly embraced the idea that she, like all white people, is a racist. As one article summarizing her work put it, "If you're a white person in America, social justice educator Robin DiAngelo has a message for you: You're a racist, pure and simple."

But DiAngelo's core message was directed at those who dared to deny her prescription for self-identifying as a racist. Refusing to take any disagreement with her intellectual framework at face value, she insisted that pushback against it was, as the title of her most influential book suggests, merely evidence of "white fragility." As John McWhorter has summarized her view, "If you object to any of the 'feedback' that DiAngelo offers you about your racism, you are engaging in a type of bullying 'whose function is to obscure racism, protect white dominance, and regain white equilibrium.'" The effect of DiAngelo's book was to mainstream a non-falsifiable theory: All white people are racist. And if you disagree, that merely proves how racist you are.

When three policemen murdered George Floyd in the streets of Minneapolis on May 25, 2020, inspiring millions of Americans to protest against racial injustice, it was Kendi and DiAngelo who became overnight celebrities, setting the terms of mainstream discourse. Published in 2018, *White Fragility* became one of the most sold books of 2020, occupying top places on the *New York Times* bestseller list for more than a year. Kendi's *How to Be an Antiracist* was only a little less popular, spawning a franchise that included bestsellers such as *Antiracist Baby*. ("Babies are taught to be racist or antiracist—there is no neutrality," states the picture book, which is marketed to children who are one to six years old, before encouraging them to "confess when being racist.")

Kendi and DiAngelo appeared on major television programs from *The View* to *The Late Show with Stephen Colbert*. Their books received rave reviews in prestigious publications and made their way to antiracist reading lists shared by the country's biggest corporations. In light of the uncritical adulation their ideas received all across the country, it is hardly surprising that many people who had deep concerns about the popularized form of the identity synthesis came to feel that they had no choice but to remain silent. The identity trap had fully conquered the mainstream.

So far, this book has told the story of two remarkable transformations. In part I, I showed how the nature of left-wing thought changed over the course of the past half century, giving rise to the "identity synthesis" that had taken hold in many universities by 2010. In part II, I explained how a popularized version of these ideas could escape the ivory tower, coming to exert tremendous influence over the norms and ideas governing life in the United Kingdom and especially the United States today.

For the next section of the book, I propose to turn to a rather different task: the evaluation of the most influential claims made by the proponents and popularizers of the identity synthesis. Can applications of the identity synthesis to a wide range of topics from free speech to cultural appropriation help to make the world a fairer place? Or are they—as I shall argue—likely to prove dangerous and counterproductive?

KEY TAKEAWAYS

- After Donald Trump's election, millions of people mobilized to protest his administration. But when hopes for his quick removal from office faded, a small number of these activists turned their anger toward the inside, targeting anybody in their immediate surroundings who had violated the new progressive sensibilities.

- Individuals are very susceptible to peer pressure. As a result, groups of like-minded people often take more radical positions than those initially held by any of their members. Internal critics therefore play a very important role in keeping groups from going off the rails. But while groups are often open to such dissenters, they start to mistrust or even to punish them when they feel that they are under external threat.

- These group dynamics can help to explain why many institutions grew so intolerant of anybody who disagreed with the key precepts of the identity synthesis after Trump's election. Understandably feeling under threat from his administration, they came to think of any internal critic as a traitor or saboteur. An identity orthodoxy descended on many institutions.

- The enforcement of the identity orthodoxy was given an intellectual superstructure by two bestselling authors. According to Ibram X. Kendi, every person is either racist or antiracist; this made it easy to accuse anybody who disagreed with his prescriptions for how to remedy injustice of being a bigot. And according to Robin DiAngelo, anybody who denies that all white people are racist must be motivated by a self-serving refusal to acknowledge the truth. This helped to turn the popularized version of the identity synthesis into a non-falsifiable theory: in many milieus, any public disagreement with it would henceforth be seen as a form of self-incrimination. The mainstreaming of the identity synthesis was complete.

PART III

The Flaws of the Identity Synthesis

n the spring of 2019, a public high school in Florida hosted a kind of cultural show-and-tell. The school's students were encouraged to wear an item of clothing, bring in a culinary dish, or display some symbol from their ancestral culture that they found personally meaningful.

One of the teachers at the school, an immigrant from Nigeria, had an idea for how best to showcase his own culture. He asked a few of his favorite students, two of whom were white, whether they would be willing to wear the ceremonial garb of his ancestral tribe. They enthusiastically said yes.

When the two white students came to school dressed in the clothes their teacher had given them, they were met with instant hostility. Classmates told them they were committing "cultural appropriation." Some teachers accused them of mocking African culture. They were hauled into the principal's office.

The students' teacher did his best to intercede on their behalf. It had been his idea, he assured the principal. The clothes were part of his own culture. If he was honored by his students wearing them, why should anyone who isn't even part of his tribe have a reason to be offended on his behalf?

The principal disagreed. For white students to wear traditional African clothing, she declared, is an offensive form of cultural appropriation. Even though their teacher had encouraged them to do so, they should have known better. She suspended the students.

This incident is but one small example of the much wider way in which the popularized form of the identity synthesis is transforming the reigning norms and ideals of mainstream society, from neighborhood schools all the way to government offices. In this part of the book, I critically examine five such concepts, norms, and policy frameworks. While I could easily have discussed a number of others, these five collectively give a clear sense of what it would look like to reorder the world in accordance with the conclusions that many progressives have drawn from the identity synthesis.

All five applications are inspired by the identity synthesis and are now in the process of transforming mainstream institutions. All five have intuitive appeal because they give voice to real concerns about genuine injustices. But all five would ultimately fail to address the grievances that motivate them, and even undermine the goals they supposedly serve. Like the ideology from which they derive, they are a trap. These claims are:

1. *Standpoint theory*: Citizens drawn from different groups can never truly come to understand one another. Those who are comparatively privileged should therefore defer to the factual assessments and political demands of those who are comparatively marginalized.

2. *Cultural appropriation*: Groups do (or should) enjoy a form of collective ownership over their cultural products and artifacts, from distinctive modes of dress to particular culinary dishes. This puts restrictions on how people who do not belong to those groups can legitimately make use of them.

3. *Limits on free speech*: The state should make laws that rein in misinformation and protect minority groups from being exposed to hurtful or bigoted speech. Even when it comes to forms of expression that remain legally permitted, society should uphold a "consequence culture" that makes people less likely to express views that others will see as offensive.

4. *Progressive separatism*: Social and educational institutions should encourage people to identify themselves by the ethnic, racial, religious, sexual, and gender groups to which they belong. Spaces that are reserved for members of such groups can play an important role in helping people gain political consciousness and take on persistent injustices.

5. *Identity-sensitive public policy*: To redress persistent socioeconomic inequalities between different communities, the state must favor historically disadvantaged groups. We therefore need to adopt "identity-sensitive" policies, like prioritizing members of marginalized ethnic minorities for scarce medical resources, which make the way the state treats people depend on the group to which they belong.

Many of these views are motivated by rational concerns and legitimate needs. Members of marginalized groups, for example, really do face forms of injustice that are easy for members of dominant groups to overlook. And yet it is a mistake to believe that achieving justice for members of historically marginalized groups requires rejecting principles such as free speech and the aspiration to understand each other across racial or cultural boundaries. As I shall argue in this part of the book, the best way to remedy persistent injustices consists of a renewed commitment to core universal principles. It is such universal principles that allow us to think about topics from cultural appropriation to race-sensitive public policies in a more principled—and productive—manner.

If we put in the work, I argue in the next six chapters, we can come to understand the experiences of our compatriots and build a more meaningful form of political solidarity. Instead of patrolling who is allowed to make use of which cultural traditions, we should celebrate the joys of mutual cultural influence. Rather than living in fear of extremists who express loathsome sentiments, we should trust that we can beat them back without giving up on the right to free speech. Far from encouraging the creation of separate identities and institutions, we should foster real integration and encourage people to see what they have in common. And instead of making the treatment that individuals receive from the state depend on their sexual orientation or the color of their skin, we should embrace policies that benefit everyone who is in need, whatever the identity group to which they belong, while helping to remedy the lingering effects of past domination.

Building a fair society will take great willpower and serious effort. And yet the set of solutions that is now in the ascendant in areas from free speech to cultural appropriation would merely serve to aggravate existing problems. Rather than helping to build a society in which members of different groups are better able to understand and support each other, it would entrench current divisions and deepen mutual hostility.

Chapter 8

HOW TO UNDERSTAND EACH OTHER

n 1967, the producers of a surprise Broadway hit took their show to a faraway country for the first time. They were nervous about how it would be received. *Fiddler on the Roof* focuses on the life of an Orthodox Jewish family in a Central European shtetl at the turn of the twentieth century. Would theatergoers in Tokyo be able to relate to the internal struggle of the show's protagonist, a devout Jew who has to come to terms with his three daughters choosing deeply "unsuitable" husbands?

They need not have worried. As Joseph Stein, who wrote the musical's book, recalls, "I got there just during the rehearsal period and the Japanese producer asked me, 'Do they understand this show in America?' And I said, 'Yes, of course, we wrote it for America. Why do you ask?' And he said, 'Because it's so Japanese.'"

Stein interpreted this story as a testament to the ability of art and literature to cross boundaries of language, religion, and race. The show he created had somehow managed to tap into something "universal: the breakdown of tradition, the differences between generations, the eagerness to hang on to a religious background. These things are very much a part of the human experience."

By interpreting the story this way, Stein—a lifelong leftist—drew on a long tradition that sees the differences between people as less important than their commonalities. *Homo sum, humani nihil a me alienum puto*, a character in a play by the ancient Roman playwright Terence famously said: "I am human, and nothing human is alien to me." For centuries, this humanist tradition was especially cherished on the left. But of late, a big part of the left—and, increasingly, much of the mainstream—has turned on universalism. The (admittedly kitsch) insistence in "We Are the World" that we are "all a part of God's great big family" is gradually being supplanted by an emphasis on the way in which the members of privileged groups, like straight white men, are incapable of understanding the experiences of oppressed groups.

In corporate diversity trainings, the focus has shifted from celebrating cultural differences to recognizing the impossibility of overcoming ingrained racism and implicit bias. In the workshops of the country's most prestigious MFA programs, professors advise aspiring novelists to "write what you know." In Hollywood, actors from Tom Hanks to Eddie Redmayne to Kristen Bell have apologized for portraying characters whose sexual orientation, gender identity, or ethnic origin they did not share. Alison Brie has even publicly atoned for voicing an Asian American character on *BoJack Horseman*, an animated series whose protagonists largely consist of speaking animals.

In progressive political circles that are deeply steeped in the popularized form of the identity synthesis, the emphasis on the impossibility of mutual comprehension goes even further. The core claim is that a member of a privileged group will never be able to understand a member of an oppressed group, however hard they may try to do so. As Janetta Johnson, a prominent Black activist in San Francisco, put it in a debate about how white allies can help to fight for racial justice, "Don't come to me, because you will never understand my perspective." A number of viral articles and bestselling books go so far as to suggest that it is pointless for members of minority groups to share their experiences with members of the majority. "Even if they can hear you, they're not really listening," the British Nigerian author Reni Eddo-Lodge claimed in *Why I'm No Longer Talking to White People About Race*. "It's like something happens to the words as they leave our mouths and reach their ears."

This newfound emphasis on the impossibility of mutual comprehension is no mere cultural lament; increasingly, it justifies an explicitly political upshot. Because it is supposedly impossible for members of different groups to understand each other, those who are "more privileged" are asked to defer to those who are less so. The job of a loyal ally is to "listen," to "affirm the beliefs of the less privileged," and to "amplify their demands." In practice, the stress on "lived experience" often amounts to claims both that members of different identity groups will never be able to understand each other and that those who belong to more privileged groups should defer to those who belong to more marginalized ones.

There is a kernel of truth to the emphasis on "lived experience." How we experience the world is mediated by our identity. This gives all of us a moral obligation to listen carefully when members of different groups call our attention to injustices they encounter. But there are two big problems with the way in which many writers and activists are now invoking lived experience to justify much more far-reaching conclusions. The first is that the core claims of the popularized form of "standpoint theory" are unconvincing. With few exceptions, even feminist philosophers who are deeply committed to the idea that our social identity influences what we know reject the form of standpoint theory that has quickly become influential over the past decade. Empathy with the plight of others may take hard work, but it remains both possible and politically indispensable. The second problem is that standpoint theory fails as a set of practical guidelines for how to take effective political action in the real world. In particular, its growing influence is unlikely to empower the marginalized and may even make it harder to sustain the forms of true political solidarity we need to overcome real injustices. But before we turn to the arguments against standpoint theory, we must understand what these ideas entail and where they come from.

THE ORIGINS OF STANDPOINT THEORY

Philosophers interested in epistemology, or the theory of knowledge, have traditionally focused on fundamental questions about what we know about the world. In seventeenth-century France, René Descartes famously wondered how we can rule out that our perception of the world might be a hallucination induced by an evil demon. Today, philosophers debate such questions as the difference between "true belief" (when our beliefs happen to be true because we get lucky) and genuine "knowledge" (when our beliefs are both true and justified in the right ways).

In reflecting on these issues, philosophers have traditionally assumed that we are all, broadly speaking, in the same boat; they were not especially interested in what it would take for you, rather than for me, to have well-justified beliefs. But in the 1970s, feminist philosophers such as Donna Haraway started to argue that the ability of people to gain insights about some important social or political issues depends on the identity group to which they belong. Women, for example, supposedly share a set of common experiences that give them access to insights that are inaccessible to men.

In most societies, one argument for this position goes, women bear the main responsibility of caring for children. As a result, they have knowledge about the virtues of care, and the injustice of traditional gender norms, that escape men. To emphasize how each person's ability to understand the world depends on some such social "standpoint," feminist theorists called the field of inquiry they founded "standpoint epistemology."

As Sandra Harding put this intuitive argument in her introduction to *The Feminist Standpoint Theory Reader*, "The social location of women or other oppressed groups . . . could be the source of illuminating knowledge claims not only about themselves but also the rest of nature and social relations." Theorists and activists writing within other identity-based traditions quickly appropriated the same core insights for themselves. Today, Harding writes, "race, ethnicity-based, anti-imperial, and Queer social justice movements routinely produce standpoint themes."

The basic intuition behind standpoint epistemology is compelling. Think of three simple examples: A Black man on his way to work is stopped and searched by the police. A young woman is sexually harassed on the subway. An immigrant who speaks imperfect English is mocked by a government bureaucrat.

Clearly, our social identity shapes the experiences we are likely to have.

Someone who has never had to worry about being arbitrarily stopped by cops is less likely to empathize with the apprehension that a police uniform evokes in some Black men. Someone who has little reason to worry for their physical safety is less likely to understand how scary it is to be approached on the subway. And someone who fluently speaks the language of the country in which they live is less likely to be aware of the fear some immigrants feel before having to engage in mundane social interactions.

In its more modest versions, standpoint epistemology reminds us of an important and intuitive insight. It really is easy for the comparatively privileged to remain blind to the challenges faced by those who are less fortunate. Similarly, it really is frustrating to share heartfelt concerns that are based on one's own experiences, only to be dismissed by people who have not made the effort to listen with an open mind. And yet those philosophers and social theorists who have thought hardest about standpoint epistemology tend to reject the core claims of its popularized version, which goes far beyond that plausible intuition.

Writers and activists, Harding notes, have increasingly embraced what she calls a "folk" version of standpoint epistemology: a simplified—and often much more radical—set of ideas about the impossibility of mutual comprehension that quickly became highly influential outside academia. As Lidal Dror, an African American philosopher at Princeton University, puts it, "In everyday conversation, political debates, activist circles, and even philosophical settings, speakers will at times appeal to their social location as epistemic support for a claim. We have all heard someone say something to the effect of, 'as a Black person I know . . . ,' 'as a woman I know . . . ,' 'as a minority [of some type], I know . . . ,' before making a claim about society, group relations, or justice."

There is significant variation in the exact nature of these views. But four interlocking claims are particularly central to the forms of standpoint theory* that now routinely influence public debate:

---

* In this chapter, I will refer to claims widely embraced by feminist philosophers as standpoint epistemology. I will refer to the popularized and often more radical version of these claims—which are much more influential in activist circles and mainstream institutions, and constitute the main subject of this chapter—as standpoint theory.

1. There is a set of significant experiences that (virtually) all members of (particular) oppressed groups share.

2. These experiences give members of the group special insight into the nature of their oppression and other socially relevant facts.

3. Members of the group cannot fully or satisfactorily communicate these experiences to outsiders, even insofar as they have important political implications.

4. When an oppressed group makes political demands based on the identity its members share, outsiders should defer to them.

Do these claims hold water?

WHY STANDPOINT THEORY MAKES FOR BAD PHILOSOPHY

The first core claim of standpoint theory runs into trouble because it is extremely hard to identify meaningful experiences that all members of a socially relevant group share. Feminist philosophers originally tried to ground the special perspective of women in the fact that they have historically been expected to be in charge of rearing children, for example. But other feminist philosophers such as Elizabeth Spelman soon pointed out that there have been, all through history, many women who never had children. In a similar vein, men may be less likely to raise children on their own than women, but it is not clear why any particular single dad should have less insight into the burden of caregiving than any particular single mom. As Rachel Fraser, an associate professor of philosophy at Oxford University who herself defends a more moderate form of standpoint epistemology, told me, "You're going to have to abandon the simple idea that there's some kind of experiential core that all and only women have."

The second core claim of standpoint theory has also been called into doubt. Even insofar as many members of a relevant group do have common experiences, it is not clear that these bestow an overall advantage in understanding the world. Especially in deeply stratified societies, members of privileged groups may—unjustly and perversely—have some important forms of knowledge that are inaccessible to those who belong to marginalized groups. They may, for example, have better educational opportunities because members of the marginalized minority are excluded from quality schools and universities. They are also likely to have better access to the spaces in which unjust decisions are made and oppression is perpetuated. "Though an exploited factory worker has informative experiences about class oppression," Dror points out, "the factory owner—who uses their wealth and bargaining advantage to cut health benefits and pay less than a living wage—will also have experiences that provide insights into how class oppression operates." While the marginalized will have an epistemic advantage with respect to some important aspects of their oppression, the privileged may well have an epistemic advantage with respect to other pertinent aspects of the social world; effective action against injustice would ideally draw on both sets of insights.

The third core claim of standpoint theory is misleading in a somewhat more subtle way. It is true that it is impossible to know exactly what certain kinds of experiences, such as sexual harassment or police profiling, feel like if you haven't been subjected to them. This gives a certain plausibility to the widespread intuition that the experience of being oppressed or marginalized can't fully be shared. Rendered in philosophical language, there are, even when it comes to relatively simple things, real limits to the extent to which "experiential" knowledge is communicable. To know what it feels like to eat a blueberry, you need to have tasted a blueberry.

But the same does not apply to what philosophers call "propositional" knowledge. Such knowledge is typically thought to consist of statements that are true or false; to know that blueberries are in the genus *Vaccinium*, for example, you need never have eaten or even laid eyes upon a blueberry. The key question, then, is whether the most important insights drawn from experiential knowledge can—especially insofar as they are relevant to social and political debates—be shared in the form of propositional knowledge. Thankfully, there is good reason to believe that the answer is yes.

Fraser gives a striking example of how this distinction between experiential and propositional knowledge becomes relevant in debates about important questions of public policy. Many feminists favor restrictions on the sale of sexual services but worry that laws that criminalize sex workers will stigmatize them in dangerous ways. For that reason, they favor the so-called Nordic model, which makes it legal for sex workers to offer their services but illegal for clients to buy them. This seems like an elegant solution, discouraging sex work without marginalizing the vulnerable women who engage in it.

But of late, Juno Mac and Molly Smith have put forward strong arguments against the Nordic model. Based on their own experiences as sex workers, they claim that these laws are likely to do significant harm. Where sex work is outlawed, potential clients have a strong reason to solicit prostitutes in hidden or remote places. They are also in a stronger negotiating position because the fear of being punished drives down the number of potential customers. Due to these mechanisms, which most feminists had overlooked, the Nordic model, according to this argument, puts sex workers at greater risk of harm.

Fraser points out that Mac and Smith would have been unlikely to come up with these insights if they had never been sex workers. But she also insists that the politically relevant implications of those insights can easily be grasped by people who do not share Mac and Smith's experiences. Though you or I may not share their experiential knowledge, we are able to understand and act on the propositional knowledge they derived from it. "The role of experience in politics," Fraser concludes, "should not be overstated." Who we are will shape what we learn about the world, but it need not constrain our ability to communicate those insights to others.

All of this is good reason to doubt the first three claims of standpoint theory. "While the oppressed may often have a *contingent* epistemic advantage deriving from their tendency to have more informative experiences of the workings of social marginalization," Dror concludes his consideration of the subject, "there are only extremely limited grounds for thinking that they have an epistemic advantage derived *in principle* from being oppressed." Fraser is even more skeptical about the way in which standpoint-flavored claims are now commonly made in public. People, she points out, "often want to say that the fruits of oppression are a kind of virtue, a kind of admirable illness. I think that's just not there in the intellectual tradition. There's a kind of naïveté to that perspective that is very difficult to actually find in the academic work."

There are compelling philosophical reasons to be skeptical about the first three core elements of standpoint theory. But we are yet to consider the fourth claim: that the comparatively privileged should defer to the claims of the comparatively marginalized. This claim requires a different kind of analysis because it is fundamentally political rather than philosophical in nature. And as it happens, the political reasons against standpoint theory weigh even more heavily than the philosophical ones: put simply, standpoint theory just isn't a realistic guide for how members of different identity groups can make common cause with each other.

WHY STANDPOINT THEORY MAKES FOR BAD POLITICS

Addressing progressive activists at Netroots, Ayanna Pressley, a politician from Massachusetts who entered the House of Representatives in the blue wave of 2018, encouraged them to speak in the name of their identity groups:

> If you're not prepared to . . . represent that voice, don't come, because we don't need any more brown faces that don't want to be a brown voice. We don't need Black faces that don't want to be a Black voice. We don't need Muslims that don't want to be a Muslim voice. We don't need queers who don't want to be a queer voice.

Pressley's speech embraced a political vision that puts identity groups at the very heart of representative democracy. In her view, African Americans should get to decide the most important questions concerning their community, Asian Americans those that are of special relevance to them, and so on. Those who are not members of these groups should, in keeping with the dictates of standpoint theory, largely defer to their demands.

But even as Pressley advocated for this vision, she implicitly acknowledged the biggest problems it struggles to resolve. Clearly, she believes that some Black or brown or Muslim or queer politicians don't represent the interests of their groups in an adequate manner; in her language, these politicians don't want to be a Black (or brown or Muslim or queer) voice. But this of course raises a crucial follow-up question: Who gets to decide whether a Black politician does or does not represent the "authentic" Black voice?

Pressley, a member of the informal group of far-left congresspeople popularly known as the Squad, has one set of views about what it looks like for a politician to represent the authentic Black experience. Democratic members of Congress such as Jim Clyburn and the late John Lewis, who hold considerably more moderate positions, take a different view. Black conservatives such as Congressman Byron Daniels and Senator Tim Scott take an even more starkly different view. The key problem with Pressley's position consists of the difficulty in determining who can call themselves a legitimate spokesperson for a particular group. (The same problem is even more acute in the U.K. because the Conservative Party has been much more successful than the Republican Party at diversifying its leadership and attracting a large number of voters from ethnic minority groups.)

That might seem like an abstract concern. But in practice, the determination of who is a legitimate representative and what policies or norms a group favors is almost always made by people who are comparatively privileged. The rapid adoption of the term "Latinx" is a canonical example for this phenomenon in the United States. Most activist groups that claim to represent Hispanics have quickly adopted the term. So have the (mostly non-Hispanic) leaders of many mainstream institutions, from the dean of the Harvard Kennedy School to the president of the United States. But according to opinion polls, only about 2 percent of "Latinx" people prefer the new locution to older designations like "Hispanic."

In societies with significant inequalities of power and status, it is the affluent and well connected who are in the best position to determine who gets to speak on behalf of various identity groups. And so, "the Black voice" or "the brown voice" is, in the end, likely to be picked by some combination of powerful members within and outside a particular identity group. As the legendary civil rights activist Bayard Rustin wrote, "The notion of the undifferentiated black community is the intellectual creation of both whites . . . and of certain small groups of blacks who illegitimately claim to speak for the majority."

This is related to another serious worry about the effects that standpoint theory is likely to have in the real world: Its view of collective action gives short shrift to what true political solidarity entails. When members of other groups call on you to be their ally, you should, according to standpoint theory, say something along the following lines: "I do not understand your experiences and I am in no position to evaluate your demands. But since I recognize that you are more oppressed than me, I will endeavor to be a good ally and support what you ask for."

But such a thin model of political solidarity is unlikely to be effective. Most people simply won't be willing to delegate their judgment about what actions or policies they should support to a representative of a different group. They are especially unlikely to do so when they can't understand the reasons for the demand or when they disagree with it based on their own moral or religious views. For the most part, admonitions to defer to the views of the oppressed are likely to go ignored.

There may be a few exceptions. A small number of people who are deeply immersed in the identity synthesis might insist that they really do defer to members of other groups. But they will still face the problem of having to determine whom they consider a "true" Black or brown or Muslim or queer voice—and will almost certainly anoint spokespeople whose political prescriptions happen to dovetail with their own. In practice, demands to defer to an oppressed group succeed, at most, in encouraging activists to point at someone with whom they already agree and pretend that this ends the argument.

ONLY HARD-WON EMPATHY
CAN GROUND REAL SOLIDARITY

Standpoint theory sounds enticing. It proffers the prospect of a society in which we do what we can to listen to the experiences of the oppressed, constantly foregrounding their demands. At first glance, this seems like a promising recipe for building a more just society.

And yet the version of standpoint theory that is so often voiced in popular discourse today is likely to prove counterproductive. It wrongly claims that people from different groups are incapable of empathizing with each other's experiences of injustice—and that it would be better for them to stop trying. Embracing a vision of political solidarity based on thoughtless deference rather than hard-won empathy makes it harder to bring about real political progress. Thankfully, we can do better. Far from resigning ourselves to the idea that we either can't or shouldn't relate to members of different identity groups, we need to embrace a more ambitious form of political solidarity as one of the foundational values of a thriving democracy.

Building this kind of political solidarity—and this is the misdirected insight that lends standpoint theory its intuitive appeal—will require all of us to be humble. We do not, as a matter of course, see or know the obstacles faced by most of our fellow citizens. In important ways, our experience of the world really is mediated by our identity. This gives all of us a moral obligation to listen to each other with full attention and an open mind. But the point of this hard work is communication, not deference. As long as we put in the work, we *can* come to understand each other's experiences, especially insofar as they are politically relevant.

Understanding each other is the first step. Acting on the insights derived from our mutual empathy is the next. In a pluralistic society, you and I are likely to be motivated by different political aspirations and religious convictions. But that need not be a problem. After all, each moral or religious tradition has its own ways of expressing why some things are desirable and others are unjust. This is especially true when it comes to forms of racial, religious, or sexual discrimination that adherents of most moral traditions should find loathsome. When our fellow citizens tell us about the genuine injustices they face, we are perfectly capable of empathizing with their experiences—and of recognizing the way in which they violate our own aspirations for the kind of society in which we want to live.

KEY TAKEAWAYS

- Starting in the 1970s, feminist philosophers began to criticize traditional approaches to the theory of knowledge. Who we are, they argued, influences what we can know. Because women are usually expected to be primary caregivers, for example, they have more insights into the injustice of gender norms.

- These ideas were soon popularized in the form of standpoint theory. As activists now often claim, members of dominant groups cannot understand the experiences of members of marginalized groups. To be good allies, members of dominant groups should "defer" to members of marginalized groups, especially when they describe social injustices or make political demands.

- Standpoint theory consists of three key philosophical claims: First, there are significant experiences that members of oppressed groups share. Second, these experiences give members of the group special insight into the nature of their oppression as well as other politically relevant facts. And third, members of the group cannot fully or satisfactorily communicate these experiences to outsiders.

- Even most feminist philosophers who advocate some forms of standpoint epistemology reject the core claims of its popularized version. There are, they argue, no meaningful experiences that all members of particular identity groups, like women, share. Members of marginalized groups need not have superior insight into the true structure of society, in part because they might be excluded from spaces where important decisions are made. And though there are limits to the extent to which they can share "experiential" knowledge (for example, what it feels like to be discriminated against), they can communicate the "propositional" knowledge they derive from such experiences (for example, the fact that such forms of discrimination are unjust).

- Standpoint theory also entails a fourth claim, which is more political in nature: that members of dominant groups should defer to members of marginalized groups in the name of political progress. But in a pluralistic society, it is unclear who can legitimately speak on behalf of relevant identity groups. In practice, most members of dominant groups are going to either ignore demands to defer to members of marginalized groups or anoint people with whom they already agree as the "true" spokespeople of those groups.

- We should therefore insist on a more ambitious account of political solidarity and the role of empathy. True solidarity would have two elements: First, each of us would listen to members of other identity groups with an open mind, empathizing with the forms of oppression to which they may be subject. And second, each of us would strive to remedy genuine injustices, not out of a misguided sense of deference, but because they violate our own aspirations for the kind of society in which we want to live.

Chapter 9

THE JOYS OF MUTUAL INFLUENCE

n the summer of 2020, I discussed the concept of "cultural appropriation" with a set of smart, inquisitive undergrads. After reading three philosophical accounts outlining what is bad about cultural appropriation, the students were even more convinced of something that most of them had already assumed coming into the class: there is something deeply pernicious about the idea that a member of one identity group might use tunes, symbols, fabrics, or flavors that are characteristic of a culture to which they do not belong, especially if they hail from a comparatively "privileged" group.

Then Selena, a thoughtful sophomore who rarely spoke up in class but always had a smart point to make when she did, raised her hand. "I think I sort of have a personal story about cultural appropriation," she said softly. Intrigued, I encouraged her to share.

That term, Selena had been working as an intern at the university's art museum. As part of a drive to make its collection come to life, the marketing team asked members of the public to re-create its artworks. Because not as many people as hoped were sending submissions, Selena's boss encouraged her to contribute, even sharing a list of suggestions. Selena happily agreed, picking out a photograph that particularly spoke to her: *Plant Contest* by Cao Fei—a self-portrait of the Chinese artist and her mother, lying on the floor surrounded by flower petals and beauty products.

Because she was living at home for the semester due to the pandemic, Selena asked her mother, a Chinese immigrant, to re-create the picture with her. A few hours after she submitted the piece, the museum's director sent her a congratulatory email, telling her how beautiful a picture she had taken and promising that it would soon be added to the museum's website. Selena was elated. Then she got an angry email from an Asian American curator at the museum. It was deeply wrong, the curator said, for Selena to appropriate the work of a Chinese artist. She should be ashamed of herself.

Selena, who is mixed race and looks ethnically ambiguous, was confused. Gingerly, she pointed out that her mother was a Chinese immigrant and that she too identified as Asian American. But the curator was not having it. Because Selena's dad is not Chinese, the curator insisted, she did not have a right to re-create the painting.

While Selena was telling her story, the mood in the classroom shifted. A few minutes earlier, my students had been sure that cultural appropriation is reprehensible. Now they were growing concerned about how the concept might be abused. "If we're not allowed to draw on the culture of 'another' group," one student, whose parents had migrated to the United States from Mexico, asked, "who gets to decide who counts as a member of which group?" Another student, who grew up in Europe and Latin America but traces his roots to Africa, seemed even more perturbed: "I'm just really troubled by the idea that my university would apply some kind of racial purity test in deciding whether or not Selena gets to re-create that picture."

Ever since human beings developed distinct cultures, they have worried that their purity might soon be spoiled. In ancient Greece, Therpandrus caused offense by adding an extra string to his lyre. In sixteenth-century China, the emperor ordered all seafaring ships destroyed because of fears about the cultural changes that foreign trade missions might induce. In nineteenth-century Germany, Richard Wagner worried that Jews might spoil the authenticity of German culture.

A new version of the same old anxiety about cultural influence is once

again at the forefront of political debate. Far-right populists love to denounce the ways in which immigration and the growth of minority groups
are supposedly eroding social norms, supplanting native languages, or dis-
placing local cuisines. The greatest danger of the moment, they claim, is
"globalism." Even mainstream politicians increasingly like to portray themselves as brave defenders of traditional mores: in one of her first official acts
as the president of the European Commission, Ursula von der Leyen tasked
a member of her cabinet with "protecting the European way of life."

Traditionally, it has been the right that opposed and the left that defended new cultural influences. But in recent years, many progressives have
also started to worry about ways in which cultures might cross-pollinate.
While they celebrate a great variety of traditional cultures, and seek to improve the representation of various ethnic and religious minorities, they
have started to warn about the dangers of "cultural appropriation." As one
professor put the point, the cultures of others should be considered "off
limits." How did such concerns come to conquer the left?

HOW THE LEFT CAME TO WORRY
ABOUT CULTURAL APPROPRIATION

After World War II, socialists were under pressure to explain why the proletarian revolutions predicted by Karl Marx had failed to materialize in so
many countries. From Antonio Gramsci to the Frankfurt School, many
thinkers looking for an explanation turned to the ability of mainstream
cultural institutions to co-opt workers and confuse them about their true
class interests. One of the most influential efforts to do so was started, in
Birmingham, by Stuart Hall, a British Jamaican sociologist. But whereas many
of Hall's predecessors had focused on high culture, the "Birmingham
School of Cultural Studies" paid a lot more attention to popular culture.

At first, the Birmingham School was resolutely Marxist. But as postmodernism and postcolonialism started to reshape the main concerns of
the left over the course of the 1970s and 1980s, cultural theorists in Hall's
tradition became more receptive to concerns about how members of dominant identity groups could exercise a form of cultural hegemony over

members of marginalized identity groups. As the UCLA professor Vinay Lal points out, one of the questions that stood at the heart of Edward Said's *Orientalism* had been, "Who represents whom with what authority, with what right, and with what consequences?" From that question, it was but a small stop to conclude that, as Robert S. Nelson, a Yale professor of architecture and art history, has put it, "in every cultural appropriation there are those who act and those who are acted upon, and for those whose memories and cultural identities are manipulated by aesthetic, academic, economic, or political appropriations, the consequences can be disquieting or painful."

By 2010, these themes had become deeply influential in a variety of academic departments, from comparative literature to African American and media studies. When a new set of ideas about identity escaped the ivory tower and became popularized over the course of the following decade, the charge that somebody had committed "cultural appropriation" became a recurring feature of small online communities. Like the identity synthesis as a whole, cultural appropriation had gone pop.

By now debates about cultural appropriation have gone mainstream and cover a very wide range of supposed offenses. Over the past couple of years, musicians have been shamed for copying the styles of minority groups, chefs have been boycotted for emulating the cuisines of different nations, and novelists have had their book contracts canceled for featuring protagonists whose "identity" did not match their own. As part of its "Archive Repair Project," *Bon Appétit*, the American culinary magazine, apologized for allowing a Gentile writer to publish a recipe for hamantaschen, a traditional Jewish dessert. In Germany, *Der Spiegel* worried that Gentiles who donned a kippa in a show of solidarity after a man had been assaulted for wearing the traditional Jewish head covering were guilty of cultural appropriation. And in the U.K., *The Guardian* has weighed in on whether Jamie Oliver, a star chef, can cook jollof rice; whether Gordon Ramsay, another star chef, should be allowed to open a Chinese restaurant; and whether it was offensive for Adele, a star singer, to wear a traditional Jamaican hairstyle to the Notting Hill Carnival. In many milieus, it is now widely accepted that decent people should avoid committing any form of "cultural appropriation."

Some cases of so-called cultural appropriation do undoubtedly amount to real injustices. It was, for example, immoral for white musicians in the United States to steal the songs of Black artists who were barred from big careers because of racial discrimination or for collectors in the United Kingdom to loot art from the country's former colonies. But does the concept of cultural appropriation actually help to express what is wrong in such cases? And should societies forever be on guard against the possibility that a member of the majority group may take inspiration from the cultures of ethnic or religious minorities?

The answer to both of these questions is no. In the face of varied anxieties about the way in which cultures influence each other, it is high time for a full-throated defense of cultural hybridity. For far from explaining the nature of genuine injustices, the concept of cultural appropriation actually muddles our thinking, making it much harder to understand what renders those cases unjust. And rather than being something we should guard against, the ever-present reality of mutual inspiration is one of the most attractive features of diverse societies.

THE PROBLEMS WITH "CULTURAL APPROPRIATION"

Concerns about cultural appropriation are often rooted in anger about real injustices or genuinely offensive behavior. In the spring of 2017, for example, members of Baylor University's Kappa Sigma fraternity hosted a "Cinco de Drinko" party, a malicious parody of an (itself dubiously authentic) holiday celebrating Mexican American heritage. Lots of students came to the frat house sporting ponchos and sombreros. Some of the girls had dressed up as maids. Two boys clad in construction outfits were dancing on a table.

Many students at the school understandably felt that they were being mocked. "My dad is a painter and my mom, she cleans offices for a living," Grace Rodriguez, a sophomore at the school, said. "She doesn't do it because . . . cleaning is great. . . . She does it because she wants something better for me." Grace is right. The "Cinco de Drinko" party was clearly tasteless and offensive. But does the concept of "cultural appropriation" help us understand *why* it was offensive?

In the nascent literature about cultural appropriation, philosophers have tried to explain the nature of the harm that is involved. Some claim that it is a form of exploitation, stealing the rightful intellectual property of a marginalized group for the profit of privileged individuals. Others claim that it is a form of oppression that can "silence, speak for, and misrepresent" different groups. Other still argue that it impinges on the "intimacy" of the relevant group.

To be coherent, all of these different accounts need to defend the same basic claim: that some groups of people should enjoy formal or informal ownership over particular cultural practices or artifacts, giving them decision-making power over who gets to partake. After all, we need some account of who has the right to engage in a particular cultural practice, and how its owners will determine under what circumstances outsiders should be allowed to partake in it, if we are to get any clarity about when its uses are legitimate, and when they aren't. This raises a host of difficult questions that have not been satisfactorily answered—and, I believe, never will. These include the following: How does a group come to enjoy ownership over a set of cultural products? Who counts as a member of that group? What is the decision-making mechanism for determining who can legitimately partake in its cultural products? And how will those who violate these rules be punished? To illustrate how hard it is to answer these questions in a satisfactory way, I will focus on just two of them: the problem of original ownership and the problem of group membership.

The Problem of Original Ownership

Philosophers have long developed theories about how people came to have legitimate claims on property before the creation of modern states and the explicit legal codes they uphold. In the famous formulation of John Locke, for example, someone acquires property when he "mixes his labor" with a physical object, like a patch of land, thus gaining rightful enjoyment over its fruits. Today, lawyers still spend a lot of time thinking about the intricacies of contract law, ironing out the details of who owns what under which circumstances. To get a concept of cultural appropriation off the ground, we need some equivalent of these formal and informal regimes of property rights: a plausible account for why, even in the absence of explicit laws to that effect, some group has a plausible moral claim to a collective form of ownership over certain cultural memes or artifacts.

At first sight, this doesn't seem too difficult. Even in the absence of formal property rights, we might believe that groups of people gain a rightful claim of ownership over some cultural practice or artifact by the effort that went into creating it. If the Vietnamese invented banh mi, they should enjoy some rights over who gets to put it to what uses.

Plausible as it may look at first glance, this account of the origins of collective ownership turns out to be self-undermining in most cases. If we grant that group rights to cultural artifacts exist, we can help to explain why it might be inappropriate for Americans with roots in Europe, Africa, or Latin America to turn a profit by selling the sandwich; indeed, a number of chefs and business owners have, of late, been raked over the coals for doing so, especially when their efforts were deemed insufficiently "authentic." But because the banh mi is served on something suspiciously resembling a French baguette, this raises the question of why its inventors should have had the right to create the dish in the first place.

Since its dawn, human culture has evolved by remixing and reappropriating a rich array of cultural influences. So if we were to apply the same rules to the groups that first produced cultural artifacts whose use the critics of cultural appropriation now seek to limit, we would quickly find that the supposed victims of cultural appropriation have themselves perpetrated the very same sin.

This points to an insight that is as simple as it is important: Nearly all of the greatest dishes, customs, and inventions on which humanity can pride itself have roots in multiple cultures. Trying to assign particular instances of culture to one group in a clean way is a fool's errand. For the same reason, it would fundamentally undermine our collective creativity if humans were to be restricted from drawing on the cultures of all groups in the future.

As the British-Ghanaian-American philosopher Kwame Anthony Appiah, whose paternal ancestors were leaders of the Ashanti tribe that invented kente cloth, has written,

> Trying to find some primordially authentic culture can be like peeling an onion. The textiles most people think of as traditional West African cloths are known as Java prints; they arrived in the 19th century with the Javanese batiks sold, and often milled, by the Dutch. The traditional garb of Herero women in Namibia derives from the attire of 19th-century German missionaries, though it is still unmistakably Herero, not least because the fabrics used have a distinctly un-Lutheran range of colors. And so with our kente cloth: the silk was always imported, traded by Europeans, produced in Asia. This tradition was once an innovation. Should we reject it for that reason as untraditional? How far back must one go? Should we condemn the young men and women of the University of Science and Technology, a few miles outside Kumasi, who wear European-style gowns for graduation, lined with kente strips (as they do now at Howard and Morehouse, too)? Cultures are made of continuities and changes, and the identity of a society can survive through these changes. Societies without change aren't authentic; they're just dead.

The Problem of Group Membership

It is easy to see why a local artisan or cultural innovator should, even if they do not have the legal tools to enforce it, gain a moral right to the fruits of their creation. If a poor peasant creates a pattern of dress, or discovers the salutary qualities of a local herb, and this discovery brings benefits to millions of people, she deserves to be honored and rewarded for that work. But it is far from clear that the creative act of an individual—or even of a small group—should transmit such rights to the kinds of large identity-based categories to which critics of cultural appropriation seek to assign an informal property right.

Humans have an ingrained tendency to distinguish between an ingroup and an out-group. But the way in which they draw the distinction between who is in and who is out always depends on local contexts. This means that the artisans who created much of the cultural heritage of humanity were extremely unlikely to identify with the kinds of broad groups that are salient to us in mass societies embedded in a much more interconnected world. Rather than believing themselves to be part of the large ethnic or racial categories codified by the U.S. Census Bureau or the British Office for National Statistics, these artisans likely saw themselves as members of a specific indigenous tribe or as residents of a particular village.

Critics of cultural appropriation believe that the unknown peasant woman who first created the rebozo, the shawl-like garment worn by many women in Mexico, has somehow passed the rights to her creation on to those people we might today call Hispanic, making it inappropriate for white women to make use of it. But it is thoroughly unclear by what strange alchemy her invention should give a group to which she did not know she belonged a form of collective ownership over the fruits of her creation.

This raises another problem, which may seem theoretical or abstract, but is likely to create concrete and oft-absurd dilemmas in real life: Who gets to count as one of the collective "owners" of a practice or artifact? Can Mexican Americans whose ancestors hail from Europe partake in cultural practices that were invented by Mayans? May Brahmins perform dances that were developed by members of lower castes (and vice versa)? Should members of the southwest African tribe of Chewas be allowed to sell dishes concocted by neighboring Tumbukas? And does somebody who is mixed race, like Selena, get to re-create the artwork of a "fully" Asian artist?

In philosophy, one powerful way to notice that you have gone astray is when the moral principle you defend pushes you to evaluate the world by means of increasingly absurd criteria. That is the case here. Anyone who takes the idea of cultural appropriation seriously is forced to adjudicate such questions as whether Selena is sufficiently Asian to re-create Cao Fei's artwork, or whether it would be appropriate for a Mexican immigrant whose ancestors hail from Spain to make a living selling *cochinita pibil*, a popular dish reputed to have been inspired by Mayan cuisine. And that, in my mind, is one of the best reasons to look for a better way to articulate the real harm that is at play in many of the situations that have—wrongly, I believe—come to be described as instances of "cultural appropriation."

A BETTER WAY OF EXPRESSING WHAT'S WRONG

A consistent application of the language of cultural appropriation pushes us to ask absurd questions and draw the wrong conclusions. If the concept has nonetheless become so prominent, it is because there are some cases of supposed cultural appropriation that really are unjust. Is there some way to express what is wrong with them that is less likely to lead us astray?

Let's get back to that Cinco de Drinko party. The students who participated in it really did do something wrong, and the idea of cultural appropriation has spread so quickly in good part because it promises to explain *what* made their behavior so hurtful. But a closer look reveals that the idea of cultural appropriation does not capture what was most offensive about the party, and that there is a better way of expressing what philosophers would call its "wrong-making feature."

According to the language of cultural appropriation, what was so wrong about the party is that students who are not Latino appropriated some of the most iconic elements of Mexican culture for their own purposes. But this would have a highly implausible implication. Ponchos and sombreros are part of traditional Mexican culture. Maids' outfits and construction vests are not. So from the perspective of cultural appropriation, the students who wore ponchos or sombreros were doing something wrong but those who wore maids' outfits or construction vests were not. But is that really true?

Obviously, it isn't. While wearing a poncho or a sombrero may arguably be tacky and insensitive, it need not entail any ridicule or disrespect. Wearing a maid's outfit or a construction vest to a Mexican-themed party, by contrast, is a far more pointed and cruel insult. As Grace Rodriguez recognized, the intention was clearly to imply that Latinos are (or perhaps should be) cleaners or manual laborers, not college students or professionals.

But if some of the most offensive behavior at the Cinco de Drinko party didn't consist of any form of cultural appropriation, we need a different explanation for what made it wrong. The one that seems to fit much better is, simply, that their choice of dress expressed deeply prejudiced and hurtful ideas about Latinos. The problem is neither that they wore a sombrero nor that they donned a maid's outfit; it is that they did both to portray Latinos as a group of uneducated people who deserve to be mocked.

A similar dynamic is at play in virtually all cases in which the media invokes the specter of cultural appropriation. When a critic at *The Toronto Star* got a small business shut down in the middle of the pandemic for the crime of serving an inauthentic version of pho, the popular Vietnamese soup, for example, she justified her anger by invoking the times classmates in elementary school had mocked her for the contents of her lunch box. But while it is of course deeply wrong for kids to mock their classmate because they are not accustomed to the food she eats at lunch, shutting down a business that serves inauthentic pho will not help to save other children from that injustice. (If anything, the opposite is likely true: the more a particular cuisine enters a country's cultural mainstream, even in a form that is inauthentic, the less likely it is that future children will be mocked for eating one of its dishes at lunch.)

Some of the most iconic instances of cultural appropriation similarly misidentify the wrong-making feature. Rock 'n' roll artists like Pat Boone have, for example, been blamed for getting famous by appropriating musical styles that were popular among African Americans, or even stealing songs from Black musicians who were barred from fame and wealth due to the color of their skin. Once again, it is both beyond doubt that these Black musicians were harmed and very much in doubt that the concept of cultural appropriation best describes the nature of that harm. For justice would have consisted not in stopping Boone from popularizing that music, allowing millions of people to share in its joy, but rather in challenging the social and legal barriers that stopped African American performers like

Little Richard, Big Mama Thornton, and Muddy Waters from enjoying the rightful fruits of their creative efforts.

––––––––––

Throughout human history, different groups of people have influenced and emulated each other's cultures. This is especially true in Canada and the United States, which have always been a mix of the influences their residents brought to these countries from across the world. But it is also true in countries whose leaders pretend that their culture is somehow "pure." Traditional Polish culture, for example, involves a religion whose origins lie in the Middle East, a system of numerals that was imported from the Arab world, a script that stems from southern Europe, and a cuisine that heavily features a certain starchy vegetable that is native to the New World.

It should be little surprise that some of the most celebrated epochs of human history have come at times, and in places, that allowed different cultures to inspire each other. From the Baghdad of the ninth century to the Vienna of the nineteenth century to London and New York in the twenty-first century, it was cultural hybridity that allowed multiethnic societies to thrive and shine.

For all these reasons, the joy of mutual influence is not a sin against which diverse societies should be on guard; it is the key promise they hold out to us if we get things right. Instead of condemning cultural appropriation, we should seek to build a society in which members of every group are valued equally—and all are free to draw inspiration from the cultures of their compatriots.

KEY TAKEAWAYS

- The left has traditionally celebrated art's ability to speak to people beyond the boundaries of race and religion. But of late, many left-leaning milieus, especially in the arts, have endorsed the idea that any instance in which a member of a dominant group uses, co-opts, or partakes in the culture of a marginalized group constitutes a dangerous form of "cultural appropriation."

- The concept of cultural appropriation gains superficial plausibility from the fact that artists who belong to marginalized groups have often been cheated out of the fruits of their creation. But as it is now applied, it misdescribes what made those situations wrong and inhibits valuable forms of cultural exchange.

- The concept of cultural appropriation is based on an implicit notion of collective ownership over particular products and ideas. But it is unclear how the inventions of particular individuals who lived at a different time and place (like indigenous craftswomen in Central America) should convey ownership over such products to the kinds of broad identity categories (like Latinos) that are most salient today. Because virtually all cultural artifacts and ideas are themselves inspired by a broad range of preexisting cultures, it is also unclear why a particular innovation should give rise to such a form of collective ownership.

- In philosophical terms, cultural appropriation misidentifies the "wrong-making feature" of unjust situations. When supposed instances of cultural appropriation really are bad, the injustices at stake can be explained in simpler terms, such as discrimination against Black artists or an intent to mock Latinos. When it is impossible to express the supposed wrong involved in cultural appropriation in such simple terms, it is a mistake to pathologize otherwise healthy forms of cultural exchange.

- The ability of people from different cultural backgrounds to inspire each other is one of the most attractive features of diverse societies. While genuine injustices motivate the opponents of cultural appropriation, we should proudly defend the joys of mutual cultural influence.

Chapter 10

SPEAK FREELY

When I first set foot in Sopron, a city in western Hungary that has enjoyed enormous economic growth since the fall of the Berlin Wall, I marveled at the beauty of its round churches and cobblestoned streets. The spruced-up town looked like a shining example of the successful transition from communism to democracy. Then I started approaching passersby to ask what they thought of their government. When they saw the BBC logo on my microphone—I was traveling through four countries in Central Europe for a radio documentary—most refused to talk to me.

Finally, I found a middle-aged construction worker who agreed to have a quick chat as long as I switched off the mic. "We're scared," he told me. "If I criticize the government on the BBC, I might be out of a job tomorrow." Though he was not employed by the state, the man explained, his company often worked on public building projects. If local politicians got wind that one of the company's employees had criticized the government, they might demand that he be fired. It was a risk he couldn't take.

Around the world, authoritarian populists such as Hungary's Viktor Orbán are attacking free speech. Their first victims have typically been investigative journalists or outspoken opposition leaders. But, like Orbán, many have eventually started to crack down on the speech of ordinary citizens. Like the people of Sopron, the people of Bangkok and Manila, of Mumbai and Istanbul have had to become careful about what they say.

Even in the United States, there are growing attempts to use the law to stifle what people can say. A number of Republican state legislatures have, for example, passed bills that restrict how public employees can discuss race or sexuality. On the face of it, many of these laws are merely determining what kind of content teachers should impart in public schools, something the state has a legitimate interest in regulating. But the kind of speech they prohibit is defined in a worryingly broad manner.

In the state of Tennessee, for example, a law passed in 2022 prohibited any teaching materials that promote "division between, or resentment of, a race, sex, religion, creed, nonviolent political affiliation, social class, or class of people." Similarly, in the state of Florida, a 2022 bill outlaws "classroom instruction by school personnel or third parties on sexual orientation or gender identity" in kindergarten and the first three grades; even in later years, it is illegal when done "in a manner that is not age appropriate." Because the language in both of these bills is very vague, there is a real danger of them chilling legitimate forms of expression, from teachers mentioning their same-sex partners to discussing historical injustices like slavery.

Thankfully, key constitutional protections put limits on the extent to which coercive authorities can punish private citizens for what they say. The First Amendment prohibits Congress from making any law "abridging the freedom of speech, or of the press." The constitutions of all fifty states include similar provisions. (While the bills in Tennessee and Florida regulate what public employees can say when they are on the clock, for example, it would be unconstitutional for them to put similar restrictions on what they can say when they are off the job.) Even at the height of Donald Trump's power, most Americans did not need to fear that their government would punish them for speaking their minds.

But in other countries, strict laws regulating hate speech and personal insults do often constrain what ordinary citizens can say to a concerning extent. In February 2021, for example, three police officers in Merseyside, in the north of England, took to the streets with a public service announcement. Clad in official uniforms, with their faces covered by masks meant to protect them against the pandemic, they posed in front of a giant billboard. BEING OFFENSIVE IS AN OFFENSE, it announced. (The billboard did not specify what should be considered offensive, or who would be the judge of that.)

Laws in Germany are even more restrictive, and even more likely to go wrong. In Stuttgart, leftist activists have been prosecuted for selling anti-fascist merchandise that depicts a stick figure throwing the swastika, a symbol that is forbidden in Germany, into a trash can. In Berlin, police have investigated the publishers of a gay magazine for describing the late pope Benedict as a homophobe. Meanwhile, in Hamburg, police turned up at the doorstep of a local resident with a search warrant. His alleged crime? When a government minister criticized city residents for partying during the pandemic, he responded by tweeting, "You are such a dick."

Meanwhile, censorship has quickly become institutionalized in some of the most important venues for public debate. Social media platforms like Twitter and Facebook have quickly become indispensable for public debate; when they ban certain viewpoints, they make it very hard for these ideas to reach a wide audience. And yet the CEOs of most major tech companies have vowed to ban a broad and poorly defined set of ideas they consider "misinformation." Over the course of the past few years, they have, with that justification, artificially limited discussion of the origins of the coronavirus and scandals surrounding the son of a presidential candidate.

Especially in the United States, a censorious spirit has gone mainstream. Major television networks and streaming providers have removed episodes of shows they consider offensive. Publishers have canceled the release of hotly anticipated novels because a few online reviewers deemed them insensitive. Venues have canceled shows by comedians because their employees claimed that they might express "dangerous" views. Universities have disinvited speakers because they had expressed widely held opinions about affirmative action in the pages of a national magazine. A large number of people have been summarily fired from their jobs for offenses either trivial or imaginary.

Incidents of censorship or social shunning attract most attention when they involve someone famous. But in the main, they affect ordinary people who never make the news. More than three out of five Americans now say that they abstain from expressing their political views for fear of suffering significant adverse consequences. A majority of college students report having self-censored in the past, with only one out of every four saying that they are comfortable discussing controversial topics with their classmates. Even at *The New York Times*, about half of the paper's own employees believe that many of their colleagues are "afraid to say what they really think."

This is a problem. To feel empowered to engage in political debate, it is, as political theorists have long recognized, not enough for them to be protected from the police throwing them in jail. They also shouldn't have to fear that voicing a view that happens to stray from the fickle consensus of the day will get them socially shunned or fired from their job. As John Stuart Mill pointed out during the Victorian era, society

> practices a social tyranny more formidable than many kinds of political oppression, since, though not usually upheld by such extreme penalties, it leaves fewer means of escape, penetrating much more deeply into the details of life, and enslaving the soul itself. Protection, therefore, against the tyranny of the magistrate is not enough: there needs protection also against the tyranny of the prevailing opinion and feeling; against the tendency of society to impose, by other means than civil penalties, its own ideas and practices as rules of conduct on those who dissent from them.

This is why a free society requires a genuine *culture* of free speech. And it is in this realm that Americans, as well as the inhabitants of many other democracies, now face an acute danger.

There are many reasons for this lamentable state of affairs, including the way in which social media makes it easier for hard-liners to mobilize collective anger against anyone who flouts the in-group consensus—something that has increased the cost for daring to dissent with your own tribe on both sides of America's increasingly bitter partisan divide. But as a longtime member of the left who is deeply committed to the value of free speech, I find one reason for this transformation especially remarkable: large parts of the American left have openly turned against the ideal of free speech.

From abolitionists fighting for their right to lambaste slavery in the 1850s to student protesters opposing the war in Vietnam in the 1960s, the American left has long championed the value of free speech. "Liberty is meaningless where the right to utter one's thought and opinions has ceased to exist," Frederick Douglass once said. Calling free speech "the dread of tyrants," he insisted that it is, "in the eyes of all thoughtful men, the great moral renovator of society and government."

But over the past decade, the defense of free speech has, in the imagination of many leftists, taken on a right-wing hue. Alexandria Ocasio-Cortez, perhaps the most prominent young progressive in the United States, has repeatedly put free speech in scare quotes and insinuated that the First Amendment is "merely a service for the powerful." Owen Jones, a columnist at *The Guardian* and one of the most influential leftist writers in the United Kingdom, claimed that "'free speech' warriors" care only about "the right to say bigoted and stigmatising things about minorities." Ellen K. Pao, a former CEO of Reddit and a committed leftist, expressed the increasingly common dismissal of free speech even more succinctly. "At the end of the day," she wrote on Twitter, "the free-speechers really just want to be able to use racist slurs."

These arguments are a serious mistake. As philosophers have long recognized, a true culture of free speech has important benefits, allowing us to recognize our errors and develop a deeper understanding of our own beliefs. Even more important are the bad things that would happen if we gave up on free speech. When censors rule the day, the powerful decide who gets to speak, the stakes of elections grow existential, and social progress moves out of reach. But before we can answer the new critics of free speech, we need to understand their arguments: So where does the growing progressive hostility against "free speechers," as Pao derogatively called us, come from?

THE ROOTS OF THE "PROGRESSIVE" REJECTION OF FREE SPEECH

The most influential rejection of free speech from the left was formulated by Herbert Marcuse. When Adolf Hitler ascended to power, Marcuse, a German Jew, was about to take a position at the prestigious Institute for Social Research, more commonly known as the Frankfurt School. Instead, he was forced to flee to the United States, moving to California and reinventing himself as the intellectual apostle of the New Left. According to Marcuse, principles such as free speech might be appropriate for a society that is truly free. But, Marcuse claimed in "Repressive Tolerance," the Western democracies of his time were defined by class domination and media propaganda. Under such circumstances, "freedom (of opinion, of assembly, of speech) becomes an instrument for absolving servitude"; free speech, he concluded, merely serves to entrench oppression.

The solution, according to Marcuse, was for a "subversive majority" to gain power, by violent means if necessary, and to withdraw "toleration of speech and assembly from groups and movements which promote aggressive policies, armament, chauvinism, discrimination on the grounds of race and religion, or which oppose the extension of public services, social security, medical care, etc." It would then be up to an intellectual vanguard to "identify policies, opinions, movements which would promote" true tolerance. (Indeed, according to Marcuse, a number of major movements such as the recent "Chinese and Cuban Revolutions" had already succeeded in establishing "the democratic educational dictatorship of free men.")

A quarter century later, a prominent literary scholar formulated another highly influential rejection of free speech. According to Stanley Fish, the very idea of free speech is logically incoherent. Because "abstract concepts like free speech do not have any 'natural' content," Fish claims, echoing Foucault, they are forever "filled with whatever content and direction" the victors of political struggles decide to give them. Building on the tradition of critical legal studies, he argued that it is impossible to draw a principled boundary between the kind of expression that falls under the protection of free speech provisions like the First Amendment and the kind of speech that can legitimately be regulated.

It is, for example, widely held that the First Amendment does not protect "fighting words": forms of expression that are "likely to provoke the average person to retaliation." The problem, according to Fish, is that the judgment as to what utterances are likely to provoke the average person to such an extreme extent will inevitably be highly subjective. This, Fish claims, is not an isolated case: the boundary between what must be permitted and what can be forbidden is always a matter of politics. And so free speech is supposedly meaningless—an empty incantation that cleverly conceals the real power dynamics that are at work. "Free speech," Fish concludes, "is just the name we give to verbal behavior that serves the substantive agendas we wish to advance."

The lasting influence of these two strands of critique is evident in contemporary attacks on free speech. Marcuse's idea that "true" tolerance requires intolerance toward offensive views, for example, now holds tremendous cultural sway. As the British Labour MP Nadia Whittome recently tweeted, "We must not fetishize 'debate' as though debate is itself an innocuous, neutral act. The very act of debate in these cases is an effective rollback of assumed equality and a foot in the door for doubt and hatred." The debt to Marcuse is even more obvious in the work of Ibram X. Kendi, such as when he claims that "racist ideas are both false and dangerous. I don't consider racist ideas to be a form of free speech. I consider it to be a form of unfree speech."

Similarly, Fish's idea that those who favor free speech merely have different preferences about where to draw the line between permissible and impermissible speech—and that this indeterminacy serves the interests of the powerful—has quickly gone mainstream. "When is the free speech of the oppressed protected?" one student group that disrupted an event because it featured a speaker from the ACLU asked. "We know from personal experience," they answered their own question, "that rights granted to wealthy, white, cis, male, straight bodies do not trickle down to marginalized groups."

Taken together, these ideas amount to a dismissive view of free speech that has become astoundingly influential over the course of a decade. This view portrays anybody who is concerned about formal or informal restrictions on free speech as a right-wing reactionary who secretly hopes to maintain existing hierarchies of oppression. Some deny that cases in which people suffer severe personal and professional punishments for trivial or imaginary offenses amount to a concerning form of "cancel culture." Others actively celebrate such cases as examples of a healthy "consequence culture." (As Denise Branch, a prominent "antiracism consultant," told *Forbes*, for example, "'Consequence culture' is needed to build safer, more inclusive, equitable and accountable workplaces.") Both deny that instances of this phenomenon—like social media platforms censoring certain forms of content, private companies firing employees, or publishers dropping authors because some people consider them controversial—pose a threat to free speech on the grounds that they do not involve the formal exercise of state power.

Can defenders of a broad ideal of free speech answer the points made by their critics? Yes. Traditional arguments for free speech that focus on the benefits of this ideal retain much of their relevance today. But there are, I believe, even stronger arguments for free speech: ones that focus on the disastrous consequences of forgoing free speech rather than the positive consequences of maintaining it. And as it happens, these arguments are especially pertinent at a time when society is deeply polarized and the stakes of politics are perilously high.

WHY RESTRICTING SPEECH IS SO DANGEROUS

When they make the case for free speech, philosophers have traditionally explained its value by enumerating the benefits that would flow from it. Two arguments are especially common. The first argument points out just how many societies have jailed, tortured, or murdered people—from Socrates to Galileo—for expressing what later generations came to embrace as the truth. Should we really be so arrogant as to think that we are the first generation to get things absolutely right? Clearly, the answer is no.

If great moral and scientific advances have, in the past, so often been de-layed because an obstinate majority shut down free expression, limits on free speech would pose the same risk today.*

The second argument points to the value of letting people express their views even when these turn out to be wrong. This seems paradoxical. What could we possibly lose by shutting down opinions that turn out to be false? The answer is that true beliefs can, if they are never challenged, turn into dead dogma. "Truth, thus held," John Stuart Mill argues in *On Liberty*, "is but one superstition the more, accidentally clinging to the words which enunciate a truth." Having such weak foundations, it can be swept aside all the more easily if, at some point in the future, it does come under attack.

Both of these classic arguments for free speech retain their relevance today. In the two decades since I started college, I have seen large segments of society change their minds about weighty issues, from the moral accept-ability of homosexuality to the dangers caused by carbon emissions. I have no doubt that we will, twenty or forty years hence, look back at many of our current beliefs with the same sense of wonder about how people could have been so wrong about something so important. Similarly, the tempta-tion to assent to socially desirable views without pausing to think about what we are actually saying is all around us. Like Mill, I worry that this prioritizes the public recitation of fashionable slogans over the achieve-ment of real change, making it hard to resist pernicious ideas if they are clad in the clothes of a righteous cause.

But I also recognize that these arguments can seem precious at a time when the stakes of politics feel especially high. Wouldn't it (as Fish might insist) be worth sacrificing some of these lofty goals to combat racism, to curb demagoguery, and to curtail the rise of authoritarian populism? And isn't it (as Marcuse would say) in any case naive to think that there is a genuine "marketplace of ideas" at a time when powerful media conglomerates

---

* Indeed, as John Stuart Mill points out in *On Liberty*, the most consequential harm from persecuting the heterodox is not to those who suffer death or humiliation at the hands of an angry mob; it is to everyone else. "Who can compute what the world loses in the multitude of promising intellects combined with timid characters, who dare not follow out any bold, vigorous, independent train of thought, lest it should land them in something which would admit of being considered irreligious or immoral?" (John Stuart Mill, *On Liberty* [London: Broadview Press, 1859], 32–33.)

are doing what they can to shape the opinions of their viewers and readers?

These are fair questions. Democracies do have important goals that will at times seem to clash with free speech. And clearly, the assumption that more debate will always allow the truth to win out is helplessly naive. These reasonable objections explain why the lofty defenses of free speech on which philosophers have historically focused are insufficient. But as it happens, the best case for free speech focuses not on the positive consequences that often flow from its maintenance but rather on the negative consequences that are likely to result from its absence.

Three negative consequences of abandoning free speech are particularly important at a moment when levels of political polarization are at record highs. All three are intimately connected to the way in which restrictions on free speech entrench the dominance of those who are already powerful. For if those who hold power are able to censor what they consider noxious views, then

1. the ideas of the powerful are going to be systematically favored over those of the powerless, perpetuating the kind of injustice that progressive opponents of free speech rightly abhor;

2. the stakes of who gets to hold power vastly increase, incentivizing political partisans to refuse to accept the outcome of elections or even engage in violence; and

3. society will lose a crucial safety valve that allows the victims of bad public policies to protest the status quo, making it harder to achieve much-needed social change.

Empowering the Powerful

A lot of the things that people write on Twitter and Facebook or say on YouTube and TikTok are, to use a phrase that is popular on social media, "trash." The world would be a better place if they were judicious enough to shut up. And if we could devise some harmless way to make sure that nobody ever had to encounter their views, I would be all for it.

There's only one problem. If we are to make sure that worthless utterances don't find an audience, we need to appoint some set of people or institutions to determine what posts (or articles or books) are so worthless or dangerous that they deserve to be censored. And even though I may have my own views about the line between the desirable and the disgusting, or the provocative and the trollish, I simply don't trust anybody else to make that decision on my behalf. The single most compelling reason against restrictions on free speech stems from the impossibility of appointing smart and selfless censors.

Whether located in the beige cubicles of Washington, D.C., or the gleaming open-floor offices of Silicon Valley, the people who are sufficiently powerful to serve as censors would quickly supplant the interests of society with their own concerns. As political scientists and organizational sociologists have shown again and again, people who are in charge of influential social institutions tend to guard their power jealously. Similarly, the bureaucrats who would run the (fictitious) Federal Censor's Bureau, or the executives who might be in charge of Facebook's (equally fictitious) Speech Facilitation Committee, would likely want to ensure that they can continue to do their jobs. And that would make it extremely tempting for them to censor any voices that criticize their right to censor.

To make things worse, the committees that determine the rightful bounds of free speech would, because they have a lot of power and influence, become subject to intense political competition. Even if the original people running the Federal Censor's Bureau or Facebook's Speech Facilitation Committee were to be extremely public-spirited, each side of our deep political divide would soon jockey to place its own loyalists in these bodies. Instead of protecting society from the nastiness of partisan rivalries and tribal hatreds, these institutions would, themselves, become subject to those very pressures.

Ironically, this problem should be especially compelling to leftists who hold deeply pessimistic views about the current state of Western democracies. Advocates of the popularized version of the identity synthesis insist that countries like the United States and the United Kingdom are fundamentally shaped and defined by racism. Even left-leaning institutions like Harvard University, *The New York Times*, and the BBC, they claim, perpetuate white supremacy. And yet many of those same writers and activists seem to assume that the censors tasked with determining the bounds of acceptable discourse would somehow be free from these vices. This is simply naive. While progressives might be able to censor ideas they dislike within left-leaning institutions or professions, a society that gets into the habit of censoring unpopular viewpoints would be just as likely to suppress their own points of view.

Raising the Stakes of Elections

The core promise of electoral democracy is that you can always live to fight another day. You might feel that, as the political cliché goes, "the next election is the most important of our lifetimes." You may be convinced that the policy decisions made over the next four years will enrich or impoverish millions of lives. All of that may even make you go to extreme lengths to ensure victory: to campaign, to donate money, and perhaps to smear your opponent. But does it also make you willing to break the rules of the democratic game, stopping your enemy from taking power even if he wins a free and fair election?

As the events of January 6, 2021, remind us, the answer to this question has, during the long and turbulent history of democracy, depressingly often been yes. Once partisan polarization grows so intense that many people consider a victory by the opposition intolerable, the danger of (attempted) coups or even civil wars rises precipitously. When the stakes of politics grow sufficiently high, citizens become much less likely to stick to the rules.

Thankfully, democracies have figured out some basic mechanisms to reduce the likelihood of such a tragic outcome. And they have done so, in good part, by adopting institutions that lower the stakes of political competition, making it easier to tolerate a victory by the other side. For as long as you trust the system of checks and balances to limit the power of any government, you know that there is no such thing as a final winner. Even if you lose an election, you will, a few years hence, have another opportunity to fight for your values and persuade your compatriots of the justice of your cause.

This is a rarely noted reason why limits on free speech are so counterproductive. In a highly polarized country, free speech allows irresponsible actors to smear their political opponents and even to vilify groups for which they harbor an irrational hatred. There is good reason why we sometimes find it hard to tolerate the way in which some of our compatriots abuse the license granted to them by protections for free speech. But precisely because it is so important not to let the stakes of political competition escalate, an absence of free speech would be even worse. For if I have good reason to fear that my opponent's victory would give him the power to stop me from speaking out for my beliefs, I would have much stronger reason to go to any length—including violence—to stop him from taking control in the first place.

Closing the Safety Valve

Governments impose strict regulations regarding a wide variety of human activities, from the home you are allowed to build for yourself to the drugs that pharmaceutical companies can sell. When these regulations are ill-conceived, their costs can be very high. For example, governments sometimes prohibit the construction of new homes that would make it more affordable to live in major centers of economic opportunity, or fail to license lifesaving drugs in a timely manner because they wrongly fear that these would have adverse health effects. Despite the seriousness of such unintended consequences, most of us believe that the government can legitimately regulate many areas of our lives. So why shouldn't it be allowed to restrict noxious speech in the same manner?

One answer to this question distinguishes between the harm done by bad speech and the harm done by bad actions. Unlike an unsafe drug, an offensive tweet does not kill. This is true. But another, less commonly noticed, reason is even more important: limits on free speech are harmful in a way that other policies are not because they undermine the ability of a society to course correct.

Free speech acts as a safety valve that helps to alert all of us when something in our society has gone well and truly awry. So when certain positions or policies are put beyond reproach, the prospect for social progress diminishes. Those who believe that building more housing would bring down rent and increase economic opportunity can no longer make their arguments to their fellow citizens. Those who have amassed evidence that a banned drug is safe to use can no longer present it to regulators. In this way, limits on free speech raise the risk of locking societies into dangerous errors across a broad range of realms.

FREE SPEECH PRINCIPLES FOR A FREE SOCIETY

One spring morning when I was fifteen years old, I spent hours standing by my bedroom window watching ten thousand protesters assemble in the street below my apartment. They had come to Munich, the historical "capital" of the Nazi movement, from all over the country to protest an exhibition about the crimes Germany's army had committed during World War II.

The men sported skinheads and wore black boots. They waved the flag of the German Reich. Their banners said things like OUR GRANDFATHERS WERE HEROES and HONOR AND GLORY BE TO THE WEHRMACHT. The Holocaust, in which much of my family had perished, had at that point ended only fifty years ago.

Ever since that day, I have viscerally understood how intimidating the public display of racial hatred can be. And so I retain real sympathy for some of the core arguments against free speech: I can see how it takes an emotional toll on students to see speakers who incite hatred against them visit their campus. And it fills me, too, with disgust when far-right trolls invoke free speech to deflect from criticism about their hateful choices.

And yet I continue to believe that a robust culture of free speech remains an essential foundation for a thriving democracy. On the surface, the vague hate speech laws that have over the past decades been adopted in long-standing democracies, from Germany to Great Britain, merely promise to ban truly noxious speech from the public sphere. But any restriction the state imposes on people is ultimately backed by the threat of forcible imprisonment. And if we start punishing people for saying what they believe, we don't just raise the stakes of our politics in a perilous way; we also end up empowering people and institutions that are unlikely to have our best interests at heart.

For that reason, a society that values free speech would protect its citizens' ability to express unpopular opinions across a number of different dimensions. It would make sure that the state cannot throw them in jail for their views. It would limit the ability of private companies and institutions, from Twitter to Mastercard, to wield outsized power over what views can be expressed in the key forums in which public debate now takes place. And it would support a true culture of free speech in which people aren't intimidated into agreeing with their compatriots by the use of illiberal tactics like cancellation campaigns.

The Government Must Not Have the Right to Lock You Up for What You Say

In many European countries, the introduction of far-reaching and ill-defined hate speech laws now poses a serious threat to freedom of speech. Even in the United Kingdom, where free speech has traditionally been highly prized, the police regularly investigate citizens for "offensive" speech that falls afoul of extremely vague rules about what is permissible. But as thinkers from Voltaire to James Baldwin recognized, the right to offend has always stood at the very core of any serious notion of free speech. Because those who are in power will always regard any serious challenge to them as offensive, any ban on vague categories of speech like "insult" and "blasphemy" is likely to be used against truth tellers as well as trolls. Even when bans affect content that really is deeply noxious, like genuine hate speech, it is far from clear that they help to solve the deeper problem; in fact, research suggests that extremists merely find more clever ways of expressing their hateful views, and may even grow more likely to engage in political violence.

Modern states wield tremendous power. They employ large armies and vast police forces, set coercive rules telling their citizens how they must behave, and fine or lock up those who do not obey. This makes it especially dangerous when states are at liberty to punish citizens for what they say. In many areas, the liberty to speak your mind must be absolute. For that reason, democracies from Britain to Germany should emulate America's First Amendment, adopting much more far-reaching protections against state-sponsored forms of censorship. No state should have the power to lock its citizens up for what they say.

Some nongovernmental institutions that are not legally bound by the First Amendment should also commit themselves to honoring absolute protections for free speech. The core purpose of universities, for example, is to produce knowledge. Given how easily that purpose is subverted by social pressure or the fear of being fired, they should voluntarily adopt strong protections for "academic freedom" (as many of them have, at least on paper). If universities are to serve their core mission, it is better to have some professors spreading falsehoods or saying offensive things than to risk that nobody can call into doubt a popular consensus that might well be wrong.

There Must Be Limits to the Power of Private Actors to Censor Political Debate

When the state punishes its citizens for expressing unpopular opinions, however noxious, free speech is under especially serious threat. But in many countries, the most dangerous punishments against unpopular speech are meted out through more informal mechanisms. Most of the time, those who are punished for their opinions face a suspended account on social media or a termination letter in the mail rather than a cop knocking on their door.

The power of private actors, like social media platforms or credit card companies, is more limited than that of the government. But in other ways, it is even more pernicious. After all, democratic citizens accused of violat-

ing state-sponsored restrictions on free speech at least have a chance to defend themselves in a court of law. By contrast, citizens who are fired, have
their social media accounts suspended, or can no longer access basic financial services like credit cards often have little or no recourse; their fate
hinges on anonymous people making decisions in accordance with rules
and procedures that may not even be fully public. Anybody who cares
about upholding a genuine culture of free speech must therefore care about
reining in the ability of private actors to punish people for expressing unpopular views or to police the boundaries of legitimate debate. Thankfully,
governments can help to constrain private power without overstepping the
strict limits on what they themselves can legitimately do in this realm.

The first step should be to ban companies from firing their employees
for saying unpopular things. Governments could accomplish this by including the political views of employees in the list of protected characteristics, as some jurisdictions including Seattle and Washington, D.C., have
already done. Obviously, employers should be able to restrict what their
staff do or say while they are on the job. But unless the nature of their work
is openly political—as might, for example, be the case for a campaigning
organization—they should not be able to fire their employees for views
they express as private citizens. This would go a long way toward giving
citizens the confidence to express themselves without fear of material ruin.

Second, key financial institutions like Mastercard, the credit card
company, and Stripe, the payment processing service, effectively serve as
public utilities. Anybody who wants to engage in basic commercial trans-
actions, from renting a car to booking a flight, needs a credit card. Anybody who wants to earn income online needs to use a payment processing
company. Citizens who are barred from using these services would effectively be unable to go about their daily lives, to travel freely, or to maintain
a viable business. Therefore, these companies should—like other public
utilities, such as gas and electricity companies—be limited in their ability
to decline doing business with would-be customers. Though they must be
allowed to refuse service to customers on commercial grounds, such as a
persistent refusal to pay their bills, they should not be able to do so because
they dislike their views.

This leaves the biggest source of private power over free speech: social media. Facebook and Twitter function as key venues for political debate. And yet they frequently ban users on arbitrary grounds. They have also prohibited the expression of controversial points of view about matters of intense public interest. And while they have justified these measures with the noble goal of fighting "misinformation," the concept is defined so nebulously that they have, in practice, ended up taking sides in highly important and complex public debates. For much of 2020 and 2021, for example, Facebook and YouTube banned users for suggesting that an inadvertent leak in a biological lab performing "gain of function" research might have caused the COVID pandemic. But though it remains unclear whether that theory is true, it is now being taken seriously at the highest echelons of the American intelligence community.

To make things worse, much of the debate over the power of social media is obviously unprincipled. As long as censorship on Twitter was perceived by many people to favor the sensibilities of the left, conservatives complained about this abuse of private power while progressives pointed out that private companies could decide what content to host without violating the First Amendment. Once Elon Musk bought the company, the positions quickly reversed, with conservatives emphasizing that he could do what he wanted and progressives emphasizing that it is dangerous for a private actor to have such outsized power over public debate.

My stance has been consistent: I believe that it is a clear threat to the culture of free speech for private companies to decide what can or can't be said about issues from public health to trans rights. This is why I believe that social media companies should voluntarily adopt stringent restrictions on their own ability to censor. Such rules would leave them free to ban users for forms of illegal, extreme, or uncivil behavior such as spreading child pornography, libeling people, or engaging in doxing. Social media platforms would also remain free to use algorithms that amplify content on the basis of such properties as being less divisive, for example by favoring posts that elicit few negative responses. But they would no longer be able to ban users or delete posts because of the substantive political views they express.

If companies decline to regulate themselves in a clear and transparent way, legislators should consider stepping in. In the United States, Section 230 now ensures that platforms like Twitter and Facebook are not legally liable for the content posted by their users; some other jurisdictions have adopted similar rules. If major platforms continue to censor their users in capricious or untransparent ways, democratic governments should (even though this too would have drawbacks) give serious thought to attaching clear conditions to this immunity. By picking and choosing what posts to allow or promote on their platforms on the basis of the viewpoints they express, rather than some content-neutral criterion like the amount of engagement they garner, Twitter and Facebook are effectively acting as publishers; this makes more compelling the case that they should, like every other publisher, be held responsible for the content they spread.

Building a Culture of Free Speech

Governments must not be able to throw people in jail for what they say. Private actors like giant corporations should be constrained in their ability to shape the contours of public debate. But to uphold a genuine culture of free speech, we also need protections against the kind of "tyranny of the prevailing opinion" that Mill identified as a serious threat more than 150 years ago.

Doing so requires us to think about the line between two core liberal commitments: free speech and free association. On the one hand, a culture of free speech is only possible when citizens don't have to fear that any errant remark will get them shunned by their friends and colleagues. In Mill's words, we must guard against "the tendency of society to impose . . . its own ideas and practices as rules of conduct on those who dissent from them." On the other hand, every citizen must get to decide for themselves with whom they do—and don't—want to be friends. If you say something I find abhorrent, it is my good right to denounce you on social media and to stop inviting you to dinner. So is it possible to maintain a robust culture of free speech without curtailing the freedom of association?

Yes. A robust culture of free speech must absolutely allow for the expression of strong views, including intense criticisms of others' perceived faults. It might be deeply hurtful when thousands of strangers denounce your tweet or Instagram post. But insofar as it goes, being criticized on the internet is an expression of, rather than an attack on, freedom of speech.

There are, however, ways in which extreme forms of social pressure and collective punishment can add up to a real attack on the culture of free speech. This is often the case when people are not just being criticized for but rather "canceled" because of what they said. According to Jonathan Rauch, a senior fellow at the Brookings Institution, at least four warning signs help to distinguish healthy instances of what he calls a "critical culture" from worrying indications that people are being "canceled" for their views:

- *Punitiveness*: Cancellations often involve severe punishments such as suffering the revocation of titles or honors or being fired from a job.
- *Deplatforming*: Cancellations often involve demands to "deplatform" offending individuals so that they cease to be able to express their views.
- *Organization*: Cancellations often involve collective efforts to punish offending speakers through coordinated petitions or social media campaigns.
- *Secondary boycotts*: Cancellations often seek to exert pressure on any institutions or publications with which the person who is being criticized is affiliated, aiming to render that person "radioactive."

Rauch emphasizes that none of these criteria constitute a bright line test for whether something falls into the realm of fair criticism or adds up to a worrying attempt at cancellation. But put together, these indicators do help to express the difference in spirit and effect. Unlike a healthy critical culture, Rauch points out, cancellation "is about shaping the information battlefield, not seeking truth; and its intent—or at least its predictable outcome—is to coerce conformity."

It is not the role of the state to combat these illiberal forms of cancel culture. It would be inappropriate for the law to make it impossible for people to call others out for their words or their associations, even if the instigating incident is trivial or silly. But nor do we need to resign ourselves to a future in which such witch hunts continue to shape the public sphere.

All of us have a responsibility to maintain a culture of free speech as best we can. Even if we are deeply upset with what somebody has said, we should refrain from engaging in the kinds of tactics Rauch describes, and push back against anybody (including our own allies) who stoops to such illiberal tactics. Standing up to those who instigate campaigns of cancellation is never easy. But collectively those of us who recognize the urgency of restoring a genuine culture of free speech have the power to do so.

KEY TAKEAWAYS

- The culture of free speech is under serious threat around the world. In Western democracies, part of this threat comes from a surprising source: while the left has long championed the importance of free speech, recognizing its centrality in historical struggles against oppression, many progressives have of late derided its defenders as "free speechers" and advocated for a "consequence culture" that holds people to account for unpopular statements.

- Traditional arguments about free speech are mostly about the benefits of this social practice, such as the ability to make scientific progress. While these arguments remain relevant, the strongest reasons to hold on to free speech, especially at a time of deep polarization, have to do with the bad things that would happen in its absence.

- Because the people making decisions about what speech to allow or to ban are by definition powerful, limits on free speech usually serve to entrench their hold over society; it is naive to think that a pervasive social practice of censorship would systematically serve the "right" causes. Limits on free speech also increase the stakes of elections. If members of a political movement believe that losing the next election will hamper their ability to keep advocating for their cause, they will become much less likely to abide by its outcome. Finally, free speech functions as a crucial safety valve that allows people to organize against all kinds of injustices; limiting free speech therefore makes it harder to achieve social progress.

- It is possible to take proactive steps to uphold a genuine culture of free speech. States should not be able to punish their citizens for what they say, however heinous. The power of private actors like big corporations to undermine the culture of free speech must be limited, for example by rules that make it illegal for companies to fire employees for their political views or for providers of basic financial services to refuse service to customers on ideological grounds; similarly, social networks should voluntarily limit their ability to favor some political causes over others. Finally, all of us can help to stand up for a culture of free speech by being on guard against the key tactics that make the difference between a healthy critical culture and an unhealthy cancel culture.

Chapter 11

THE CASE FOR INTEGRATION

Progressive educators have traditionally conceived of their mission as emphasizing what all people have in common. The philosopher John Dewey, long one of the most influential writers on American pedagogy, once wrote that "the intermingling in the school of youth of different races, differing religions, and unlike customs creates for all a new and broader environment." A century later, Barack Obama repeatedly echoed Dewey's sentiments, emphasizing on one occasion that "our goal is to have a country that's not divided by race," and noting on another occasion that "when children learn and play together, they grow, build, and thrive together."

Over the course of the past few years, this universalism has fallen out of favor. Many progressives have come to believe that the traditional emphasis on our common humanity amounts to an erasure of the injustices facing oppressed groups. They also worry that members of marginalized groups are at constant risk of serious psychological harm when they have to study or work in institutions that remain dominated by members of the ethnic or cultural majority. These political and psychological precepts often lead to an organizational upshot: rather than focusing on efforts to integrate society, progressives have increasingly militated for the creation of spaces and organizations in which members of minority groups can remain among themselves.

This trend is especially striking in education. Over the last decade, many schools have introduced race-segregated affinity groups, some as early as kindergarten. In extreme cases, school principals who claim to be fighting for social justice have, as Kila Posey experienced in Atlanta, even put all the Black children in the same class. A similar set of trends is now changing the nature of higher education. World-renowned universities are building dorms reserved for their Black or Latino students, hosting separate graduation ceremonies for "students of color," and even excluding some students from physical education classes on the basis of their race. In the place of liberal universalism, parts of the American mainstream are quickly embracing what we might call "progressive separatism."

These practices thankfully remain less common outside the United States. But they are starting to spread beyond the country's borders. Canada's National Arts Centre, in Ottawa, for example, has recently started to offer race-segregated performances. As the website of the publicly funded institution proudly announces, a performance of Aleshea Harris's *Is God Is* will be reserved for "an all-Black identifying audience." In Europe, meanwhile, the new form of progressive separatism is more likely to focus on culture than on race. As part of its embrace of a "multicultural" vision for Great Britain, for example, the last Labour government introduced state-funded faith schools that are reserved for (respectively) Jewish, Hindu, Sikh, and Muslim students.

Of late, this progressive separatism has gone yet another step further. At first, educators merely thought it would be beneficial for members of historically marginalized groups to embrace their ethnic identity; to encourage members of historically dominant groups, like whites, to define themselves by their skin color would have seemed highly suspect. But of late, progressive educators and diversity trainers have started to insist that white people, too, "embrace race." As the academics Cheryl Matias and Janiece Mackey wrote, white teachers should, like their nonwhite colleagues, "engage in racial identity work" and learn "how to take racial responsibility of whiteness."

Some aspects of progressive separatism may be inevitable. Everyone has a right to decide with whom they want to spend time. Anybody can choose to deepen their ties with people who share their religion, culture, or ethnicity. In a pluralistic society, freedom of association will always lead to some amount of "homophily," the well-documented tendency of people to seek out those who resemble them. But the practices that are now in vogue go much further. In particular, many progressive educators believe that they must proactively encourage students to define themselves by virtue of the identity groups into which they were born.

The rise of progressive separatism is rooted in two complementary intellectual transformations: the embrace of strategic essentialism and new worries about omnipresent threats to the psychological safety of marginalized groups. But the fundamental findings of comparative politics and group psychology help to explain why this kind of separatism is likely to be dangerously counterproductive. For in the long run, it will succeed only in encouraging a zero-sum competition between different ethnic blocs. The only realistic alternative is to double down on the long-standing dream of integration—encouraging students and citizens to think of themselves in terms of broader groups that include members from many different backgrounds.

THE RISE OF PROGRESSIVE SEPARATISM

Progressive separatism has an unlikely intellectual history. Like much of the left, the main proponents and popularizers of the identity synthesis have long emphasized that the biological idea of race is a dangerous fiction. As Ta-Nehisi Coates succinctly put the point in *Between the World and Me*, "Race is the child of racism, not the father." Popular notions of race, such critics argue, were created in long and unjust historical processes, making categories like "Hispanic" and "African American" the product of a complex interplay of social forces and political interests. As Kimberlé Crenshaw wrote in one of the foundational articles of critical race theory, categories of race and gender that "we consider natural or merely representational are actually socially constructed."

There are two very different ways of thinking about the political implications of this insight. According to parts of the left, the lack of a biological basis for popular notions of race is a strong reason to stop using such categories. Because race is socially constructed, and has long been used for the purposes of unjust domination, we should aim to transcend the concept altogether. In their work on what they call "racecraft," for example, Barbara and Karen Fields lament the prevalence of pre- and pseudoscientific assumptions about race, seeking to point out "the oddness of social beliefs and practices that Americans continue to take for granted." Their explicit goal is for "our fellow Americans to explore how the falsehoods of racecraft are made in everyday life, in order to work out how to unmake them."

In its most radical form, the aspiration to make race less salient even consists of a form of "race abolitionism," the insistence on building a society in which race has lost virtually all of the importance it now holds. "I will no longer enter into the all-American skin game that demands you select a box and define yourself by it," the writer Thomas Chatterton Williams, whose African American father grew up in segregated Texas, has vowed. "There are not fundamentally, inherently, essentially, Black or white lives. There is human life, and we have different ethnicities and cultural traditions, but we have to abolish the idea of race, full stop, or we're always going to have the residue of racism."

Another set of scholars, meanwhile, took the opposite inference from the premise that race lacks a meaningful biological basis. Because so many people have internalized artificial notions of race, they hope to enlist such identities in the fight against the status quo. Following the lead of Gayatri Chakravorty Spivak, they advocate a form of strategic essentialism. Even though they too believe that "essentialist" accounts of identity, like those that claim a biological basis for race, are mistaken, they hope that a greater emphasis on those categories can strengthen historically oppressed groups in their fight for justice. "Subordinated people," Crenshaw insisted, should embrace socially constructed categories of race and gender.

At first, most scholars who embraced strategic essentialism continued to pay lip service to a future in which the importance of these categories would gradually attenuate. But over time, many of them have dispensed with the strategic element. Though they regularly acknowledge that identities are socially constructed, they effectively treat race as a natural category,

and have given up the hope that a truly just society would render it less salient. What we should aim for, according to them, is not a society in which
ethnic identity recedes into the background because it no longer structures
society in fundamental ways; rather, it is a society in which citizens will forever be highly attuned to differences in ethnic, gender, and sexual identity.

At the same time as advocates of the identity synthesis embraced strategic essentialism, they also expanded their conception of the nature of
harm and prejudice. According to an older set of assumptions, prejudice
consisted of bigoted beliefs or behavioral patterns, such as affirming that
members of some culture or race are inferior. Harm required a physical
injury, a significant psychological trauma, or the accrual of a clear socioeconomic disadvantage (such as not being hired for a job on account of racism). But over time, sociologists and psychologists inspired by the identity
synthesis began to argue that this way of thinking about harm and prejudice overlooked more subtle forms of injustice.

According to them, prejudice could consist of implicit biases that are
hidden to those who harbor them, or even of the expression of seemingly
innocuous political attitudes that find majority support in the population.
Widely cited articles cast skepticism of affirmative action and the idea that
America is a land of opportunity as paradigmatic examples of a "microaggression." Anyone who is exposed to such forms of prejudice or injustice
was portrayed as being at risk of suffering serious harm, vastly expanding the
realm of what is considered a threat to "safety." Gradually, left-leaning institutions came to see it as their task to protect people in their care from these
ever-present dangers, and started to fear that interactions with members of
other identity groups were especially likely to cause such harms. In the formulation of Greg Lukianoff and Jonathan Haidt, they embraced a new and
increasingly pervasive form of "safetyism."

The idea of strategic essentialism and the expansion in notions of harm
both helped to shape how organizational leaders responded to the demands
of a diversifying workplace. Over the course of the last fifty years, institutions that had for the most part been the preserve of white men started to
open their gates to a much broader set of members. Campuses of elite universities in both Britain and the United States went from being reasonably

monochrome to extremely diverse. The upper reaches of the corporate world, which had once been predominantly staffed with white Anglo-Saxon Protestants, came to have executives drawn from every corner of the globe. These changes are a big reason for celebration. But the social ascent of people from a much broader range of backgrounds did not put the question of inequality to rest. In particular, many women and members of ethnic minorities came to feel—often for very good reason—that the dominant culture of these institutions remained inhospitable to them.

In response, leaders of universities, foundations, and corporations could have focused on reducing the role that race plays within their organizations and making them more welcoming to members of minority groups; indeed, that is the route that many of them initially took. But as the twin influence of strategic essentialism and safetyism grew, many of them changed course. They now opted to create more spaces in which members of such groups could engage in consciousness building (as demanded by the advocates of strategic essentialism) and would be protected from the threat posed by members of dominant groups (as inspired by safetyism). An activist group at Williams College summarized this rationale especially clearly: dorms that are reserved for Black students, it argued, are necessary for the college to fulfill its "obligations to the well-being and safety of its students."

One way of understanding the rise of progressive separatism, in other words, is to see it as the love child of strategic essentialism and safetyism. The result has been a rapid transformation in the norms of highly influential institutions, including government entities. In Seattle, for example, the office of the mayor recently defended race-segregated trainings for its employees and other forms of "race-based caucusing" by noting that such practices have long since become "a part of the City of Seattle's workplace culture."

THE PROGRESSIVES WHO CHAMPION WHITE IDENTITY

The key precepts of progressive separatism are no longer that new. In some form or another, progressives have embraced separatist trends for at least three decades; in a book published in 1996, for example, the liberal senator Daniel Patrick Moynihan already discussed and criticized them at length. But over the past few years, the progressive opposition to universalism has been extended in a crucial way.

Early advocates of strategic essentialism believed in the need for consciousness-raising exercises that would allow marginalized groups to fight against the discrimination they suffered. For that reason, they encouraged only those who had historically been oppressed to embrace their ethnic identity. An explicit emphasis on, or avowal of, white identity remained the preserve of the far right.

In the past two or three decades, by contrast, progressive separatists have also started to encourage whites to identify by their ethnic origin. According to them, whites who believe that the color of their skin does not define them are oblivious to the ways in which they profit from the subjugation of "people of color." An emphasis on their own whiteness is therefore seen as the first step on the long road toward disowning "white privilege." As Charley Flint, an early pioneer of the new academic field of "whiteness studies" put it, "We want to racialize whites. How can you build a multiracial society if one of the groups is white and it doesn't identify itself as a race?"

The exhortation for white people to embrace their race has quickly come to be advocated by some of America's most prominent writers and activists. Robin DiAngelo, the influential author and diversity consultant whose course was used to train employees of Coca-Cola, for example, consistently emphasizes the importance of whites developing a stronger identification with the color of their skin. As she writes in *White Fragility*, whites are "rarely asked to think about ourselves or fellow whites in racial terms. . . . But rather than retreat in the face of discomfort," whites should embrace that racial label. "Being seen racially is a common trigger of white fragility, and thus, to build our stamina, white people must face the first challenge: naming our race." (As I mentioned in the introduction, this trend has even begun to influence the world of progressive pedagogy, with prestigious private institutions like Bank Street School for Children, on Manhattan's Upper West Side, founding all-white "Advocacy Groups" and encouraging their students to "own" their "European ancestry.")

But will a greater emphasis on the differences between ethnic groups, or a widespread embrace of "whiteness," really inspire members of dominant groups to make the world more just? Or might the spread of progressive separatism, on the contrary, encourage them to guard their dominant status as best they can? These key questions are as much empirical as they are normative. To answer them, we can't just argue about the kind of society we would like to create; we also need to understand how human beings form groups, when they treat outsiders well or badly, and what kinds of institutions can foster mutual solidarity. Thankfully, social psychologists and political scientists have (as I chronicled in my last book, *The Great Experiment*) given compelling answers to these questions—answers that help to demonstrate that the embrace of progressive separatism is a dangerous trap.

WHAT SOCIAL SCIENCE CAN TEACH US ABOUT HOW TO FOSTER EMPATHY AND COHESION

The students at Johns Hopkins University, where I teach, are extremely diverse. They are drawn from every state in America and sixty-four countries around the world. They practice all of the world's major religions and hail from a great variety of ethnic groups. In 2019, only about 41 percent of undergraduates were white. So it is perhaps unsurprising that these students think of themselves as some of the most tolerant people in the world—and in some ways, perhaps they are.

But when I teach classes on topics like diversity and democracy, I often ask these students to debate a seemingly trivial question: Is a hot dog a sandwich? At first, the students are usually bemused by the question. Then they take to answering it with gusto. One student will usually make a passionate case for why hot dogs are, indeed, sandwiches. ("A hot dog is two pieces of bread with meat in between. That's exactly what a sandwich is!") Another student will respond just as forcefully. ("Hot dogs are vertical, and they only have one piece of bread. That's nothing like a sandwich!")

After five or ten minutes of debate, I have the students play a simple distribution game. They can either give $8 to classmates who agree with them about whether a hot dog is a sandwich and $10 to those who disagree. Or they can give $7 to those who share their opinion and $5 to those who don't. A majority opts for the latter option. My students, though supposedly so tolerant, are willing to take home less money to make sure that classmates who disagree with them about the nature of the hot dog fare worse than them.

Human Beings Are Groupish

The point of the exercise is to introduce students to a powerful set of findings in social psychology. Human beings, I explain, are "groupish." They are primed to form strong bonds with their own group, even when its criterion for membership (such as a shared conviction in the "sandwichness" of the hot dog) is trivial. On behalf of members of their own groups, they often prove capable of staggering feats of ingenuity and awe-inspiring acts of altruism. But in dealing with people whom they think of as members of an outside group, they are capable of frightening cruelty and callousness. This tendency to favor the in-group over the out-group helps to explain much of what is noble and most of what is vile in human history.

The simple game we play in class also helps to illustrate a second feature of groups. In many contexts, the groups that sustain our most fervent loyalty are of long-standing and obvious significance. They consist of people who have a common set of ancestors or share each other's religious beliefs, who have fought major battles together or suffered from the same forms of oppression. But often, more recent circumstances are just as important in determining the nature and significance of these groups. Political incentives, economic interests, and media narratives can decide where the lines between different groups are drawn, and even which aspect of our identity is most salient. As a result, groups that are peaceful allies in one time and place can become bloody enemies a few years later or a dozen miles away.

All of this makes it extremely important to think about how members of different groups come to have prejudices against each other and under what circumstances they might be able to reconceive of yesterday's enemies as tomorrow's allies. What set of policies and practices should we adopt if we want to maximize the chances that the members of highly diverse societies, from Germany to Australia, will treat each other with empathy and respect?

The Promise of Intergroup Contact

When the psychologist Gordon Allport volunteered at a local center for refugees in the 1940s, he came into contact with a group against which he harbored deep-seated prejudices. But as he spent more time with members of that group, he came to realize that his negative views had been ill-founded. Perhaps, Allport wondered, a similar mechanism might also help other people overcome their irrational prejudices.

Over the next fifty years, social psychologists painstakingly demonstrated that this is indeed the case. American soldiers who were exposed to German civilians after World War II came to have much more positive views of them than those who mostly remained in their barracks. White residents of integrated housing projects in New York came to have much more positive views about African Americans than those who lived in segregated projects in Newark. Catholic and Protestant students in Northern Ireland who were asked to work together on a simple task came to have more positive views of each other than those who did not have a similarly cooperative encounter. The evidence from hundreds of studies all over the world is overwhelming: when people who hold prejudices about outsiders come into contact with them under the right circumstances, they develop a much more positive view of them.

But the same studies also point to important caveats. For there were also certain circumstances in which these improvements in the relationship between groups that had historically been hostile to each other failed to materialize. When white employees worked with Black colleagues at a similar skill level, this had a positive effect on their views, for example, but when they exclusively worked with Black colleagues who served in subordinate roles, their prejudices did not attenuate.

When Intergroup Contact Does (and Doesn't) Work

Building on Allport's initial intuitions, and analyzing hundreds of studies, psychologists gradually confirmed that four key conditions help to ensure that intergroup contact has positive effects. Each of these needs to apply to the particular situation in which they encounter each other, even if it is not (yet) true in the relations between these two groups more broadly:

- *Equal status*: Members of different groups need to enjoy equal status, for example because they are teammates or colleagues working in a similar capacity.
- *Common goals*: Members of different groups need to have common goals, such as winning a match or completing a group project.
- *Intergroup cooperation*: Members of different groups need to actively cooperate to accomplish their common goals, for example by teammates passing a ball to each other or colleagues collaborating on a presentation.
- *Support from authorities and customs*: Members of different groups need to be encouraged to get along by the relevant authorities, such as a team's coach or a workplace's boss.

Anybody who is serious about fostering better relations between different identity groups needs to take this research extremely seriously. But sadly, the practices encouraged by the advocates of progressive separatism fly in the face of these insights. Instead of encouraging citizens of diverse democracies to reconceptualize themselves as part of a broader whole, progressive separatism encourages them to see each other as members of mutually irreconcilable groups. And instead of creating more situations in which they can cooperate as equals, it encourages them to self-segregate and primes them to focus on the status inequality between them. The key precepts of progressive separatism fly in the face of fifty years of research about how to build cross-ethnic and cross-cultural solidarity.

WHY THE PRACTICES PROPOSED BY PROGRESSIVE SEPARATISTS ARE COUNTERPRODUCTIVE

Much of American life, from residential neighborhoods to church pews, has long been painfully segregated. But since the 1960s, institutions that do have a diverse membership have usually tried to maintain the kinds of practices that social psychologists familiar with the literature on intergroup contact might recommend. The leaders of sports teams or military units, for example, encourage people to see themselves first and foremost as Yankees or as marines, emphasizing the mission they share.

Some psychologists even built on these findings to foster greater harmony in the classroom. Elliot Aronson, for example, realized that schoolchildren would be less likely to bully classmates if they recognized that they needed every single member of the group to thrive so that they themselves can succeed. He therefore championed a form of "jigsaw pedagogy" in which students would try to solve puzzles that require every student to contribute a part of the answer based on information to which only he or she has access; if any student wants to gain points, they have to ensure that all of them are included.

By contrast, the social norms and institutional rules made fashionable by progressive separatism fly in the face of the key conditions that are required for intergroup contact to succeed. It is not only that many changes, like safe spaces and separate dorms, reduce how often students from different groups are exposed to each other in social settings. It is also that the kinds of rules and rituals that elite institutions are putting into place could have been custom designed to minimize the promise of greater mutual understanding through intergroup contact because they directly violate the conditions discovered by Allport and his followers. Take four examples:

1. *Unequal status*: For members of different groups to enter into meaningful contact that reduces their mutual prejudices, they need to have equal standing within that situation (even if they don't enjoy equal status in society as a whole). But many progressive separatists now actively oppose

creating circumstances in which this would be the case. According to
them, any interaction between a member of a historically dominant
group and a member of a historically marginalized group should include
an explicit emphasis on their difference in status. In both Britain and
America, for example, whites are now often asked to "acknowledge their
privilege." This makes it harder for members of different groups to enjoy,
even temporarily, the equality of status that is necessary for intergroup
contact to build mutual understanding and solidarity.

2. *Different goals*: The environments that are most conducive to fostering
   mutual sympathy require people from different backgrounds to reconceive of themselves as pursuing common goals as part of the same team.
   Rather than thinking of themselves as white or Black, straight or gay,
   they should, at least within that situation, define themselves as members
   of the same college class or sports team. But according to the advocates
   of progressive separatism, the emphasis on such commonalities is highly
   suspect. If you say that "we are all Americans" or "we all go to Haver-
   ford," they claim, you are downplaying the importance of race and
   sweeping social conflicts under the carpet. Instead, powerful institutional leaders now encourage people to think of themselves in terms of
   their racial identities, and to emphasize the ways in which the interests
   and preferences of different groups clash. This makes it harder for members of different groups to see themselves (however temporarily) as sharing a broader identity or pursuing common goals.

3. *Intergroup competition*: The benefits of intergroup contact are most likely
   to materialize when people from different backgrounds are actively
   working together; this is what has made Aronson's "jigsaw pedagogy,"
   in which groups of students need the input of every child to solve a
   puzzle, so successful. The new forms of progressive separatism reduce
   the number of occasions for members of different identity groups to engage in such cooperation. More important, they send the message that
   creating an inclusive atmosphere in an institution is not a joint goal to

be solved by all of its members, but rather one to be pursued by different identity groups, all of which cooperate primarily within their own ranks.

4. *Lack of support from authorities and customs*: Finally, for intergroup contact to have positive effects, it is crucial for the people who are exposed to each other to get the message that they are expected to get along. When an institution communicates to its members that harmonious cooperation is one of its values or a boss tells employees that they better find a way to work together effectively, this creates healthy incentives that help trust to develop. But in the era of progressive separatism, many institutions are creating procedures that actively invite or even reward conflict. College campuses, for example, teach students from minority groups that prejudice against them often comes in seemingly innocuous or even invisible forms, encouraging them to be constantly on guard against subtle signs of prejudice or "white supremacy culture." Some universities have even gone so far as to create anonymous hotlines that allow students to report their classmates when they believe they have engaged in a microaggression. This erodes the trust that people need to manage conflicts in a cooperative manner. Because many institutions now send their members the message that they are unlikely to get along, it is hardly surprising that they often don't.

Over the past few years, it has, in a striking number of cases, been the most privileged and progressive institutions—from Smith College to the Guggenheim Museum—that experienced the greatest difficulties with mutual tolerance and comprehension. That might, at first sight, look puzzling. Why do people at ethnically diverse campuses like Yale and Oxford struggle to get along while ethnically diverse employees at McDonald's or Burger King tend to do just fine? Allport's intergroup contact theory helps to provide part of the answer: it is because many ordinary businesses and institutions still try to facilitate the conditions for greater mutual understanding, while some of the most elite ones are systematically undermining them.

WHY ENCOURAGING WHITES TO
EMBRACE RACE IS LIKELY TO BACKFIRE

The conflict in these elite spaces is aggravated by the rapid adoption of the misguided idea that whites placing greater emphasis on their ethnic identity would help bring about racial progress. The distinction between white and nonwhite Americans is a fundamental part of American history (though some commentators have powerfully argued that it would make more sense to think of the central distinction as dividing Black and non-Black Americans). For centuries, it determined to what extent people had access to opportunities, to civil rights, and even to the most basic components of freedom, like the right to raise their own children. It is surely true to suggest that, for better or mostly for worse, white Americans have always been aware of their racial status.

But this isn't the whole of the story. For much of American history, whites were the overwhelming majority of the population. In 1860, for example, 86 percent of Americans were white; as late as 1960, that figure still stood at 85 percent. By comparison to virtually every other Western society, this majority population was characterized by an astonishing heterogeneity of ethnic origin, cultural tradition, and religious conviction. Even as Americans were aware of their whiteness, their strongest markers of self-identification tended to be Catholic or Protestant, Jewish or atheist, English or German, Italian or Irish. This raises serious questions about whether it would be politically fruitful for these Americans to "embrace race," starting to think of themselves, explicitly and primarily, as whites— as many racially segregated affinity groups and corporate diversity trainings now encourage them to do.

The relevant research strongly suggests that this is not the case. Nothing in human nature determines that people who happen to be white will always be motivated by racial solidarity with other people who share a similar skin color. It is perfectly possible for them to define membership in the relevant in-group in terms that have nothing to do with race. They can come to think of themselves as New Yorkers, devout Catholics, or proud Americans, for example. And while each of these identities excludes some people, all of them encompass millions of people who belong to just about every conceivable racial (as well as gender and sexual) group.

At the same time, social psychology also suggests that it is very rare for people to act against the interests of what they regard as the most salient group to which they belong. If they primarily conceive of themselves in terms of an ethnically inclusive marker of collective identity, many Americans who happen to be white might come to stand in genuine solidarity with people who are not. But they are far less likely to do so if they come to think that their whiteness is their most important attribute. My students began to discriminate against "outsiders" when they were primed to think of themselves as belonging to a group marked by their shared belief in the sandwichness of the hot dog; similarly, white Americans are more, not less, likely to engage in out-group discrimination against "people of color" if they are primed to think of belonging to a group defined by the color of their skin as their primary identity.

This is why the fashionable insistence that more Americans (or, for that matter, more Britons and Canadians) identify as white is likely to prove dangerously counterproductive. The teachers at Bank Street who place young kids in an all-white "Advocacy Group" hope that a greater self-identification as white, coupled with an awareness of the injustices suffered by nonwhite people, will transform these students into courageous activists for social progress. In a few individual cases, this may well prove to be the case. But this solution is extremely unlikely to work at scale. For every child who redoubles their commitment to racial progress because they come to think of their white skin as their most salient characteristic, there are likely to be two or three who grow determined to defend the interests of that racially defined group.

"I am not certain whether or not self-flagellation can have a beneficial effect on the sinner (I tend to doubt that it can), but I am absolutely certain it can never produce anything politically creative," Bayard Rustin, the great civil rights activist, has written. "It will not improve the lot of the unemployed and the ill-housed. On the other hand, it could well happen that the guilty party, in order to lighten his uncomfortable moral burden, will finally begin to rationalize his sins and affirm them as virtues. And by such a process, today's ally can become tomorrow's enemy."

Progressive separatism is a dead end. Its vision of the future is neither realistic nor attractive. And partial success—a world in which whites do come to define themselves by their ethnic identity yet fail to dismantle the advantages that have historically flowed from it—may transport us into the worst of all possible timelines. A society whose most influential members conceive of it as consisting of two fundamentally opposed blocs of "whites" and "people of color" is much more likely to become mired in destructive interethnic competition than it is to overcome the injustices of the past. Thankfully, there is an alternative: a society that tries to overcome the segregation that has historically defined it, encourages its members to develop greater compassion for each other, and inspires them to place more emphasis on the markers of identities they share than on those that divide them.

THE CASE FOR INTEGRATION

Across the Western world, democracies have become vastly more diverse over the course of the last fifty years. In much of Europe, the proportion of the population with immigrant stock has grown by an order of magnitude. In Canada and the United States, a population that was once predominantly European in origin now increasingly consists of people who hail from Asia, Africa, and Latin America. But while societies have become a lot more ethnically diverse, the actual lives of people have become intertwined at a much slower rate.

In the United States, the legacy of segregation still permeates social reality in a million ways. From Boston to St. Louis, some neighborhoods are predominantly white, others overwhelmingly Black or Latino. All across the country, pastors preach a message of racial reconciliation to congregations that are startlingly homogeneous. Even at the dining halls or holiday parties of fancy colleges or major corporations, people who belong to the same identity group flock to each other with depressing regularity.

The situation in Europe is better in certain ways, yet worse in many others. Residential segregation is less pronounced. But, especially on the Continent, European elites remain far more homogeneous than North American ones. And on average, the children and grandchildren of immigrants feel more deeply alienated from the countries in which they were born.

These persistent forms of segregation are deeply concerning. Children who grow up without going to school or playing with those who belong to different ethnic groups are much more likely to develop noxious prejudices. Meanwhile, communities that are cut off from the mainstream are likely to lack resources and economic opportunities, especially if they are historically marginalized. "If a firm is overwhelmingly white and recruits new employees by employee referral," the philosopher Elizabeth Anderson writes in *The Imperative of Integration*, "segregation at work, school, and church and in neighborhoods practically guarantees that few blacks will learn about the firm's job openings."

It is understandable that these injustices have inspired a good deal of anger, and even a modicum of fatalism. Especially the first members of minority groups who gained access to elite institutions like Ivy League colleges did face both outright hostility and more subtle forms of condescension. Perhaps it was inevitable that some of them would come to embrace calls for a supposedly progressive form of separatism—and that an influential group of white leftists who feel deeply ashamed of their country's failings would quickly amplify and institutionalize such demands. But as most Americans from all ethnic groups realize, the best way to combat the lingering reality of segregation is to redouble our efforts to integrate society, not a shortsighted attempt to sidestep the difficulties that this process inevitably entails. What would that look like?

In a free society, people are at liberty to associate with whomever they choose, and to identify themselves in whatever way they wish. There is nothing wrong with some adults spending most of their time among those with whom they share key ascriptive traits. And when it comes to culture, the pride that many Americans take in their heritage is a big part of what makes the country so vibrant. Given the history of the United States, hopes for a complete abolition of race are probably unrealistic for the foreseeable future; especially when it comes to groups that have suffered centuries of injustice, it is easy to see why they are likely to retain some pride in their shared ancestry.

For all of those reasons, society should celebrate its ethnic and religious diversity, and even look upon certain forms of homophily with benevolence. But it would be a big mistake to let celebrations of diversity or respect for each citizen's right to exercise the freedom of association turn into an embrace of progressive separatism. The goal of the country's most influential institutions, from corporations to philanthropic foundations, should be to foster integration and inspire an emphasis on the identities that compatriots drawn from different ethnic (and religious and sexual) groups share with each other.

This is especially important when it comes to educational institutions. American colleges, for example, have historically assigned students from very different backgrounds to shared rooms in their first year. Now most of them allow incoming students to request roommates of like mind and usually like background they have met on social media or at local meetups. It is time for colleges to abandon these counterproductive changes, returning their focus to practices that are likely to integrate rather than to separate.

Similarly, one important goal of elementary and secondary education should be to create as many opportunities as possible for students from different groups to have meaningful contact with each other. Teachers should of course emphasize the contributions that different cultures have made—and continue to make—to the United States. But instead of pushing students to place their primary allegiance in the "correct" ethnic labels, they should seek to inspire them to place the biggest importance on identities they share with their classmates and compatriots. This means that they should resolutely reject fashionable practices like race-segregated affinity groups in favor of inclusive and collaborative activities that are far more likely to build mutual respect and affection. (And yes, rightly understood, this more truly inclusive pedagogy is fully compatible with teaching an honest account of the country's past, one that features both its great accomplishments and its terrible injustices.)

Making meaningful progress on integration will, especially in countries that continue to suffer from some measure of segregation, also require substantial changes of public policy. The American system of financing public schools, for example, is in urgent need of reform. In virtually all countries, schools are governed by comparatively large entities like cities, counties, regions, or even states. Only in the United States, with its hodgepodge of different school districts, does the quality and the ethnic composition of local public schools depend so heavily on the income of residents in a tiny area.

Housing policy is also important. In the past, outright discrimination was the main reason for residential segregation. Today, strict zoning laws and byzantine regulations regarding new building projects help to explain why some neighborhoods remain predominantly white. Giving people more opportunities to interact as neighbors and classmates hinges, in part, on seemingly wonkish measures such as more permissive zoning laws.

The ultimate shape of a free society will always depend on the choices its citizens make. But over the past few decades, some of the richest and most influential institutions have fully embraced the radical form of progressive separatism. They do what is in their power to make young people, including whites, define themselves in terms of their ethnic identities. This is a big mistake.

While a free society will always be respectful of its citizens' cultural and religious differences, the human penchant for homophily ensures that people will naturally sort themselves into different groups. To ensure mutual tolerance and build solidarity among citizens drawn from different ethnic groups, powerful institutions need to see themselves as a counterweight to groupishness. Their goal must be to push for integration, not to encourage people to lean more deeply into what separates them from each other. If diverse societies are to succeed, their citizens will one day be less, rather than more, conscious of their ethnic differences than they are now.

KEY TAKEAWAYS

- Many important institutions have recently embraced practices, from affinity groups to Black-only dorms, that separate people on the basis of their skin color or sexual identity. They believe that it is their duty to encourage people to define themselves in terms of the identity groups into which they are born and to protect them from the ever-present danger of harm posed by members of dominant groups. Historically, this new form of "progressive separatism" can be understood as the love child of two major intellectual influences: strategic essentialism and safetyism.

- Human beings are groupish: they tend to favor members of the in-group and discriminate against members of the out-group. But whom they think of as insiders and how they feel about outsiders depends on historical circumstance. In particular, contact between different groups can reduce long-standing prejudices when four conditions are met: they enjoy equal status within the situation; they have common goals; they have to work together to achieve them; and they are expected to get along.

- The norms and customs encouraged by progressive separatists systematically violate the four conditions that allow members of different groups to forge a bond. They encourage members of different identity groups to see each other as always having a big difference in status; they discourage an emphasis on shared forms of identity that make common goals more salient; they reduce opportunities to work together; and they create incentives for conflict.

- Some progressive separatists don't just encourage members of historically marginalized groups to define themselves in terms of their ethnicity; they also encourage whites to do so. This is highly counterproductive. These practices are motivated by the hope that whites who are deeply conscious of their racial identity will become antiracist activists. But in practice a greater identification with their skin color is likely to make them fight for their collective interests, encouraging more zero-sum conflict between different demographic groups.

- A better solution to the persistent problem of segregation is a redoubled commitment to integration. The goal must be to create more contexts and opportunities in which people from different groups can interact and cooperate.

Chapter 12

THE PATH TO EQUALITY

When an earthquake hits, doctors have to decide whom to treat first. In the early stages of the coronavirus pandemic, hospitals in Italy and some parts of the United States were forced to make heartrending choices about the distribution of ventilators. And when a long-awaited vaccine finally promised to deliver the world from its suffering, public health authorities needed to determine who should be first in line to access its scarce doses.

Countries from Canada to Italy came up with remarkably similar plans. To begin with, they would make the vaccine available to medical staff. Intensive care units were stretched to their limits. Key personnel were scarce. For everyone's benefit, it was paramount to minimize the number of doctors and nurses who had to stay home because they might have been exposed to the virus. In the next phase, the elderly would become eligible. Because the likelihood of dying from COVID increases exponentially with age, a majority of the disease's victims were of retirement age. Protecting those who are most at risk as quickly as possible promised to save the most lives.

Only one country radically deviated from this plan: the United States. In its preliminary recommendations, the key committee advising the Centers for Disease Control proposed putting eighty-seven million "essential workers"—a broad category that would include bankers and film crews—ahead of the elderly.

The ethical considerations that go into this kind of triage are complex. Though I studied moral and political philosophy for much of my academic career, I would hate to be in a position to decide these questions. And if scientific models had suggested that vaccinating essential workers before the elderly led to a much more rapid fall in the number of infections, I too might have been willing to countenance deviating from the example set by so many other countries. But what was striking about the recommendations initially adopted in the United States wasn't just the substance of them; it was that they would, according to the CDC's own reasoning, lead to thousands of additional deaths.

A presentation to the Advisory Committee on Immunization Practices (ACIP) by Kathleen Dooling, a senior public health expert at the CDC, suggested that two important considerations favored prioritizing the elderly, the course of action that virtually every other industrialized country adopted. First, Dooling acknowledged, prioritizing people over the age of sixty-five would be much more practicable. It is difficult to determine who should count as an essential worker and even more difficult to reach out to those people who do. It is much easier to inform the public that everyone above a certain cutoff becomes eligible for the vaccine on a particular date and to verify their age at their appointment. On "implementation," Dooling's presentation awarded three points to putting the elderly first and a generous two points to prioritizing essential workers.

Second, Dooling admitted that prioritizing the elderly would likely save thousands of lives. Depending on the exact scenario, it would, her presentation showed, reduce the number of Americans who would die from COVID over the following months by between 0.5 percent and 6.5 percent. The obvious implication is that this provided a very weighty reason for putting the elderly first. But that is not how the presentation put it. Dismissing the prospect of additional deaths on the scale of September 11 as "minimal," Dooling maintained that from a scientific point of view there was not much difference between the two possible courses of action. On "science," she gave both alternatives three points.

Finally, Dooling turned to her last metric: "ethics." The key problem, the presentation highlighted in red font, is that "racial and ethnic minority groups are underrepresented among adults > 65." Because the elderly are a less diverse group than the younger group of essential workers, it would be immoral to put them first. On "ethics," Dooling gave three points to essential workers and only one point to the elderly. (Her presentation did not appear to consider the fact that her suggested course of action would, according to her own data, lead to a much larger number of deaths, an "ethical" consideration.)

On the basis of this tortuous reasoning, essential workers scored eight points, one more than the elderly. Dooling advocated putting essential workers first. ACIP unanimously accepted the recommendation.

When ACIP's recommendations went public, a few intrepid journalists pushed back against them. These plans, they pointed out, inscribed racial discrimination at the very heart of American public policy. They accepted that thousands of people would needlessly die. And though they were dressed up in the language of the identity synthesis, they would, ironically, be likely to have a deadly impact on historically marginalized groups.

Old people are much, much more likely to die from COVID than young people. So the overall death toll for Black people would rise even if two thousand young Black delivery drivers got the vaccine instead of one thousand old Black retirees. Under ACIP's plans, a moderate increase in the *proportion* of Latinos and African Americans who got the vaccine in the first months after its release would likely go hand in hand with an increase in the *total number* of Latinos and African Americans who die from COVID. It is hard to overstate how perverse the implications are: the policy was so focused on reducing the disparity in the number of vaccines that members of different races would receive that it likely resulted in an increase in deaths in the very groups whose welfare it was supposedly designed to prioritize.

In the end, ACIP partially relented to public criticism. It issued new recommendations that gave Americans over the age of seventy-four a slightly higher priority than the original plan had suggested. But even these new plans prioritized the elderly far less than other countries. They likely led to needless deaths on a significant scale. How could this jaw-droppingly misguided decision happen?

Dooling's presentation is one of the most remarkable public documents I have seen in years of studying political science. It is also an example of a wider trend. A few months later, for example, the Republican governor of Vermont announced that all "Black, Indigenous residents and other people of color" would be given access to COVID vaccines at a time when most white residents continued to be ineligible for them; when the policy proved controversial, he dismissed its critics as "racist." And when, a few months after that, promising treatment options for COVID like Paxlovid first became available, a number of states (as I discussed in the introduction) resorted to the new playbook as a matter of course: guidelines issued by the State of New York, for example, urged doctors to prioritize twenty-year-old Asian American patients without preconditions over sixty-year-old white patients without preconditions.

Examples from health care are particularly striking because the most basic interests of citizens—potentially their very survival—are at stake. But over the past few years, governments have incorporated similar "race-sensitive" and, more broadly, "identity-sensitive" policies in a large number of areas. For example, the federal government at first distributed limited emergency funds for small businesses affected by the pandemic on the basis of the revenue loss they had suffered. When the Biden administration took office, the White House quickly changed the program's eligibility criteria. Now businesses owned by women or ethnic minorities would jump to the front of the line.

How did key public agencies from the CDC to the White House become convinced that it is wise to allocate public goods from lifesaving drugs to emergency loans for small businesses on the basis of gender or skin color? To understand the new penchant for identity-sensitive policies, we need to put these decisions in the context of a much broader debate about how, and whether, public policy should take characteristics like skin color into account.

THE RISE OF EQUITY AND THE EMBRACE
OF IDENTITY-SENSITIVE PUBLIC POLICY

For much of American history, explicit racial discrimination was inscribed in the law. At the time of the country's founding, Black Americans were excluded from full civic rights in the North and held as slaves in the South. Starting in the late nineteenth century, a series of bills explicitly aimed to keep immigrants from China and other nonwhite nations out of the country. During World War II, 100,000 Americans of Japanese origin were rounded up and transported to internment camps.

Americans who fought these injustices came from vastly different traditions and backgrounds. They were Black and white, secular and religious, Christian and Jewish. What united them is a strong faith in equality. It was time, they insisted, to live up to the promise the Founding Fathers had made when they claimed that "all men are created equal." As Barack Obama put the point in his moving speech on the fiftieth anniversary of the march from Selma to Montgomery, "The Americans who crossed this bridge . . . marched as Americans who had endured hundreds of years of brutal violence, countless daily indignities—but they didn't seek special treatment, just the equal treatment promised to them almost a century before."

As the nation and its courts grappled with how to turn the aspirations of the civil rights movement into reality, intense fights over public policy took center stage. Should cities bus kids to faraway schools to fight racial segregation? Should states give special loans or tax breaks to minority-owned businesses to rectify a legacy of discrimination? And should public universities engage in affirmative action to make their campuses more diverse? The right answers to these questions have been contentious from the start, and remain so today. Liberals and conservatives tend to disagree. So do federal judges appointed by Democrats and Republicans.

But both liberals and conservatives have historically expressed the hope that such policies would be temporary. A 2003 Supreme Court decision upholding race-sensitive admissions policies at the University of Michigan Law School, which was written by Sandra Day O'Connor and joined by Ruth Bader Ginsburg, explained that "racial classifications, however compelling their goals, are potentially so dangerous that they may be employed no more broadly than the interest demands.... All governmental use of race must have a logical end point." At the time, O'Connor and Ginsburg expected that "25 years from now, the use of racial preferences will no longer be necessary to further the interest approved today."

Nearly twenty-five years have passed since O'Connor's opinion, and it is now obvious that her prediction was wrong. Far from fading, the use of racial preferences has surged. While there was once a kind of consensus that race-sensitive policies are only appropriate as a temporary remedy when no alternatives are available, an influential group of activists, politicians, and intellectuals are now seeking to inscribe race and other forms of group identity at the very heart of public policy as a matter of routine.

Indeed, scholars who helped to shape the identity synthesis, including Derrick Bell and Kimberlé Crenshaw, have over the past decades mounted a radical attack on the idea that it might ever be appropriate to be "colorblind." Race, they argue, still shapes every citizen's opportunities and experiences in profound ways. Because the culture of the United States is deeply suffused with white supremacy, even well-meaning whites treat their Black and brown compatriots in racist ways. Any race-blind policy would, they conclude, only serve to compound the fact of structural disadvantage with the fiction that it doesn't exist.

As a result, it has in many quarters become taboo to claim to be colorblind. According to official guidance that UCLA offered to its students, for example, they should always treat their classmates as "racial/cultural beings"; a failure to do so qualifies as a "microaggression." According to Ibram X. Kendi, "The language of color blindness—like the language of 'not racist'—is a mask to hide racism"; it follows that "a color-blind Constitution" would merely serve to maintain "a White-supremacist America." Dani Bostick echoes the growing consensus even more starkly, asserting that the idea of color blindness "is actually racist."

Inspired by these ideas, even mainstream Democrats have embraced a new set of goals. Ever since the French Revolution, the left has touted "equality" as one of its core values. But over the past decade, many politicians, activists, and writers have instead begun to emphasize what they call "equity." Though both of these terms admit of many different definitions, making their meaning somewhat dependent on context, the most common interpretation of equity entails a commitment to eliminating group-level disparities, especially between different races and ethnicities. As Adolph Reed Jr., a Black Marxist who has long taught at the University of Pennsylvania, has pointed out, it should be thought of as a form of "disparitarianism."

This form of disparitarianism has quickly gone from the seminar room to the heart of government. Joe Biden and Kamala Harris have repeatedly emphasized that they view racial equity as a core goal of their administration. Putting the value of equity in explicit contrast with the value of equality, for example, Kamala Harris proclaimed, "I'm proud to stand with and by President Joe Biden as we make equity one of the cornerstones of our vision for our administration." And so it is hardly a surprise that Biden, on his first day in office, signed an executive order that obligated "the Federal Government [to] pursue a comprehensive approach to advancing equity" by adopting an "ambitious whole-of-government equity agenda."

To promote equity, Democrats now routinely promise to pursue "race-conscious" and "race-sensitive" policies. In practice, what it means for a policy to be race sensitive varies widely. Sometimes, it merely means making sure that policies don't turn out to have discriminatory effects, as might, for example, be the case when laws requiring motorcyclists to don helmets don't include exceptions for Sikhs who must wear turbans for religious reasons. But increasingly, such policies explicitly make the way the state treats people depend on the color of their skin (or the ethnic composition of the neighborhood in which they reside).

Taken together, these ideas explain what motivated the CDC's reasoning. Age is, by far and away, the strongest predictor for who dies from COVID. White people are overrepresented among the elderly. It follows that a policy that isn't explicitly based on race would have given a slightly higher proportion of vaccines to white Americans. Giving priority to essential workers, who are disproportionately Latino or African American, by contrast, would ensure that a slightly higher share of vaccines goes to "people of color," marginally reducing disparities in access to vaccines between white and Black Americans. In the fashionable language of the day, the policy would serve to promote equity—even though, making it harder for older Latinos and African Americans to get access to the vaccine by prioritizing younger Latinos and African Americans, it might have the perverse result of killing a greater number of people in both ethnic groups.

The case for equity and other identity-sensitive public policies deserves to be taken seriously. If race-neutral policies really made us incapable of perceiving racism or of boosting the opportunities of historically disadvantaged groups, it would be hard to justify them. But that is not the case. It is possible for a state to recognize and combat the racism that continues to characterize most societies without making how it treats people turn on the identity group to which they belong. Public policies that benefit all needy citizens irrespective of their race or gender are more likely to address poverty, and perhaps even to reduce disparities between different groups, than the identity-sensitive policies that are now in vogue. Conversely, a society that aims for equity instead of equality is unlikely to reduce the vast socioeconomic disparities between the rich and the poor. It could even make citizens from all groups worse off. And far from being merely theoretical, these problems are already showing up in real-world applications of race-sensitive public policies.

THE DIFFERENCE BETWEEN BEING RACE-BLIND AND BEING RACISM-BLIND

The discussion of race blindness usually lumps two very different questions together. The first is about how we should *understand* the world. The second is about how we should *act* in it.

If we are to build a just society, we obviously need to be able to identify and remedy racism. In the excellent formulation of the British Nigerian writer Ralph Leonard, those who fail to live up to this important imperative are "racism blind." Whether by design or omission, their eyes aren't open to the racial injustices that characterize many aspects of developed democracies.

Racism blindness, Leonard argues, is deeply pernicious because it stops us from recognizing when people are experiencing discrimination on the basis of the ethnic groups into which they were born. This is why (as I argued in my chapter on standpoint theory), we all have a moral duty to listen to the stories of our compatriots very carefully. Even though we might imagine that we already know what the world looks like for members of other identity groups, understanding their hardships—and building the foundations for true political solidarity—takes time and effort.

But while we need to weed out racism blindness, we should not, Leonard insists, give up on building a society in which we "treat everyone equally, judging people by individual attributes" rather than by race. It takes a lot of sensitivity to racism to ensure that people aren't treated poorly due to attributes like the color of their skin. But being sensitive to the realities of racism is so important precisely because the aim should be to build a world that is *truly* insensitive to race.

The same distinction between race blindness and racism blindness is highly pertinent when it comes to public policy. To ensure that governments don't inadvertently discriminate against those who have historically been treated unjustly, they do need to pay attention to race. If policymakers pretend that race doesn't exist, they will neither be able to spot willful discrimination nor be able to recognize when a policy has an unfair and disproportionate impact on one demographic group. To understand why it seems worrisome that federal laws meted out much higher penalties for crack than for cocaine, for example, it is important to know that Black Americans were comparatively more likely to use crack, while white Americans were comparatively more likely to use cocaine. People who design and implement policies should make every effort to ensure that they do not have an unfairly disparate impact on some demographic group; insofar as that is all that "race-conscious" policies seek to accomplish, they aren't a reason for concern.

But as Leonard points out, a determination to spot and combat ongoing forms of discrimination is perfectly compatible with a refusal to base public policy on immutable characteristics like race. The solution to disparate punishments for the use of crack and cocaine, for example, is not to distinguish between white and Black users of crack; it is to give out proportionate punishments for users of both drugs—or to stop putting nonviolent drug users in jail altogether. For thinkers like Leonard, it is a virtue to be fully aware of the ways in which race shapes society and the effects of public policy, but it is a vice for the state to distinguish between how it treats particular citizens on the basis of their race.

To favor race-neutral public policies is neither to be complacent in combating ongoing racial discrimination nor to blind ourselves to the persistent realities of racism. This is a distinction that everybody should, in principle, be willing to acknowledge. And it is made all the more powerful because race-blind policies that aim to alleviate poverty and offer opportunity can, to a much greater extent than many now realize, help to address historical injustices.

RACE-NEUTRAL POLICIES CAN HELP
FIGHT RACIAL INEQUALITY

The effects of past discrimination continue to shape the United States and many other democracies around the world. In light of the centuries of slavery and Jim Crow, for example, it is hardly a coincidence that African Americans, on average, remain less well-off than members of most other demographic groups. Any framework for public policy that fails to provide some hope for overcoming inequalities that stem from such historical injustices will remain vulnerable to forceful criticism. But as it happens, race-neutral policies, not just race-sensitive ones, are capable of attenuating the effects of historical disadvantage.

Many people have a difficult start in life because they suffer from entrenched disadvantages. If you grow up in an impoverished neighborhood that has high crime and terrible schools, you deserve special assistance to ensure you have a fair shot at succeeding in life. We need ambitious public policies to create genuine equality of opportunity. We also need to make sure that every citizen who is willing to make a genuine contribution to society can, even if they don't become an investment banker or a plastic surgeon, lead a good life.

Given the disparities in income between different ethnic groups, it might be tempting to think that racial criteria would be effective at directing assistance to those who need it most and are most deprived of opportunity; this is the morally powerful intuition behind the recent embrace of race-sensitive policies. But this elides the fact that averages hide a tremendous amount of variation. In both the United States and the United Kingdom, for example, there is now both a large and thriving nonwhite middle class and a growing white underclass. A race-sensitive set of policies that simply provides additional benefits to Black people would help a good number of people who grew up with tremendous opportunities—while neglecting a huge number of people who grew up in intergenerational poverty.

Consider the United States, where the poverty rate is much higher among Black than among white Americans. A little more than one in five Black Americans are in poverty while a little less than one in ten white Americans are. But because there are still over five times more white than Black Americans, an antipoverty policy that targets the roughly ten million poor Black Americans would fail to assist the even greater number of twenty-three million poor white Americans.

Race-neutral policies wouldn't just help to ensure that all needy people can hope for assistance; ironically, they would also help to lessen disparities between different ethnic groups. African Americans, for example, are more likely to live in deprived neighborhoods or to have poor parents than white Americans. Race-neutral policies that direct extra funding to schools in deprived neighborhoods or offer scholarships to college students who grew up in poverty would therefore disproportionately benefit African Americans. If they are sufficiently ambitious, they can, without having to distinguish between different citizens on the basis of their race, make a big contribution to reducing unjust disparities.

Finally, it might be thought that race-sensitive policies are necessary in a context like the United States to overcome the persistent legacy of extraordinary historical crimes, such as slavery. There is indeed especially strong reason to remedy the lingering effects of slavery. When individuals are wronged, they or their descendants should to the extent possible be compensated for the moral and financial injuries that were inflicted on them. This provides a strong reason to pay descendants of people who have been enslaved reparations for the terrible injustices done to their ancestors. But note that such reparations would not be based on purely racial characteristics; the descendants of recent immigrants from Kenya or Nigeria, for example, should not be eligible for them. If some Americans deserve compensation from their government, it is not because they are Black or "people of color"—but because their ancestors were victims of terrible crimes.

The most common objections to dealing with racial injustice within a universalist framework are less convincing than they first appear. People who insist that the state should not make how it treats its citizens depend on the color of their skin do not need to blind themselves to the pernicious persistence of racism. And far from being toothless, state programs that benefit all citizens who are in need can do enormous good, and even help to remedy racial disparities. Conversely, a closer examination of the equity framework shows that it is much less convincing than it first appears: both in theory and in practice, it fails to deliver on the promises that make it so attractive.

WHY EQUITY FAILS IN THEORY

The especially strong appeal of equity in the United States has a lot to do with the nature of injustice in the country. For centuries, African Americans have been treated abominably. It is no coincidence that Black Americans continue to earn somewhat lower wages, and to have much less wealth, than white Americans. This is clearly unjust. The appeal of the "equity" framework is that it seems to capture why.

But while the concept of equity has some intuitive plausibility, an uncritical focus on it would lead to very bad outcomes. The first problem with equity has been emphasized by egalitarian philosophers like Reed. They care deeply about the growth of inequality in developed democracies, from Germany to the United States. At the moment, they argue, the rich are getting richer while the poor are getting poorer. The goal of government policy should, according to them, be to reverse that concerning trend.

On first glance, it might seem that this should make egalitarians look favorably upon the rise of equity. But as Reed and like-minded critics point out, equity and equality don't necessarily go hand in hand. One way to make sure that white and Black Americans have similar levels of wealth would be for society to get a lot more equal, lifting poor Black people out of poverty. But another way to make sure that white and Black Americans have similar wealth would be for a small number of Black people to become extremely rich.

Marxists like Reed are aware of the fact that the latter course of action would ask much less of the rich and powerful, allowing them to keep most of their wealth. This, they worry, makes it much more likely that societies will try to achieve equity through such comparatively cosmetic changes that don't actually reduce overall inequality. And if America manages to create a few dozen Black billionaires while millions of Americans of all races continue to live in poverty, they conclude, precious little is gained for most people: "The disparitarian ideal is that blacks and other nonwhites should be represented on every rung on the ladder of economic hierarchy in rough proportion to their representation in the general population." But "a society where making black and white people equal means making them equally subordinate to a . . . ruling class is not a more just society, just a differently unjust one."

The other problem with equity is rooted in what philosophers call the "leveling-down objection." Imagine a (highly stylized) society composed of two people. Andrea has $10, giving her a very comfortable lifestyle. Bruce has $5, making it necessary for him to budget extremely carefully to get through the month. Many people will think that this difference in living standards is unjust unless there is some good reason for Andrea to earn twice as much as Bruce; some may even think that it is the task of public policy to redress the difference between them. Now, on a strictly egalitarian conception of justice, one way to achieve this goal would be to make both Andrea and Bruce much poorer. If they both had $3, the unjust inequality between them would no longer exist (even though they might both go hungry). But would justice really be served if a public policy achieved equality by "leveling down" in this manner?

The same objection applies to equity. There is something to the intuition that it seems unfair that members of one ethnic group should, unless there is a compelling explanation for the disparity, be much more affluent, on average, than members of another ethnic group. But public policies based predominantly on equity would merely seek to reduce the disparity between these groups, and one way to reduce that disparity is by making sure that everyone becomes much less well-off than they currently are. The leveling-down objection rears its head again.

This objection might seem a little abstract. It would be tempting to think that it doesn't really apply to the real world. After all, nobody sets out to remedy racial disparity by making everyone equally poor. But as it happens, the way in which the CDC advised public health authorities to distribute lifesaving vaccines is a striking example of what happens when policymakers are so focused on equity that they end up ignoring the leveling-down objection. By reducing the disparity between different ethnic groups, prioritizing essential workers over the elderly really did serve equity. But because the policy had the foreseeable consequence of increasing mortality among all ethnic groups, making everyone worse off, it was obviously immoral.

WHY EQUITY FAILS IN PRACTICE

Even as race-sensitive policies fail to deliver on their promises, they have a lot of serious drawbacks. One problem is, simply, that they force everybody to conceive of themselves as part of a particular ethnic or racial group. In countries in which the most important rights and duties that citizens enjoy depend on their membership in a particular identity group, people who do not clearly fall into one group, or who refuse to define themselves by the group to which they "objectively" belong, can barely function.

In Lebanon, where Shias, Sunnis, and Maronite Christians are subject to different sets of laws governing important areas of personal life, the state often refuses to recognize marriages between members of different communities. Similarly, in India, the government has barred prospective migrants based on their religion, and made it easier for some religious groups to obtain citizenship. This is not only extremely unjust to such individuals;

it also demonstrates that policies that make how the state treats citizens depend on their race or religion can be a big impediment to a society's ability to attenuate historical divisions.

Another problem is that policies that favor members of one group usually also disfavor members of another group. Race-sensitive admissions policies at American universities, for example, have helped to ensure that a critical mass of Black students attend the country's most august institutions. This is a laudable achievement. But those same policies have, simultaneously, made it much harder for Asian American applicants to win access to those same schools. As a raft of evidence suggests, Asian Americans don't just need to outperform African Americans to gain admission to elite colleges in the United States; they also need to do a lot better than their white peers. Their prospects are further diminished by admissions officers judging applicants on soft criteria like whether they possess "grit" or "effervescence"— criteria on which universities like Harvard just so happen to rank Asian American applicants far lower than those of any other racial group.

When public policy is formulated in race-neutral terms, members of all demographic groups have a stake in its success. Unemployment insurance is appealing to a lot of people because we all know that we might one day lose our job. Truly universal benefits like Social Security are even better at sustaining political support because practically every citizen hopes to reach retirement age. But when public policy is formulated in race-sensitive terms, each group has an interest in mobilizing along ethnic lines to fight for its own interests. And in a democracy, fights over the distribution of scarce resources are, virtually by definition, usually won by more numerous and more powerful rather than less numerous and less powerful groups— making it, at best, an extremely risky tool for overcoming historical injustice. As Hubert Humphrey, a passionate advocate of desegregation, reportedly insisted when he shepherded the Civil Rights Act through the Senate, giving preferential treatment to a group on the basis of its ascriptive characteristics can very easily go awry. "Do you want a society that is nothing but an endless power struggle among organized groups?"

All of this helps to explain why it has, even in highly diverse states like California, proven very difficult to sustain support for race-sensitive policies. In the 1990s, the Golden State was in the midst of a deep political backlash against its rapidly rising demographic diversity. In 1994, Proposition 187, popularly known as Save Our State (SOS), banned undocumented immigrants from accessing welfare benefits, from using nonemergency health care, and from enrolling in public education. Two years later, a majority of Californians voted to ban government entities and public universities in the state from engaging in affirmative action.

Since then, California has undergone a profound political sea change. The state is now deeply liberal. A majority of its population is Black, Asian, or Hispanic. With the exception of an obscure insurance commissioner called Steve Poizner and a famous governor called Arnold Schwarzenegger, not a single Republican has won statewide office since 1994. A prominent group of activists saw this political transformation as an opportunity to repeal the state's ban on affirmative action. They secured the support of key institutional players, from Kamala Harris to the major newspapers and many of the biggest corporations in the state. Backed by deep-pocketed donors, they outspent opponents of affirmative action by more than ten to one.

But it was all to no avail. In a referendum held on the same day that Joe Biden beat Donald Trump by 64 percent to 34 percent in the state, a clear majority of Californians voted to maintain the ban on giving preferential treatment to some people based on their race or ethnicity. The failure of the referendum suggests a final drawback of race-sensitive policies: in a democracy, supposedly progressive measures that are incapable of winning popular majorities—even in a highly diverse and left-leaning state like California—simply aren't capable of delivering on the benefits they promise in a sustainable manner.

The benefits of equity-inspired public policies are less obvious than they at first appear. Conversely, the costs are more serious than is usually acknowledged. Does that mean that they should never be permissible?

IMPERFECT, EXCEPTIONAL, AND RARE

In the United States, more than just about any other developed democracy, key questions of morality and public policy are often reduced to debates about the best interpretation of particular phrases in the country's founding documents. Instead of considering the deep moral reasons that militate for or against the death penalty, Americans discuss whether it constitutes "cruel and unusual punishment." And instead of tackling the deep ethical and metaphysical reasons to favor or oppose abortion rights, they argue about whether banning the practice would amount to an impermissible violation of the "right to privacy."

For that reason, I am at times impatient with the legal framing of moral debates in the United States. We would often come to better decisions—and a greater understanding of our respective positions—if we ignored the jurisprudence. But questions about the desirability of race-sensitive policies are an interesting exception. Both the Fourteenth Amendment to the Constitution and the subsequent case law on its interpretation have created a powerful moral framework that neatly captures the most important considerations.

Ruth Bader Ginsburg strongly favored affirmative action. Antonin Scalia strongly opposed it. Even so, both agreed on a basic set of criteria for how the Supreme Court should evaluate programs that give minority applicants a leg up. As the Supreme Court held in *Adarand Constructors Inc. v. Peña*, the Fourteenth Amendment "protects *persons*, not *groups*." This creates a strong presumption against any attempt by public authorities to treat members of different groups differently from each other: "Government may treat people differently because of their race only for the most compelling reasons."

Any government program that distinguishes between different people on the basis of their race must therefore meet three stringent criteria. First, it must serve a "compelling interest." This means that distinguishing between different citizens on the basis of their race must serve an essential or necessary purpose of public policy, not merely be motivated by considerations that are reasonable or rational.

Second, these programs need to be "narrowly tailored" to accomplish that compelling state interest. This means that the relevant government entity needs to have made a serious effort to serve the compelling interest that is at stake in a way that does not require an explicit distinction between different people on the basis of their race.

And third, the courts need to apply "strict scrutiny" to any such governmental programs. As the Supreme Court wrote in 1989, "We apply strict scrutiny to all racial classifications to 'smoke out illegitimate uses of race by assuring that [government] is pursuing a goal important enough to warrant use of a highly suspect tool.'"

The legal fight over race-sensitive public policies has mostly consisted of different judges giving different answers as to whether such programs meet these stringent tests. Because the Supreme Court has long had a light liberal lean, it has mostly deferred to universities when they argued that they have a compelling interest in practicing affirmative action to ensure that they have a diverse student body. Conservative judges have steadily dissented from these rulings on the grounds that such policies do not serve a sufficiently compelling state interest or that their goals could effectively be pursued in other ways. Because conservatives are now in the majority on the court for the first time in two generations, they may soon put much stricter limits on affirmative action. (A decision on a landmark case, *Students for Fair Admissions v. Harvard University*, is likely to be announced before this book is published.)

Americans will continue to disagree about the circumstances in which race-sensitive policies serve an interest so compelling, and the alternatives are so inadequate, that race-sensitive policies are appropriate. There will be hard cases in which many people feel deeply torn, as I myself do in the case of affirmative action. But the moral framework embraced by both Ruth Bader Ginsburg and Antonin Scalia remains the best guide for how to think through these issues. And it strongly suggests that even those who are convinced that race-sensitive public policies are justified in particular contexts must recognize their serious costs—and hope that the need for them shall prove temporary.

The U.S. Constitution rightly promises to treat each citizen as an individual rather than as a member of a group. In a liberal democracy, civic rights should be based on citizenship, not on religion, ethnicity, or skin color. This creates a strong presumption against identity-sensitive policies.

KEY TAKEAWAYS

- In recent years, America has started to pursue race-sensitive public policies at all levels of government. Even decisions with existential stakes, such as who should get priority for lifesaving vaccines, are now being made on the basis of considerations of equity. And while the initial justification for such policies assumed that they would prove temporary, its advocates increasingly envisage this approach as a standard operating procedure for governments going forward.

- Advocates of equity make two claims that are meant to show why universal policies are morally unacceptable. First, more universal policies supposedly force us to ignore the role that racism continues to play in reality. And second, they are supposedly incapable of attenuating disparities between different identity groups or dealing with the long-run repercussions of past injustices, like slavery. But on closer inspection, universal policies turn out to be more attractive than they first appear. They do not make us incapable of recognizing or remedying the existence of racial discrimination. They can help to attenuate racial disparities because a universal welfare state will in any case channel more resources to groups whose members are disproportionately in need. And finally, they are even conformable with reparations for past injustices, which should be based on individual descent rather than broad identity categories.

- At the same time, the ideal of equity turns out to be far less attractive than it seems at first sight. Philosophically, it suffers from two major drawbacks: First, because equity merely focuses on the disparities between different ethnic groups, it is possible to achieve equity by making a few members of a historically marginalized groups very rich; an equitable society could therefore be a highly unequal one. Second, it is possible to achieve equity by making members of all groups worse off; an equitable society could therefore be a very poor one.

- These objections are not merely theoretical. Some of the first applications of equity, including the guidance on vaccines issued by the Centers for Disease Control, likely led to worse outcomes for all demographic groups.

Race-sensitive public policies also tend to entrench divisions between different identity groups, making future conflict more likely. Finally, such policies tend to be highly unpopular among all demographic groups, making it harder to sustain support for a generous welfare state and the improvements it promises in the long run.

- The legal framework embraced by both progressive judges like Ruth Bader Ginsburg and conservative judges like Antonin Scalia can set better guidelines for when to adopt race-sensitive public policies. There should always be a strong presumption against the state making how it treats people depend on identity markers like the color of their skin. This presumption can be superseded only when three strict conditions are met: There must be a compelling state interest in pursuing the policy. The policy must be narrowly tailored to achieve that interest. And race-neutral alternatives to the policy must be unavailable. For all these reasons, it is both a moral and a practical mistake to turn identity-sensitive public policies into standard operating procedure.

Chapter 13

ON STRUCTURAL RACISM, GENDER, AND MERITOCRACY

In the last chapters, I have focused on five common applications of the identity synthesis to contemporary cultural and political debates. It is, I argue, a mistake to give up on the hope that members of different ethnic groups can come to have genuine empathy for each other; to put forms of cultural influence between members of different groups under a general pall of suspicion; to underestimate the dangerous consequences that stem from giving up on a genuine culture of free speech; to embrace calls for a supposedly progressive form of separatism that undermines efforts at genuine integration; and to make race-sensitive public policies the government's default mode of operation.

In each case, I have instead advocated for a solution that takes concerns about persistent injustices seriously without giving up on long-standing universal norms. It is possible for citizens to develop genuine empathy for each other if they make the time and effort to listen to the experiences of their compatriots. We can address genuine exploitation or ridicule without stigmatizing healthy cultural exchange as a dangerous form of "cultural appropriation." Politicians and leaders of key social institutions can express their passionate disagreement with racism or other forms of bigotry without giving up on the First Amendment or undermining a culture of free speech. Society can respect the freedom of association and encourage members of minority cultures to take pride in their heritage without succumbing to pernicious forms of progressive separatism. Finally, public policies can protect citizens against discrimination, and address persistent inequalities, without routinely making the way the state treats people depend on markers of their identity such as the color of their skin.

The topics I have covered in these pages are both important and widely debated. But because advocates of the identity synthesis hope to remake the traditional ways in which democracies deal with a vast array of subjects, applications of their ideology are also influential in many other contexts. I could easily have added five extra chapters to this part of the book.

It would be overkill to go into detail on each of these potential applications of the identity synthesis. But three more are especially prominent or consequential and need to be briefly addressed before we can move on: the claim that racism has nothing to do with individual motivations or biases; the claim that an individual's gender should in all contexts supersede any consideration of their biological sex; and the claim that we should completely give up on the ideal of meritocracy.

STRUCTURAL RACISM

Many advocates of the identity synthesis rightly point out that an account of racism that focuses purely on individual beliefs or motivations runs the danger of concealing important forms of injustice. Even if everyone has the best of intentions, the aftereffects of historical injustices can ensure that many immigrant students attend underfunded public schools or that many members of ethnic minorities suffer disadvantages in the housing market. It therefore makes sense, they argue, to add a new concept to our vocabulary: structural racism.

As the *Cambridge Dictionary* explains with reference to the closely related concept of systemic racism, it consists of "policies and practices that exist throughout a whole society or organization, and that result in and support a continued unfair advantage to some people and unfair or harmful treatment of others based on race." By pointing out that some forms of racism are "structural" in this way, we are better able to capture—and hopefully remedy—circumstances in which members of some racial groups suffer significant disadvantages for reasons other than individual bias.

In the past ten years, many advocates of the identity synthesis have effectively claimed that this more recent concept of structural racism should altogether supplant the older concept of individual racism. Rather than acknowledging that there are two different forms of racism, each of which deserves careful attention and needs to be combated, they have come to conceptualize racism in an exclusively structural form. "Racism," one online guide puts the growing consensus, "is different from racial prejudice, hatred, or discrimination" because it must involve "one group having the power to carry out systematic discrimination through the institutional policies and practices of the society and by shaping the cultural beliefs and values that support those racist policies and practices."

In its most radical form, this claim explicitly entails the implication that it is impossible for a member of a historically marginalized group to be racist toward a member of a historically dominant group. Because racism does not have anything to do with individual attributes, and members of groups that are comparatively powerless are incapable of carrying out "systematic discrimination" against members of groups that are comparatively powerful, even the vilest forms of hatred need not count as racist. As Manisha Krishnan put the point in *Vice*, "It is literally impossible to be racist to a white person."

The result has, again and again, been a form of selective blindness when members of minority groups have expressed bigoted attitudes toward supposedly more privileged groups, including those that are themselves minorities. When Tamika Mallory, one of the founders of the Women's March, was criticized for calling the proudly anti-Semitic (as well as homophobic and misogynistic) Louis Farrakhan "the greatest of all time," for example, she defended herself by telling *The New York Times* that "white Jews, as white people, uphold white supremacy."

This inability to recognize the importance of the more traditional conception of racism has serious consequences. For example, it makes it impossible to name what is happening when members of one minority group are the victims of hate crimes committed by members of another minority group that has historically suffered greater disadvantages. In the United States, for example, Asian Americans are usually said to be more "privileged" (or even more "white adjacent") than African Americans. As a result, mainstream newspapers have been reluctant to report on hate crimes committed by African Americans against Asian Americans during the COVID pandemic, only rarely labeling such attacks as racist. This has hampered the country's ability to take effective action against such attacks and exacerbated tensions between these groups.

SEX, GENDER, AND THE DEBATE OVER TRANSGENDER RIGHTS

The debate about sex, gender, and transgender rights suffers from a strikingly similar set of conceptual confusions. Feminists rightly stress that we miss important aspects of the world when we exclusively focus our attention on biological sex. To understand how men and women have long related to each other, we must also consider gender, the set of social expectations about how individuals who are biologically male or female do or should act.

A recognition of the importance of gender opens up space for a contestation of traditional gender norms. As feminists have long argued, subverting traditional gender norms can be an effective way to challenge the unfair expectations that have historically been put on women. And as trans activists have pointed out of late, some people who are born biologically male are profoundly unhappy if they are forced to comply with masculine gender norms. Justice therefore demands that they be allowed, if they so wish, to live as women. (The same holds for biological women who wish to live as men, or for people of either biological sex who, wishing to eschew both masculine and feminine gender norms, are "nonbinary.")

But as in the case of structural racism, the trouble starts when the well-founded recognition of the importance of a newer concept (in this case gender) turns into an ideologically motivated denial of the importance of the older concept (in this case biological sex). Over the past few years, a growing number of writers and activist organizations have insisted that in human beings there is no utility to thinking about sex as a biological concept; many have also embraced the further claims that there are no reasons to think of sex as a binary and that any policy that takes biological sex into account should therefore be considered transphobic.

In this view, the existence of people who are intersex demonstrates that biological categories like male and female are an oppressive social construct. And because people should be allowed to live in accordance with their internal sense of gender, any recognition that this may not match their biological sex affronts their dignity. As Agustín Fuentes, a biological anthropologist at Princeton University, has argued, "A simple binary view creates a fictitious template . . . that manifests in miseducation about basic biology." It should be resisted because it might lead to "the creation of anti-transgender laws." Sometimes, activists even claim that anybody who thinks that a person's biological sex can retain relevance in certain contexts is denying the right of trans people to exist; this accusation, which is especially popular on social media, uses the different meanings of the word "exist" to insinuate that those who take a different view on the role of biological sex want particular individuals who identify as trans to die.

But the denial of biological sex is wrongheaded. Both scientists and medical professionals, for example, know that biological sex is a key determinant of important human attributes, from the prevalence of heart disease to the ability to become pregnant. A small percentage of individuals—according to estimates, less than one in a thousand people—have an intersex condition that means that they do not clearly fall into the category of a biological male or a biological female. But as is also true in many other contexts, including questions about when free speech blends into blackmail or defamation, it is a mistake to believe that the existence of "hard cases" that do not fall into a clear category means that the underlying dichotomy is incoherent. It would be wrong to say that the existence of people who have some hair means that there is no such thing as people who either are bald or have a full head of hair; similarly, it is wrong to say that the existence of people who are intersex means that there is no such thing as people who are biologically male or biologically female.

Something similar applies to the claim that it is always offensive to distinguish between women who are and women who are not transgender. Take a celebratory tweet sent by GLAAD, one of the most vocal defenders of transgender rights in the United States: "History! Dr. Rachel Levine has been confirmed as the next Assistant Secretary of Health. She is the first out transgender federal official confirmed by the Senate." This tweet seems straightforward. But it has meaning only because of an implicit assumption, apparently shared by GLAAD: just as it sometimes makes sense to distinguish between women who are lesbian and those who are not, it sometimes makes sense to distinguish between women who are transgender (like Levine) and those who are not (like all the other women whom the Senate has confirmed as federal officials in the past).

Taken together, these insights can help to offer a more coherent account of how to think about public policy and transgender rights. Sex and gender are both important categories. For the most part, this is not a social problem. People whose sense of their own gender does not match their biological sex should be allowed to live as they wish. All of us should treat them in a respectful and welcoming manner. There is good reason to celebrate the rapid growth in social acceptance of trans men, trans women, and people who are nonbinary.

There are, however, some areas of public policy in which the demands of sex and gender do potentially clash. In some medical settings, for example, doctors need to know the biological sex of their patients to be able to diagnose their condition accurately and treat them effectively. In many sports, biological males who transitioned after undergoing puberty enjoy significant physical advantages when they compete against biological females. And finally, there are certain spaces, such as prisons, in which biological women have well-founded apprehensions or understandable religious concerns about having to share intimate spaces with people who have male sexual organs.

The best way to deal with those situations in which the demands of sex and gender do clash is to recognize that they involve a genuine trade-off between the legitimate interests of two different groups. Most of the time, this recognition can set the stage for humane compromises that are respectful toward the needs and the dignity of both. But identifying such compromises becomes impossible if hospitals, sports leagues, or prison wardens insist that the notion of biological sex is an oppressive social construct that must never be considered when making rules.

MERITOCRACY

For centuries, America drew immigrants on the promise that even the lowliest dishwasher could become a millionaire. But if the American dream figured so prominently in the imagination of mankind, a big part of the reason is that the United States also afforded a good life to people who did not climb all the way to the top. Today, each of these promises is starting to sound hollow. Even as American dishwashers have become less likely to turn into millionaires, American waiters and factory workers have become a lot less financially secure. Over the past three decades, the incomes of most Americans have been more or less stagnant. Meanwhile, the costs of housing, education, and medical care have risen rapidly. Many Americans without a college degree now face serious difficulties in sustaining a decent standard of living.

In an age in which the promise of social mobility is so often broken—not only in the United States, but also in Canada, the United Kingdom, and other democracies around the world—many people understandably feel that the vocabulary of meritocracy can at times turn into an easy way of justifying a steep and unjust social hierarchy. As a result, writers and politicians from all sides of the political spectrum have of late started to attack the meritocratic ideal. As the title of a viral interview with the Yale legal scholar Daniel Markovits put it, "Meritocracy Harms Everyone." Or, as the Harvard philosopher Michael Sandel argues in *The Tyranny of Merit*, "even a fair meritocracy . . . induces the mistaken impression that we have made it on our own." To break its tyranny, we must recognize that "the meritocratic ideal is not a remedy for inequality; it is a justification for inequality."

Advocates of the identity synthesis are especially prone to reject the idea of meritocracy. "Objective truth, like merit, does not exist," Richard Delgado and Jean Stefancic write in their influential *Critical Race Theory:*

An Introduction. From that premise, it is but a small step to claim, as one recent article in the *American Journal of Public Health* put it, that "the promise of equality inherent in meritocratic ideology serves to elide racism." In its most radical form, critics of meritocracy even suggest that the ideal is itself racist because it actively serves to deepen racial disparities. As one business consultant put it, applying race-neutral standards for job applicants in the name of meritocracy might seem like an "inherently unbiased policy"; in truth, "it's absolutely racist."

The shortcomings of our supposedly meritocratic system make a strong case for change. Sandel is, for example, right to point out that many democracies, including Britain and the United States, now give the children of the wealthy a big leg up, only to sanctify their success in the language of merit, allowing them to believe that they have earned their cushy place in the world thanks to their hard work and superior talent. To give all citizens a chance to thrive, we must ensure that a good life does not remain the exclusive preserve of those who win the race to the top. If we want to live in a just society, we need to make sure that anyone who does an honest day's work gets to live in a decent home, has access to quality medical care, and can send their kids to a good school. And if we want to live up to the promise of a fair democracy, neither the quality of education that children receive nor the likelihood that they will live to be a hundred years old should depend on the color of their skin.

But even if we succeed in transforming the economy in this radical way, there will still be some positions in society that carry much greater reward and prestige than others. On what basis should these be allocated? Meritocracy, it seems to me, is the worst system for distributing these kinds of positions except for all the alternatives.

One essential reason to hold on to some basic form of meritocracy is, quite simply, to preserve an incentive for young people to develop socially valuable skills. In many countries, people have little reason to study or strive because social advancement depends primarily on power and connections. In those countries, people are less likely to develop their talents, and economic growth slows to a snail's pace. If merit is rewarded, by contrast, young people have a reason to invest time and effort into developing their talents. And that not only helps to ensure that we have enough doctors, engineers, craftsmen, and plumbers to take care of our collective needs; it also gives a much larger number of people the satisfaction of excelling at a craft or a profession they worked hard to master.

Another reason to uphold meritocracy is rooted in the kinds of explanations that institutions can legitimately invoke to justify their decisions to those who are denied the positions they covet. If you try out for a spot on a sports team, you will likely be disappointed to find out that you didn't make the cut. But whether you have good grounds to complain depends on why somebody else was chosen instead of you. If the coach tells you that your competitor is more likely to help the team win, her decision is justified by the purpose of this particular social institution. If, on the other hand, the coach tells you that she picked your competitor because he offered more money to be on the team, comes from a family with the right connections, or happens to have the right skin color, you have good reason to feel wronged.

Looking at the United Kingdom or the United States today, it is tempting to conclude that meritocracy has led these countries astray. But the opposite comes closer to the truth: The legitimate aspirations of millions of people have been betrayed because too few people can access material comfort, and those positions that do come with special power or privilege are not distributed in a sufficiently meritocratic fashion. The problem is not that Britain or America is too meritocratic; it's that they aren't meritocratic enough.

———

In the first three parts of the book, I have explained the origins of the identity synthesis; shown how it went from being a relatively marginal ideology to a highly influential one; and critically evaluated some of the most important ways in which it has reshaped widespread assumptions about culture and politics. In the process, I have also started to formulate the kernel of a systematic response to its most important claims. Over the course of the last six chapters, I demonstrated how those of us who are committed to universal values can conceptualize and combat the injustices that motivate many advocates of the identity synthesis without giving up on our ideals.

Indeed, my critique of popular claims about important topics, from cultural appropriation to meritocracy, can serve as a model for how to mount a principled response to the identity synthesis. The trick is to take the concerns that motivate such demands seriously; to expose the logical flaws they entail and the practical difficulties they would inspire; and to demonstrate how a more universalist approach can better serve to articulate injustices and improve the world. In the remainder of the book, I will build on that foundation to make a full-fledged case for how to escape the identity trap.

KEY TAKEAWAYS

- The concept of structural racism rightly points out that forms of racial discrimination can persist even though no individual person has negative views about members of marginalized groups. This is an important addition to our conceptual repertory for describing real injustices. But advocates of the identity synthesis go wrong when they claim that the new concept of structural racism should supplant older notions. It is possible for members of marginalized groups to hold dangerous prejudices against members of groups that are comparatively "privileged." A failure to recognize this makes it harder to understand the world or to combat certain kinds of hate crime.

- Some people feel that their gender does not match their biological sex. We should allow them to live as they wish and celebrate the greater acceptance of trans people. But it is a mistake to think that the importance of the concept of gender makes the concept of biological sex incoherent or unimportant. In some contexts, including medicine, institutions need to take an individual's biological sex into account. A recognition of the enduring relevance of both sex and gender can help us to find humane compromises in situations that feature genuine trade-offs between the legitimate interests of different groups, such as prisons or sports competitions.

- The promise of social mobility is broken for many people. This makes it tempting to blame meritocracy, claiming that the ideal merely serves to uphold an unjust system. But if taken seriously, this remedy would have disastrous effects. A world in which top positions are not even supposed to go to the most deserving would be less affluent because unqualified people would ascend to important positions of leadership and everyone would have fewer incentives to develop their talents. A better solution is to hold on to the ideal of meritocracy, striving to create a society in which people truly have equal opportunities—and those who don't end up in the most prestigious or lucrative positions also get to lead a good life.

- The critiques of the main applications of the identity synthesis in part III can serve as a model for how to respond to similar cases. The key is to take the concerns and injustices that motivate these positions seriously; to show where the supposed remedies to these problems go wrong; and to demonstrate how a universalist approach can do better at addressing these injustices than the newly fashionable solutions that are rooted in the identity synthesis.

PART IV

In Defense of Universalism

The identity synthesis has a rich intellectual history. But attempts to apply the core assumptions of this tradition to topics from free speech to race-sensitive public policy have proved counterproductive. Far from solving the real injustices that persist in many countries, it now threatens to exacerbate them. In its current form, the new obsession with identity is a trap. So, in the fourth and final part of this book, I make a wholehearted plea for a universalist alternative to the assumptions and the prescriptions of the identity synthesis.

Advocates of the identity synthesis have historically been especially hostile to an ideology that they blame for many of the injustices of the contemporary world: liberalism. In chapter 14, I explain the nature of these criticisms and show how liberals—as well as others who believe in the importance of universal values and neutral rules—can put forward a compelling response to them.

My own politics are based on the conviction that principles such as the political equality of all citizens, the ability to rule ourselves through democratic institutions, and the central role individual freedom should play in the world remain the best guide to building a better future—especially if we recognize that these ideals are yet to be fully realized. That is why, in chapter 15, I go on to make the case for philosophical liberalism.

Before we proceed, I need to issue an obligatory clarification about what I mean by the term "liberalism." Confusingly, the word has become associated with a partisan political identity in a number of countries. In France, a liberal tends to be right-wing on economic questions. In the United Kingdom, a liberal is sometimes thought to be a supporter of the Liberal Democrats, a political party that competes for votes with both Labour and the Conservatives. In the United States, a liberal is often interpreted as being left-wing on both economic and cultural issues. Indeed, some left-wing writers and politicians whom I would consider *il*liberal because of their advocacy for the popularized form of the identity synthesis are frequently labeled "liberals" by mainstream media outlets. For my part, I use the term "liberal" to refer to a set of key philosophical principles that many people across the political spectrum share. Proud progressives, passionate moderates, and devoted conservatives can all, in my sense of the term, be liberals.

Liberalism, in the sense in which I will defend it, is based on the rejection of natural hierarchy. Rather than believing that some people have a right to rule over others by virtue of their noble birth or their spiritual enlightenment, liberals are convinced that we are born equal. They therefore insist on political institutions that allow all of us to determine the rules that govern us; guarantee each of us the liberty to live our lives in accordance with our own convictions; and assure members of any identity group that the treatment they will receive from the state should not depend on their gender, their sexual orientation, or the color of their skin.

Liberalism is, these days, much maligned on both the left and the right. But in truth its ideals remain extremely appealing, and the institutions they have inspired are responsible for much of the moral and material progress the world has made over the course of the past three centuries. The path toward building a just future remains long and uncertain. But it is paved with a determination to implement liberal principles more fully, day by day, and year by year—not with a misguided resolve to jettison these aspirations in the name of an ideology whose vision of the future is simultaneously less ambitious and less realistic.

Chapter 14

A RESPONSE TO
THE IDENTITY SYNTHESIS

From the inception of the identity synthesis, its advocates have been very clear about whom they see as their main target: liberals. The movement, Richard Delgado and Jean Stefancic write in their influential *Critical Race Theory: An Introduction*, has always believed that "complacent, backsliding liberals represented the principal impediment to racial progress." It was only decades later that some of its members began to broaden their focus beyond "liberalism and its ills."

Not every core claim of the identity synthesis stands in conflict with every basic principle of philosophical liberalism. But there is a reason why advocates of this ideology, from Derrick Bell all the way to Robin DiAngelo and Ibram X. Kendi, have so consistently focused their attacks on liberals. In their judgment, it is the basic liberal commitment to universalism that is responsible for the supposed failure of major democracies to make any substantive progress on offering members of marginalized groups some modicum of equality. So what is the core of the identitarian case against liberalism? And do liberals have a convincing response to it?

The set of ideas that animates the identity trap is sprawling. That complexity makes it hard to respond to the identity synthesis in a systematic fashion; it may even suggest that the ideology does not have a core to which it is worth responding. But the impetus behind these ideas is no more scattershot than that animating many other political ideologies. So anyone who wants to demonstrate that liberals can mount a convincing response to the identity synthesis must start by restating its core commitments.

Thankfully, philosophy can assist in this endeavor. Philosophers have long thought about how to restate a sprawling set of ideas in a way that remains true to its core. In the influential formulation of Rudolf Carnap, we should aim at a "rational reconstruction of an entity which has already been constructed in a partly intuitive, partly rational way in daily life or in the sciences." The clarity and precision of this reconstruction, Carnap suggested, would make it possible to assess its core claims in a more productive manner than might otherwise be possible. So, to start, I want to offer a "rational reconstruction" of the identity synthesis.

THE CORE OF THE CASE AGAINST LIBERALISM

It may feel as though I have already done enough to describe the identity synthesis. In part I, I traced its origins and gave an account of its main themes. In part II, I showed how these ideas transformed as they were popularized on social networks and in mainstream media outlets. In part III, I examined some of its most important applications to areas from free speech to race-sensitive public policy. But while there will inevitably be some overlap with these previous discussions, what I propose to do here is different. For the kind of rational reconstruction I am about to undertake focuses not on the main themes or principal implications of an ideology but rather on its underlying logic. And in the case of the identity synthesis, such an analysis reveals three foundational claims.

1. The key to understanding the world is to examine it through the prism of group identities like race, gender, and sexual orientation.*

Many ideologies entail an account of the prism through which we must view the world to make sense of it. To early Christian writers, it seemed impossible to understand major historical events without paying attention to religious facts about their protagonists. To Marxists, it seems impossible to understand major historical events without paying attention to questions relating to the ownership of the means of production, the relative size of the proletariat, or the ability of an intellectual vanguard to spread class consciousness. A similar insistence on a particular prism for interpreting the world makes up the first key postulate of the identity synthesis. But according to its adherents, it is not grace or class that provides the most important lens for understanding historical events; rather, it is group identities like race, gender, and sexual orientation.

This explanatory focus on categories of group identity is meant to explain big historical events, from the dissolution of empires to the election of Donald Trump. It even extends to seemingly trivial interactions or interpersonal disputes. When one friend interrupts another to finish their sentence, some might interpret this as a way to affirm their mutual understanding; linguists call this a "rapport interruption." But if the gender or ethnic identity of the two speakers differs, many adherents of the identity

---

* It might be tempting to add another prism to this list: religion. But while advocates of the identity synthesis do often mention religious minorities, this interest is mostly epiphenomenal. Rather than being driven by a concern with religious freedom, it is an outgrowth of a deeper concern with race and ethnicity.

Indeed, advocates of the identity synthesis usually conceive of the religious communities on whose behalf they do speak as marginalized *ethnic* or *racial* minorities. This helps to explain why, presuming them to be predominantly brown or Black, advocates of the identity synthesis do often talk about Muslim minority groups in the United Kingdom and the United States. And it also helps to explain why the tradition is not especially interested in individual religious dissenters, like heretics; or religious groups that they think of as belonging to ethnic or racial majority groups, including Jews.

Meanwhile, sexual orientation is a key and irreducible prism through which advocates of the identity synthesis see the world. However, the extent to which advocates of the identity synthesis see people as members of marginalized groups always depends on the relative power and social prestige they hold. As a result, the focus on homosexuality within the tradition has significantly lessened as the gay rights movement won important victories and gay men have, especially if they are white, come to be seen as comparatively affluent and powerful. (Similarly, cisgender lesbians are now sometimes portrayed as being privileged compared with trans women, resulting in less emphasis on, or even concern for, their claims and interests.)

synthesis will interpret such an interaction as an exercise of power; after all, as Robin DiAngelo has claimed, anytime a white person interrupts a Black person, they are bringing the whole apparatus of white supremacy to bear on them.

2. Supposedly universal values and neutral rules merely serve to obscure the ways in which privileged groups dominate those that are marginalized.

Many societies adopt neutral rules that promise to treat all of their members equally irrespective of the identity group to which they belong. But according to adherents of the identity synthesis, the way people are treated always and unavoidably depends on their race, gender, and sexual orientation. Rather than being a useful check on the tendency of people to favor their own, universal values and neutral rules merely serve to hide the true purpose of the social order they uphold: to perpetuate the power and the privilege of dominant identity groups.

The way in which advocates of the identity synthesis mistrust free speech is particularly instructive. Traditionally, I showed in part III, most parts of the left have defended free speech as a crucial, if inevitably imperfect, tool in the arsenal of the weak and downtrodden. They recognized that it was precisely the universality of this norm that made it harder for the powerful to find excuses that would allow them to silence dissenters—though few people were ever so naive as to believe that they would never try to do so. Now big parts of the left have, under the influence of the identity synthesis, come to believe that norms like free speech are actively harmful. They don't just emphasize the obvious point that the universal aspirations of free speech are often violated in practice, for example because the powerful may at times flout the stated norms of their society by punishing the marginalized for criticizing them. Rather, they argue that the norms of free speech must be jettisoned altogether because they merely cloak what is really going on, actively helping to entrench the power of the privileged.

3. To build a just world, we must adopt norms and laws that explicitly make the way the state treats each citizen—and how citizens treat each other—depend on the identity group to which they belong.

When supposedly universal values or neutral rules turn out to discriminate against members of particular identity groups, it might be tempting to institute reforms that will ensure that they actually operate in a fair manner. But according to adherents of the identity synthesis, this would be a fool's errand. Because forms of discrimination like patriarchy, cis normativity, and white supremacy are so deeply ingrained, societies will never be able to apply neutral standards in an evenhanded manner. The only remedy is to dismiss any aspiration to live up to universal values or neutral rules. Instead, societies should explicitly and permanently make the way in which people are treated depend on the identity groups to which they belong, favoring members of those that have historically been marginalized.

This principle helps to justify race-sensitive public policies, like the decision by some health authorities in the United States to prioritize "people of color" for lifesaving vaccines and anti-COVID drugs. It also applies to many less obviously political areas, from education to the social norms governing office life. In diversity trainings, for example, the focus has increasingly shifted from encouraging a form of mutual respect that aims for equal treatment to an awareness of the ever-present potential for implicit bias and microaggressions that encourages people to be highly aware of the specific identity markers of their interlocutor.

THE LIBERAL RESPONSE TO THE IDENTITY SYNTHESIS

There are rational reasons why the identity synthesis has proven to have such a strong appeal. Countless people really have been oppressed on the basis of identity markers like race and gender. Dominant groups really do frequently refuse to acknowledge that painful truth. And it really is true that ethnic or religious majorities can enlist supposedly neutral standards as smoke screens that allow them to perpetuate their domination. When the identity synthesis is compared with caricatural versions of universalist ideologies like liberalism—or with the many ways in which empirical reality falls short of our aspirations—it comes to look very attractive.

But liberalism has coherent responses to these ideas. Building on the criticisms I have made of particular applications of the identity synthesis in part III, these responses take well-founded criticisms of past and persistent injustices seriously while offering a more constructive way forward; recognize the great importance that markers of group identity play in the real world without taking them to be the key to all of cultural and political life; beware the tendency of all institutions to favor the powerful while recognizing the ability of universal values and neutral rules to push societies closer toward treating all people as genuine equals; and encourage us to live up to the ideals on which liberal democracy is based rather than to abandon them because we will inevitably fail to do so perfectly. Indeed, the liberal response to the identity synthesis can be summarized in the form of a restatement of the three core postulates of the identity synthesis.

1. To understand the world, we must pay attention to a broad set of categories, including—but not limited to—forms of group identity like race, gender, and sexual orientation.

Markers of identity like race have often cleaved the world into in-group and out-group. And so it should not come as a surprise that many of the worst wars and injustices have pitted members of different racial or religious groups against each other. And yet the identities we are born with aren't everything. For at other times, the most salient groups have been formed on the basis of categories that advocates of the identity synthesis tend to neglect. These include economic categories like class; theological considerations such as disputes about who should be regarded as the rightful heir to the Prophet Muhammad; and ideological considerations such as whether a country should be ruled by a monarch or by elected representatives.

All of this makes philosophical liberals, like me, skeptical of any conception of what truly matters in human affairs that focuses on a single dimension. We agree with advocates of the identity synthesis that it is impossible to understand many fundamental aspects of human life without paying due attention to categories of group identity such as race, gender, and sexual orientation. But we also agree with many Marxists that it is impossible to understand other fundamental aspects of human life without paying due attention to economic categories such as social class; with nationalist historians that it is impossible to understand still other fundamental aspects of human life without paying due attention to ideological categories such as patriotism; with religious historians that it is impossible to understand still other fundamental aspects of human life without paying due attention to theological categories such as the beliefs that people hold about the nature of their religious duties; and so on.

Our understanding of our own societies owes much to scholars who rigorously demonstrate the ways in which they are shaped by forces like ethnic competition and racial discrimination. But other categories, from economic class to political ideology, are equally important. To make sense of our world—from everyday social interactions to the causes of major political events—we must be attuned to the potential importance of this much broader set of considerations, letting the specific facts of each situation guide us toward the appropriate prism for understanding it.

2. In practice, universal values and neutral rules do often exclude people in unjust ways. But an aspiration for societies to live up to the standards they profess can allow them to make genuine progress in treating their members fairly.

Every society in history has presented itself in a more flattering light than its reality warranted. But there are important differences between them. In some times and places, rulers invoke ideals that bear so little resemblance to what is actually happening in the real world that most citizens learn to tune out their empty incantations. In other times and places, a society's self-conception does help to structure some of its fundamental institutions; to constrain the actions of its rulers in meaningful if incomplete ways; and to give dissenters and activists a powerful vocabulary in which to express their grievances.

This is how to think about liberalism and its failure to live up to its ideals. Like every other society, liberal democracies contain powerful people and groups who do what they can to serve their own interests. As in every other society, these powerful people and groups often try to obscure the ways in which their privileges violate the principles they profess. Neither now nor ever before has formally adopting a set of rules and values sufficed to ensure that everyone is actually treated in accordance with them.

These shortcomings help to explain why, even in avowedly liberal societies, many members of historically marginalized communities continue to experience poverty and deprivation, discrimination and outright racism, police violence and mass incarceration. True liberals will face up to this state of affairs with an unflinching recognition of its injustice, growing all the more determined to build a fairer future. And yet liberals should reject the conclusion, so central to the identity synthesis, that these universal values and neutral rules are merely a smoke screen that helps to sustain the privileges of the oppressive majority. For in truth, the liberal democratic commitment to universal values like free speech and neutral rules such as prohibitions on racial discrimination has inspired tremendous progress over the course of the past three centuries.

Universal values and neutral rules have fueled the overthrow of deeply unjust institutions, like racial segregation or the exclusion of women from the professional world. Again and again, they have given those who suffered such injustices a powerful vocabulary that has proven capable of mobilizing the oppressed and stirring the conscience of the historically dominant. It is this popular attachment to universal values that made it possible for civil rights activists to push for equality by asking their compatriots to explain by what logic they should remain excluded from full citizenship—and for gay rights activists to overcome centuries of homophobia by asking why they should have to hide their love. While universal values and neutral rules are no silver bullet—in the face of deep and persistent injustice, none exists—they have played a key role in making democracies more decent places for all of their members.

3. To build a more just world, societies should strive to live up to their universalist aspirations instead of abandoning them.

Over the course of half a century, most liberal democracies, from Germany to the United States and from the United Kingdom to Australia, have made great strides toward treating their members as true equals. Fifty years ago, the vast majority of Americans believed that intermarriage between members of different "races" was immoral, with nineteen out of twenty respondents telling pollsters that it was wrong. In Western Europe, most citizens thought that only people who are descended from the same ethnic stock could come to be true members of their nations, making it impossible for immigrants to truly integrate. On both sides of the Atlantic, most citizens believed that homosexuality was deeply immoral, that gays and lesbians who admit to their sexual orientation should be shunned from public life, and that it was absurd to suggest that they should be allowed to marry.

Today, most citizens of these countries believe that there is nothing wrong with homosexuality, have become completely accustomed to seeing gays and lesbians serve in the highest echelons of their societies, and cheer the fact that gay marriage has long since become reality. In Western Europe, most citizens have broadened their conception of membership in the nation, recognizing that immigrants with roots in faraway parts of the world can become true compatriots. And in the United States, the vast majority of citizens now believe that interracial marriage is perfectly normal, with only about one in twenty respondents continuing to say that it is wrong.

This remarkable change in views has gone hand in hand with equally big changes in real life. In Western Europe, members of ethnic minority groups are rapidly ascending the socioeconomic ranks, with the children of immigrants likely to experience upward mobility at higher rates than the children of similarly situated "natives." In the United States, immigrants from El Salvador, Vietnam, and Nigeria experience social mobility at about the same rate as Italians and Irish did a century ago. Indeed, in America, Asian women now earn as much as or even more than white men, and immigrants from such different places as India and Nigeria are much more likely to be in the top quintile of the income distribution than white Americans whose ancestors have been in the country for generations. As a result, virtually all democracies have become much more diverse at the top, with women, immigrants, sexual minorities, and members of historically marginalized ethnic groups vastly more likely to be lawyers and doctors, business leaders and elected officials than in the past.

The biggest difficulty faced by liberal democracies lies in how to remedy the lasting consequences of discrimination and injustice. Many groups that have been horrifically oppressed in the past continue to suffer severe disadvantages in the present. In the United States, for example, African Americans, on average, earn lower salaries and dispose of much less wealth than white Americans; this is in good part because a significant percentage of African Americans continue to suffer from severe poverty, to live in deprived neighborhoods, and to lack access to high-quality schools. The fight against these persistent injustices is urgent.

But even in the area in which it is easiest and most appropriate to blame liberal democracies for their shortcomings, it would simply be wrong to claim that the past half century has failed to bring about significant progress. Over the past five decades, a large African American middle class has come into existence. Today, the median Black American has a white-collar job, lives in a reasonably affluent suburb, and is doing significantly better than his or her parents. As a result, African Americans are much more upbeat about their future prospects than you might expect by listening to adherents of the identity synthesis. According to recent polls, they are more likely to be optimistic about the future of America, or to believe that their best days are ahead, than white Americans.

I fully understand why emphasizing such progress often rubs people the wrong way. It's easy to imply that the only motivation of those who emphasize the progress we have made must be to minimize the injustices that persist. But there are many important reasons to gain an accurate view of reality, one that is neither blithely optimistic nor cynically pessimistic. Perhaps the most important is that we need an accurate assessment of recent changes to know whether the tools we have deployed to make progress are working. And as it happens, an accurate assessment of the past fifty years suggests that the push to live up to universal values and neutral rules is capable of bringing about enormous improvements.

A view of the world that falsely states that there has been no progress easily lends itself to the conclusion that the universal values and neutral rules to which liberal democracies subscribe are just a fig leaf for the maintenance of oppression, and that they should therefore be abandoned. A more realistic assessment comes to a different conclusion. It acknowledges that it's not enough to pay lip service to universal values and neutral rules. But it also recognizes that earnest attempts to live up to these standards have helped liberal democracies make rapid and real, if inevitably imperfect, progress. The best hope to keep making such progress lies not in abandoning liberalism but in redoubling our efforts to live up to its animating ideals. To understand how to do that, it is time to explain the nature of this much-maligned and oft-misunderstood ideology in its own terms.

KEY TAKEAWAYS

- Advocates of the identity synthesis have long thought of philosophical liberals as their main adversaries. To evaluate the identity synthesis and its attack on liberalism, it makes sense to boil this tradition down to its main claims. Such a "rational reconstruction" would focus on three propositions. First, the key to understanding the world is to examine it through the prism of group identities like race, gender, and sexual orientation. Second, supposedly universal values and neutral rules merely serve to obscure the ways in which privileged groups dominate those that are marginalized. And third, to build a just world, we must adopt norms and laws that explicitly make the way the state treats each citizen—and how citizens treat each other—depend on the identity group to which they belong.
- Liberals can give a convincing response to this attack while taking the most valuable insights from the identity synthesis on board. To understand the world, they point out, we must pay attention to a broad set of categories, including—but not limited to—forms of group identity like race, gender, and sexual orientation. In practice, universal values and neutral rules do often exclude people in unjust ways, but an aspiration for

societies to live up to the standards they profess can allow them to make genuine progress in treating their members fairly. And to build a more just world, societies should strive to live up to their universalist aspirations instead of abandoning them.

- The identity synthesis portrays itself as an ambitious ideology that seeks to make the world a better place. But its vision is ultimately neither realistic nor desirable. One of the core appeals of liberalism is that it aims higher.

Chapter 15

A BRIEF CASE FOR
THE LIBERAL ALTERNATIVE

The story of humanity is an annal of cruelty and injustice. Most societies in history have been deeply hierarchical, giving a small group vast powers over the rest. They were extremely violent, enslaving outsiders, treating their own peasants as serfs, sometimes even requiring the sacrifice of children for ritual purposes. They were mired in endemic conflict, from battles between adjacent tribes and villages to destructive wars that engulfed the whole world. For the most part, the norms of the community took precedence over the desires of the individual, with those who dared to deviate, whether they be heretics or homosexuals, punished with utmost cruelty.

These cruelties knew no bounds of time or place, of creed or race. Christian crusaders converted scores of people at sword point, killing those who would not submit. American colonists fought violent campaigns of eradication against indigenous people and maintained a brutal system of chattel slavery. On the Indian subcontinent, a rigid caste system relegated a vast swath of the population to the status of untouchables for over a thousand years. In China, emperors persisted in vast construction projects even though they claimed hundreds of thousands of lives. In sub-Saharan Africa, the members of rival tribes waged endemic war against each other for centuries. Slaves have existed in pharaonic Egypt and ancient Athens, in the Roman Republic and in China's Shang dynasty, in western Africa and southern Asia, among the Incas of South America and the Creeks of Georgia. Some form of slavery officially persisted until 1981, when Mauritania finally abolished the system; unofficially, it continues to exist in parts of the world until this day.

Starting in the early modern period, many thinkers came to believe that learning and technology would help to remedy these injustices. But even as the human ability to understand and manipulate the natural world rapidly expanded, mass atrocities and periods of intense suffering persisted. The twentieth century saw the discovery of penicillin and DNA, the invention of the space station and the internet. It also bore witness to two world wars that claimed more than 100 million victims; to the first ever attempt to eradicate an entire ethnicity through industrial means; to genocides in Armenia and Rwanda; and to politically induced famines that killed millions of people in China and Bengal, in Ukraine and Kazakhstan, in Greece and Ethiopia.

Observing the persistence of these horrors, many people came to believe that some political ideology might be able to remake the world from scratch. The ranks of those who thought that they had a historical calling to liberate humanity by imposing upon it their vision of all that is right and good include theocrats and nationalists, monarchists and utopian socialists. Of all these dreamers and idealists, it was communists like my own grandparents who proved to have the biggest influence on the events of the last century. In every single country in which their ideas were tried, they failed to deliver on their enticing promises. North Korea and the Soviet Union, Maoist China and the East Germany of Erich Honecker delivered despotism in lieu of emancipation, and deprivation in the place of affluence.

For anyone who takes a long, hard look at these dashed hopes and destroyed lives, it may appear that humans are by their nature evil, and tempting to despair of our future prospects. But I am not invoking the long history of human horrors to preach fatalism or to insinuate that our flawed character makes us irredeemable. The reason is more constructive: the long history of human horrors can teach us something fundamentally important about what to do next.

Anybody who seeks to avoid such disasters in the future should ask what kinds of societies have been comparatively successful in avoiding the worst of which humanity is capable. Are there societies that, flawed though they may remain in all kinds of important respects, have a proven track record of making genuine progress toward giving their members the opportunity to build an affluent, peaceful, and self-determined life? And, if so, what principles have helped to animate the institutions of these societies?

It is striking how consistent the answer to these questions is. There are many societies today that afford their members far greater freedom and dignity, affluence and security than humans have enjoyed at virtually any juncture since the beginning of recorded history. They are daily proof that the future need not resemble the past. And on closer inspection, it turns out that one set of institutions has proven much better than its competitors at creating such societies: those that are guided by the philosophically liberal emphasis on individual freedom and collective self-government.

THE CORE PRINCIPLES OF LIBERALISM

Humans need government. Without some central authority, we would be unable to keep the peace between rival bands of warriors, or to provide basic public goods. Even the most ingenious human would fail to thrive if she had to live in fear of being murdered by her neighbors or lacked access to schools, hospitals, and basic medical care.

But the need for government also gives rise to a—perhaps to *the*— fundamental problem of politics: Who gets to rule? Humans are both cacophonous and vainglorious. That is to say that we both differ in our opinions and share a devotion to advancing our own interests. This makes it unsurprising that we are also prone to fighting with each other over who should be in control. Every political system needs to give some account, explicit or implicit, of how to resolve this tension between the need for government and the human propensity to fight over who constitutes it.

Most societies have historically found a seemingly simple solution to this fundamental problem: they posited that some people naturally have more of a claim to rule than others. The leaders of these societies claim, for example, that their noble birth gives them a natural, even divine, right to rule; that their membership in a hereditary caste marks them out for the privilege of being in charge; or that their religious wisdom makes them natural shepherds for the flock of the faithful. What all such claims have in common is a commitment to solving the problem of disagreement through the recognition and maintenance of a natural hierarchy rooted in factors such as noble birth, caste status, or religious enlightenment.

Philosophical liberalism is founded on the rejection of this premise. Liberals recognize that human beings differ in speed and strength, in intelligence and moral character. But they insist that no such difference is sufficiently stark or apparent to justify one person or group ruling over everybody else. The best foundation of a legitimate political order, liberals claim, is not some supposedly natural hierarchy—but the recognition that, in matters of politics, we are all "created equal."

What does this foundational commitment to political equality mean, in concrete terms, for the kinds of institutions that we should embrace? Over time, liberals have derived three ambitious conclusions from this simple starting point. First, liberals deny that anybody can invoke their noble birth or their superior wisdom to force others to obey. Instead, they think of power as emanating from the people and insist on the egalitarian principle of "one person, one vote." Some citizens may be richer, smarter, or taller than others. Elections may even confer some special privileges and responsibilities to those who hold high office. But in a well-functioning democracy, officeholders are elevated to their status on the basis of a free vote of their peers and can, if they fall out of favor, just as quickly be removed from power by the same mechanism. Rather than being governed by kings, aristocrats, or priests, humans should collectively be able to decide what kinds of rules they should obey; this helps to settle the vexed question of how to maintain an effective government without coming to blows over who gets to rule.

The same argument that leads liberals to believe that no one has an inherent right to rule also creates a powerful argument for individual liberty. If nobody enjoys a stark or apparent superiority over everyone else, this doesn't just limit who has a special claim to rule; it also calls into question why anybody should get to have the last word on how everyone else should live. Taken seriously, a commitment to political equality thus implies that each of us should have the right to determine what we wish to say, which relationships to pursue, and how and whether we wish to worship. It is in recognition of this fundamental precept that liberal democracies put strict limits on how much authority the state can, even if it enjoys the blessing of the majority, exercise over its citizens. This is the second institutional inference that liberals draw from their fundamental premises: even laws that are legitimate because they are derived from the will of the people need to leave key decisions about how to live, whom to worship, and what to say up to each individual.

Finally, a government that takes the equality of its citizens seriously will also refrain from privileging some (groups of) citizens over others. A monarch who believes that he can determine the true answer to fundamental moral or religious questions, such as the truth of the Bible or the veracity of the Quran, will naturally be tempted to prefer subjects who live in accordance with the moral strictures it implies. Similarly, a dictator who believes that the members of some ethnic or cultural group are superior to those of another will understandably be tempted to grant them special privileges that ensure that they will thrive. But a government that refrains from such judgment calls cannot play favorites. To respect the political equality of citizens is to grant each of them the same rights and duties, irrespective of the religious, ethnic, or cultural group to which they belong. Liberals' insistence on universal values and neutral rules does not flow from blind obeisance to some idiosyncratic tradition; it derives from one of the most fundamental premises of modern political thought: that, for political purposes, all human beings are born equal.

WHY THE CORE PRINCIPLES OF LIBERALISM HELP TO CREATE THRIVING SOCIETIES

The fundamental principles of liberalism are attractive in their own right. Most people want a meaningful say over the rules that structure their societies. They want to feel that their government is treating them with the same respect and consideration it extends to their neighbors. And they don't like being told what to say or whom to worship (unless they fantasize that the government will impose beliefs they already hold and customs they already practice on everybody else).

But the case for liberalism is even stronger than that. Some cynics might claim they don't care about their ability to participate in the government, to have basic autonomy over their own lives, and to enjoy the same rights and duties as members of other identity groups. But even they must contest with a strong empirical argument that favors liberalism. For, by comparison to societies structured by other kinds of ideals, those guided by liberal values have done much better at achieving outcomes such as avoiding the worst forms of government abuse, keeping the peace, and holding intergroup competition in check. That is no coincidence.

1. *A commitment to collective self-determination helps to avoid the worst forms of government abuse.* In a society based on some principle of natural hierarchy, there is no easy mechanism for removing rulers who are abusive or incompetent. In a society based on political equality, by contrast, the people retain the ability to elect and dismiss governments as they please. This gives governments that seek to stay in office an incentive to deliver for their citizens—and citizens who are unhappy with their governments a peaceful way to throw them out. There is good reason to think that these mechanisms help to reduce the risk of calamitous government failures, from the extreme oppression that has so often upheld supposedly natural hierarchies of power to the economic mismanagement that has so often induced bouts of destructive hyperinflation. According to a famous study by the Nobel Prize–winning economist Amartya Sen, for example, an effective commitment to collective self-determination even radically reduces the chance of famine.

2. *A commitment to individual freedom helps to keep the peace.* In a society that does not guarantee the freedom of speech or worship, anybody who wants to stay true to their conscience must curry favor with the powerful or wrest control of the machinery of the state, enormously

raising the stakes of political competition. Historically, this has led to constant conflicts, from the religious wars of early modern Europe to the sectarian battles in today's Middle East. In a liberal democracy, by contrast, every citizen knows that they can lead their life as they see fit, expressing opinions even if they are deeply unpopular and worshipping their god even if their compatriots believe such behavior to be blasphemous. The one price we all have to pay for this freedom and tranquility is to abstain from using force to deprive others of their enjoyment of the same—a price that is hardly trivial for those who feel a calling to proselytize their moral or religious convictions, but that most have historically become willing to pay when faced with the consequences of violent and protracted struggles for power.

3. *A commitment to government neutrality helps to avert the most destructive forms of intergroup competition.* In many times and places, the benefits that citizens can expect to receive from the government depend on their proximity to power. If a monarch shares their faith, if a representative of their tribe wins a close-run election, or if their village votes for the incumbent political party, they can hope to receive government patronage; otherwise, they are likely to be neglected or exploited. These forms of government partiality increase the chances of ethnic clashes, regional rebellions, and civil wars. They make it harder to sustain key public goods like good roads and quality schools. And they encourage citizens to see those of their compatriots who belong to groups that are different in some salient way as competitors, even enemies. Thankfully, governments can reduce the danger of these pitfalls by binding themselves to universal values and neutral rules. When the government grants the same rights and duties to members of every group, it reduces the incentive to fight for control over the levers of power, builds greater support for public goods that benefit all citizens, and makes it easier for them to see each other as potential partners rather than perennial competitors.

Many factors, including the higher likelihood that democratic institutions survive in a country that is already affluent and highly educated, help to explain why liberal democracies are hugely overrepresented among the world's most successful countries. But perhaps the biggest reason why liberal democracies thrive has to do with the principles that animate them. The values of political equality, individual freedom, and collective self-determination make a huge contribution to fostering tolerance and prosperity, helping liberal democracies avoid the terrible suffering that has so often bedeviled humanity in the past.

THE SUCCESS OF LIBERAL DEMOCRACIES

Indulge me for a minute. Think of a country, other than your own, in which you'd love to live. Somewhere you could imagine spending a lifetime of study and work, of developing your interests and (if you are so inclined) raising a family. Which would you pick?

I can't pretend to know the answer you gave. There are so many wonderful cultures and countries in the world, and every single one has serious problems alongside its alluring qualities. But the one thing on which I am willing to take a bet is that, more likely than not, the country you chose has a government that is deeply shaped by the precepts of philosophical liberalism.

Authoritarian countries, like Vietnam and Ethiopia, might rank high in a list of places to visit as a tourist. Some affluent dictatorships, like China and Saudi Arabia, might seem appealing for a professional sojourn of a few months or a few years. But when they think about how and where they want to live, most people will, as surveys of the dream destinations for would-be immigrants reveal, choose countries like France and Germany, Canada and the United Kingdom, Australia and the United States: countries, that is, in which they could speak freely, enjoy great autonomy in how they lead their private lives, and contest the decisions of a government they consider out of touch.

There is good reason for that. Statistics show that liberal democracies outperform their rivals on key metrics that virtually every human being values. All twenty of the countries in which people report being the happiest are democracies. Out of the thirty countries with the highest human development index, twenty-seven are liberal democracies. Out of the thirty countries with the longest life expectancy, twenty-nine are liberal democracies. Even on economic metrics, which are often thought to favor efficient autocracies, democracies enjoy a striking advantage: out of the twenty-five countries with over four million inhabitants that have the highest GDP per capita, twenty-two are democratic. (The exceptions are a semi-authoritarian city-state, Singapore, as well as two dictatorships that have become rich on oil, Kuwait and the United Arab Emirates.)

It matters to have the resources to feed and clothe yourself. It matters to have access to a quality education. It matters how long you live and how happy you are. But what matters most is that these social achievements add up to more than the sum of their parts. For it is only when you can take care of your basic needs, live in a community that is comparatively peaceful, and are free to develop your talents that you have the best chance to order your life in accordance with your convictions and aspirations.

Some people seek to pursue a high-flying career; others to maximize the time they spend with their families. Some dream of being a rock star; others focus on complying with the strictures of their religion. A liberal society does not impose a particular account of human flourishing on its citizens. But it does vastly better than any alternative system at providing them with the rights, the liberties, and the resources they need to pursue what they themselves consider a flourishing life.

No advocate of collective self-determination, individual freedom, and political equality should be so naïve as to believe that these values have ever been fully realized in any part of the world. At the same time, we must avoid an ahistorical cynicism that would blind us to the stark contrast between liberal democracies and the other systems of government that have historically dominated the world. This means that liberals must hold two beliefs in our heads at the same time. We should celebrate the way in which our principles have helped to bring about vast improvements in the world. And we should remember that liberalism is a force of progress, not of the status quo—vowing that we will continue to do what we can to bring the world into fuller alignment with our ideals.

The identity synthesis presents itself as a progressive ideology that tries to remake the world in a radical fashion. But this radical paint job fails to obscure its deep pessimism or the poverty of its ambitions. At the heart of its vision stands an acceptance of the enduring importance of dubious categories like race. It tries to sell people on a future in which people will forever be defined by the identity groups to which they belong; in which different communities will always be mired in zero-sum competition; and in which the way we treat each other will forever depend on our respective skin colors and sexual proclivities.

Liberalism, by contrast, is based on a much more ambitious set of aspirations for the future. At their best, philosophical liberals believe, humans are driven by their capability to make common cause with people who have different beliefs and origins rather than their membership in specific groups. People who hail from different parts of the world and now think of themselves as members of different identity groups can build real solidarity with each other. Universal values and neutral rules can make the world a better place if they are applied with conviction and implemented with care. Perhaps most important, identity categories that have historically been the basis for injustice and oppression, like race, can over time become less salient than they are today—not because we contrive to ignore the injustices they still inspire, but because we work hard to overcome them.

This brings me to the last set of questions I wish to address in this book. How likely are we to remain stuck in the identity trap? And how can liberals—and others who disagree with the fundamental premises of the identity synthesis—fight back against it while staying true to our principles?

KEY TAKEAWAYS

- The history of humanity is an annal of cruelty. But these persistent injustices are no reason to despair. For there are some societies that have, by historical standards, made enormous progress in treating their members as equals. These societies have embraced political institutions inspired by the basic tenets of philosophical liberalism.

- The core of the liberal tradition is a rejection of the forms of supposedly natural hierarchy that have traditionally justified historical rulers; according to liberals, all humans are created equal. Liberals derive three fundamental principles for just institutions from this premise: They believe in collective self-determination, allowing all of us to make the rules by which we live. They believe in individual freedom, allowing each of us to determine how we want to lead our lives. And they believe in political equality, ensuring that the way the state treats people does not depend on the identity group to which they belong.

- These principles are attractive in their own right. But they also have important empirical benefits. In particular, collective self-determination helps to avoid the worst forms of government abuse, from politically motivated persecutions to famines. Individual freedom helps to keep the peace, allowing each of us to stay true to our conscience even if we are in the minority. And political equality helps to avert the most destructive forms of intergroup competition, making sure that all of us get a fair shake even if we don't run the government.

- Liberal democracies vastly outperform alternative regime forms on metrics that most people have strong reason to value. Nearly all of the richest and happiest countries in the world are liberal democracies. So are those with the highest human development index. This is no mere coincidence: liberal institutions have helped sustain peace and affluence.

Conclusion

HOW TO ESCAPE THE IDENTITY TRAP

Eboo Patel was born in Chicago, the son of a Muslim immigrant from India who came to the country as a poor student and worked his way up to relative riches by taking out franchises on Subway sandwich stores. He was raised in the city's affluent suburbs, enjoying the opportunities of an upper-middle-class life while deeply self-conscious about the ethnic and religious differences that separated him from most of his classmates.

So when Patel first learned about "institutionalized racism" and "structures of oppression" as a sociology major at the University of Illinois, the vocabulary of the identity synthesis helped him make sense of his own experiences. White supremacy, he read in one class, consisted of the belief that "cultural patterns associated with white people" are the norm, marking those associated with other groups as inferior. He thought to himself, "Doesn't that basically describe *my entire life*?"

Patel's view of his childhood changed radically. One time, he now remembered, he had accompanied his father to a conference of South Asian businessmen. When an audience member wanted to know why he had taken out a franchise on a Subway store rather than starting a sandwich shop of his own, his father retorted with a question: "Which white people do you know are going to buy sandwiches from a brown guy born in India named Sadruddin?"

At the time, his father's response had seemed unremarkable to Patel. But now he came to see it as a testament to the racism that surrounded him everywhere he looked: "The deeper I read, the more I saw the entire world through that lens. I soon couldn't see much else. Racism permeated everything. My principal identity was as a victim of racism."

Patel, in other words, fell into the identity trap. He stopped noticing the ways in which his upbringing had been one of opportunity and privilege. He became censorious, sitting in judgment of anybody who did not share his values or his worldview in every respect. When one of his progressive professors, a Black woman who had kindly agreed to conduct an independent study with him, staged a play that was meant to center on the experience of children, he thought that he would make her proud by finding fault with it: "What about all the families where kids don't have their own rooms?" he asked at a question-and-answer session after the show. "Or the black and brown families that don't have houses? Don't you realize that your play is only further oppressing them?"

A few days later, Patel's professor emailed him. She gently explained that she was hurt by his comments. Instead of passing judgment on the efforts of others, he should try his hand at creating something better. The email made a big impression. "I know that there is a role for people who sit in the audience and criticize the show, but it was starting to dawn on me that that's not who I wanted to be. I wanted to be the person putting something on the stage."

Gradually, Patel realized that the ideology that seemed to explain his world had serious blind spots of its own. It's not just that its portrayal of the world did not allow for any gray tones. It's that it seemed to lead Patel away from the kind of life he himself wanted to live. The concepts he had learned in college encouraged Patel to see the worst in people. But as he matured, he realized that he wanted to encourage people to be their best selves—and aspired to build something of value himself.

Now that Patel himself has become a father, he is determined to impart a more positive outlook to his children. "I would be remiss in my duties if I allowed my kids to fall into the same victim mind-set that I succumbed to as a college student," he recently wrote. "I want my two sons to understand that responsible citizenship in a diverse democracy is not principally about noticing what's bad; it's about constructing what's good."

Maurice Mitchell has undergone a similar evolution. As a longtime progressive activist, a key organizer of the Movement for Black Lives, and now the head of the Working Families Party, Mitchell used to believe that the core precepts of the identity synthesis could help him combat injustice. But today he is deeply worried about the way in which its ideas are reshaping America, including some of the progressive organizations he knows intimately. As he wrote in a recent article, "Executives in professional social justice institutions, grassroots activists in local movements, and fiery young radicals on protest lines are all advancing urgent concerns about the internal workings of progressive spaces." Drawing on their own experiences, they lament how "toxic" the atmosphere within such organizations has become, making it hard to get anything done.

One of the main culprits for this failure, Mitchell argues, is a simplistic understanding of identity. In the article, he takes particular aim at the way in which many activists and politicians invoke their heritage as a justification for their political position. "What's implied," Mitchell writes, "is that one's identity is a comprehensive validator of one's political strategy—that identity is evidence of some intrinsic ideological or strategic legitimacy. Marginalized identity is deployed as a conveyor of a strategic truth that must simply be accepted." But though this assumption may be popular, it is dangerously flawed: "Identity is too broad a container to predict one's politics or the validity of a particular position. . . . Genuflecting to individuals solely based on their socialized identities or personal stories deprives them of the conditions that sharpen arguments, develop skills, and win debates."

Patel and Mitchell are no outliers. Many other reluctant critics of the identity trap now find themselves in a similar position. Because they are highly progressive and deeply conscious of the injustices still shaping America, they initially greeted the arrival of the identity synthesis with curiosity or even enthusiasm. Now they are growing seriously concerned about the destructive influence it has had on causes and communities in which they are invested. The more deeply we have gotten stuck in the identity trap, the more opposition it is generating. Will this backlash be enough to reverse the trends of the past decade, relegating the influence of the identity synthesis to a strange yet short-lived moment in the history of the United Kingdom, the United States, and other democracies around the world?

THREE POSSIBLE FUTURES FOR THE IDENTITY TRAP

The identity synthesis has been adopted in the highest echelons of society at remarkable speed. Many schools have embraced the logic of progressive separatism, encouraging their students to see themselves primarily in terms of their ethnic or sexual identity. Key cultural institutions have accepted the idea that forms of cultural appropriation are inherently harmful, and will continue to patrol novels and movies, artworks and exhibitions for possible violations of this new norm. Major corporations have institutionalized diversity, equity, and inclusion trainings based on the ideas of Robin DiAngelo and Ibram X. Kendi and will continue to spread that Manichaean worldview to their employees. Finally, big swaths of the Democratic Party have imbibed the rhetoric of equity and will likely stay committed to identity-sensitive public policies that make the way the state treats people depend on such factors as the color of their skin.

Increasingly, the influence of the identity synthesis is also being felt outside the United States. In Canada, public schools in the province of Ontario, following the advice of a senior member of the ruling Liberal Party, staged ceremonial burnings of supposedly "offensive" books in a "flame purification ceremony." In Britain, serious threats of violence from students at her own university forced a well-known philosopher to resign her teaching post because of her views on the nature of gender and biological sex. In Switzerland, the performance of a rock band was canceled at the last moment because its lead singer, who is white, has worn dreadlocks since he was a teenager. And in Spain, a publishing house decided that it was morally unacceptable for a white man to translate the work of a prominent Black poet.

In light of these disheartening developments, many observers have concluded that it is too late to escape the identity trap. The game, they suggest, is effectively up. As Andrew Sullivan has observed, "We all live on campus now."

But what confident predictions about the lasting victory of the identity synthesis seem to miss is the way in which its very success has gradually put off people like Patel and Mitchell. The changes to America's elite culture that took place over the course of the past decade have been so rapid that they were virtually complete before most people even had a chance to understand their nature or their consequences. But as the influence of the identity synthesis has grown, the perverse effect it is having on myriad communities and organizations across the country is coming into clearer view. As a result, many people who were initially reluctant to express their displeasure about the identity trap are starting to recognize its serious drawbacks, and even to muster the courage to speak out against it.

This pushback is already showing first signs of success. Over the past couple of years, many companies and nonprofit organizations have attracted public outrage for unfairly dismissing their employees or slandering their business partners; as a result, institutional leaders around the country are starting to recognize that giving in to moral panics on social media carries as much risk as refusing to do so. Meanwhile, the courts are playing an important role in rolling back some of the most blatant excesses of the identity synthesis, including mandatory trainings by public agencies that effectively compel state employees to pay lip service to this ideology. The more advocates of the identity synthesis try to put their aspirations into practice, the clearer it becomes that they stand in direct tension with the moral convictions of the great majority of Americans.

Over the past year or so, there have even been signs that the identity trap is starting to fall out of fashion. On social media, performative acts of self-flagellation by white journalists who once garnered thousands of likes for their supposed bravery now encounter polite eye rolls or outright mockery. Cultural journalists briefly obsessed over a small scene of New York writers and artists who congregated around the Dimes Square neighborhood in lower Manhattan during the pandemic, in part because their "vibe" seems to stand in stark contrast to the "woke" ethos that had ruled the city's artistic and literary scenes in the preceding years. Points of view that were once considered too controversial or "heterodox" for the pages of *The Washington Post* and *The New York Times* are slowly making their way into mainstream publications. Even leaders of the Democratic Party are taking note that the scolding tone that has dominated left-of-center discourse for the past decade is doing serious damage to its political prospects. Appearing on *Pod Save America*, a progressive podcast run by four of his former staffers, a few weeks before the 2022 midterms, Barack Obama warned that "sometimes people just want to not feel as if they are walking on eggshells. They want some acknowledgment that life is messy and that all of us, at any given moment, can say things the wrong way."

This provides the fodder for a diametrically opposed set of predictions about the likely future of the identity synthesis. As its excesses escape campus, come into public view, and generate more and more pushback, the opponents of the identity trap will, in this scenario, win an unconditional victory. The influence of the identity synthesis is likely to wane over the course of the coming years. "In the 1960s, left-wing radicals wanted to overthrow capitalism. We ended up with Whole Foods," David Brooks notes in *The New York Times*. Similarly, "the co-optation of wokeness seems to be happening right now."

Most of the predictions about the likely future of the identity trap oscillate between these two poles, foretelling either its lasting victory or its imminent demise. But there is also a third possibility, one that may be more plausible than either of these extremes. In this scenario, many of the core assumptions of the identity synthesis have become so entrenched in the ideology and the institutions of mainstream America that they are here to stay. Some illiberal norms, including unforgiving social sanctions for unpopular speech, the need to pay lip service to a Manichaean version of antiracism, and the occasional witch hunt against innocents, are likely to remain part of the culture of America's most influential institutions for the foreseeable future.

At the same time, the growing resistance to the identity trap will make it more feasible to undo some of its worst excesses. Other illiberal norms, including the most extreme prohibitions on forms of so-called cultural appropriation and the most blatant attempts by the state to discriminate between citizens on the basis of their race, are likely to prove short-lived. The next decades will, in other words, consist of a protracted fight over the extent to which the worlds of culture and education, business and politics will be governed by the core ideas and assumptions of the identity synthesis.

According to this third scenario—which I consider the most likely— the forces favoring the identity trap and the forces favoring its retrenchment will continue to clash for many years to come. After decades in which ideological debates felt marginal to politics, we are back to having a serious and protracted dispute about the nature of our societies and the best way to govern them. The overall outcome will be neither a complete rout for the identity synthesis nor its definitive victory. Rather, the conflict over the extent to which we should reject liberalism and embrace the identity synthesis is likely to shape the front lines in some of the most important intellectual debates and political battles of the coming decades. The precise way in which these boundaries are drawn will depend on the passion and the skill with which each side makes its case—and that makes it all the more important for the opponents of the identity trap to act in a smart and principled manner.

HOW TO ARGUE AGAINST THE IDENTITY TRAP

Many people have come to the conclusion that the identity trap presents a real danger to their most fundamental values. They want to speak out against it, whether in public, at the workplace, or within their group of friends. But they are nervous about doing so. After all, they don't want to risk alienating their friends or sabotaging their careers. And they certainly aren't so obsessed with politics that they want to turn themselves into full-time crusaders against "wokeness."

I understand their apprehension. Over the last five years, the newspapers have been full of stories of decent people losing their livelihoods over trivial or imaginary offenses against prevailing sentiments. Given that journalists are much more likely to report on famous people and institutions, most of these concerned well-known figures or brand-name organizations.

But it would be wrong to conclude that these illiberal practices touch only the rich and famous. Far from the spotlight of major media outlets, a similar fate has befallen the lives of innumerable ordinary individuals in every corner of the social and professional world, from local schools to yoga studios and from communities built around gaming to those focused on sewing. As I know from my own reporting, many of these victims were "civilians" in the "culture wars"—like the Latino electrician who was fired from the San Diego Gas & Electric Company because someone wrongly accused him of flashing a white power symbol.

So I do not blame anyone who chooses to stay on the sidelines in the hope that the current frenzy will, over time, die down of its own accord. But though the desire to minimize risk to one's own career or reputation is understandable, there is a simple problem with it. In the language of economists, we now face a classic case of the prisoner's dilemma. For each of us, it may well be rational to free ride on the efforts of others by keeping our criticisms of the identity trap quiet. But if all of us do so, the small minority of activists who have a deeply ideological commitment to the most crude forms of the identity synthesis will continue to have outsized influence. The current frenzy may well die down over time. But it will only do so if reasonable people point out the dangers of the identity trap.

This is a key reason why I decided to write this book. It is also the main reason why I hope that you will (if you agree with its principal conclusions) find a way to fight back against the dangers of the identity trap within your own personal and professional spheres. Speaking your mind will carry some risk. But there is a way to do so that maximizes the chances of making a difference and minimizes the chances of experiencing adverse consequences. So here are six pieces of advice for arguing and organizing against the identity trap in a way that is full-throated, doesn't court unnecessary risk, and has some chance of actually persuading your interlocutors.

1. Claim the Moral High Ground

There is a strange phenomenon I have observed among many different kinds of people, including critics of the identity trap, who disagree with the views that are prevalent in their social circles: something like an internalized sense of shame. It can be scary to disagree with your friends and colleagues. When there is strong social pressure to repeat certain slogans or pay lip service to certain views, a refusal to join in the chorus can, even to the would-be objector, come to feel like a kind of moral failing. And so many of the people who dare to speak up against prevailing views cede the moral high ground before they even open their mouths.

The first group of people who suffer from such internalized shame might be called reluctant heretics. They are so nervous about disagreeing with prevailing sentiments that they practically seem to apologize for their own ideas. Even when they do speak out, they hedge every point in so many concessions that their own position slips out of view. By adopting this tactic, reluctant heretics hope to insulate themselves from criticism. But that often turns out to be counterproductive. For by signaling that they themselves seem to regard their views as somehow illicit, they encourage the enforcers of orthodoxy to use moral shaming or rank intimidation to shut them down.

There is also a second group of objectors—one that may, at first glance, seem to be much more uncompromising, but simply expresses its internalized shame in a different manner. Call them the defiant heretics. The feeling that they are supposed to hide their real views has understandably embittered them. Convinced that everything they say will in any case be poorly received, they express themselves in the form of aggressive lectures or angry barbs. But this tactic is even more counterproductive. For by agreeing to play the part of the bad guy from the start, they give up on a chance to persuade their interlocutors of the justice of their position.

The best way to avoid these pitfalls is to overcome the internalized feeling of shame. So when I notice that I feel nervous about arguing for a position that is unpopular among many of my friends and colleagues (as I have in parts of this book), I remind myself that I am proud of the views I hold. I have thought about them long and hard. They are rooted in a noble tradition that has done a tremendous amount of good for the world. And though I recognize that I am, like everyone else, likely to be wrong about some important things, the views I hold are—virtually by definition—the ones that seem to me most likely to prove right. This makes it a little easier to speak from a position of calm confidence.

2. Don't Vilify Those Who Disagree

It's tempting to think of people with whom you profoundly disagree as having some kind of moral or intellectual defect. That makes it easy to belittle or even dehumanize them. If your interlocutors hold their views due to stupidity or moral deviance, there is little reason to treat them with decency.

But things aren't as simple as that. For virtually all of human history, the vast majority of people in every culture and on every continent were convinced of some beliefs that we would now regard as heinous. Even in my own lifetime, prevailing opinions about important issues have transformed radically; indeed, many people who now vilify others for straying from the views they consider sacrosanct themselves held such "deviant" views until a few years ago. It would be both silly and haughty to conclude that so many of our ancestors and compatriots are simply evil or stupid.

The most radical advocates of the identity synthesis often refuse to accept that people may disagree with them for legitimate reasons; it is precisely their tendency to confuse political disagreement with moral failure that has transformed public discourse for the worse over the course of the past decade. But that makes it all the more important for those of us who are critical of the identity trap to avoid making the same mistake. We too must remember that smart and decent people can come to radically different conclusions about all kinds of important issues—including the question of whether the identity synthesis is a force for good or for ill.

3. Remember That Today's Adversaries Can Become Tomorrow's Allies

No matter how hard you try, it is nearly impossible to make a friend or family member change their mind about an important issue in the middle of an argument. That makes it tempting to be cynical about the prospects of persuasion. Because people rarely switch their position, making political progress appears to be a matter of battling rather than of convincing your adversaries.

Some have argued that this is especially true when it comes to the most devoted advocates of the identity synthesis. Because there is something religious about the fervor with which what he calls "the Elect" have embraced their cause, John McWhorter warns, normal forms of persuasion are futile. The only question is how to limit their influence on the rest of society.

Happily, the evidence does not bear out such skepticism about the prospects for persuasion. Though few people acknowledge defeat in the middle of an argument, most do shift their worldview over time. According to a recent YouGov poll, for example, more than three in four Americans report that they have changed their mind on an important issue of public policy over the course of their lives. Since other studies show that people have a tendency to downplay how much they have changed their mind, the true figure is probably even higher.

Over time, such changes can—and often do—amount to a real shift in worldview. Political scientists have, for example, long found that people in the United Kingdom and the United States tend to become more conservative as they age. But though this is true on aggregate, the overall drift to the right can conceal that there are also many people who shift left over the course of their lives. The more you zoom out, the more ideological change and political persuasion look like the rule rather than the exception. Especially when it comes to fundamentals, such a process of change and persuasion usually takes place so gradually that it can seem imperceptible. You might start by rejecting some point of view as obviously disgusting; transition to recognizing why decent people might believe in it; and finally, to your own surprise, come to embrace it yourself.

Over the last couple of years, I have witnessed a similar transformation in how many of my friends think about the identity trap. Because they are on the left and are deeply conscious of the great injustices that persist in their societies, many of them were at first well disposed toward the identity synthesis. But then they gradually witnessed how destructive its influence has proven in their own communities and started to recognize to what extent its applications clashed with other values they hold. Gradually, they transformed from boosters to critics of the identity trap. Despite Mc-Whorter's worries, they are far from alone. After all, even some of the most prominent and sophisticated critics of the identity trap, like Eboo Patel and Maurice Mitchell, once endorsed its core principles and dismissed its dangers out of hand.

4. Appeal to the Reasonable Majority

On social media and cable news, it can seem as though society were cleaved into two mutually antagonistic halves. Most Americans are either "woke" or "MAGA." They think that American history is defined by the inequities of 1619 (the year when Africans were first brought to America in chains) or the heroism of 1776 (the year the Declaration of Independence was signed). They either get offended by every trivial thing or don't care when members of minority groups suffer injustice and discrimination. A similarly polarized set of views increasingly seems to dominate public discussion in other countries. In Britain, for example, some believe that the nation's character is defined by the cruelties of imperialism, while others think it consists exclusively of the heroism of the Battle of Britain.

There is a reason for this impression. A small number of people really do take extreme views on the most controversial issues of the day. And because of the way politics and the media work, these voices are given an outsized platform and now hold considerable sway.

But thankfully, most people have sensible views on complex issues, including those that touch on history and national identity. According to one recent study, for example, the great majority of Americans, including most Republicans, believe that "it's important that every American student learn about slavery, Jim Crow, and segregation"; "Martin Luther King and Rosa Parks should be taught as examples of Americans who fought for equality"; and "America is better today because women, immigrants, and Black Americans have made progress towards equality." At the same time, the great majority of Americans, including most Democrats, also believe that "George Washington and Abraham Lincoln should be admired for their roles in American history"; "we don't need to be ashamed to be American"; and "students should not be made to feel personally responsible for the actions of earlier generations." This nuanced approach to the nation's history is all the more striking because it belies popular perceptions on both sides—with a majority of Democrats doubting that Republicans want to teach the history of slavery, and a majority of Republicans doubting that Democrats want to tout the accomplishments of George Washington.

Far from being predominantly white, members of this reasonable majority are highly diverse. Studies suggest that in both Britain and the United States members of ethnic minority groups are not only less likely to take far-right views; they are also less likely to embrace the key tenets of the identity synthesis. When More in Common, a nonprofit that aims to counteract polarization, studied America's ideological tribes, for example, it found that so-called progressive activists—who are skeptical of long-standing norms and institutions because they believe them to be "established by socially dominant groups such as straight white men for their own benefit"—were disproportionately white, affluent, and highly educated. Asian Americans, Hispanics, and African Americans, by contrast, were all less likely than whites to share this worldview.

In the past, politicians have often appealed to a "silent majority" to perpetuate discrimination against minority groups. But today, the silent majority in countries like the United States, the United Kingdom, and many other democracies in the world is neither woke nor intolerant. Rather, it is both surprisingly reasonable and highly diverse. Most people from all walks of life both want members of minority groups to be treated with respect and reject the core tenets of the identity synthesis. Opponents of the identity trap should seek to persuade this reasonable majority.

5. Make Common Cause with Other Opponents of the Identity Synthesis . . .

When I criticize the dangers of the identity trap, I do so from the perspective of a philosophical liberal. But in a big and diverse democracy, politics must inevitably involve building a broad coalition. So liberals like myself should be open to making common cause with others who worry about the rise of the identity trap for principled reasons of their own. And as it happens, the fundamental propositions of the identity synthesis don't just put that ideology on a direct collision course with the basic liberal values that anchor my politics; they also stand in deep contrast with core strands of other influential political and religious traditions, from Marxism to conservatism, and from Christianity to Buddhism.

Many critics of the identity synthesis have decried it as a form of "Marxism." It is easy to see why. Marxism and the identity synthesis share both a disdain for the traditional institutions of parliamentary democracy and a deep enmity to liberalism. Some Marxist thinkers, like Frantz Fanon, Paulo Freire, and Herbert Marcuse, even continue to influence advocates of the identity synthesis. But to equate the two ideologies is to miss that the differences and tensions between them are at least as important as their similarities.

The principal roots of the identity synthesis lie in the postmodern rejection of grand narratives, including Marxism. Its adherents believe that identity-based categories like race, gender, and sexual orientation, not economic categories like class, are the key prism for understanding the world. That helps to explain why Marxist writers, from old stalwarts like Adolph Reed Jr. to young scholars like Olúfẹ́mi Táíwò, have become some of its most forthright critics. As Reed has lamented, "The disposition to catalog and aggregate neatly rounded-off identities is in no meaningful way radical." (I offer a fuller account of the relationship between Marxism and the identity synthesis in the appendix.)

Like Marxists, conservatives have an ambivalent relationship to questions of identity. Some conservatives fall into an identity trap of their own by maintaining that the ethnic, cultural, or religious groups that traditionally dominated their countries hold greater value and should therefore continue to have special powers and privileges. But many other conservatives recognize that countries like France, Great Britain, and the United States have (albeit imperfectly) been organized according to the universalist principles of liberal democracy for a very long time. They have therefore come to the conclusion that classic conservative principles like a commitment to gradual change and a skepticism about utopian promises give them good reason to defend this long-standing political settlement.

This makes such conservatives skeptical about "post-liberal" thinkers on the right, such as Sohrab Ahmari, Adrian Vermeule, and Curtis Yarvin, who seek to use the coercive power of the state to impose their vision of the good life on everybody else. At the same time, it also puts principled conservatives on a collision course with left-wing advocates of the identity synthesis who believe that we must sacrifice traditional norms such as free speech and race-neutral public policy to the pursuit of social justice.

The identity trap, such conservatives warn, holds out a utopian vision of a perfectly just society. But in practice, it would merely succeed in tearing down the guardrails that have for the past decades allowed members of different ethnic and religious groups to live alongside each other in relative peace. As David French, the conservative *New York Times* columnist who is one of the most principled defenders of philosophical liberalism in the United States, has put this lament, both the "post-liberal right and [the] post-liberal left fundamentally prioritize the power of the state over the liberty of the individual." The inevitable result is that both would diminish "free speech, economic freedom, private property, and religious liberty."

Some of the world's most storied political traditions thus stand in tension with the core precepts of the identity synthesis; so do some of its most influential religious traditions. The Old Testament, for example, claimed that all human beings are made in the image of the divine, a point that went on to inspire generations of political thinkers from the framers of the U.S. Constitution to Martin Luther King Jr. The New Testament, meanwhile, repeatedly emphasized the irrelevance of markers of group identity like race and ethnicity. (Perhaps the most prominent expression of this comes in Galatians, when the apostle Paul writes that "there is neither Jew nor Greek, there is neither bond nor free, there is neither male nor female: for ye are all one in Christ Jesus.")

Other religious traditions, from Islam to Buddhism, express the idea that the fundamental equality between human beings is more important than their ethnic or cultural differences in their own way. The Baha'i faith, for example, puts special emphasis on "the principle of the oneness of the world of humanity." In one of the tradition's most influential works, Abdu'l-Bahá, the son of the faith's founder, asks, "Is not the same sun shining upon all? Are they not the sheep of one flock? Is not God the universal shepherd?"

In short, there is a kind of overlapping consensus among critics of the identity synthesis. A surprisingly wide and varied set of political and religious traditions give their adherents reasons to view with deep skepticism any worldview that puts group identities like race and ethnicity at its moral and epistemological center. Philosophical liberals should welcome these allies with open arms. But though we should celebrate that some will make common cause with us for principled reasons of their own, we must avoid a temptation that would lead us astray from our own ideals: that of endorsing any point of view, no matter how crude or unprincipled, that happens to be critical of the identity synthesis.

6. . . . But Don't Become a Reactionary

Norman Davies, one of the most distinguished historians of Central Europe, was once asked what he considered the biggest shortcoming of his colleagues. Davies thought about the many brave and accomplished scholars from Central Europe who had spent a lifetime chronicling the abuses of the region's communist regimes, trying to demonstrate that Marxists who see everything through the monomaniacal prism of class misrepresent important aspects of reality. Then he gave a surprising answer: "Marxism."

Did Davies believe that Marxism had shaped Central Europe so profoundly that even the most avowedly anti-Marxist historians were unable to escape its influence? I don't think so. On the contrary, Davies was lamenting that the best Central European historians had become so consumed with their righteous resistance to Marxism that they found it difficult to focus on anything else. Marxism deformed their scholarship because they couldn't let go of criticizing it.

A similar danger now confronts some critics of the identity trap. Its opponents are united by what they oppose, not by what they endorse. This creates a temptation to outsource their moral judgments to their opponents. Instead of militating for a positive vision of the future, these critics of the identity trap have started to rail against anything that somehow seems "woke." In other words, they have become guilty of what, drawing on an idea by Emily Yoffe, I once called 180ism: "the tendency of many participants in public debate to hear what their perceived enemies have to say and immediately declare themselves diametrically opposed."

The alternative is simple: Opponents of the identity synthesis need to be guided by a clear and consistent compass of their own. In my case, this compass consists of liberal values like political equality, individual freedom, and collective self-determination. For others, it will consist of Christian faith or Marxist conviction, of conservative principles or the precepts of Buddhism. But what all smart opponents of the identity trap will share is a determination to avoid letting their understandable frustration at the ideas they dislike consume them to such an extent that they lose sight of the fundamental commitments that should guide their own actions.

HOW ORGANIZATIONS CAN ESCAPE THE IDENTITY TRAP

One of the stranger aspects of the way in which social media has transformed America over the past decade is the fear of many institutional leaders to exercise their authority. While writing this book, I have spoken to extremely powerful people—including CEOs of big companies, presidents of leading universities, and directors of major nonprofits—who privately complained to me about the influence of the identity trap. Each of them was worried about the way in which a few junior staff members were able to intimidate their colleagues and poison morale. Each of them feared that this was making it harder for their organization to serve its mission. And yet all of them felt unable to push back or speak up about their misgivings.

It is understandable that these institutional leaders are scared to speak their mind, especially when doing so might earn them accusations—however unfair—of being sexist or racist. But the real risks of doing too much have now become an excuse for the equally dangerous path of doing too little. And in the end, institutional leaders who are afraid to uphold rational rules or punish those who blatantly disregard them will succeed only in emboldening activists who are intent on usurping what remains of their authority, making their organizations even more acrimonious and dysfunctional.

This is why institutional leaders need a plan. They must think through what they will do if they find themselves in the midst of a social media maelstrom before they are being bombarded from all sides. Better still, they should proactively take action to set clear expectations, restore their authority, and make it less likely that such crises will arise in the first place. An incomplete list of the actions and principles they should adopt would, at the least, include the following five points:

1. *Clearly communicate that employees are expected to be tolerant toward different points of view.* Organizations should proactively cultivate a spirit of tolerance and viewpoint diversity. Private businesses should make it clear that employees are expected to be comfortable with having co-workers who have different political values and convictions. Nonprofit organizations, media outlets, and publishers should emphasize that their staff will sometimes need to work on causes or products with which they may personally disagree. Universities should adopt free speech principles and actively communicate the value of open debate to their students, faculty, and administrators.

2. *Solicit real feedback instead of letting activists hijack the conversation.* Organizations should put in place mechanisms, such as regular anonymous surveys, for employees to offer honest feedback. These mechanisms should convey a sense of overall sentiment within the organization rather than becoming a forum for the most radical or disaffected people to hijack the conversation. Often, the findings of these surveys will help to defuse tension. In one big nonprofit organization, for example, many young white staff members complained about pervasive forms of white supremacy, but most Black staff members reported being happy with the organization's culture.

3. *Stop employees from bullying each other on social media.* In the last five years, many organizations have been pushed into crisis as employees used social media to intimidate their colleagues or bully them into parroting their views. Clear and consistent social media guidelines can make it more likely that conflicts will be resolved in a collegial manner within the organization. While these guidelines must not restrict the right to private political speech, they can and should prohibit employees from publicly attacking their employer or criticizing their colleagues.

4. *Don't discipline anybody before the facts are clear and passions have cooled.* Organizations should adopt clear procedures for dealing with complaints and accusations against their staff in a fair and evenhanded manner. Especially when employees are accused on social media of having said or done something morally unacceptable, it is tempting to rush to action. The point of these procedures is to delay any definitive decision until the relevant facts have been investigated. Often, this will have the added benefit of ensuring that the initial uproar has subsided, making it a little easier for the organization to come to the decision that is appropriate given the facts of the case rather than the one that seems most likely to placate strangers on Twitter, Facebook, and Instagram.

5. *Don't apologize unless you've done something wrong.* Organizations and their leaders should never apologize for something that isn't morally wrong or that they did not in fact do. Though the intent of issuing such apologies is usually to calm a firestorm on social media, the effect often is to fan its flames. The same goes for other members of the organization. Institutional leaders should never encourage or incentivize their subordinates to issue such insincere apologies; when they do, employees should be very skeptical of any promises that signing off on such apologies will save them from being fired.

All of this is, admittedly, more easily said than done. But I do think that these actions and principles can help to prepare institutional leaders for the kinds of difficult situations that they will, given the nature of the times, sooner or later face. Imagine, for example, that you are a university president facing the kind of controversy that has consumed many campuses over the course of the past decade. A student organization has invited a speaker with views that you find genuinely noxious. Many other student organizations are planning to protest. It is likely that some will try to use force to disrupt the event. What do you do?

If you side with the protesters, you risk condoning a clear attack on academic freedom. If you stand with the invited speaker, you risk associating yourself with his noxious views. You are seemingly doomed if you do and doomed if you don't.

But in truth there is a rather simple way for you to both stand up for academic freedom and express your distaste for the views of the visiting speaker: You should publicly emphasize the importance of free speech, making it clear that any student who resorts to violence or stops the visiting speaker from expressing his views will incur a serious punishment. At the same time, you are free to express your personal disagreement with the visiting speaker, promising to join any student protest that peacefully contests his ideas.

Will this make everyone happy? Of course not. But it will communicate the values of the institution, significantly reduce the likelihood of a violent confrontation, and start to build a healthier campus culture: one in which people are warmly encouraged to speak up or protest, but firmly dissuaded from pursuing their goals by the use of force. And along the way, it might just reestablish your authority as an institutional leader—allowing you to take an active role in building an internal culture that is both rational and resilient.

WHAT WE GIVE UP IF WE FALL
FOR THE IDENTITY TRAP

This book is deeply personal to me. The history of ethnic and religious prejudice has profoundly shaped the lives of my ancestors. My forefathers suffered centuries of restrictions on what they could do and where they could live. My great-grandparents were murdered for being Jewish. My grandparents lost virtually their entire families in the Holocaust. Even my own parents had to remake their lives from scratch when, in their early twenties, they were expelled from the only country they knew as home.

My family's history gives me deep empathy for the victims of racial and religious discrimination. It is impossible to understand the world without being attuned to the real ways in which categories like race, religion, and sexual orientation have historically shaped how people are treated. Nothing can justify averting our eyes from the serious injustices that, even today, persist in every country on earth.

But when it becomes monomaniacal, a due focus on categories of group identity turns into a dangerous distortion of reality. By encouraging us to interpret every historical fact and every personal interaction through the lens of race, gender, and sexual orientation, advocates of the identity synthesis make it impossible to understand the world in all of its complexity. And by portraying society as being full of bigots who pose a constant threat to members of every conceivable minority group, they encourage more and more people to feel adrift in a relentlessly hostile world.

This is why the risk posed by these distortions is ultimately as much personal as it is political. To those who suffer from feelings of isolation, the identity synthesis promises much-needed orientation, even enlightenment. As Eboo Patel experienced when he first encountered these ideas as an undergraduate, they can seem to give people a deeper understanding of their place in society and grant them greater access to their true selves. But as Patel also came to learn, the promise of consolation eventually reveals itself as a chimera.

The identity trap seduces complex people into seeing themselves as wholly defined by external characteristics whose combinations and permutations, however numerous, will never amount to a satisfactory depiction of their innermost selves. Its supposedly validating focus on our identity as a product of the various group attributes into which we are born leaves little space for the individual tastes and idiosyncratic temperaments that actually make us unique. The problem with the ideas that have gained so much power over the past decade is not, as some critics of the identity synthesis like to suggest, that they treat each of us as though we were "our own special snowflake." It is that they proffer the illusion that we will be fully recognized in our uniqueness while reducing us to actors reading simplistic scripts about what it is to be male or female, brown or Black, gay or straight, cis or trans.

The identity trap poses serious dangers. It undermines important values like free speech. Its misguided applications have proven deeply counterproductive in areas from education to medicine. If implemented at scale, it won't provide the foundation for a fair and tolerant society; it will inspire a zero-sum competition between mutually hostile identity groups.

To escape this danger, we must aspire to surpass the prejudices and enmities that have for so much of human history boxed us into the roles seemingly foreordained by the religion of our ancestors or the color of our skin. We should keep striving for a society in which categories like race, gender, and sexual orientation matter a lot less than they do now because what each of us can accomplish—and how we all treat each other—no longer depends on the groups into which we were born. We must not let the identity trap lure us into giving up on a future in which what we have in common finally comes to be more important than what divides us.

Appendix

WHY THE IDENTITY SYNTHESIS
ISN'T MARXIST

Many critics of so-called wokeness contend that the identity synthesis is a form of "cultural Marxism." Their basic claim is simple: if you take class and economics out of Marxism, and swap in race and identity, you arrive at the ideas that are now transforming the American mainstream.

It is easy to see why a lot of people have come to this conclusion. Many thinkers in the Marxist tradition continue to exert significant influence on the key themes and applications of the identity synthesis. To name but a few examples, advocates of the identity synthesis often criticize capitalism in terms that are clearly downstream from the work of Karl Marx and Friedrich Engels. The focus on cultural hegemony in many academic disciplines is in part inspired by Antonio Gramsci. Critiques of free speech often invoke the work of Herbert Marcuse. And one of the most widely read texts in American education schools is by Paulo Freire.

There are also some striking similarities between the core views of the two traditions. Perhaps most important, both Marxism and the identity synthesis are deeply skeptical of the core promise of liberal democracy. Both distrust universal values and neutral norms as a kind of fig leaf that allows the group that is truly in charge to hold on to power. And both infer that these rules and norms need to be overthrown, making them hostile to core liberal ideals.

But for all of these similarities, the differences between the identity synthesis and Marxism weigh just as heavily. Let's start with the respective origins of these traditions. As I showed in part I, it simply isn't true that the main intellectual roots for the identity synthesis are Marxist. On the contrary, its original impetus stems from postmodern thinkers like Michel Foucault and Jean-François Lyotard who were deeply concerned about what they called "grand narratives," including both liberalism and Marxism, that then enjoyed a strong hold over intellectual life in Paris.

This opposition to grand narratives made thinkers like Foucault and Lyotard highly skeptical of the liberal principles on which postwar democracies in Europe claimed to be based. This helps to explain why advocates of the identity synthesis have from the beginning been very dismissive of the core institutions of Western democracies. But Foucault and Lyotard were also deeply opposed to another ideology, which was even more influential over their interlocutors: Marxism. Indeed, their contemporaries, including Jean-Paul Sartre, rightly interpreted the rejection of universal truth and the skepticism about stable categories of identity as a full-frontal attack on the fundamental assumptions underwriting Marxism; after all, postmodernism also amounted to a critique of those who claimed to speak on behalf of the proletariat or made confident proclamations about the determinist laws of historical progress that supposedly foretold the imminent arrival of communism.

The structural similarities between the identity synthesis and Marxism are admittedly striking. As I show in part IV, a rational reconstruction of the identity synthesis would focus on three key claims:

1. The key to understanding the world is to examine it through the prism of group identities like race, gender, and sexual orientation.

2. Supposedly universal values and neutral rules merely serve to obscure the ways in which privileged groups dominate those that are marginalized.

3. To build a just world, we must adopt norms and laws that explicitly make the way the state treats each citizen—and how citizens treat each other—depend on the identity group to which they belong.

It would be easy to offer a rational reconstruction of the core claims of Marxism that looks strikingly similar:

1. The key to understanding the world is to examine it through the prism of social class.

2. Supposedly universal values and neutral rules merely serve to obscure the ways in which privileged classes dominate those that are oppressed.

3. To build a just world, we must adopt norms and laws that explicitly make the way the state treats each citizen—and how citizens treat each other—depend on their economic condition.

This seems like a pretty compelling case that those who talk about "cultural Marxism" are onto something. But while the structure of Marxism really does resemble the structure of the identity synthesis, their substantive dissimilarities are ultimately more important.

The first substantive dissimilarity is obvious. The two traditions disagree about the fundamental prism through which to see the world: the category that motivates human action and whose members must be liberated if we are to bring about a better world. Marxists believe that the economic category of class is fundamental. Meanwhile, adherents of the identity synthesis focus on group identities like race, gender, and sexual orientation, including class in their list at most as a kind of afterthought.

This difference has widely been noted. (In fact, those who compare the identity synthesis to Marxism implicitly acknowledge it by adding that the Marxism of which they speak is *cultural* in nature.) But there is also a second substantive dissimilarity, which is just as important but has mostly been overlooked.

Marxists have traditionally theorized the proletariat as a universal class. The goal of the revolution, according to them, is to overcome all class antagonism by putting proletarians in charge and abolishing all class distinctions. This gives Marxism a utopian promise of a future in which classes disappear and all humans can finally stand in solidarity with each other—a utopian promise that the identity synthesis notably lacks.

Some scholars, like Karen and Barbara Fields, advocate for the parallel goal of "race abolitionism": echoing the utopian goal that Marxists embrace with regard to class, they hope for a future in which this category of analysis has ceased being useful. But adherents of the identity synthesis strenuously reject that goal as misguided or unrealistic. Embracing a form of strategic essentialism that has ceased to be strategic, they have resigned themselves to a future in which the most basic aspects of reality, from how two friends should interact to who should receive scarce medical goods, should forever depend on categories of identity. As a result, adherents of the identity synthesis are stuck with a vision of the future in which social and political reality will forever continue to be structured by conflict, or at least by significant tensions, between different identity groups. They therefore lack the utopian promise that made Marxism so intoxicating.

The wings of birds and the wings of butterflies share many anatomical features. This makes it tempting to assume that they must have a common ancestor. But that is not the case. In evolutionary biology, they are considered a core example of "convergent evolution." The shape of their wings evolved, independently from each other, to perform the same function: to allow them to fly.

Something similar is true for Marxism and the identity synthesis. The two ideologies have important structural similarities because they share a core purpose: to oppose and overcome philosophical liberalism. But this should not tempt us to oversimplify the relationship between the two traditions. Far from being a mere adaptation of Marxism, the identity synthesis is a new challenge to liberal democracy that we must take seriously—and oppose—on its own terms.

Acknowledgments

To write a book is a lonely process. To write a book that swims against the current can be doubly lonely. So I have, in working on this manuscript, felt even more grateful than I usually do to have wonderful colleagues, loyal friends, and trusted readers.

My first thanks goes to Scott Moyers, a visionary editor who—precisely because he did not agree with every word I wrote—pushed me at each turn to make this book smarter, deeper, more subtle, and more persuasive. It is always true that a good editor helps to shape a project; it is rarely as true as it has been in this case.

I am also profoundly grateful to Stuart Proffitt. Stuart was indefatigable in comments big and small, helping to push me towards greater clarity on many key points and immensely improving the flow of the whole manuscript.

This book would not exist without Andrew Wylie. At a time when fear of criticizing the identity synthesis was palpable in publishing, Andrew never wavered in his support or his belief in its importance. He offered valuable guidance on the manuscript from its inception and proved to be a passionate advocate when its fate hung in the balance.

I am also immensely grateful for the wonderful teams at Penguin Press, Allen Lane, and the Wylie Agency. At Penguin Press, I am especially grateful to Mia Council for her helpful comments and for patiently shepherding the book through the publication process and to Elisabeth Calamari for being the best, bluntest publicist any author can hope for. At Allen Lane, I am indebted to Alice Skinner for her feedback and assistance; to Annabel Huxley for being such a thoughtful and energetic advocate for the book; and to the design team which came up with a beautiful cover. At the Wylie Agency, James Pullen and Claire Devine have been a delight to work with, helping to make sure that this book sees the light of day in its best possible form in many editions and translations; I am deeply indebted to their patience and persistence.

It is a special pleasure to work on international editions with publishers across the world. I am grateful for my third collaboration with Muriel Beyer, Adèle van Reeth, Séverine Courtaud, Jeanne de Saint-Hilaire, and Benjamin Peylet at Editions L'Observatoire as well as with Carlo Feltrinelli, Camilla Cottafavi, Adolfo Frediani, Elisa Martini, and Serafina Ormas at Feltrinelli. I am also grateful to Tom Kraushaar, Marion Preuß, and Katharina Wilts at Klett-Cotta; to Barend Wallet and Léon Groen at Het Spectrum; and to the whole team at Paidos.

I am also deeply grateful to the wonderful institutions I get to call home. Johns Hopkins University has been an incredible academic base since I came on board as a faculty member in 2019. My special thanks goes to Ron Daniels, Hahrie Han, and Stephen Ruckman, to my wonderful colleagues at both the SNF Agora Institute and at SAIS—and of course to the hundreds of students it has been my pleasure to teach, and from whom I have learned so much.

The Council on Foreign Relations is a second institutional home to which I am deeply grateful. Conversations with and comments from Richard Haass, James Lindsay, and Shannon O'Neill have improved this project in key respects; I am very grateful to Barbaralee Diamonstein-Spielvogel for being a generous and visionary supporter of the CFR's Democracy Program; and I owe a big debt to my research assistants Gideon Weiss and Anya Konstantinovsky for their help and patience.

One publication is cited more than any other in the pages of this book:

Persuasion. So it is no overstatement that I am especially indebted to my friends and colleagues who have helped me think through so many different aspects of contemporary politics over the course of the past years, including David Hamburger, Luke Hallam, Sam Kahn, Emily Yoffe, Sahil Handa, Seth Moskovitz, Bea Frum, Francisco Toro, and Moises Naim. Special thanks goes to my all-star podcast team, including John Taylor Williams, Brendan Ruberry, and (previously) Rebecca Rashid.

For the past half decade, *The Atlantic* has been the indispensable publication where I have been able to develop many of my ideas and to find an audience for them. I am grateful to Jeff Goldberg, Yoni Applebaum, Juliet Lapidos, Matt Seaton, and many others for giving me ideas and making sure that they are presented in their best possible form.

The team at the Lavin Agency has been ever resourceful in making sure that my work reaches that most vital and old-fashioned of things: an in-person audience. I am especially indebted to David Lavin, Charles Yao, Tom Gagnon, and Kenneth Calway.

I have been very lucky to have excellent research assistants to help on this project. Brittin Alfred, Devontae Lacasse, and Maggie O'Brien have been very helpful in assembling sources and assisting with references. A very special thanks is due to Anders Knospe, who has accompanied this project from the inception until the last copyedits. It is a rare blessing to have a collaborator on whom you can rely so fully; it is even rarer to have one who feels more like a writing partner—helping to generate ideas, to steelman every position, and to stress-test every argument. I look forward to appearing in the acknowledgments to his first book before long.

Last but not least, a great number of people have helped to shape this book, from the initial proposal to the final manuscript, whether through formal comments (large and small) or through years of being in conversations about the world. They are responsible for a lot of what's best in the book, and for many of the happiest moments I had while writing it. They include Shira Telushkin, David Plunkett, Katarina Podlesnaya, Francis Fukuyama, Eleni Arzoglou, Sam Koppelman, Benjamin Shinogle, Ian Bassin, Anne Applebaum, Samantha Holmes, Carl Schoonover, Carly

Knight, Jonathan Rauch, Bernardo Zacka, Samantha Rose Hill, George Packer, Rachel Prtizker, Martin Eiermann, Jonathan Haidt, Lidal Dror, Rachel Fraser, David Miliband, Garry Kasparov, David Hamburger, Amelia Atlas, Seth Klarman, Noam Dworman, Mike Berkowitz, Russ Muirhead, Manual Hartung, Marie Thibault de Maisieres, Thomas Chatterton-Williams, Tom Meaney, and Guillermo del Pinal.

Notes

Introduction: The Lure and the Trap

1 **Kila Posey asked:** All quotations from Kila Posey based on interview with the author, Jan. 2023, unless otherwise noted. Posey also provided further supporting materials, including email exchanges and audio recordings. See also Lateshia Beachum, "Atlanta Principal Accused of Separating Black Kids from Other Students in 'Discriminatory' Practice," *Washington Post*, Aug. 13, 2021, www.washingtonpost.com/education/2021/08/12/atlanta -principal-black-students; and Vanessa McCray, "Parent Alleges Atlanta School Designated 'Black Classes,' Others Dispute That Claim," *Atlanta Journal-Constitution*, Aug. 19, 2021, www.ajc.com/education/parent-alleges-atlanta-school-designated-black-classes -others-dispute-that-claim/ODR2JJVNXJBQ7DAQRRNPQ6Q764/.

1 **"disbelief that I was having":** Niara Savage, "'It Was Just Disbelief': Parent Files Complaint Against Atlanta Elementary School After Learning the Principal Segregated Students Based on Race," *Atlanta Black Star*, Aug. 10, 2021, atlantablackstar.com/2021/08 /10/it-was-just-disbelief-parent-files-complaint-against-atlanta-elementary-school-after -learning-the-principal-segregated-students-based-on-race/.

2 **calculus classes reserved:** "Mathematics / Courses—Evanston Township High School," accessed Jan. 26, 2023, www.eths.k12.il.us/Page/3025.

2 **emailed invitation emphasized:** Diane Adame, "Wellesley School District Faces Civil Rights Complaint from Parent Group," WGBH, May 20, 2021, www.wgbh.org/news /education/2021/05/20/wellesley-school-district-faces-civil-rights-complaint-from -parents-group.

2 **establish narrow limits:** *Brown v. Board of Education of Topeka*, 347 U.S. 483 (1954).

2 **inspired legal challenges:** See, for example, Nick Valencia, "Atlanta School Under Federal Investigation After Allegations Principal Assigned Black Students to Classes Based on Race," CNN, Dec. 5, 2022, www.cnn.com/2022/12/01/us/atlanta-school-federal -investigation-separate-classes-reaj/index.html.

2 **divided by race:** Shanon L. Connor and Julie Parsons, "Loving the Skin They're In: Race-Based Affinity Groups for the Youngest Learners," NAIS, Aug. 18, 2020, www

.nais.org/learn/independent-ideas/august-2020/loving-the-skin-theyre-in-race-based
-affinity-groups-for-the-youngest-learners/.

2 **"A play-based curriculum"**: Connor and Parsons, "Loving the Skin." Gordon's efforts
have long been heralded by the National Association of Independent Schools. In 2004,
the Gordon School received a "Leading Edge" award from the NAIS for its work on equity and inclusion. Julie Parsons, "Identity, Affinity, Reality," NAIS, Winter 2012, www
.nais.org/magazine/independent-school/winter-2012/identity,-affinity,-reality/.

2 **on Dalton's website**: "About DEI at Dalton," Dalton School, accessed Jan. 28, 2023,
www.dalton.org/about/diversity-equity-and-inclusion/about-dei-at-dalton.

2 **fittingly called EmbraceRace**: EmbraceRace is linked as a resource by Dalton. See "DEI
Hosts 'What Is Racial Identity Development' Parent Workshop," Dalton School, Feb.
11, 2021, www.dalton.org/dalton-news?pk=1398973. EmbraceRace is hardly a niche
group. According to its 2021 impact report, the organization has received funding from
organizations like the LEGO Community Fund, Gap, Price Chopper, and Adobe ("2021
Impact Report," EmbraceRace, 5, accessed Jan. 26, 2023, embracerace-prod.imgix.net
/assets/2021-ER-Impact.pdf, 10). It has also received glowing press coverage, with its
resources recommended in newspapers including *The Washington Post* and *The New York
Times*. See Martha Conover, "Nine Things Parents Should Consider When Searching for
Anti-racist Media for Their Kids," *Washington Post*, July 2, 2020, www.washingtonpost
.com/lifestyle/2020/06/12/9-things-parents-should-consider-when-searching-anti-racist
-media-their-kids/; and Perri Klass, "The Impact of Racism on Children's Health," *New
York Times*, Aug. 12, 2019, www.nytimes.com/2019/08/12/well/family/the-impact-of
-racism-on-childrens-health.html.

3 **"We are racial beings"**: Sandra Chapman, "Understanding Racial-Ethnic Identity Development," EmbraceRace, May 23, 2017, www.embracerace.org/resources/recording
-and-resources-understanding-racial-ethnic-identity-development.

3 **Bank Street School**: For instance, Shael Polakow-Suransky, the current president of the
Bank Street College of Education and himself an alumnus of the school, served as second-
in-command of New York City's Education Department between 2010 and 2014.

3 **"own" their "European ancestry"**: Paul Sperry, "Elite K–8 School Teaches White Students They're Born Racist," *New York Post*, July 1, 2016, nypost.com/2016/07/01/elite-k-8
-school-teaches-white-students-theyre-born-racist/. See also Bank Street College of Education, "Letter to the Community About Our Racial Justice and Advocacy Program,"
July 3, 2016, www.bankstreet.edu/news-events/news/letter-to-the-community-about
-our-racial-justice-and-advocacy-program.

3 **Beverly Daniel Tatum**: Beverly Daniel Tatum, *Why Are All the Black Kids Sitting Together in the Cafeteria?*, rev. ed. (New York: Basic Books, 2017), 96.

3 **"putting my daughters in a class"**: Posey, interview with the author, Jan. 2023.

4 **"racial beings"**: For instance, a UCLA guide to recognizing microaggressions asserts the
importance of recognizing individuals as "racial/cultural being[s]." "Tool: Recognizing
Microaggressions and the Messages They Send," UCLA, https://web.archive.org/web
/20150611163315/https://www.ucop.edu/academic-personnel-programs/_files/seminars
/Tool_Recognizing_Microaggressions.pdf.

4 **doctor was flabbergasted**: Jon Levine, "NYC Will Consider Race When Distributing
Life-Saving Covid Treatments," *New York Post*, Jan. 1, 2022, nypost.com/2022/01/01/nyc
-considering-race-in-distributing-life-saving-covid-treatment/. New York State guidelines did not give pharmacists the power to decline filling prescriptions from doctors
based on the race of a patient. But because these guidelines did suggest that doctors should
prioritize some nonwhite patients over similarly situated white ones, doctors could
reasonably interpret such a question as a form of pressure to rethink their prescription
practices.

5 **drugs like Paxlovid**: Paxlovid, the first COVID pill, was authorized for emergency use
on December 22, 2021, though the supply of the drug was initially "extremely limited."

See, for example, Berkeley Lovelace, "FDA Authorizes First Covid Pill, from Pfizer, for Emergency Use," NBCNews.com, Dec. 23, 2021, www.nbcnews.com/health/health -news/fda-authorizes-first-covid-pill-pfizer-emergency-use-rcna8760.

5 **most countries outside:** For instance, *Vox* characterized the Advisory Committee on Immunization Practices' initial recommendation that essential workers should be prioritized over older adults as "a major departure from how other countries were prioritizing vaccination." Kelsey Piper, "Who Should Get the Vaccine First? The Debate over a CDC Panel's Guidelines, Explained," *Vox*, Dec. 22, 2020, www.vox.com/future-perfect /22193679/who-should-get-covid-19-vaccine-first-debate-explained. For more on this, see the beginning of chapter 12.

5 **like advanced age:** Different provinces in Canada can prioritize different people. But the federal government strongly suggests that the elderly and those who have preexisting conditions should take precedence. Megan DeLaire, "What You Need to Know About Getting COVID-19 Antiviral Medication Paxlovid in Canada," CTV News, July 28, 2022, www.ctvnews.ca/health/what-you-need-to-know-about-getting-covid-19-antiviral -medication-paxlovid-in-canada-1.6006441.

5 **like African Americans:** Gregorio A. Millett et al., "Assessing Differential Impacts of COVID-19 on Black Communities," *Annals of Epidemiology* 47 (2020): 37–44, doi.org /10.1016/j.annepidem.2020.05.003; Maritza Vasquez Reyes, "The Disproportional Impact of COVID-19 on African Americans," *Health and Human Rights* 22, no. 2 (2020): 299–307.

5 **groups of British Asians:** The data from Britain is interesting because it suggests that differences in medical outcomes by race are strongly mediated by differences in socioeconomic status. In the U.K., residents with origins in Pakistan and Bangladesh have a much lower "disability-free life expectancy" than white British patients. But residents with origins in India, who tend to have a higher socioeconomic standing, fare much better. For similar reasons, so-called Black African residents of the U.K., most of whom are descendants of relatively recent immigrants, do better, not worse, than average on key metrics like "health-related quality of life scores." See Veena Raleigh and Jonathon Holmes, "The Health of People from Ethnic Minority Groups in England," King's Fund, Sept. 17, 2021, www.kingsfund.org.uk/publications/health-people-ethnic-minority-groups-england.

5 **Bram Wispelwey and Michelle Morse:** "Sensitive to these injustices, we have taken redress in our particular initiative to mean providing precisely what was denied for at least a decade: a preferential admission option for Black and Latinx heart failure patients to our specialty cardiology service. The Healing ARC will include a flag in our electronic medical record and admissions system suggesting that providers admit Black and Latinx heart failure patients to cardiology, rather than rely on provider discretion or patient self-advocacy to determine whether they should go to cardiology or general medicine." Bram Wispelwey and Michelle Morse, "An Antiracist Agenda for Medicine," *Boston Review*, March 17, 2021, www.bostonreview.net/articles/michelle-morsebram-wispelwey-what -we-owe-patients-case-medical-reparations. See also Lauren A. Eberly et al., "Identification of Racial Inequities in Access to Specialized Inpatient Heart Failure Care at an Academic Medical Center," *Circulation: Heart Failure* 12, no. 11 (2019): e006214.

6 **"should be assessed":** Lori Bruce and Ruth Tallman, "Promoting Racial Equity in COVID-19 Resource Allocation," *Journal of Medical Ethics* 47, no. 4 (2021): 212, doi.org /10.1136/medethics-2020-106794.

6 **"a racially equitable triage protocol":** Bruce and Tallman, "Promoting Racial Equity in COVID-19 Resource Allocation," 208.

6 **"families will remember being denied":** Bruce and Tallman, "Promoting Racial Equity in COVID-19 Resource Allocation," 212.

6 **rejected "race-neutral" frameworks:** FDA, *Fact Sheet for Healthcare Providers Emergency Use Authorization (EUA) of Sotrovimab*, 2022, www.fda.gov/media/149534 /download.

6 **"not mean simply treating everyone equally"**: "Public Health Vending Machine Initiative in New York City," accessed Jan. 28, 2023, fphnyc.org/wp-content/uploads/sites/76/2021/12/Public-Health-Vending-Machine-Initiative-in-NYC-RFP-FINAL.pdf.

6 **New York State Department of Health:** Though the ostensible justification for this policy was to prioritize ethnic groups that had experienced higher mortality rates from COVID, this group included Asian Americans, who had been dying from COVID at lower rates than other ethnic groups since the beginning of the pandemic. See, for example, Latoya Hill and Samanta Artiga, "COVID-19 Cases and Deaths by Race/Ethnicity: Current Data and Changes over Time," KFF, Aug. 22, 2022, www.kff.org/coronavirus-covid-19/issue-brief/covid-19-cases-and-deaths-by-race-ethnicity-current-data-and-changes-over-time/.

6 **Otherwise identical New Yorkers:** "COVID-19 Oral Antiviral Treatments Authorized and Severe Shortage of Oral Antiviral and Monoclonal Antibody Treatment Products," New York Department of Health, Dec. 27, 2021, www.mssnyenews.org/wp-content/uploads/2021/12/122821_Notification_107774.pdf. See also Wang Ying and Zuma Press, "New York's Race-Based Preferential Covid Treatments," *Wall Street Journal,* Jan. 7, 2022, www.wsj.com/articles/new-york-race-based-covid-treatment-white-hispanic-inequity-monoclonal-antibodies-antiviral-pfizer-omicron-11641573991.

To give the authorities that adopted these racial criteria for who should get treatment their due, some ethnic groups, like Latinos and African Americans, did suffer markedly higher rates of hospitalization and death than other ethnic groups, including both whites and Asian Americans, at the beginning of the pandemic. It is only right that authorities were keen to protect the most vulnerable Americans from the ravages of the disease.

But that does not justify the empirically misguided, morally dubious, and politically inflammatory policies that public health officials and hospital systems all across the United States actually adopted. As most studies suggest, racial differences in outcomes were mostly a result of other socioeconomic attributes or political attitudes. Latinos and African Americans were especially vulnerable at the beginning of the pandemic because they are more likely to work in blue-collar professions or to live in cramped housing units, making it harder for them to avoid getting infected. In fact, education levels predicted the likelihood of dying from COVID much better than race throughout the early stages of the pandemic, with college-educated Latinos and African Americans being hospitalized and dying at lower rates than whites who have only a high school degree.

What's more, the racial composition of fatalities changed significantly over the course of the pandemic, with the share of white Americans who were hospitalized or killed because of COVID steadily rising over time. Indeed, whites were especially vulnerable in the later stages of the pandemic because they are comparatively old and were less likely to get vaccinated (Akilah Johnson and Dan Keating, "Whites Now More Likely to Die from Covid Than Blacks: Why the Pandemic Shifted," *Washington Post*, Oct. 24, 2022, www.washingtonpost.com/health/2022/10/19/covid-deaths-us-race). Meanwhile, Asian Americans fared comparatively well throughout, in part because they are, on average, more affluent and more likely to get vaccinated.

The actions of America's key medical authorities ignored such complexities. For the most part, they did not prioritize people on the basis of living in cramped conditions or having a lower socioeconomic status. They even failed to distinguish between ethnic groups that did initially suffer a higher risk of serious disease than whites, like African Americans, and those that had a markedly lower risk of serious disease all along, like Asian Americans. Faced with a complicated reality, they defaulted to a simplistic and inflammatory binary: "whites" are privileged, and "people of color" are oppressed.

6 **part of a wider trend:** Minnesota was among a number of states that adopted "race-sensitive" protocols for distributing scarce treatments at the height of the Omicron wave. As official guidelines issued by the state's Department of Health stated, "Race and ethnicity alone, apart from other underlying health conditions, may be considered in determining

eligibility." (Minnesota, along with New York and Utah, had drawn from the FDA's acknowledgment that race could be used as a criterion to determine prescription treatment. Aaron Sibarium, "Minnesota Backtracks on Racial Rationing of COVID Drugs," *Washington Free Beacon*, Jan. 14, 2022, freebeacon.com/coronavirus/minnesota-backtracks -on-racial-rationing-of-covid-drugs/.) Under the scheme, a twenty-year-old Asian American woman was to take precedence over a sixty-four-year-old white man, even though the latter would, according to all available metrics, be an order of magnitude more likely to die from COVID.

Utah adopted its own version of a "race conscious" plan for doling out lifesaving drugs. Under the state's system, which prioritized patients depending on the number of points they scored, some of the most serious risk factors counted for very little. Being severely immunocompromised or suffering from congestive heart failure, for example, counted for one point; being Asian American, by contrast, counted for two.

On the ground, this form of guidance was at times applied in even more extreme form. SSM Health, a large Catholic hospital chain with facilities in Illinois, Missouri, Oklahoma, and Wisconsin, instructed its physicians that they should prescribe scarce antibody treatments like Sotrovimab and Regeneron only to patients who garnered at least twenty points on a proprietary scoring system. The scheme gave patients one point for having serious preconditions like hypertension, obesity, or asthma; being Black, Asian American, Hispanic, or Native American counted for seven points. As a result, a forty-year-old man with no preexisting conditions would qualify for Sotrovimab if his ancestors hailed from Spain; meanwhile, a forty-nine-year-old man with asthma, obesity, and hypertension would not qualify if his ancestors hailed from neighboring France. See Aaron Sibarium, "Hospital System Backs Off Race-Based Treatment Policy After Legal Threat," *Washington Free Beacon*, Jan. 14, 2022, freebeacon.com/coronavirus/hospital -system-backs-off-race-based-treatment-policy-after-legal-threat/.

6 **Vermont encouraged young:** Phil Galewitz, "Vermont to Give Minority Residents Priority for COVID Vaccines," *Scientific American*, April 6, 2021, www.scientificamerican.com /article/vermont-to-give-minority-residents-priority-for-covid-vaccines/.

6 **urged states to put essential workers:** Yascha Mounk, "Why I'm Losing Trust in the Institutions," *Persuasion*, Dec. 23, 2020, www.persuasion.community/p/why-im-losing -trust-in-the-institutions. See also the detailed description of this policy at the beginning of chapter 12.

7 **an amicus brief:** James W. Lytle, "Litigation Challenges Prioritization of Race or Ethnicity in Allocating COVID-19 Therapies," *Bill of Health*, March 28, 2022, blog.petrieflom .law.harvard.edu/2022/03/28/new-york-state-covid-therapy-litigation/.

7 **emergency funds available:** In the Biden administration's own language, the American Rescue Plan included "the creation of an initial funding prioritization period for Restaurant Revitalization Fund applications from historically underserved business owners and women- and veteran-owned small businesses." "The Small Business Boom Under the Biden-Harris Administration," White House, April 2022, www.whitehouse.gov/wp -content/uploads/2022/04/President-Biden-Small-Biz-Boom-full-report-2022.04.28 .pdf.

7 **City of San Francisco:** "San Francisco Launches New Guaranteed Income Program for Trans Community," City and County of San Francisco, Nov. 16, 2022, sf.gov/news/san -francisco-launches-new-guaranteed-income-program-trans-community.

7 **victims of a "cancel mob":** For instance, the Los Angeles City Council member Gil Cedillo's appeal to "cancel culture" after facing calls to resign for his comments about Black and indigenous people was a disingenuous ploy to portray himself as a victim. See Julia Wick, "'Why I Did Not Resign': Gil Cedillo Suggests He's a Victim of 'Cancel Culture,'" *Los Angeles Times*, Dec. 12, 2022, www.latimes.com/california/story/2022 -12-12/former-councilmember-gil-cedillo-issues-three-page-letter; Los Angeles Times Editorial Board, "Resign, Councilmembers Nury Martinez, Kevin De León, and Gil

Cedillo," *Los Angeles Times*, Oct. 10, 2022, www.latimes.com/opinion/story/2022-10
-10/nury-martinez-kevin-deleon-gil-cedillo-should-resign. Neither was the impeachment
of President Trump for incitement of an insurrection an attempt to "cancel the president
and anyone who disagrees with them," as Representative Jim Jordan has claimed. Associated Press, "Watch: Jordan Says Second Trump Impeachment Is a Product of 'Cancel
Culture,'" PBS, Jan. 13, 2021, www.pbs.org/newshour/politics/watch-jordan-says-second
-trump-impeachment-is-a-product-of-cancel-culture.

7 **the Associated Press:** "AP Deletes 'the French' Tweet and Apologises After It Is Widely
Mocked," BBC News, Jan. 28, 2023, www.bbc.com/news/world-europe-64436973.

7 **Massachusetts Institute of Technology:** Yascha Mounk, "Why the Latest Campus
Cancellation Is Different," *Atlantic*, Oct. 19, 2021, www.theatlantic.com/ideas/archive
/2021/10/why-latest-campus-cancellation-different/620352/.

7 **it already shapes:** On both the ACLU and Coca-Cola, see chapter 5.

8 **National Health Service:** See, for example, Andrew Gregory, "NHS to Close Travistock
Gender Identity Clinic for Children," *Guardian*, July 28, 2022, www.theguardian.com
/society/2022/jul/28/nhs-closing-down-london-gender-identity-clinic-for-children;
and Keira Bell, "My Story," *Persuasion*, April 7, 2021, www.persuasion.community/p
/keira-bell-my-story.

8 **National Arts Centre:** Claire Clarkson, "National Arts Centre Event for Patrons Identifying as Black Only," *Canada Today*, Jan. 27, 2023, canadatoday.news/on/national
-arts-center-event-for-patrons-identifying-as-black-only-197957/.

8 **To be on the left:** For a few contemporary defenses of this strain of left-wing thought, see
Amartya Sen, *Identity and Violence: The Illusion of Destiny* (New York: Norton, 2006);
Kwame Anthony Appiah, *Cosmopolitanism: Ethics in a World of Strangers* (New York:
Norton, 2006); Tony Judt, *Ill Fares the Land* (New York: Penguin Books, 2010); and
Brian Barry, *Culture and Equality: An Egalitarian Critique of Multiculturalism* (Cam-
bridge, Mass.: Harvard University Press, 2002).

8 **things we share:** This politics of unity is evident in Barack Obama's keynote address at
the 2004 Democratic National Convention: "Alongside our famous individualism,
there's another ingredient in the American saga. A belief that we are connected as one
people. . . . [T]here's not a liberal America and a conservative America—there's the
United States of America. There's not a black America and white America and Latino
America and Asian America; there's the United States of America." Barack Obama,
"Keynote Address at the 2004 Democratic National Convention" (speech, Boston, July
27, 2004), American Presidency Project, www.presidency.ucsb.edu/documents/keynote
-address-the-2004-democratic-national-convention.

8 **alongside serious discrimination:** See chapter 3. Frederick Douglass criticized the same
disconnect between ideals and practice a century before: "The blessings in which you this
day rejoice are not enjoyed in common. The rich inheritance of justice, liberty, prosperity,
and independence bequeathed by your fathers is shared by you, not by me. The sunlight
that brought life and healing to you has brought stripes and death to me. This Fourth of
July is yours, not mine. You may rejoice, I must mourn." Frederick Douglass, "What to
the Slave Is the Fourth of July?" (speech, Rochester, New York, 1852).

8 **long been inhospitable:** This too has a long tradition. See, for example, Sojourner Truth,
"Ain't I a Woman?" (speech, Akron, Ohio, 1851). But critiques of the left from the perspective of various identity groups, including women and ethnic minorities, became
more pronounced in the 1960s and 1970s. See, for example, Frantz Fanon, *The Wretched
of the Earth*, trans. Constance Farrington (New York: Grove Press, 1963); Robin Archer,
*Out of Apathy: Voices of the New Left Thirty Years On: Papers Based on a Conference Orga-
nized by the Oxford University Socialist Discussion Group* (London: Verso, 1989); and
Lynne Segal, Sheila Benson, and Dorothy Wedderburn, "Women in the New Left," Verso
website, Oct. 26, 2017, www.versobooks.com/blogs/3460-women-in-the-new-left.

8 **awareness and understanding:** This sentiment is most obvious in the Black Power move-

ment. As Stokely Carmichael and Charles V. Hamilton wrote, Black Power is "a call for black people in this country to unite, to recognize their heritage, to build a sense of community. It is a call for black people to begin to define their own goals, to lead their own organizations and to support those organizations." Stokely Carmichael and Charles V. Hamilton, *Black Power: The Politics of Liberation in America* (New York: Random House, 1992), 23.

8 **encourage gay or Black:** See chapter 2 on "strategic essentialism."

9 **"little black boys and girls":** Martin Luther King, "I Have a Dream," Aug. 28, 1963, transcript provided by "Read Martin Luther King Jr.'s 'I Have a Dream' Speech in Its Entirety," NPR, Jan. 16, 2023, www.npr.org/2010/01/18/122701268/i-have-a-dream -speech-in-its-entirety.

9 **depend on the groups:** See chapter 12 for a discussion of race conscious policy.

9 **about "identity politics":** See, for example, Christine Emba, "In Defense of Identity Politics," *Washington Post*, Dec. 6, 2016, www.washingtonpost.com/news/in-theory /wp/2016/12/06/in-defense-of-identity-politics; David French, "Identity Politics Are Ripping Us Apart," *National Review*, May 19, 2016, www.nationalreview.com/2016/05 /identity-politics-race-ripping-us-apart/.

9 **describe themselves as "woke":** John McWhorter, "How 'Woke' Became an Insult," *New York Times*, Aug. 17, 2021, www.nytimes.com/2021/08/17/opinion/woke-politically -correct.html.

9 **No generally accepted term:** See, for example, Perry Bacon, "What We Really Mean When We Say 'Woke,' 'Elites,' and Other Politically Fraught Terms," *Washington Post*, Sept. 19, 2022, www.washingtonpost.com/opinions/2022/09/19/decoding-political-phrases -midterms-perry-bacon/.

9 **many different kinds of groups:** It might be natural to add "religion" to this list. For a more detailed discussion of the importance that religion as well as sexual orientation does and does not play in the identity synthesis, see footnote on p. 243.

10 **These injustices are undoubtedly real:** For good summaries of each, see Madeline E. Heilman and Suzette Caleo, "Gender Discrimination in the Workplace," *Oxford Handbooks Online*, 2018, doi.org/10.1093/oxfordhb/9780199363643.013.7; Elizabeth A. Nowicki and Robert Sandieson, "A Meta-analysis of School-Age Children's Attitudes Towards Persons with Physical or Intellectual Disabilities," *International Journal of Disability, Development, and Education* 49, no. 3 (2002): 243–65, doi.org/10.1080 /1034912022000007270; Devah Pager and Hana Shepherd, "The Sociology of Discrimination: Racial Discrimination in Employment, Housing, Credit, and Consumer Markets," *Annual Review of Sociology* 34, no. 1 (Jan. 2008): 181–209, doi.org/10.1146/annurev.soc .33.040406.131740; Wesley Myers et al., "The Victimization of LGBTQ Students at School: A Meta-analysis," *Journal of School Violence* 19, no. 4 (July 2020): 421–32, doi .org/10.1080/15388220.2020.1725530.

10 **Explicit restrictions on:** "Voting Rights Act (1965)," National Archives and Records Administration, www.archives.gov/milestone-documents/voting-rights-act#; "Civil Rights Act (1964)," National Archives and Records Administration, www.archives.gov/milestone -documents/civil-rights-act; *Loving v. Virginia*, 388 U.S. 1 (1967).

10 **large Black middle class:** See Yascha Mounk, *The Great Experiment: Why Diverse Democracies Fall Apart and How They Can Endure* (New York: Penguin Press, 2022), chap. 8.

10 **to earn less:** Palash Ghosh, "Black Americans Earn 30% Less Than White Americans, While Black Households Have Just One-Eighth Wealth of White Households," *Forbes*, Dec. 10, 2021, www.forbes.com/sites/palashghosh/2021/06/18/blacks-earn-30-less-than -whites-while-black-households-have-just-one-eighth-of-wealth-of-white-households /?sh=57a2b847550c.

10 **attend an underfunded school:** Ashley Nellis, "The Color of Justice: Racial and Ethnic Disparity in State Prisons," Sentencing Project, Oct. 13, 2021, www.sentencingproject .org/reports/the-color-of-justice-racial-and-ethnic-disparity-in-state-prisons-the

-sentencing-project/; Laura Meckler, "Study Finds Black and Latino Students Face Significant 'Funding Gap,'" *Washington Post*, July 22, 2020, www.washingtonpost.com /education/study-finds-black-and-latino-students-face-significant-funding-gap/2020 /07/21/712f376a-caca-11ea-b0e3-d55bda07d66a_story.html; Erika Harrell, "Black Victims of Violent Crime," Bureau of Justice Statistics Special Report, Aug. 2007; Gabriel L. Schwartz and Jaquelyn L. Jahn, "Mapping Fatal Police Violence Across U.S. Metropolitan Areas: Overall Rates and Racial/Ethnic Inequities, 2013–2017," *PLOS One* 15, no. 6 (2020), doi.org/10.1371/journal.pone.0229686.

11 **vastly more inclusive:** On schools, see, for example, Ludmila Nunes, "New Directions for Diversity, Equity, and Inclusion in Higher Education," Association for Psychological Science, Jan. 6, 2021, www.psychologicalscience.org/observer/words-to-action. On corporations, see, for example, Pippa Stevens, "Companies Are Making Bold Promises About Greater Diversity, but There's a Long Way to Go," CNBC, June 15, 2020, www .cnbc.com/2020/06/11/companies-are-making-bold-promises-about-greater-diversity -theres-a-long-way-to-go.html. Although both of these articles still state there are improvements to be made, they also recognize the efforts to make schools and corporations more inclusive.

11 **harder for first-generation:** See, for example, Ross Perlin, *Intern Nation: How to Earn Nothing and Learn Little in the Brave New Economy* (New York: Verso, 2012).

11 **"strong and slow boring":** Max Weber, "Politics as a Vocation," in *From Max Weber: Essays in Sociology*, trans. and ed. H. H. Gerth and C. Wright Mills (New York: Oxford University Press, 1946), 27.

12 **treated with special consideration:** For a more detailed account of the origins of these claims, see parts I and II. For a more detailed account of the three fundamental principles on which the identity synthesis is based, see part IV.

13 **drawing lines between different groups:** See chapters 7 and 11.

13 **great courage and altruism:** Jonathan Haidt, *The Righteous Mind: Why Good People Are Divided by Politics and Religion* (New York: Penguin Press, 2013), 189–220.

13 **"us" and "them":** See my discussion of the minimal group paradigm in Mounk, *Great Experiment*, chap. 1.

14 **on a pedestal:** See Yascha Mounk, *The People vs. Democracy: Why Our Freedom Is in Danger and How to Save It* (Cambridge, Mass.: Harvard University Press, 2018), chaps. 1 and 6.

14 **a zero-sum competition:** When advocates of the identity synthesis encourage people to define themselves by their ethnic, gender, or sexual identity, they mostly have members of historically marginalized groups in mind. But when prestigious social institutions try to promote that kind of group consciousness, and public policies explicitly prioritize the needs of people who are members of certain communities, the effect is unlikely to remain contained. In a society organized around such communitarian lines, members of historically dominant groups are, sooner or later, likely to explicitly embrace their own racial, gender, and sexual identities, clamoring for as big a piece of the pie as they can get. And because these historically dominant groups are, almost by definition, likely to remain both numerous and powerful for a long time to come, they have every chance of succeeding. The identity synthesis not only encourages forms of competition that are likely to herald new forms of social strife; it may ultimately make it harder for marginalized groups to obtain justice and equality.

14 **"real" or "authentic":** People who are born into a marginalized minority within a minority, such as Dalits or Ismaili Muslims, are likely to face a related problem: many members of society will presume that they identify with a broader community that often mistreats them.

15 **victims are ordinary people:** See, for example, my account of Emmanuel Cafferty, a Latino electrical worker who was fired after an activist took a picture of him doing the OK symbol, a gesture with a long and innocuous history that has of late been appropriated by some niche groups as a sign of support for the so-called white power movement.

Yascha Mounk, "Stop Firing the Innocent," *Atlantic*, June 27, 2020, www.theatlantic
.com/ideas/archive/2020/06/stop-firing-innocent/613615.

16 **Today, dangerous demagogues continue:** Yasmeen Serhan, "The Trump-Modi Play-book," *Atlantic*, Feb. 25, 2020, www.theatlantic.com/international/archive/2020/02
/donald-trump-narendra-modi-autocrats/607042/; Steven Erlanger, "What Should Europe Do About Viktor Orban and 'Illiberal Democracy'?," *New York Times*, Dec. 23, 2019, www.nytimes.com/2019/12/23/world/europe/tusk-orban-migration-eu.html.

17 **radio documentary, two books:** See, for example, Mounk, *People vs. Democracy*; Mounk, *Great Experiment*; Yascha Mounk, "Pitchfork Politics," *Foreign Affairs*, Aug. 18, 2014. www.foreignaffairs.com/articles/united-states/2014-08-18/pitchfork-politics; Roberto Stefan Foa and Yascha Mounk, "The Danger of Deconsolidation: The Democratic Disconnect," *Journal of Democracy* 27, no. 3 (2016): 5–17; Roberto Stefan Foa and Yascha Mounk, "The Signs of Deconsolidation," *Journal of Democracy* 28, no. 1 (2017): 5–15; Yascha Mounk, "The Week Democracy Died: Seven Days in July That Changed the World as We Know It," *Slate*, Aug. 14, 2016, www.slate.com/articles/news_and_politics /cover_story/2016/08/the_week_democracy_died_how_brexit_nice_turkey_and _trump_are_all_connected.html; Yascha Mounk, "How a Teen's Death Has Become a Political Weapon," *New Yorker*, Jan. 21, 2019, www.newyorker.com/magazine/2019/01 /28/how-a-teens-death-has-become-a-political-weapon; Yascha Mounk, *The Populist Curtain*, BBC Radio 4, www.bbc.co.uk/programmes/m00048p9; Jordan Kyle and Yascha Mounk, "The Populist Harm to Democracy: An Empirical Assessment," Tony Blair Institute for Global Change, Dec. 26, 2018; Yascha Mounk, "Attack of the Zombie Populists," *Atlantic*, Oct. 26, 2022, www.theatlantic.com/ideas/archive/2022/10/boris -johnson-donald-trump-zombie-populists/671865/; and Yascha Mounk, *The Good Fight*, podcast, open.spotify.com/show/3nhfO2XVPsv2wZafZ5n7Hk.

18 **accelerated the takeover:** See chapter 7.

18 **are deeply polarized:** Yascha Mounk, "The Doom Spiral of Pernicious Polarization," *Atlantic*, May 21, 2022, www.theatlantic.com/ideas/archive/2022/05/us-democrat -republican-partisan-polarization/629925/.

18 **go hand in hand with:** For a longer version of this argument, see Kenan Malik, "Racism Rebranded: How Far-Right Ideology Feeds Off Identity Politics," *Guardian*, Jan. 8, 2023, www.theguardian.com/world/2023/jan/08/racism-rebranded-how-far-right-ideology -feeds-off-identity-politics-kenan-malik-not-so-black-and-white.

19 **form of "cultural Marxism":** Alexander Zubatov, "Just Because Anti-Semites Talk About 'Cultural Marxism' Doesn't Mean It Isn't Real," *Tablet*, Nov. 29, 2018, www .tabletmag.com/sections/news/articles/just-because-anti-semites-talk-about-cultural -marxism-doesnt-mean-it-isnt-real. For a widely circulated version of this view, see Ruminate, "Postmodernism and Cultural Marxism | Jordan B Peterson," YouTube, video, 43:46, July 7, 2017, www.youtube.com/watch?v=wLoG9zBvvLQ.

PART I: THE ORIGINS OF THE IDENTITY SYNTHESIS

26 **simply a form of "cultural Marxism":** See, for example, James Lindsay, "The Complex Relationship Between Marxism and Wokeness," *New Discourses*, July 28, 2020, newdiscourses .com/2020/07/complex-relationship-between-marxism-wokeness/.

Chapter 1: Postwar Paris and the Trial of Truth

27 **imposing communist satellite regimes:** See, for example, Anne Applebaum, *Iron Curtain: The Crushing of Eastern Europe, 1944–56* (London: Allen Lane, 2012).

27 **"When it came to changing":** Tony Judt, *Postwar* (New York: Penguin Press, 2005), 401.

28 **had collaborated with:** See, for example, Julian Jackson, *France: The Dark Years, 1940– 1944* (Oxford: Oxford University Press, 2001).

28 **heroic resistance movement:** See, for example, H. R. Kedward, *The French Resistance and Its Legacy* (London: Bloomsbury Academic, 2022), 455–61.

28 **to Louis Althusser:** Althusser, for instance, was a longtime member of the French Communist Party. As the philosopher William Lewis put it, "During the 1950s, Althusser lived two lives that were only somewhat inter-related: one was that of a successful, if somewhat obscure academic philosopher and pedagogue and the other that of a loyal Communist Party Member." William Lewis, "Louis Althusser," in *Stanford Encyclopedia of Philosophy*, Aug. 22, 2022, plato.stanford.edu/entries/althusser/.

28 **Marxism, he avowed:** Quoted in Judt, *Postwar*, 401. On Sartre, see also Annie Cohen-Solal, Norman MacAfee, and Annapaola Cancogni, *Jean-Paul Sartre: A Life* (New York: New Press, 1985).

28 **a shocking speech:** "Khrushchev's Secret Speech, 'On the Cult of Personality and Its Consequences,' Delivered at the Twentieth Party Congress of the Communist Party of the Soviet Union," Feb. 25, 1956, Wilson Center Digital Archive, digitalarchive .wilsoncenter.org/document/115995. He also reported that "of 1,966 delegates with either voting or advisory rights, 1,108 persons were arrested on charges of anti-revolutionary crimes."

28 **leaked transcripts of the speech:** As the journalist Vivian Gornick, recalling her and her family's struggle to come to terms with Khrushchev's speech, wrote in 2017: "I was 20 years old in February 1956 when Nikita Khrushchev addressed the 20th Congress of the Soviet Communist Party and revealed to the world the incalculable horror of Stalin's rule. Night after night the people at my father's kitchen table raged or wept or sat staring into space. I was beside myself with youthful rage. 'Lies!' I screamed at them. 'Lies and treachery and murder. And all in the name of socialism! In the name of *socialism*!' Confused and heartbroken, they pleaded with me to wait and see, this couldn't be the whole truth, it simply couldn't be. But it was." Vivian Gornick, "When Communism Inspired Americans," *New York Times*, April 29, 2017, www.nytimes.com/2017/04/29/opinion /sunday/when-communism-inspired-americans.html.

29 **unquestioningly loyal to the Kremlin:** When the Soviet Union invaded Hungary in 1956, Sartre justified the invasion, accusing the country's government of having a "rightist spirit." Judt, *Postwar*, 321–22.

29 **a deeply unhappy child:** For an overview of Foucault's life and work, see Didier Eribon, *Michel Foucault* (Cambridge, Mass.: Harvard University Press, 1989); David Macey, *Michel Foucault* (London: Hutchinson, 1993); and James Miller, *The Passion of Michel Foucault* (Cambridge, Mass.: Harvard University Press, 1993).

29 **"in fierce and lofty isolation":** Miller, *Passion*, 39.

29 **"The students pose against":** Miller, *Passion*, 39–40. (Title of *Folie et déraison* in French in the original.)

29 **Foucault's years at university:** Miller, *Passion*, 40–56.

30 **studied with Jean Hyppolite:** Leonard Lawlor and John Nale, eds., "Jean Hyppolite (1907–1968)," in *The Cambridge Foucault Lexicon* (Cambridge: Cambridge University Press, 2014), 639–40.

30 **joined the French Communist Party:** Miller, *Passion*, 57. See also David Scott Bell and Byron Criddle, *The French Communist Party in the Fifth Republic* (Oxford: Oxford University Press, 1994), esp. chaps. 4 and 5.

30 **"Over anyone who pretended":** Miller, *Passion*, 57.

30 **he would be an adversary:** For the rest of the 1950s, Foucault worked as a kind of diplomat, serving in a number of government-sponsored institutes of French culture and language across Europe, while continuing to work on his doctoral dissertation. After a station in Uppsala, he came to Poland to direct the French Institute at Warsaw University in 1956. His experience of living in a socialist satellite state helped him realize how strongly the local population resented being under the thumb of the Soviet Union and how repressive a regime that had promised the emancipation of the proletariat turned out

to be in practice. Going beyond his rejection of communist orthodoxy, Foucault increasingly came to doubt the overall project. "Marxism exists in nineteenth century thought," he concluded, "as a fish exists in water; that is, it ceases to breathe anywhere else." Quoted in Sara Mills, *Michel Foucault* (New York: Routledge, 2003), 15.

30 **age of consent:** The petition to lower the age of consent was signed by a number of Foucault's contemporaries, including Gilles Deleuze, Jacques Derrida, Simone de Beauvoir, Jean-Paul Sartre, and Jean-François Lyotard. While the petition does not mention a specific age, it references, sympathetically, the "Affaire de Versailles," an incident that involved adults having sex with twelve- and thirteen-year-olds. "Lettre ouverte à la Commission de révision du code pénal pour la révision de certains textes régissant les rapports entre adultes et mineurs" [An open letter to the Penal Code Revision Commission regarding the revision of texts governing relations between adults and minors], *Archives Françoise Dolto*, Association des Archives et Documentation Françoise Dolto, Paris. On Foucault's support for Ayatollah Khomeini, see Jeremy Stangroom, "Michel Foucault's Iranian Folly," *Philosophers' Magazine*, Oct. 15, 2015, www.philosophersmag.com/opinion/80-michel-foucault-s-iranian-folly.

31 **supported opposition movements:** Miller, *Passion*, 327.

31 *Madness and Civilization*: Michel Foucault, *Madness and Civilization: A History of Insanity in the Age of Reason*, trans. Richard Howard (New York: Random House, 1965), 116.

31 **standard accounts of psychiatry:** In earlier epochs, scholars believed that those whose behavior deviated from contemporary norms were "in contact with the mysterious forces of cosmic tragedy" (as per the consensus in the Renaissance) or choosing to renounce reason (as per the consensus in the seventeenth century). By contrast, modern scientists, who argue that madness should be understood as a "mental disease," making it the job of doctors to heal patients from their affliction, believe that they are being much more tolerant and humane. See, for example, Gary Gutting and Johanna Oksala, "Michel Foucault," in *Stanford Encyclopedia of Philosophy*, Aug. 5, 2022, plato.stanford.edu/entries/foucault/.

31 **not to heal:** "That is, on one hand madness is immediately perceived as difference: whence the forms of spontaneous and collective judgment sought, not from physicians, but from men of good sense, to determine the confinement of a madman; and on the other hand, confinement cannot have any other goal than a correction (that is, the suppression of the difference, or the fulfillment of this nothingness in death)." Foucault, *Madness and Civilization*, 116.

31 **appearance of scientific progress:** Miller, *Passion*, 62.

31 **criminal justice system:** In between studying madness and systems of punishment, Foucault published one of his most ambitious methodological works, and the one that, becoming a surprise bestseller, turned him into an international star: *The Order of Things: An Archaeology of the Human Sciences*. Some of its views about the socially contingent nature of truth claims are discussed later.

31 **tarred and feathered, even beheaded:** Michel Foucault, *Discipline and Punish: The Birth of the Prison*, trans. Alan Sheridan (New York: Vintage Books, 1995), 6–9.

31 **"to punish less, perhaps":** Foucault, *Discipline and Punish*, 82.

31 **a panopticon developed:** Jeremy Bentham, *The Panopticon Writing*, ed. Miran Bozovic (London: Verso, 1995), 29–95.

31 **act of self-imposed discipline:** "At the other extreme [of discipline], with panopticism, is the discipline-mechanism: a functional mechanism that must improve the exercise of power by making it lighter, more rapid, more effective, a design of subtle coercion for a society to come" (Foucault, *Discipline and Punish*, 209). "In this panoptic society of which incarceration is the omnipresent armature, the delinquent is not outside the law; he is, from the very outset, in the law, at the very heart of the law, or at least in the midst of those mechanisms that transfer the individual imperceptibly from discipline to the law, from deviation to offence" (Foucault, *Discipline and Punish*, 301).

32 **serve as his metaphor:** "Borne along by the omnipresence of the mechanisms of discipline, basing itself on all the carceral apparatuses, it has become one of the major functions of our society. The judges of normality are present everywhere. We are in the society of the teacher-judge, the doctor-judge, the educator-judge, the 'social worker'–judge; it is on them that the universal reign of the normative is based." Foucault, *Discipline and Punish*, 304.

32 **"to transform individuals":** Foucault, *Discipline and Punish*, 172.

32 **third big topic:** Michel Foucault, *The History of Sexuality*, trans. Robert Hurley (New York: Random House, 1978).

32 **high time for:** See, for example, Anne-Claire Rebreyend, "May 68 and the Changes in Private Life: A 'Sexual Liberation'?," in *May 68* (London: Palgrave Macmillan, 2011), 148–60. Alternatively, for one of many popular treatments of the theme, see the movie *The French Dispatch*.

32 **narrative is all wrong:** As Foucault sets up his analysis, "One can raise three serious doubts concerning what I shall term the 'repressive hypothesis.' First doubt: Is sexual repression truly an established historical fact? Is what first comes into view—and consequently permits one to advance an initial hypothesis—really the accentuation or even the establishment of a regime of sexual repression beginning in the seventeenth century?" Foucault, *History of Sexuality*, 10.

32 **Victorian scientists were obsessed:** "But medicine made a forceful entry into the pleasures of the couple: it created an entire organic, functional, or mental pathology arising out of 'incomplete' sexual practices; it carefully classified all forms of related pleasures; it incorporated them into the notions of 'development' and instinctual 'disturbances'; and it undertook to manage them." Foucault, *History of Sexuality*, 41.

32 **idea of a "homosexual":** "Homosexuality appeared [after Carl Westphal's 1870 *Archiv für Neurologie*] as one of the forms of sexuality when it was transposed from the practice of sodomy onto a kind of interior androgyny, a hermaphrodism of the soul. The sodomite had been a temporary aberration; the homosexual was now a species." Foucault, *History of Sexuality*, 43.

32 **"Pleasure," Foucault once insisted:** Quoted in Mark Jordan, "Our Identities, Ourselves?," *Boston Review*, May 27, 2020, www.bostonreview.net/articles/mark-d-jordan-our-identities-ourselves/.

32 **skeptical of calls:** As Jeffrey Weeks, a sympathizer of Foucault, put it, "We can no longer accept the liberatory politics of . . . Reich and Marcuse, nor believe in transcendent sexual liberation." Jeffrey Weeks, "The Contribution of Michel Foucault to Recent Sexual Theory" (paper delivered at the conference "History of the Present: Sex, Law, Literature, and Contemporary Social Issues," University of California, Berkeley, March 29–31, 1985), 7.

33 **depended on prevailing "discourses":** "The central issue, then (at least in the first instance), is not to determine whether one says yes or no to sex, whether one formulates prohibitions or permissions, whether one asserts its importance or denies its effects, or whether one refines the words one uses to designate it; but to account for the fact that it is spoken about, to discover who does the speaking, the positions and viewpoints from which they speak, the institutions which prompt people to speak about it and which store and distribute the things that are said. What is at issue, briefly, is the over-all 'discursive fact,' the way in which sex is 'put into discourse.'" Foucault, *History of Sexuality*, 11.

33 **just as constraining:** "Where there is power, there is resistance, and yet, or rather consequently, this resistance is never in a position of exteriority in relation to power." Foucault, *History of Sexuality*, 95.

33 **disappointed and even enraged:** In the preface to the German edition of *The History of Sexuality*, Foucault addressed critics, writing, "This is what happened in France, where critics who had suddenly been converted to seeing the struggle against repression as beneficial (without going so far as to demonstrate any great zeal in this department) reproached me for denying that sexuality had been repressed." Foucault goes on to clarify

that he does not deny repression, but instead understands it in a context of power, which is always exercised more broadly. Preface to the German edition of *The History of Sexuality* (Frankfurt: Suhrkamp, 1983).

33 **nature of power:** For a good recent discussion of the influence of Foucault's conception of power, see Colin Koopman, "Why Foucault's Work on Power Is More Important Than Ever," *Aeon*, March 15, 2017, aeon.co/essays/why-foucaults-work-on-power-is-more -important-than-ever.

33 **systematically subjugated a particular category:** Notably, many advocates of the identity synthesis conceptualize the world in a similar form, putting "people of color" in the place of the subjugated class that Marxists would reserve for workers or feminists would reserve for women.

33 **"produced from one moment":** Foucault, *History of Sexuality*, 93.

33 **"Where there is power":** Foucault, *History of Sexuality*, 95.

33 **"is never in a position":** Foucault, *History of Sexuality*, 95–96. Having given up on the prospect of wholesale liberation or emancipation, the most that Foucault is able to offer his readers is the prospect that new forms of resistance will produce "cleavages in a society that shift about, fracturing unities and effecting regroupings, furrowing across individuals themselves, cutting them up and remodeling them." Foucault, *History of Sexuality*, 96.

34 **"Simplifying to the extreme":** Jean-François Lyotard, *The Postmodern Condition*, trans. Geoff Bennington and Brian Massumi (Minneapolis: University of Minnesota Press, 1984), xxiv.

34 **veracity of scientific findings:** The scientific method, Lyotard argued in *The Postmodern Condition*, makes claim to universal validity: it holds itself out as an objective standard that can assess the accuracy of all kinds of claims about the world, including those that are not themselves presented in a scientific register. If contemporary science is able to corroborate the articles of a widely held religious faith or the assumptions of a narrator telling a compelling story, then these are legitimate; if it is not, then they are mere mistakes or superstitions.

But these standards of judgment, Lyotard argued, are ultimately self-undermining. If all claims can only be valid so long as they are justified by a rigorous scientific assessment, that must also be true for the standards that constitute the scientific method itself. But subjecting these standards to such a test proves impossible. While it is possible to test, say, the boiling point of water in an experimental manner by applying the scientific method, there is no empirical test for the rules that constitute the scientific method itself. See Lyotard, *Postmodern Condition*, 53–60.

35 **Deleuze now concluded:** Michel Foucault, *Language, Counter-memory, Practice: Selected Essays and Interviews*, trans. Donald F. Bouchard and Sherry Simon (Ithaca, N.Y.: Cornell University Press, 1977), 206.

35 **"the masses no longer need":** Foucault, *Language, Counter-memory, Practice*, 207.

35 **hotly anticipated debate:** Martin Mortenson, "Noam Chomsky—Noam vs. Michel Foucault (Eng. subs)," YouTube, video, 6:50, April 17, 2007, www.youtube.com/watch ?v=kawGakdNoT0. See also Noam Chomsky and Michel Foucault, *The Chomsky- Foucault Debate: On Human Nature* (New York: New Press, 1974).

36 **"I had never met such an amoral":** Yascha Mounk, "Noam Chomsky on Identity Politics, Free Speech, and China," *The Good Fight*, Nov. 6, 2021, podcast, 54:07, www.persuasion .community/p/chomsky#details.

Chapter 2: The End of Empire and the Embrace of "Strategic Essentialism"

39 **a few countries in Europe:** In 1914, for example, European countries are estimated to have controlled around 84 percent of the world's land surface. Philip Hoffman, *Why Did Europe Conquer the World?* (Princeton, N.J.: Princeton University Press, 2015), 2.

39 **the United Kingdom still ruled:** Mark Harrison, ed., *The Economics of World War II: Six Great Powers in International Comparison* (Cambridge: Cambridge University Press, 1998), 3.

39 **smaller European nations:** On Belgian rule in the Congo, see Adam Hochschild, *King Leopold's Ghost: A Story of Greed, Terror, and Heroism in Colonial Africa* (Boston: Mariner Books, 1998). On Portuguese rule in Angola, see Inge Tvedten, *Angola: Struggle for Peace and Reconstruction* (Boulder, Colo.: Westview Press, 1997), chap. 2.

39 **the British Empire:** See Michael Collins, "Decolonization," in *The Encyclopedia of Empire* (Chichester, U.K.: John Wiley & Sons, 2016).

40 **French-speaking lycées:** *Encyclopædia Britannica*, s.v. "Frantz Fanon," accessed Jan. 20, 2023, www.britannica.com/biography/Frantz-Fanon.

40 **like the Sorbonne:** *Encyclopædia Britannica*, s.v. "Habib Bourguiba," accessed Jan. 20, 2023, www.britannica.com/biography/Habib-Bourguiba.

40 **École Normale Supérieure:** *Encyclopædia Britannica*, s.v. "Assia Djebar," accessed Jan. 20, 2023, www.britannica.com/biography/Assia-Djebar.

40 **study at Cambridge:** *Encyclopædia Britannica*, s.v. "Jawaharlal Nehru," accessed Jan. 20, 2023, www.britannica.com/biography/Jawaharlal-Nehru.

40 **Oxford (Indira Gandhi):** *Encyclopædia Britannica*, s.v. "Indira Gandhi," accessed Jan. 20, 2023, www.britannica.com/biography/Indira-Gandhi.

40 **University of London:** *Encyclopædia Britannica*, s.v. "Jomo Kenyatta," accessed Jan. 20, 2023, www.britannica.com/biography/Jomo-Kenyatta.

40 **Inns of Court:** *Encyclopædia Britannica*, s.v. "Mahatma Gandhi," accessed Jan. 20, 2023, www.britannica.com/biography/Mahatma-Gandhi.

40 **Mohammed Ali Jinnah:** *Encyclopædia Britannica*, s.v. "Mohammed Ali Jinnah," accessed Jan. 20, 2023, www.britannica.com/biography/Mohammed-Ali-Jinnah.

40 **liberal nationalist tradition:** For example, the leader of the Indian nationalist movement, Jawaharlal Nehru. See C. A. Bayly, "The Ends of Liberalism and the Political Thought of Nehru's India," *Modern Intellectual History* 12, no. 3 (2015): 605–26, doi .org/10.1017/s1479244314000754.

40 **promises of Marxism:** While studying in France in the 1920s, Ho Chi Minh turned toward socialism, remaining influenced by Marxism-Leninism throughout his time as President of North Vietnam. See Sophie Quinn-Judge, *Ho Chi Minh: The Missing Years, 1919–1941* (Berkeley: University of California Press, 2003).

40 **exponents of both liberalism:** Some of the most influential liberal thinkers, like Immanuel Kant and Adam Smith, were staunch opponents of colonialism. But as its critics often point out, other important philosophers working in the tradition, including Adam Ferguson and Alexis de Tocqueville, were complicit in the colonial project or even defended it outright.

    John Stuart Mill, who worked for the British East India Company for much of his life, embodies this ambivalence. He strenuously opposed earlier notions according to which natural law gave the monarchs of Europe a right to rule over distant lands as well as newer racialist theories that denigrated Asians or Africans as biologically inferior. In one of his major works, *Considerations on Representative Government*, Mill even put forward a sophisticated explanation for why permanent rule by colonizers would, even if they were well intentioned, be deeply harmful to the colonized; colonial administrators can never fully understand local conditions, he warned, and would always be more beholden to their own values or interests than to those of the people they governed. But at the same time, Mill did accept a temporary defense of colonialism based on the claim that many peoples in Asia and Africa were not yet ready to rule themselves. As he put it in *Considerations on Representative Government*, "Outlying territories of some size and population, which are held as dependencies, that is, which are subject, more or less, to acts of sovereign power on the part of the paramount country, without being equally represented (if represented at all) in its Legislature, may be divided into two classes. Some are composed of people of similar civilization to the ruling country, capable of, and ripe for representative government, such as the British possessions in America and Australia. Others, like India, are still at a great distance from that state." See John Stuart Mill, *Considerations on Representative Government* (New York: Henry Holt, 1873), 337. For a discussion of Mill's views on India, and the colonial enterprise more broadly, see Duncan Bell, "John Stuart Mill on Colonies," *Political Theory* 38, no. 1 (2010): 34–64.

40 **socialism had made excuses:** Radical intellectuals who sought to align their countries with the communist world often seized upon liberal justifications of colonialism to discredit the entire tradition. But they faced a problem of their own. For Karl Marx's view of colonialism had a strikingly similar structure to that of John Stuart Mill. Marx did not believe that European nations had an inherent right to rule over others and lamented that the internal contradictions of capitalism, with its constant need for new markets driven by periodic crises of overproduction, would continue to push Western nations to undertake colonial adventures. But at the same time, he too believed that colonialism was a necessary step toward the progress of many nations.

In his analyses of India, for example, Marx argued that the region needed to undertake vast infrastructure projects like irrigation to make economic progress, become a modern nation, and get ready for socialism. According to him, neither India's traditional form of government, which he termed "Oriental despotism," nor a land reform, which would give farmers ownership over the small patches of land they cultivate, would be able to sustain the necessary investments. The least bad option, Marx concluded, was a form of colonial domination that would help to modernize India's economy and make the country ready for communist revolution. See Karl Marx, "The British Rule in India," *New-York Daily Tribune*, June 25, 1853, www.marxists.org/archive/marx/works/1853 /06/25.htm.

40 **"Underdeveloped countries ought":** Frantz Fanon, *The Wretched of the Earth*, trans. Constance Farrington (New York: Grove Press, 1963), 99. As Fanon makes clear, "It might have been generally thought that the time had come for the world, and particularly for the Third World, to choose between the capitalist and socialist systems. The underdeveloped countries, which have used the fierce competition which exists between the two systems in order to assure the triumph of their struggle for national liberation, should however refuse to become a factor in that competition" (Fanon, *Wretched of the Earth*, 98). As the secondary literature makes clear, this ambivalence about Marxism was typical of the most influential postcolonial thinkers. According to Julian Go, for example, "Du Bois, Fanon, Césaire, Cabral, and others all read Marx or Marxist writers, deployed Marxist ideas in their writings, and affiliated with communist or socialist political parties," but these thinkers also found fault with the tradition, arguing that "the problem was Communist Marxism's failure to take difference seriously enough, a problem that stemmed from its universalizing tendencies." Julian Go, "Waves of Postcolonial Thought," in *Postcolonial Thought and Social Theory* (New York: Oxford University Press, 2016).

41 **give him an aspirational name:** For an overview of the life and thought of Edward Said, see Timothy Brennan, *Places of Mind: A Life of Edward Said* (New York: Farrar, Straus and Giroux, 2021), as well as Edward Said's autobiographical writing, including *Out of Place: A Memoir* (New York: Vintage, 2012) and *Reflections on Exile and Other Essays* (London: Granta Books, 2013).

41 **be called Edward:** Pankaj Mishra, "The Reorientations of Edward Said," *New Yorker*, April 19, 2021, www.newyorker.com/magazine/2021/04/26/the-reorientations-of-edward -said.

41 **forced to abdicate:** *Encyclopædia Britannica*, s.v. "Edward VIII," accessed Jan. 29, 2023, www.britannica.com/biography/Edward-VIII.

41 **following a British curriculum:** Mishra, "Reorientations of Edward Said."

41 **New England boarding school:** "By the end of my first month at the school, I had risen to a

kind of bad eminence as a rabble-rousing troublemaker, talking in class, hobnobbing with other ringleaders of rebellion and disrespect, perpetually ready with an ironic or noncommittal answer, an attitude I regarded as a form of resistance to the British." Said, *Out of Place*, 186.

41 **PhD in English literature:** *Encyclopaedia Britannica*, s.v. "Edward Said," accessed July 10, 2022, www.britannica.com/biography/Edward-Said.

41 **"My whole education":** Edward Said, "Between Worlds," in *Reflections on Exile and Other Essays*.

41 **"creature of an American":** Quoted in Mishra, "Reorientations of Edward Said."

41 **"When students protesting the war":** Mishra, "Reorientations of Edward Said."

42 **forbidden to speak Arabic:** "With an unexceptionally Arab family name like 'Said,' connected to an improbably British first name . . . I was an uncomfortably anomalous student all through my early years: a Palestinian going to school in Egypt, with an English first name, an American passport, and no certain identity, at all." Said, "Between Worlds," 512.

42 **his colleagues and acquaintances:** As Said wrote in *Orientalism*, "My own experience of these matters is in part what made me write this book. The life of an Arab Palestinian in the West, particularly in America, is disheartening. . . . The web of racism, cultural stereotypes, political imperialism, dehumanising ideology holding in the Arab or the Muslim is very strong indeed, and it is this web which every Palestinian has come to feel as his uniquely punishing destiny." Edward Said, *Orientalism* (London: Penguin, 2003), 27.

42 **sabbatical in Lebanon:** Said, *Reflections on Exile and Other Essays*, 3.

42 **"Michel Foucault's notion of a discourse":** Said, *Orientalism*, 3.

42 **"the general liberal consensus":** Said, *Orientalism*, 10.

43 **"that political imperialism governs":** Said, *Orientalism*, 14.

43 **embrace grand narratives:** See also notes on pp. 308–9.

43 **purpose of *Orientalism*:** "For readers in the so-called Third World, this study proposes itself as a step towards an understanding not so much of Western politics and of the non-Western world in those politics as of the *strength* of Western cultural discourse, a strength too often mistaken as decorative or merely 'superstructural.' My hope is to illustrate the formidable structure of cultural domination and, specifically for formerly colonized peoples, the dangers and temptations of employing those structures upon themselves or upon others." Said, *Orientalism*, 25.

43 **cited almost eighty thousand times:** "Orientalism," Google Scholar, accessed July 10, 2022, scholar.google.com/scholar?cluster=12103548631685263959&hl=en&as_sdt=0,44.

43 **postmodernism quickly gained popularity:** See Paul Ardoin, "Poststructuralism and Its Discontents," in *Oxford Research Encyclopedia of Literature* (2021), doi.org/10.1093/acrefore/9780190201098.013.1002. For a literary treatment, see Jeffrey Eugenides, *The Marriage Plot* (New York: Farrar, Straus and Giroux, 2011).

43 **"institutionalization and professionalization":** Said lectured on the subject at a conference in 1982. As Timothy Brennan put it in his biography of Said, "The same theories that a decade earlier seemed an intellectual adventure had given way to coded jargons of accreditation where the university was involved in little more than an assembly-line production of dubious professional 'theorists.'" Brennan, *Places of Mind*, 219.

43 **"retreat into a labyrinth":** Edward Said, *The World, the Text, and the Critic* (Cambridge, Mass.: Harvard University Press, 1983), 3.

43 **"commit himself to descriptions":** Said, *World*, 87.

44 **"vastly simplified view":** Said, *World*, 244.

44 **"justify political quietism":** Said, *World*, 245.

44 **form of discourse analysis:** In the 1990s, one anthropologist helpfully summarized how this form of discourse analysis was being used in his discipline: "In most moral models there is some way to correct evil. In the current moral model in anthropology this is done by unmasking the symbolic hegemony that hides and legitimates oppression. The morally corrective act is denunciation. One can also act morally by giving voice to those who resist

oppression; this at least identifies the oppression and the oppressors. Nowadays, one can have a moral career in anthropology; having a moral career in anthropology is being known for what one has denounced." Roy D'Andrade, "Moral Models in Anthropology," *Current Anthropology* 36, no. 3 (June 1995): 400, www.jstor.org/stable/2744050.

44 **dominant mode of inquiry:** This embrace of discourse analysis in fields like women's studies and disability studies often faced harsh criticism from more "old-school" materialist academics. See, for example, Stevi Jackson's critique of the postmodern "cultural turn" from "things" to "words": Stevi Jackson, "Why a Materialist Feminism Is (Still) Possible—and Necessary," *Women's Studies International Forum* 24, no. 3–4 (2001): 283–93, doi.org/10.1016/s0277-5395(01)00187-x. Susan Bordo has criticized this turn in similar terms: "On the sexualization and objectification of the female body contemporary feminism (with some notable exceptions) is strikingly muted. Some forms of postmodern feminism . . . are worse than muted, . . . distressingly at one with the culture in celebrating the creative agency of individuals and denying systemic pattern." Susan Bordo, *Unbearable Weight: Feminism, Western Culture, and the Body* (Berkeley: University of California Press, 2013).

44 **"wretched of the earth":** This is of course an allusion to one of the seminal texts in the postcolonial tradition, Fanon's *Wretched of the Earth.*

45 **Most postcolonial scholars:** Gayatri Spivak, "Can the Subaltern Speak?," in *Marxism and the Interpretation of Culture*, ed. Cary Nelson and Lawrence Grossberg (London: Macmillan, 1988).

45 **Calcutta in 1942:** Jon Simons, *From Agamben to Žižek: Contemporary Critical Theorists* (Edinburgh: Edinburgh University Press, 2013), 210. For overviews of Spivak's work, see also Stephen Morton, *Gayatri Chakravorty Spivak* (New York: Routledge, 2002); and Sangeeta Ray, *Gayatri Chakravorty Spivak: In Other Words* (Malden, Mass.: Wiley-Blackwell, 2009). There are also useful compendiums of her interviews, including Gayatri Chakravorty Spivak, *The Post-colonial Critic: Interviews, Strategies, Dialogues*, ed. Sarah Harasym (New York: Routledge, 2014).

45 **writing the introduction:** Jacques Derrida, *Of Grammatology*, trans. Gayatri Chakravorty Spivak (Baltimore: Johns Hopkins University Press, 1976).

45 **scholars like Spivak:** Gayatri Spivak, "Criticism, Feminism, and the Institution: An Interview with Gayatri Chakravorty Spivak," interview by Elizabeth Gross, *Thesis Eleven* 10–11, no. 1 (Feb. 1985): 178, doi.org/10.1177/072551368501000113.

45 **embrace identity markers:** This involved rejecting the notion that there might be something universal about human beings or their dignity in an even more radical way than Foucault had done. "When I first read Derrida I . . . was very interested to see that he was actually dismantling the philosophical tradition from the *inside* rather than from the *outside*, because of course we were brought up in an education system in India where the name of the hero of that philosophical system was the universal human being, and we were taught that if we could begin to approach an internalization of that universal human being, then we would be human." Spivak, "Criticism, Feminism, and the Institution," 180.

45 **"I think we have to choose again strategically":** Spivak, "Criticism, Feminism, and the Institution," 178.

46 **use essentialist concepts:** Spivak, "Criticism, Feminism, and the Institution," 184.

46 **common self-definition:** Spivak, "Criticism, Feminism, and the Institution," 184. Ironically, many scholars who are influenced by the idea of strategic essentialism would now regard the idea that all (and only) women have a clitoris as deeply offensive. See also note on p. 337.

46 **on behalf of the "oppressed":** For a critical appraisal of the influence of strategic essentialism, see Diana Fuss, *Essentially Speaking: Feminism, Nature, and Difference* (New York: Routledge, 1989).

46 **attempt to square the circle:** For a more detailed discussion of the influence that strategic

essentialism has had on activist spaces and popular discourse, see chapter 8 on standpoint epistemology.

46 **dismantle the category:** This is the position that Barbara and Karen Fields have taken with regard to race. See Karen E. Fields and Barbara Jeanne Fields, *Racecraft: The Soul of Inequality in American Life* (London: Verso, 2022). For a deeper discussion of their work, see chapter 11.

47 **embrace of strategic essentialism:** For a fuller discussion of the influence of strategic essentialism on what I call "progressive separatism," see chapter 11.

Chapter 3: The Rejection of the Civil Rights Movement and the Rise of Critical Race Theory

49 **only five African American legislators:** Representatives Dawson (D-IL), Diggs (D-MI), Hawkins (D-CA), Nix (D-PA), and Powell (D-NY) served in the Eighty-eighth Congress (Jan. 3, 1963, to Jan. 3, 1965). "Black-American Members by Congress," U.S. House of Representatives: History, Art & Archives, accessed Mar. 19, 2023, history.house.gov/Exhibitions-and-Publications/BAIC/Historical-Data/Black-American-Representatives-and-Senators-by-Congress/.

49 **unconstitutional to maintain:** *Brown v. Board of Education of Topeka*, 347 U.S. 483 (1954).

49 **banning employment discrimination:** See Title VII and the Twenty-fourth Amendment for employment and literacy tests, respectively. "Title VII of the Civil Rights Act of 1964," EEOC, www.eeoc.gov/statutes/title-vii-civil-rights-act-1964; Twenty-fourth Amendment, U.S. Constitution, constitution.congress.gov/constitution/amendment-24/.

50 **choreographed boycotts and sit-ins:** See, for example, Russell Freedman, *Freedom Walkers: The Story of the Montgomery Bus Boycott* (New York: Holiday House, 2009).

50 **"I Have a Dream":** Martin Luther King, "I Have a Dream," Aug. 28, 1963, transcript provided by "Read Martin Luther King Jr.'s 'I Have a Dream' Speech in Its Entirety," NPR, Jan. 16, 2023,

50 **won election to high office:** Georgia is represented in the Senate by Raphael Warnock, a Black pastor who was previously the senior pastor at Ebenezer Baptist Church, where Martin Luther King Jr. was co-pastor from 1960 to 1968. (He won election in a run-off against Herschel Walker, another African American; Jon Ossoff, the other senator for Georgia, has a Jewish father.) Black women make up 16.9 percent of Georgia's state legislature. Meanwhile, Virginia was the first state to elect a Black governor, Douglas Wilder, in 1990; its current lieutenant governor, Winsome Earle-Sears, is a Black woman. "Lieutenant Governor of Virginia Winsome Earle-Sears," Seal of the Commonwealth of Virginia, accessed Jan. 29, 2023, www.ltgov.virginia.gov/; Douglas Wilder, Library of Virginia, accessed Mar. 19, 2023, www.lva.virginia.gov/exhibits/political/douglas_wilder.htm; Taylor Reimann, "Georgia Leads the Nation in Black Female Legislators," Georgia Public Broadcasting, Oct. 16, 2021, www.gpb.org/news/2021/11/16/georgia-leads-the-nation-in-black-female-legislators.

50 **idea of interracial marriage:** Justin McCarthy, "U.S. Approval of Interracial Marriage at New High of 94%," Gallup, Sept. 10, 2021, news.gallup.com/poll/354638/approval-interracial-marriage-new-high.aspx.

50 **Congress contains sixty-two:** Katherine Schaeffer, "U.S. Congress Continues to Grow in Racial, Ethnic Diversity," Pew Research Center, Jan. 9, 2023, www.pewresearch.org/fact-tank/2023/01/09/u-s-congress-continues-to-grow-in-racial-ethnic-diversity/. Note that this is reasonably close to the share of African Americans in the overall population. African American legislators make up 12 percent of Congress; meanwhile, African Americans, according to the 2020 census, make up 14 percent of the overall population.

50 **because of "white flight":** "Wayne County (Detroit) lost 26.6 percent of its white population in the 1970s. Cook County (Chicago) lost 15.5 percent, and Cuyahoga County (Cleveland) 20.1 percent." Emily Badger, "Mapping 60 Years of White Flight, Brain Drain,

and American Migration," Bloomberg, Nov. 1, 2013, www.bloomberg.com/news/articles /2013-11-01/mapping-60-years-of-white-flight-brain-drain-and-american-migration. Additionally, see Matt Nowlin, Kelly Davila, and Unai Miguel Andres, "Neighborhood Change, 1970–2016," SAVI, Summer 2018, www.savi.org/feature_report/neighborhood -change-1970-2016; Patrick Reardon, "City About Equal in Terms of Race," *Chicago Tribune,* Sept. 23, 1986, www.chicagotribune.com/news/ct-xpm-1986-09-23-8603110287 -story.html.

50 **Black pupils languished:** Charles T. Clotfelter, *After Brown: The Rise and Retreat of School Desegregation* (Princeton, N.J.: Princeton University Press, 2006).

50 **much less wealth:** As of 2011, the median Black household income ($32,229) was less than two-thirds of the median white household income ($52,214) (Carmen DeNavas-Walt, Bernadette D. Proctor, and Jessica C. Smith, *Income, Poverty, and Health Insurance Coverage in the United States: 2012,* U.S. Census Bureau, Sept. 2013, 7, 32, 34). In 2019, the wealth of the median white family ($188,200) was eight times the wealth of the median Black family ($24,100) (Emily Moss et al., "The Black-White Wealth Gap Left Black Households More Vulnerable," Brookings, December 8, 2020, www.brookings.edu /blog/up-front/2020/12/08/the-black-white-wealth-gap-left-black-households-more -vulnerable/).

51 **continue to be overrepresented:** Audrey Murrell, "The 'Privilege Bias' and Diversity Challenges in College Admissions," *Forbes,* May 7, 2019, www.forbes.com/sites/audreymurrell /2019/05/07/the-privilege-bias-and-diversity-challenges-in-college-admissions/?sh =a2f2b4a139a0.

51 **cold and alienating:** For example, see Richard D. Kahlenberg, "How Low-Income Students Are Fitting In at Elite Colleges," *Atlantic,* Feb. 24, 2016, www.theatlantic.com /education/archive/2016/02/the-rise-of-first-generation-college-students/470664/; Martha Burwell and Bernice Maldonado, "How Does Your Company Support 'First-Generation Professionals'?," *Harvard Business Review,* Jan. 7, 2022, hbr.org/2022/01/how -does-your-company-support-first-generation-professionals.

51 **predominantly Black neighborhoods:** Stuart M. Butler and Jonathan Grabinsky, "Tackling the Legacy of Persistent Urban Inequality and Concentrated Poverty," Brookings, November 16, 2020, www.brookings.edu/blog/up-front/2020/11/16/tackling-the -legacy-of-persistent-urban-inequality-and-concentrated-poverty/.

51 **African Americans remain incarcerated:** As of the end of 2018, there were 465,200 Black inmates in state or federal prison. John Gramlich, "Black Imprisonment Rate in the U.S. Has Fallen by a Third Since 2006," Pew Research Center, May. 6, 2020, www .pewresearch.org/fact-tank/2020/05/06/share-of-black-white-hispanic-americans-in -prison-2018-vs-2006/.

51 **police shootings are disproportionately:** Gabriel L. Schwartz and Jaquelyn L. Jahn, "Mapping Fatal Police Violence Across U.S. Metropolitan Areas: Overall Rates and Racial/Ethnic Inequities, 2013–2017," *PLOS One* 15, no. 6 (2020), doi.org/10.1371 /journal.pone.0229686.

51 **social media has given hate speech:** Zachary Laub, "Hate Speech on Social Media: Global Comparisons," Council on Foreign Relations, June 7, 2019, https://www.cfr.org /backgrounder/hate-speech-social-media-global-comparisons; Kim Hart, "Hate Speech Soars for Young Social Media Users," Axios, Mar. 17, 2021, https://www.axios.com/2021 /03/17/hate-speech-social-media-youth-2020. "Report: Online Hate Increasing Against Minorities, Says Expert," OHCHR, March 23, 2021, www.ohchr.org/en/stories/2021 /03/report-online-hate-increasing-against-minorities-says-expert.

51 **first African American judge:** "William Henry Hastie," Howard University School of Law, accessed Mar. 24, 2023, law.howard.edu/brownat50/BrownBios/BioJudgeWmHastie .html.

51 **fight for equality:** Urban Agenda, "Derrick Bell on Racism," filmed 1994, YouTube, video, 1:42, www.youtube.com/watch?v=RVy8w0Sz9LY&t=102s.

52 **imperative to desegregate schools:** Urban Agenda, "Derrick Bell on Racism," 1:42.

52 **encounter with Hastie:** For an overview of Derrick Bell's life and work, see, for example, Richard Delgado and Jean Stefancic, eds., *The Derrick Bell Reader* (New York: New York University Press, 2005). Also, Jelani Cobb, "The Man Behind Critical Race Theory," *New Yorker*, Sept. 13, 2021, www.newyorker.com/magazine/2021/09/20/the-man-behind -critical-race-theory.

52 **only Black student:** Fred A. Bernstein, "Derrick Bell, Law Professor and Rights Advocate, Dies at 80," *New York Times*, Oct. 6, 2011, www.nytimes.com/2011/10/06/us/derrick -bell-pioneering-harvard-law-professor-dies-at-80.html.

52 **quit his government position:** Bernstein, "Derrick Bell, Law Professor and Rights Advocate, Dies at 80."

53 **three hundred cases desegregating:** "In Memoriam: Derrick Bell, 1930–2011," NYU School of Law, accessed Jan. 30, 2023, www.law.nyu.edu/news/DERRICK_BELL _MEMORIAM.

53 **newly "integrated" schools:** Cobb, "Man Behind Critical Race Theory."

53 **position as a faculty member:** Bernstein, "Derrick Bell, Law Professor and Rights Advocate, Dies at 80."

54 **"Any steps to achieve":** Derrick Bell, "Serving Two Masters: Integration Ideals and Client Interests in School Desegregation Litigation," *Yale Law Journal* 85, no. 4 (March 1976): 470, doi.org/10.2307/795339. See also 482–83 for further context.

54 **"serve two masters":** Bell, "Serving Two Masters." See in particular 482, 512–15.

54 **"Having convinced themselves that *Brown*":** Bell, "Serving Two Masters," 482.

54 **open to legal remedies:** As Bell asked, "Why, one might ask, have [civil rights lawyers] been so unwilling to recognize the increasing futility of 'total desegregation,' and, more important, the increasing number of defections within the black community?" (Bell, "Serving Two Masters," 488.) In a 2004 book, Bell laid out his view even more explicitly: Derrick A. Bell, *Silent Covenants: Brown v. Board of Education and the Unfulfilled Hopes for Racial Reform* (Oxford: Oxford University Press, 2006), 20–28.

54 **merit of desegregation:** See in particular Derrick Bell, "The Real Cost of Racial Equality," *Civil Liberties Review* 1 (1974): 79–95; Derrick A. Bell Jr., "*Brown v. Board of Education* and the Interest-Convergence Dilemma," *Harvard Law Review* 93, no. 3 (Jan. 1980): 518–33; Derrick Bell, "Racial Realism," *Connecticut Law Review* 24, no. 2 (Winter 1992): 363; and his allegorical "The Chronicle of the Space Traders," in Delgado and Stefancic, *Derrick Bell Reader*, 57–73.

54 **writings of Frederick Douglass:** For a good introduction to Frederick Douglass's speeches and writings, see his autobiographical *The Life and Times of Frederick Douglass: From 1817–1882* (London: Christian Age Office, 1881), as well as Philip S. Foner and Yuval Taylor, eds., *Frederick Douglass: Selected Speeches and Writings* (Chicago: Chicago Review Press, 2000). For his view of the Constitution and the Declaration of Independence, see in particular "What to the Slave Is the Fourth of July?" As he writes there, rejecting the view that slavery was sanctioned by the Constitution, "I hold there is neither warrant, license, nor sanction of the hateful thing; but, interpreted as it ought to be interpreted, the Constitution is a GLORIOUS LIBERTY DOCUMENT. Read its preamble, consider its purposes. Is slavery among them? Is it at the gateway? Or is it in the temple? It is neither." That is why, at the end of the speech, Douglass emphasizes that "notwithstanding the dark picture I have this day presented of the state of the nation, I do not despair of this country"; rather, he draws "encouragement from the Declaration of Independence, the great principles it contains, and the genius of American institutions."

54 **sermons of Martin Luther King Jr.:** Similarly, it is sometimes suggested that Martin Luther King Jr. grew much more radical in his rejection of American ideals and institutions in the last months before his tragic assassination. But he clearly expressed his enduring faith in their ability to inspire positive change on the eve of his death: "Because if I had sneezed, I wouldn't have been around here in 1960, when students all over the South

started sitting-in at lunch counters. And I knew that as they were sitting in, they were really standing up for the best in the American dream and taking the whole nation back to those great wells of democracy, which were dug deep by the founding fathers in the Declaration of Independence and the Constitution." Martin Luther King Jr., "I've Been to the Mountaintop" (speech, Memphis, April 3, 1968).

54 **speeches of Barack Obama:** This stance is characteristic of much of Barack Obama's writing, speaking, and political career. But it is probably expressed most clearly in his two most famous speeches on race, which bookend his presidency. The first was held when he was a presidential candidate laying out his vision of race in America in the wake of controversy over the Reverend Jeremiah Wright, whose sermons were in many ways a theological channeling of critical race theory. As Obama said in Philadelphia in March 2008, "The answer to the slavery question was already embedded within our Constitution—a Constitution that had at its very core the ideal of equal citizenship under the law; a Constitution that promised its people liberty and justice and a union that could be and should be perfected over time" (Barack Obama, "A More Perfect Union" [speech, Philadelphia, March 18, 2008], NPR, www.npr.org/templates/story/story.php?storyId=88478467). Obama returned to this theme when, during the second term of his presidency, he spoke at the fiftieth anniversary of the march on Selma. As he said at that point, "What greater expression of faith in the American experiment than [the march on Selma], what greater form of patriotism is there than the belief that America is not yet finished, that we are strong enough to be self-critical, that each successive generation can look upon our imperfections and decide that it is in our power to remake this nation to more closely align with our highest ideals?" (Barack Obama, "Remarks by the President at the 50th Anniversary of the Selma to Montgomery Marches," March 7, 2015, National Archives and Records Administration, obamawhitehouse.archives.gov/the-press-office/2015/03/07/remarks-president-50th-anniversary-selma-montgomery-marches.)

55 **"America has defaulted":** Martin Luther King, "I Have a Dream," Aug. 28, 1963, transcript provided by "Read Martin Luther King Jr.'s 'I Have a Dream' Speech in Its Entirety," NPR, Jan. 16, 2023, https://www.npr.org/2010/01/18/122701268/i-have-a-dream-speech-in-its-entirety.

55 **set of postmodern critiques:** On the institutional relationship between critical legal studies and the emerging field of critical race theory, as well as the broader influence of postmodernism on the tradition, see Kimberlé Williams Crenshaw, "Twenty Years of Critical Race Theory: Looking Back to Move Forward," *Connecticut Law Review* 43, no. 5 (July 2011): 1253–352. For critiques of critical legal studies from key scholars within the emerging discipline of critical race theory, see "Part 2: Critical Race Theory and Critical Legal Studies: Contestation and Coalition," in *Critical Race Theory: The Key Writings That Formed the Movement*, ed. Kimberlé Crenshaw et al. (New York: New Press, 1995), 63–126. See especially Harlon T. Dalton, "The Clouded Prism: Minority Critique of the Critical Legal Studies Movement."

56 **racial self-interest:** Bell, "Interest-Convergence Dilemma." See also Bell, *Silent Covenants*.

56 **fight for their country:** Bell, "Interest-Convergence Dilemma," 524–25.

56 **the American South:** Bell, "Interest-Convergence Dilemma," 525.

56 **"to provide immediate credibility":** Bell, "Interest-Convergence Dilemma," 524.

56 **"The interests of blacks in achieving":** Bell, "Interest-Convergence Dilemma," 523.

56 **"Even those Herculean efforts":** Derrick Bell, "The Racism Is Permanent Thesis: Courageous Revelation or Unconscious Denial of Racial Genocide," *Capital University Law Review* 22, no. 3 (1993): 573. With major setbacks inevitable, Bell predicted, even the most fundamental advances of the civil rights era would prove "temporary." Bell, "Racism Is Permanent Thesis," 578.

56 **"Racism," he contended:** Bell, "Racism Is Permanent Thesis," 571, 573.

56 **its idealistic hope:** Noah Adams, "The Inspiring Force of 'We Shall Overcome,'" NPR,

Aug. 28, 2013, www.npr.org/2013/08/28/216482943/the-inspiring-force-of-we-shall
-overcome.

56 "theme song": Bell, "Racism Is Permanent Thesis," 572.

57 "contemporary color barriers": Bell, "Racial Realism," 374.

57 "review and replacement": Bell, "Racial Realism," 374.

57 explicit group rights: It is worth noting, however, that Bell found the race-sensitive
policies that were implemented during his lifetime to be insufficient. For example, he
recognized that affirmative action had been helpful to African Americans. But, he maintained in 2000, "as with so many other reforms in U.S. society, though often the result of
efforts by Black people, [it] has been of far more help to Whites, particularly for White
women" (Derrick Bell, "Epilogue: Affirmative Action: Another Instance of Racial
Workings in the United States," *Journal of Negro Education* 69, no. 1/2 [2000]: 145–49,
www.jstor.org/stable/2696270).

57 form of a course: Official Register of Harvard University, *Harvard Law School Cata-
logue 1970/71* 67, no. 19 (Sept. 1970): 112–13, iiif.lib.harvard.edu/manifests/view/drs
:427001963$1i.

57 more traditional course: Lauren Michele Jackson, "The Void That Critical Race Theory
Was Created to Fill," *New Yorker*, July 27, 2021, www.newyorker.com/culture/cultural
-comment/the-void-that-critical-race-theory-was-created-to-fill.

57 found this unacceptable: Jackson, "Void."

57 those young academics: Jackson, "Void."

58 organize a summer workshop: Angela Onwuachi-Willig, "Celebrating Critical Race
Theory at 20," *Iowa Law Review* 94 (2009).

58 A new movement: Isaac Gottesman, *The Critical Turn in Education: From Marxist Critique
to Poststructuralist Feminism to Critical Theories of Race* (New York: Routledge, 2016), 124.

58 key organizational role: For an overview of key writings by Kimberlé Crenshaw, especially on the term she coined, see Kimberlé Crenshaw, *On Intersectionality: Essential
Writings* (New York: New Press, 2017).

58 "That provided a lens": Amanda Cassandra, "Kimberle Crenshaw: A Legal Jet-Setter,"
New York Amsterdam News, Aug. 5, 2005, 5.

58 coined a term: Kimberlé Crenshaw, "Demarginalizing the Intersection of Race and Sex:
A Black Feminist Critique of Antidiscrimination Doctrine, Feminist Theory, and Antiracist Politics," *University of Chicago Legal Forum* 1989, no. 1 (1989): 139–67. While
Crenshaw coined the term "intersectionality," the ideas behind the concept had already
been present in feminist theory and activism for several decades at that point. One of the
most prominent early expressions of this idea comes from the Combahee River Collective, a Black feminist group located in Boston. As they wrote in a famous declaration,
"There have always been Black women activists—some known, like Sojourner Truth,
Harriet Tubman, Frances E. W. Harper, Ida B. Wells Barnett, and Mary Church Terrell, and
thousands upon thousands unknown—who have had a shared awareness of how their
sexual identity combined with their racial identity to make their whole life situation and
the focus of their political struggles unique." Combahee River Collective, "The Combahee River Collective Statement," from Library of Congress, April 1977, https://www
.loc.gov/item/lcwaN0028151/.

58 In one case, for example: Crenshaw, "Demarginalizing the Intersection," 141.

59 "Under this view, Black women": Crenshaw, "Demarginalizing the Intersection," 143.

59 her early articles: Her early articles on the topic include "Mapping the Margins: Intersectionality, Identity Politics, and Violence Against Women of Color," *Stanford Law
Review* 43, no. 6 (1991); and "Demarginalizing the Intersection."

59 unlikely rallying cry: The concept of intersectionality is not without criticism from
within women's studies, in particular because of its ambiguity. Jennifer Nash is one of the
most prominent modern examples. See Jennifer C. Nash, *Black Feminism Reimagined:
After Intersectionality* (Durham, N.C.: Duke University Press, 2019).

59 **like Donna Haraway:** Donna Haraway, "Situated Knowledges: The Science Question in Feminism and the Privilege of Partial Perspective," *Feminist Studies* 14, no. 3 (1988), doi .org/10.2307/3178066.

60 **"The perception of any situation":** Aikaterini Antonopoulou, "Situated Knowledges and Shifting Grounds: Questioning the Reality Effect of High-Resolution Imagery," *Becoming a Feminist Architect* 7, no. 1 (Nov. 2017): 53. For the original article, see Haraway, "Situated Knowledges."

60 **"a neutral perspective":** Derrick Bell, "Who's Afraid of Critical Race Theory?," *University of Illinois Law Review* 1995, no. 4 (1995): 901.

60 **"We must learn to trust":** Charles R. Lawrence, "The Word and the River: Pedagogy as Scholarship as Struggle," *Southern California Law Review* 65, no. 2551 (1992): 2231–98.

60 **went much further:** Haraway, "Situated Knowledges."

60 **intersectionality thus came to stand:** As the women and gender studies textbook *Feminisms Matter* put it in a primer on intersectionality, "Knowledge [itself] is *located* in lived experiences and contexts." Victoria Bromley, *Feminisms Matter: Debates, Theories, Activism* (Toronto: University of Toronto Press, 2012), 48.

60 **must also be committed:** Crenshaw, "Demarginalizing the Intersection," 166–67. In the world of activism, for instance, younger employees grew concerned that the Guttmacher Institute, an NGO that seeks to promote sexual and reproductive health, was too narrowly focusing on reproductive freedom. As one employee put it, "there were questions about why the group was so abortion-focused," even as a conservative Supreme Court moved to overturn *Roe v. Wade*. See Ryan Grim, "Meltdowns Have Brought Progressive Advocacy Groups to a Standstill at a Critical Moment in World History," *Intercept*, June 13, 2022, theintercept.com/2022/06/13/progressive-organizing-infighting-callout -culture/.

61 **set of specific positions:** For example, the activist and co-chair of the 2017 Women's March Linda Sarsour denied that one could be a feminist and a Zionist: "It just doesn't make any sense for someone to say, 'Is there room for people who support the state of Israel and do not criticize it in the movement?' There can't be in feminism. You either stand up for the rights of all women, including Palestinians, or none. There's just no way around it." Collier Meyerson, "Can You Be a Zionist Feminist? Linda Sarsour Says No," *Nation*, March 13, 2017, www.thenation.com/article/archive/can-you-be-a-zionist-feminist-linda -sarsour-says-no/. Also see Eric Levitz, "The Women's Strike Can't Make Room for All Women," *Intelligencer*, March 8, 2017, nymag.com/intelligencer/2017/03/the-womens -strike-cant-make-room-for-all-women.html.

61 **In 1996, the journalist:** Larissa MacFarquhar, "The Color of the Law," *Lingua Franca*, July/Aug. 1996, linguafranca.mirror.theinfo.org/9607/criticalrace.html.

Chapter 4: The Identity Synthesis

63 **questions of identity:** Steven Best, "Culture Turn," in *The Blackwell Encyclopedia of Sociology* (2008), doi.org/10.1002/9781405165518.wbeosc201.

64 **the cultural left:** Chris Rojek and Bryan Turner, "Decorative Sociology: Towards a Critique of the Cultural Turn," *Sociological Review* 48, no. 4 (2000), 365, doi.org/10.1111 /1467-954x.00236.

64 **became less interested:** Rojek and Turner, "Decorative Sociology."

64 **a devoted home:** New departments such as women's studies were closely tied to activism from their inception. As the prominent feminist scholar Jean Robinson put it, "When women's studies was born in the mid-1970's, politics was its mid-wife." Quoted in Scott Jaschik, "'The Evolution of American Women's Studies,'" *Inside Higher Ed*, March 27, 2009, www.insidehighered.com/news/2009/03/27/evolution-american-womens-studies.

64 **founded academic units:** By 2013, 361 American institutions had formal departments focused on the experiences of African Americans, with more than 1,000 offering

programs or courses in the subject (Abdul Alkalimat et al., *African American Studies 2013: A National Web-Based Survey* [Urbana: University of Illinois at Urbana Champaign Department of African American Studies, 2013], afro.illinois.edu). More than 700 institutions now offer programs in gender studies (Michele Berger and Cheryl Radeloff, *Transforming Scholarship: Why Women's and Gender Studies Students Are Changing Themselves and the World* [New York: Routledge, 2022], 6–7). About 230 institutions offer programs in Latino studies ("Latin American Studies and Caribbean Studies Colleges," College Board, accessed July 7, 2022, bigfuture.collegeboard.org/college-search /filters?mc=Latin_American_Studies_and_Caribbean_Studies). There are also numerous programs in queer studies, disability studies, and Asian American studies.

64 **not to overstate:** There are important differences of emphasis—and in some cases even of prevailing intellectual consensus—between different departments. Scholars in gender studies like Judith Butler, for example, have long celebrated the fluidity of identity categories, especially those centered on gender. By contrast, scholars in African American or Latino studies have tended to emphasize the extent to which racial categories, though socially constructed, neither are nor should be subject to change through the agency of an individual.

64 **Boston University's Ibram X. Kendi:** Similarly, some gender studies departments are now deeply divided between academics who defend the social importance of biological sex, like Kathleen Stock, and those who argue that this distinction is discriminatory, like Katrina Karkazis.

66 **collectively make progress:** For an excellent recent defense of this position, see Jonathan Rauch, *The Constitution of Knowledge: A Defense of Truth* (Washington, D.C.: Brookings Institution Press, 2021).

66 **"expresses skepticism toward":** Mari Matsuda et al., *Words That Wound: Critical Race Theory, Assaultive Speech, and the First Amendment* (New York: Routledge, 2018), 6. Similarly, Derrick Bell argues that claims to objective truth merely try to pass "the privileged choice of the privileged . . . off as the universal authority and the universal good." Derrick Bell, "Who's Afraid of Critical Race Theory?," *University of Illinois Law Review* 1995, no. 4 (1995): 901.

66 **"Liberal democracy and racial subordination":** Richard Delgado, *The Rodrigo Chronicles: Conversations About America and Race* (New York: New York University Press, 1995), 144. In the place of a futile search for universal truths, the adherents of the identity synthesis advocate an embrace of relativism and subjectivism. As Charles Lawrence has put the point, "We must learn to trust our own senses, feelings, and experiences and give them authority." Charles R. Lawrence, "The Word and the River: Pedagogy as Scholarship as Struggle," *Southern California Law Review* 65, no. 2551 (1992): 2253. Delgado echoes a similar sentiment: Those who pretend to be guided by objective forms of inquiry, he says, "tell stories too. But the ones they tell—about merit, causation, blame, responsibility, and racial justice—do not seem to them like stories at all, but the truth." Richard Delgado, "On Telling Stories in School," *Vanderbilt Law Review* 46, no. 3 (April 1993): 666.

66 **other intellectual traditions:** Linda Martin Alcoff, for example, argues that "Latina/o philosophy is not simply distinct from Anglo-American and European philosophy"; rather, it "provides a critique of essentialist, idealized abstractions that pursue a decontextualized truth." Deborah R. Vargas and Linda Martin Alcoff, "Philosophy," in *Keywords for Latina/o Studies*, ed. Deborah R. Vargas, Nancy Raquel Mirabal, and Lawrence La Fountain–Stokes (New York: New York University Press, 2017), 159.

66 **core of "decolonial theory":** As summarized by María Lugones, "Decolonial," in Vargas, Mirabal, and La Fountain–Stokes, *Keywords for Latina/o Studies*, 44.

66 **tools of "discourse analysis":** This focus on discourse, as the philosopher Martha Nussbaum puts it, "is the virtually complete turning from the material side of life [by feminist academia], toward a type of verbal and symbolic politics that makes only the flimsiest of connections with the real situation of real women." Martha C. Nussbaum,

"The Professor of Parody," *New Republic*, Feb. 22, 1999, newrepublic.com/article /150687/professor-parody.

67 **inadvertently perpetuate discrimination:** "Elimination of Harmful Language Initiative," Stanford University, Dec. 19, 2022, s.wsj.net/public/resources/documents /stanfordlanguage.pdf.

67 **a newly popular term:** For a full discussion of the meaning of and trouble with the term "cultural appropriation," see chapter 9.

67 *Studenten* **with** *Studierende*: Julia Goncalves, "StudentInnen, Student*innen, or Student_innen: How Six German Universities Are Constructing Gender Equitable Language and Increasing Female Linguistic and Visual Representation" (2020), Chancellor's Honors Program Projects, trace.tennessee.edu/utk_chanhonoproj/2381.

67 **render ordinary language:** Some critics who broadly share leftist goals have criticized this strategy as ineffective. As one prominent scholar wrote about his own field of inquiry, "Critical disability studies writers generally seem much more interested in texts and discourses than in the ordinary lives of disabled people" (Tom Shakespeare, *Disability Rights and Wrongs Revisited* [New York: Routledge, 2014], 52). As a result, another complainant points out, scholars who are focused on discourse analysis have "diverted critical attention from identifying and challenging material forces underpinning disablement 'towards a politically benign focus on culture, language, and discourse'" (Colin Barnes, *Understanding the Social Model of Disability: Past, Present, and Future* [New York: Routledge, 2012], 23). But it would be a mistake to underestimate the enormous influence that this form of analysis has had on the world, both within the university and beyond. The fight to control the discourse has become a key part of contemporary activism, and the real power that the identity synthesis has, for better or worse, accrued in elite institutions suggests that this strategy has not proven nearly as toothless as some of its sympathetic critics suggest.

68 **are "socially constructed":** As some advocates of the identity synthesis recognize, a concept could be both socially constructed and extremely hard, or even impossible, to change. But as the concept of social construction is usually deployed, it implies the point that something that seems natural is actually subject to human agency; often, it is paired with an explicit call to action to change or overthrow it.

68 **to disrupt them:** See Judith Butler, *Gender Trouble: Feminism and the Subversion of Identity*, 2nd ed. (New York: Routledge, 1999).

69 **a permanent condition:** See Derrick Bell, *Faces at the Bottom of the Well: The Permanence of Racism* (New York: Basic Books, 2018).

69 **more pessimistic tradition:** Ta-Nehisi Coates, *Between the World and Me* (New York: Spiegel & Grau, 2014), esp. 149–52.

69 **no means limited:** See, for example, the philosopher Martha Nussbaum's biting critique of Judith Butler and her brand of feminism: "The new feminism, moreover, instructs its members that there is little room for large-scale social change, and maybe no room at all. We are all, more or less, prisoners of the structures of power that have defined our identity as women; we can never change those structures in a large-scale way, and we can never escape from them. All that we can hope to do is to find spaces within the structures of power in which to parody them, to poke fun at them, to transgress them in speech. And so symbolic verbal politics, in addition to being offered as a type of real politics, is held to be the only politics that is really possible." Nussbaum, "Professor of Parody."

69 **progress is an illusion:** Larry Kramer, "For Gays, the Worst Is Yet to Come. Again," *New York Times*, July 11, 2018, www.nytimes.com/2018/07/11/opinion/gay-rights-larry-kramer .html.

70 **jettison the aspiration:** See examples in chapter 12.

70 **"Only aggressive, color-conscious efforts":** Richard Delgado and Jean Stefancic, *Critical Race Theory: An Introduction*, 2nd ed. (New York: New York University Press, 2012), 27.

70 **touted its commitment:** See chapter 12.

71 **distinguish between citizens:** This rejection of neutral solutions is especially pronounced in legal and political contexts, and it has generally been echoed in fields from
gender to Asian American studies. But the insistence on responding to existing biases by
rejecting the very possibility of a neutral framework, rather than by trying to make such
frameworks inclusive, is also evident in more surprising contexts. As Christopher Gabbard, a leading scholar in disability studies, summarizes the point, "A disability perspective exposes classical liberalism to be an ideology rife with ableism: the belief that people
with impairments are inferior to those with typically functioning bodies and minds"
(Christopher Gabbard, "Human," in *Keywords for Disability Studies*, ed. Rachel Adams,
Benjamin Reiss, and David Serlin [New York: New York University Press, 2015], 101).
The solution, many leading exponents of disability studies argue, is not primarily to
change the physical environment in such a way that those who are blind or deaf can fully
participate in society; it is to reject the idea that it is preferable to be seeing rather than
blind, or hearing rather than deaf.

71 **logic of political organizing:** According to Judy Tzu-Chun Wu, for example, one of the
main empirical goals of the identity synthesis is to "understand how gender, race, sexuality, class, and other forms of social difference and hierarchy are mutually inflected and
intertwined." Judy Tzu-Chun Wu, "Gender," in *Keywords for Asian American Studies*,
ed. Cathy Schlund-Vials, K. Scott Wong, and Linda Trinh Võ (New York: New York
University Press, 2015).

71 **draw the inference:** See Kat Rosenfield, "How Feminism Ate Itself," UnHerd, Sept. 22,
2021, unherd.com/2021/09/how-feminism-ate-itself.

71 **with the necessary stance:** This deferral to affected parties is grounded in standpoint
epistemology; see the next section, on "Standpoint Epistemology," within this chapter as
well as the more extended discussion of standpoint theory in chapter 8.

71 **This interpretation of intersectionality:** Mark Hemingway, "Advocacy Groups' Leftward
'Mission Creep' Is Creeping Up on Free Speech," RealClearInvestigations, May. 1, 2019,
www.realclearinvestigations.com/articles/2019/04/30/how_rights_groups_mission
_creep_creeps_up_on_free_speech.html.

72 **many false beliefs:** Pamela Duncan and Alexandra Topping, "Men Underestimate
Level of Sexual Harassment Against Women—Survey," *Guardian*, Dec. 6, 2018, www
.theguardian.com/world/2018/dec/06/men-underestimate-level-of-sexual-harassment
-against-women-survey.

72 **able to communicate:** For a full discussion of the origins of standpoint epistemology
and the problems with the way in which activists have since taken the tradition's core
insights beyond what is philosophically plausible or practically useful, see chapter 8.

72 **highly influential text:** Donna Haraway, "Situated Knowledges: The Science Question
in Feminism and the Privilege of Partial Perspective," *Feminist Studies* 14, no. 3 (1988),
doi.org/10.2307/3178066. As Chela Sandoval, a prominent scholar in gender studies, put
the point, the epistemological component of intersectionality "denies any one perspective as the only answer, but instead posits a shifting tactical and strategic subjectivity that
has the capacity to re-center depending upon the forms of oppression to be confronted."
Chela Sandoval, "U.S. Third World Feminism: The Theory and Method of Oppositional
Consciousness in the Postmodern World," *Genders*, no. 10 (Spring 1991): 14.

72 **"Differences in power":** Patricia Hill Collins, "Toward a New Vision: Race, Class, and
Gender as Categories of Analysis and Connection," *Race, Sex, and Class* 1, no. 1 (1993):
36, www.jstor.org/stable/41680038.

73 **It was a cold and windy night:** This is lightly adapted from the Eliot/Jacobs version of
Aesop's fable "The Old Man and Death" and includes verbatim quotations from that
source. See Joseph Jacobs, ed., "The Old Man and Death," in *The Fables of Aesop* (London:
Macmillan, 1902), 164.

74 **"as boring a subject":** Edward Said, "Between Worlds," in *Reflections on Exile and Other
Essays* (London: Granta Books, 2013), 567.

74 **form of privileged access:** Edward Said, "The Politics of Knowledge," in *Reflections on Exile and Other Essays*, 384.

74 **"unable to share":** Edward Said, "Identity, Authority, and Freedom: The Potentate and the Traveler," in *Reflections on Exile and Other Essays*, 403.

74 **this struck Said:** Adam Shatz, "Palestinianism," *London Review of Books*, May 6, 2021, www.lrb.co.uk/the-paper/v43/n09/adam-shatz/palestinianism.

75 **"Marginality and homelessness":** Said, "Politics of Knowledge," 31.

75 **"political use of humor":** Sara Danius and Stefan Jonsson, "An Interview with Gayatri Chakravorty Spivak," *Boundary 2* 20, no. 2 (1993): 44, doi.org/10.2307/303357.

75 **"simply became the union ticket":** Danius and Jonsson, "Interview." As Spivak argued on another occasion: "One of the reasons why the strategic use of essentialism has caught on within a personalist culture is that it gives a certain alibi to essentialism. The emphasis falls on being able to speak from one's own ground, rather than on what the word strategy implies, so I've re-considered it. I think it's too risky a slogan in a personalist, academic culture, within which it has been picked up and celebrated." Gayatri Chakravorty Spivak, "In a Word. Interview," by Ellen Rooney, *Differences* 1, no. 2 (Summer 1989): 127–28.

75 **"out-of-body experience":** Jane Coaston, "The Intersectionality Wars," *Vox*, May 28, 2019, www.vox.com/the-highlight/2019/5/20/18542843/intersectionality-conservatism -law-race-gender-discrimination.

PART II: THE VICTORY OF THE IDENTITY SYNTHESIS

79 **she sounded pessimistic:** Kimberlé Williams Crenshaw, "Twenty Years of Critical Race Theory: Looking Back to Move Forward," *Connecticut Law Review* 43, no. 5 (July 2011): 1253–352.

79 **"Broad segments of the population":** Crenshaw, "Twenty Years of Critical Race Theory," 1318.

79 **close to denying:** Crenshaw, "Twenty Years of Critical Race Theory," 1324.

79 **"at odds with key elements":** Crenshaw, "Twenty Years of Critical Race Theory," 1324.

79 **"critiques of racism":** Crenshaw, "Twenty Years of Critical Race Theory," 1333. "As racial justice advocacy comes under increasing pressure from colorblind victories in both the legal and political arenas, lawyers, researchers, and advocates find themselves pushed back into their own end zone" (Crenshaw, "Twenty Years of Critical Race Theory," 1261–62). While Crenshaw expressed some optimism that critical race theorists might be able to turn the tide, she was deeply concerned about the "virtual abandonment of the racial injustice frame" in contemporary public discourse (Crenshaw, "Twenty Years of Critical Race Theory," 1341). She did, however, express her hope that "Beyond the academy, the opportunity to present a counter-narrative to the premature societal settlement that marches under the banner of post-racialism is ripe" (Crenshaw, "Twenty Years of Critical Race Theory," 1262).

Chapter 5: The Identity Synthesis Goes Mainstream

83 **"A three-minute call":** Friedman was quoting the price in 1996 dollars. In 2022 dollars, the price would have been about $559. Thomas L. Friedman, *The Lexus and the Olive Tree* (London: HarperCollins, 1999), 8.

83 **"weave the world together":** Friedman, *The Lexus and the Olive Tree*, 8.

83 **likely to connect:** Friedman even invoked his mother's newfound pastime when, in *The Lexus and the Olive Tree*, he dismissed those who were skeptical of the internet's positive potential. "To all those who say that this era of globalization is no different from the previous one, I would simply ask: Was your great-grandmother playing bridge with Frenchmen on the Internet in 1900? I don't think so." Friedman, *The Lexus and the Olive Tree*, 8.

84 **age of dialogue:** For more on this, see Clay Shirky's *Here Comes Everybody*. As an example of the capacity of the internet to drive social change, Shirky points to 2009 "flash mob" protests against the autocratic president of Belarus, Alexander Lukashenko. The challenge of internet-organized protests is clear: "Because so many people have access to the Web, the Belarusian government can't stem the formation of flash mobs in advance, and because the attendees have cameras, it can't break up the mobs without inviting the very attention it wants to avoid. In this situation, the Belarusian government is limited to either gross overreactions (a curfew in Oktyabrskaya, a ban on ice cream or the internet) or to waiting for the mob to form, then disrupting it." Clay Shirky, *Here Comes Everybody: The Power of Organizing Without Organizations* (New York: Penguin Press, 2008), 170.

84 **bridge long-standing divides:** This is not to suggest that the internet is to blame for all social or political ills. Back in 2014, I saw it as my task to puncture my students' easy optimism. If I were to teach the same class today, I would push my students to be equally skeptical of the new consensus that blames social media for just about everything that has gone wrong over the course of the past decade. For as it happens, the evidence for the new consensus is not much more solid than was the evidence for the old consensus. A comprehensive ongoing review of academic work on social media and politics, for example, has found that there is no clear consensus in existing research on how social media may lead to various forms of political dysfunction. See Jonathan Haidt and Chris Bail, "Social Media and Political Dysfunction: A Collaborative Review," unpublished manuscript, New York University, https://docs.google.com/document/d/1vVAtMCQnz8WVxtSNQev _e1cGmY9rnY96ecYuAj6C548/edit.

85 **Founded in 2007:** Josh Halliday, "David Karp, Founder of Tumblr, on Realising His Dream," *Guardian*, Jan. 29, 2012, www.theguardian.com/media/2012/jan/29/tumblr -david-karp-interview.

85 **click of a button:** "Once you cracked its interface, an amalgamation of sprawling journal entries and pithy pop culture memes, and the scattershot comments inscribed upon those artifacts by other users, was at your fingertips. You could also find your interests via tags and follow tags of interest. And those interests could be niche—extremely." Emma Sarappo, "How Tumblr Taught Social Justice to a Generation of Teenagers," *Pacific Standard*, Dec. 13, 2018, psmag.com/social-justice/how-tumblr-taught-social-justice-to-a -generation-of-teenagers.

85 **The service grew very quickly:** Joanna Stern, "Yahoo Buys Tumblr Social Network Service for $1.1 Billion," ABC News, May 20, 2013, abcnews.go.com/Technology/yahoo -buys-tumblr-social-network-service-11-billion/story?id=19215310.

85 **became a place:** In addition to features like topic tags, the broad diffusion of new ideas and identities on Tumblr was likely also aided by the website's unusually dense structures. As one computational analysis showed, Tumblr "yields a significantly different network structure from traditional blogosphere. Tumblr's network is much denser and better connected. Close to 29.03% of connections on Tumblr are reciprocate, while blogosphere has only 3%. The average distance between two users in Tumblr is 4.7, which is roughly half of that in blogosphere. The giant connected component covers 99.61% of nodes as compared to 75% in blogosphere." Yi Chang et al., "What Is Tumblr," *ACM SIGKDD Explorations Newsletter* 16, no. 1 (2014): pp. 21-29, https://doi.org/10.1145 /2674026.2674030.

85 **rooted in fandom:** Katherine Dee, "Tumblr Transformed American Politics," *American Conservative*, Aug. 11, 2021, www.theamericanconservative.com/articles/tumblr -transformed-american-politics/.

85 **place for young people:** The heavy emphasis on sexual self-exploration was also owed to the fact that the site did not censor explicit content for the first years of its existence; it only started to do so in 2018, a year after it was acquired by Verizon. Shannon Liao, "Tumblr Will Ban All Adult Content on December 17th," *Verge*, Dec. 3, 2018, www.theverge.com/2018 /12/3/18123752/tumblr-adult-content-porn-ban-date-explicit-changes-why-safe-mode.

85 **a darker side:** Carolyn Gregoire, "The Hunger Blogs: A Secret World of Teenage 'Thin-spiration,'" *HuffPost*, Feb. 9, 2012, www.huffpost.com/entry/thinspiration-blogs_n _1264459. For a discussion of the "thinspiration" movement's move to TikTok, see Laura Pitcher, "2000s Tumblr Eating Disorder Content Didn't Disappear—It Changed," *Nylon*, accessed Mar. 19, 2023, www.nylon.com/beauty/tumblr-eating-disorder-content-is -on-tiktok-how-to-navigate-it.

85 **"Tumblr became a place":** Dee, "Tumblr Transformed American Politics."

86 **"Tumblr was the first place":** Sarappo, "How Tumblr Taught Social Justice to a Genera-tion of Teenagers."

86 **"wanted to educate ourselves":** Lu clarified, "I don't see being woke as a bad thing." Sarappo, "How Tumblr Taught Social Justice to a Generation of Teenagers."

86 **"For every strange":** "Most people I spoke to shared that the first time they were exposed to anything related to identity politics . . . was on Tumblr," Dee writes. Dee, "Tumblr Transformed American Politics."

86 **short of the sophistication:** While Tumblr ideology fell short of the level of sophistication in the academic work that formed the core of the identity synthesis, it was influenced by thinkers like Crenshaw and fields like gender studies. As one young researcher found, most of the users who were major players in prominent Tumblr debates about feminism had "backgrounds in women's and gender studies on an undergraduate level, and several of them are also in grad school, pursuing academic careers." Fredrika Thelandersson, "Tumblr Femi-nism: Third-Wave Subjectivities in Practice" (master's thesis, New York University, 2013), 2.

86 **Two core themes:** "Strategic essentialism," which shed the last vestiges of its strategic nature, was also important. Though posters occasionally continued to pay lip service to the idea that race was a social construct, users were encouraged to see themselves, first and foremost, as being defined by their ascriptive identities.

86 **this intuitive insight:** For a much deeper treatment on the relationship between stand-point epistemology and this popularized form of standpoint theory, see chapter 8.

87 **"If your feminism isn't intersectional":** The quotation itself appears to have originated not from Tumblr but rather from the feminist blog Tiger Beatdown. See, for example, Aja Romano, "This Feminist's Most Famous Quote Has Been Sold All over the Internet. She Hasn't Seen a Cent," *Vox*, Aug. 12, 2016, www.vox.com/2016/8/12/12406648/flavia -dzodan-my-feminism-will-be-intersectional-merchandise.

88 **founded a website:** Matthew Newton, "Thought Catalog and the New Age of Confes-sional Media," *Forbes*, Feb. 8, 2012, www.forbes.com/sites/matthewnewton/2012/02/08 /thought-catalog-and-the-new-age-of-confessional-media/?sh=50fabd0c320d.

88 **"Our philosophy is that quality":** Zach Schonfeld, "Thought Catalog's Reckoning," *Newsweek*, May 20, 2016, www.newsweek.com/thought-catalogs-reckoning-332545.

88 **exploded in visibility:** Tim Herrera, "Inside the Contradictory World of Thought Cata-log, One of the Internet's Most Reviled Sites," *Washington Post*, Oct. 21, 2014, www .washingtonpost.com/news/the-intersect/wp/2014/10/21/inside-the-contradictory -world-of-thought-catalog-one-of-the-internets-most-reviled-sites/.

88 **most viral articles:** Interestingly, the article's author, Macy Sto. Domingo, describes it as directly inspired by "White Privilege: Unpacking the Invisible Knapsack," an influential essay by the feminist and critical race theorist Peggy McIntosh. Macy Sto. Domingo, "18 Things White People Seem to Not Understand (Because, White Privilege)," Thought Catalog, April 5, 2014, thoughtcatalog.com/macy-sto-domingo/2014/04/18-things-white -people-seem-to-not-understand-because-white-privilege/.

88 **a popularized form:** See, for example, Jen Caron, "IT HAPPENED TO ME: There Are No Black People in My Yoga Classes and I'm Suddenly Feeling Uncomfortable About It," *xoJane*, Jan. 28, 2014, https://web.archive.org/web/20140131063708/http://www.xojane .com/it-happened-to-me/it-happened-to-me-there-are-no-black-people-in-my-yoga -classes-and-im-uncomfortable-with-it; and Laura Beck, "The Problem with White Dolls," *Jezebel*, March 27, 2013, jezebel.com/the-problem-with-white-dolls-5992550.

88 **more established publications:** Randa Jarrar, "Why I Can't Stand White Belly Dancers," *Salon*, March 4, 2014, www.salon.com/2014/03/04/why_i_cant_stand_white_belly _dancers/; Kali Holloway, "10 Ways White People Are More Racist Than They Realize," *Salon*, March 11, 2015, www.salon.com/2015/03/04/10_ways_white_people_are_more _racist_than_they_realize_partner/.

89 **adorned the home page:** Roopa Singh, "4 Thoughts for Your Yoga Teacher Who Thinks Appropriation Is Fun," Everyday Feminism, March 8, 2015, everydayfeminism.com /2015/03/letter-to-my-yoga-teacher/; Kerry Truong, "People of Color Can't Cure Your Racism, but Here Are 5 Things You Can Do Instead," Everyday Feminism, March 8, 2015, everydayfeminism.com/2015/03/poc-cant-cure-your-racism/; Carmen Rios, "You Call It Professionalism; I Call It Oppression in a Three-Piece Suit," Everyday Feminism, Feb. 15, 2015, everydayfeminism.com/2015/02/professionalism-and-oppression/.

89 **I read articles:** Aliya Khan, "6 Ways to Respond to Sexist Microaggressions in Everyday Conversations," Everyday Feminism, Jan. 18, 2015, everydayfeminism.com/2015/01 /responses-to-sexist-microaggressions/; Melissa A. Fabello, "White Privilege, Explained in One Simple Comic," Everyday Feminism, Sept. 21, 2014, everydayfeminism.com /2014/09/white-privilege-explained/; Jenika McCrayer, "So You're a 'Breasts Man'? Here Are 3 Reasons That Could Be Sexist," Everyday Feminism, April 5, 2015, everydayfeminism .com/2015/04/breasts-man/.

90 **new digital magazine:** Ezra Klein, "Vox Is Our Next," *Verge*, Jan. 26, 2014, www.theverge .com/2014/1/26/5348212/ezra-klein-vox-is-our-next.

90 **why it matters:** As Ezra Klein described the importance of explainer journalism when announcing *Vox*, "New information is not always—and perhaps not even usually—the most important information for understanding a topic. . . . The news business, however, is just a subset of the informing-our-audience business—and that's the business we aim to be in. Our mission is to create a site that's as good at explaining the world as it is at reporting on it." Klein, "Vox Is Our Next."

91 **a much-heralded feature:** By 2017, three years after *Vox*'s founding, card stacks had been discontinued ("Vox's Ezra Klein Explains It All," Yahoo, accessed Dec. 18, 2022, www .yahoo.com/lifestyle/vox-ezra-klein-explains-232044265.html). Matthew Yglesias elab-orated on this point in a blog post reflecting on founding *Vox*: "To serve the needs of advertisers, you needed to serve the needs of the platforms, and that meant we just weren't masters of our destiny. Whatever the merits or flaws of the cardstack idea, it never had a chance because it didn't work with Facebook on a technical level." Instead, Yglesias writes, Facebook's algorithms seemed to favor "hard-core identity politics" at the time, incentivizing both writers and publications to embrace more radical ideas. Matthew Yglesias, "What I Learned Co-founding Vox," *Slow Boring*, Dec. 7, 2022, www.slowboring .com/p/what-i-learned-co-founding-vox.

91 **their own experiences:** Eleanor Barkhorn, "First Person, Vox's New Section Devoted to Nar-rative Essays, Explained," *Vox*, June 12, 2015, https://web.archive.org/web/20150614001232 /https://www.vox.com/2015/6/12/8767221/vox-first-person-explained.

91 **an open letter:** "A Letter on Justice and Open Debate," *Harper's*, July 7, 2020, harpers .org/a-letter-on-justice-and-open-debate/. (Along with more than a hundred other writ-ers and artists, ranging from Salman Rushdie to Noam Chomsky, I was one of the co-signatories.)

91 **employees attacked him:** Emily VanDerWerff, Twitter, July 7, 2020, 12:12 p.m., twitter .com/emilyvdw/status/1280580388495097856?lang=en. The writer, who now goes by the name Emily St. James, repeatedly emphasized that she did not want Yglesias to be punished for co-signing the letter.

91 **start his own newsletter:** Conor Friedersdorf, "Why Matthew Yglesias Left Vox," *Atlantic*, Nov. 13, 2020, www.theatlantic.com/ideas/archive/2020/11/substack-and-medias -groupthink-problem/617102/.

91 **Klein followed suit:** Ezra Klein (@ezraklein), "After nearly eight amazing years build-ing, editing, and working at @voxdotcom, I am leaving to join @nytopinion," Twitter, Nov. 20, 2020, 1:25 p.m., twitter.com/ezraklein/status/1329853360258748416?s=20.

92 **"a direct consequence of Facebook's influence":** Yglesias, "What I Learned Co-founding Vox."

93 **a remarkable explosion:** At the beginning of the 2010s, such content was overwhelm-ingly published by digital upstarts that were seen as being far outside the mainstream (as constituted by the most prestigious legacy publications). But as sites from *xoJane* to Thought Catalog exploded in popularity, mainstream publications grew keen to secure a slice of the pie. CNN, for example, expanded its "First Person" vertical in 2013. See Eve Fairbanks, "How Personal Essays Conquered Journalism—and Why They Can't Cut It," *Washington Post*, Oct. 10, 2014, www.washingtonpost.com/posteverything/wp/2014 /10/10/how-personal-essays-conquered-journalism-and-why-they-cant-cut-it/.

93 **"I will teach my boys":** Ekow N. Yankah, "Can My Children Be Friends with White People?," *New York Times*, Nov. 11, 2017, www.nytimes.com/2017/11/11/opinion/sunday /interracial-friendship-donald-trump.html.

94 **an analysis by Zach Goldberg:** Zach Goldberg, "How the Media Led the Great Racial Awakening," *Tablet*, Aug. 4, 2020, www.tabletmag.com/sections/news/articles/media -great-racial-awakening.

94 **prestigious media outlets:** Political scientists have long believed that popular beliefs about race are deeply shaped by the way in which they are presented in the media. As Paul Kellstedt showed in 2000, drawing on *Newsweek* articles, "*How* racial policy is covered in the media is extremely important [to the broader American political environment]." (Paul M. Kellstedt, "Media Framing and the Dynamics of Racial Policy Preferences," *American Journal of Political Science* 44, no. 2 (2000): 245–60, doi.org/10.2307 /2669308.) It is no surprise, then, that the rapidly changing way in which mainstream media outlets talked about race over the course of the past decade also appears to have had a massive effect on views about race among their core audience.

94 **increase in progressive views:** As Goldberg put the point, the "elite liberal media and its readership—especially its white liberal readership—underwent a profound change." However, he also cautions that "these findings, while suggestive, don't prove that the media coverage at leading liberal outlets like *The New York Times* and *The Washington Post* is *causing* shifts in racial attitudes. What it shows dispositively is that the newspapers covered here are both talking about racial inequality and race-related issues far more frequently than they have since at least 1970 as well as increasingly framing those issues using the terms and jargon associated with 'wokeness.' Additionally, it shows that the racial liberalism of white liberals has closely followed these trends in media coverage, rather than preceding them. It is beyond the scope of this article to fully explain the un-derlying causes of these changes." Goldberg, "How the Media Led the Great Racial Awakening."

94 **attitudes about race:** Matthew Yglesias, "The Great Awokening," *Vox*, April 1, 2019, www.vox.com/2019/3/22/18259865/great-awokening-white-liberals-race-polling-trump -2020.

95 **more likely to say:** Zach Goldberg (@ZachG932), "Updated whites vs. racial/ethnic outgroup feeling thermometer differential scores," Twitter, March 25, 2021, 5:30 p.m., twitter.com/zachg932/status/1375198311355969542. The same dynamic also seems to be playing out in many workplaces. As the executive director of one progressive organiza-tion, who is Black, told a journalist, "The most zealous ones at my organization when it comes to race are white." Ryan Grim, "Meltdowns Have Brought Progressive Advocacy Groups to a Standstill at a Critical Moment in World History," *Intercept*, June 13, 2022, theintercept.com/2022/06/13/progressive-organizing-infighting-callout-culture/.

95 **"White liberals have moved so far":** Yglesias, "Great Awokening."

Chapter 6: The Short March Through the Institutions

97 **"long march through"**: "To extend the base of the student movement, Rudi Dutschke has proposed the strategy of the long march through the institutions." Herbert Marcuse, *Counterrevolution and Revolt* (Boston: Beacon Press, 1972), 55.

97 **"working against the established institutions"**: Marcuse, *Counterrevolution and Revolt*, 55.

98 **co-opted by the institutions:** When Gerhard Schröder became the chair of the youth movement of the Social Democratic Party in 1971, for example, he called himself a "devoted Marxist." But by the time he had completed his march through the institutions, and become the chancellor of Germany, his old convictions had started to dwindle. Schröder now represented the moderate wing of the Social Democratic Party, clashing with left-wing figureheads like Oskar Lafontaine. His penchant for expensive suits and his close relationships to the country's corporate leaders earned him the moniker *Der Genosse der Bosse*, or the Comrade of the CEOs. By the time he left office, in 2005, the only thing that remained of his erstwhile convictions was a deep anti-Americanism; he became a lobbyist for Vladimir Putin's dictatorial regime, joining the boards of the Russian energy companies Rosneft and Gazprom. Katrin Bennhold, "The Former Chancellor Who Became Putin's Man in Germany," *New York Times*, April 23, 2022, www.nytimes.com /2022/04/23/world/europe/schroder-germany-russia-gas-ukraine-war-energy.html.

98 **social and cultural changes:** For example, the political scientist Russell Dalton uses the idea of the long march through the institutions to explain the reversion to ideologically polarized political parties in the 1970s, which supplanted the nonideological consensus-minded parties of the postwar period. Russell J. Dalton, "Generational Change in Elite Political Beliefs: The Growth of Ideological Polarization," *Journal of Politics* 49, no. 4 (1987): 976–97, doi.org/10.2307/2130780.

99 **enrollment in departments:** In women's and gender studies, for instance, the number of degrees offered grew 300 percent between 1990 and 2015. David Rutz, "Gender Studies Degrees Increased More Than 300 Percent Since 1990," *Washington Free Beacon*, March 6, 2017, freebeacon.com/politics/report-genders-studies-degrees-increased-300-percent -1990/.

99 **likely to learn:** As of a 2015 survey, 76 percent of colleges reported using distribution requirements requiring students to take a breadth of classes outside their major. Scott Jaschik, "Distribution Plus," *Inside Higher Ed*, Jan. 19, 2016, www.insidehighered.com /news/2016/01/19/survey-colleges-finds-distribution-requirements-remain-popular -new-features.

100 **failed to keep pace:** Michael Delucchi et al., "What's That Smell? Bullshit Jobs in Higher Education," *Review of Social Economy*, June 17, 2021, 1–22, doi.org/10.1080/00346764 .2021.1940255.

100 **nonteaching staff skyrocketed:** Delucchi et al., "What's That Smell?," 3.

100 **once comfortably outnumbered:** In 2018, there were 832,119 professors and 1,086,070 administrators and other professional staff, while in 1976 they numbered 434,000 and 247,322, respectively. Delucchi et al., "What's That Smell?"

100 **offered seminars on:** Samuel J. Abrams, "Think Professors Are Liberal? Try School Administrators," *New York Times*, Oct. 16, 2018, www.nytimes.com/2018/10/16/opinion /liberal-college-administrators.html.

100 **refrain from using:** Robby Soave, "The University of California's Insane Speech Police," *Daily Beast*, April 14, 2017, www.thedailybeast.com/the-university-of-californias-insane -speech-police.

100 **intervene when students:** Nick Gillespie, "Finally: An Anonymous, Online, Geo-Tagged System to Report Microaggressions at College!," Reason, March 25, 2015, https://reason .com/2015/03/25/anonymous-online-geo-system-to/.

100 **Yale, for example:** Philip Mousavizadeh, "A 'Proliferation of Administrators': Faculty Re-

flect on Two Decades of Rapid Expansion," *Yale Daily News*, Nov. 10, 2021, yaledailynews
.com/blog/2021/11/10/reluctance-on-the-part-of-its-leadership-to-lead-yales
-administration-increases-by-nearly-50-percent/.

100 **monoculture on campus:** See, for example, Abrams, "Think Professors Are Liberal?";
and Samuel J. Abrams and Amna Khalid, "Are Colleges and Universities Too Liberal?
What the Research Says About the Political Composition of Campuses and Campus
Climate," AEI, Oct. 21, 2020, www.aei.org/articles/are-colleges-and-universities-too
-liberal-what-the-research-says-about-the-political-composition-of-campuses-and
-campus-climate/.

101 **a worrying picture:** "Elite Schools Are the Most Problematic on Speech," RealClearEd-
ucation, Nov. 9, 2020, www.realcleareducation.com/articles/2020/11/09/elite_schools
_are_the_most_problematic_on_speech_110505.html. Similarly, a study by FIRE ranked
Harvard, Princeton, and Cornell "below average" on speech rights, Brown "slightly
below average," and Dartmouth "average." Columbia and the University of Pennsylvania
rounded out the bottom of the 203 schools ranked. "2022 College Free Speech Rank-
ings," Foundation for Individual Rights and Expression, accessed Dec. 16, 2022, www
.thefire.org/research-learn/2022-college-free-speech-rankings.

101 **especially successful in:** This could be because they compete for top talent, are particularly sensitive to criticism on social media, or have an ideological commitment to progressive values.

102 **for decades fought:** For a history of the ACLU, see Samuel Walker, *In Defense of American
Liberties: A History of the ACLU* (New York: Oxford University Press, 1990).

102 **"The constitutional guarantees of freedom":** David Goldberger, "The Skokie Case:
How I Came to Represent the Free Speech Rights of Nazis," American Civil Liberties
Union, March 2, 2020, www.aclu.org/issues/free-speech/rights-protesters/skokie-case
-how-i-came-represent-free-speech-rights-nazis. As Goldberger says in the same article,
the Illinois law that served as a basis for the original prohibition of the Nazi rally "used
language so sweeping that it would justify, for example, criminal prosecution of a Black
Lives Matter leader for making a speech blaming white racism for police shootings of
African Americans."

102 **continues to trumpet:** "ACLU History," American Civil Liberties Union, accessed Dec.
16, 2022, www.aclu.org/about/aclu-history.

102 **"Once a bastion of free speech":** Lara Bazelon, "The ACLU Has Lost Its Way," *Atlantic*,
May 10, 2022, www.theatlantic.com/ideas/archive/2022/05/aclu-johnny-depp-amber
-heard-trial/629808/.

102 **army of small donors:** Larry Neumeister, "ACLU Is Seeing a Trump-Era Surge in Members and Donations," AP News, Feb. 12, 2017, apnews.com/article/1dbcc13bc0104
edaabb1d55c13483101.

103 **the ACLU has called for:** The ACLU published a letter from a student at Smith College
that called for "affinity housing" for racial minorities on campus (Lucas Ropek, "Woman
at Center of Smith College Incident Calls for 'Affinity Housing' for Students of Color,"
MassLive, Sept. 14, 2018, www.masslive.com/news/2018/09/smith_college_student_pens
_let.html). On defunding the police, see "Transformational Public Safety: Reducing the
Roles, Resources, and Power of Police," American Civil Liberties Union, June 8, 2021,
www.aclu.org/news/topic/transformational-public-safety-reducing-the-roles-resources
-and-power-of-police. On student loan debt, see "Cancel Student Debt: $50k for Every
Borrower," American Civil Liberties Union, accessed Dec. 16, 2022, action.aclu.org
/petition/cancel-student-debt-50k-every-borrower. On broadband, see ACLU (@ACLU),
"Broadband access is about more than the internet – it's an issue of systemic equality,"
Twitter, March 31, 2021, 5:21 p.m., twitter.com/ACLU/status/1377370379753156608.

103 **"People without broadband access":** "Broadband Access for All Now," American Civil
Liberties Union, accessed Dec. 16, 2022, action.aclu.org/send-message/broadband-access
-all-now.

103 **"annual budget has grown"**: Michael Powell, "Once a Bastion of Free Speech, the A.C.L.U. Faces an Identity Crisis," *New York Times*, June 6, 2021, www.nytimes.com /2021/06/06/us/aclu-free-speech.html.

103 **ACLU's "rigid stance"**: Joseph Goldstein, "After Charlottesville, A.C.L.U. Braces for the Next Alt-Right Case," *New York Times*, Oct. 4, 2017, www.nytimes.com/2017/10 /04/us/aclu-charlottesville-white-supremacists.html.

103 **"a fig leaf for Nazis"**: Alex Blasdel, "How the Resurgence of White Supremacy in the US Sparked a War over Free Speech," *Guardian*, May 31, 2018, www.theguardian.com /news/2018/may/31/how-the-resurgence-of-white-supremacy-in-the-us-sparked-a-war -over-free-speech-aclu-charlottesville.

103 **shouted her down**: Jeremy Bauer-Wolf, "ACLU Speaker Shouted Down at William & Mary," *Inside Higher Ed*, Oct. 5, 2017, www.insidehighered.com/quicktakes/2017/10 /05/aclu-speaker-shouted-down-william-mary.

104 **"was concerned about donors"**: Joan Biskupic, "ACLU Takes Heat for Its Free-Speech Defense of White Supremacist Group," CNN, Aug. 17, 2017, www.cnn.com/2017/08 /16/politics/aclu-free-speech-white-supremacy/index.html.

104 **Within ten months**: The memo from the ACLU is not dated. But the first press reports about it surfaced ten months after the protests in Charlottesville. See, for example, Robby Soave, "Leaked Internal Memo Reveals the ACLU Is Wavering on Free Speech," *Reason*, June 21, 2018, reason.com/2018/06/21/aclu-leaked-memo-free-speech/.

104 **should consider factors**: The selection guidelines "were developed by a joint committee of national ACLU staff and legal directors of six affiliates," chaired by the ACLU national legal director, David Cole. "ACLU Case Selection Guidelines: Conflicts Between Competing Values or Priorities," ACLU.org, accessed Jan. 12, 2023, www.aclu.org/sites /default/files/field_document/aclu_case_selection_guidelines.pdf.

104 **the death knell**: Personal communication. See also Powell, "Once a Bastion of Free Speech."

104 **Abigail Shrier argued**: Abigail Shrier, *Irreversible Damage: The Transgender Craze Seducing Our Daughters* (Washington, D.C.: Regnery, 2020).

104 **"Stopping the circulation"**: Strangio's tweet has since been deleted. For a record, see Glenn Greenwald, "The Ongoing Death of Free Speech: Prominent ACLU Lawyer Cheers Suppression of a New Book," Nov. 15, 2020, greenwald.substack.com/p/the-ongoing -death-of-free-speech.

104 **"promotes an unfair process"**: ACLU (@ACLU), Twitter, Nov. 16, 2018, 10:40 a.m., twitter.com/ACLU/status/1063456843706585089.

104 **due process rights**: Conor Friedersdorf, "The ACLU Declines to Defend Civil Rights," *Atlantic*, Nov. 19, 2018, www.theatlantic.com/ideas/archive/2018/11/aclu-devos-title -ix/576142/; Robby Soave, "The ACLU Condemns DeVos's Title IX Reforms, Says These Due Process Safeguards 'Inappropriately Favor the Accused,'" *Reason*, Nov. 16, 2018, reason.com/2018/11/16/aclu-betsy-devos-title-ix-due-process/.

104 **"more important for ACLU staff"**: Powell, "Once a Bastion of Free Speech."

105 **share his assessment**: "Fundraising probably plays a role, but I think ideology is more important," Wendy Kaminer, a longtime board member of the ACLU, recently claimed. "I think it's an ideological shift." Mark Hemingway, "Advocacy Groups' Leftward 'Mission Creep' Is Creeping Up on Free Speech," RealClearInvestigations, May. 1, 2019, www.realclearinvestigations.com/articles/2019/04/30/how_rights_groups_mission _creep_creeps_up_on_free_speech.html.

105 **"if they are comfortable"**: Powell, "Once a Bastion of Free Speech."

105 **The Sierra Club**: In full, its mission statement vows, "To explore, enjoy, and protect the wild places of the earth; To practice and promote the responsible use of the earth's eco-systems and resources; To educate and enlist humanity to protect and restore the quality of the natural and human environment; and to use all lawful means to carry out these objectives." "About the Sierra Club," Sierra Club, accessed Jan. 12, 2023, www.sierraclub .org/about-sierra-club.

105 **"tear down the wall"**: "Tell the Biden Administration: Respect Communities on the Border. Tear Down the Wall!," Sierra Club, accessed Jan. 12, 2023, addup.sierraclub.org /campaigns/tell-the-biden-administration-honor-communities-on-the-border-tear -down-the-wall.

105 **"defund the police"**: Heather Smith, "What Does It Mean to Defund the Police?," Sierra Club, June 17, 2020, www.sierraclub.org/sierra/what-does-it-mean-defund-police.

106 **increasingly radical causes**: "American Philanthropy Turns Left," *Economist*, Sept. 4, 2021, www.economist.com/united-states/2021/09/04/american-philanthropy-turns-left.

106 **concluded in 2021**: "American Philanthropy Turns Left."

106 **about $28 billion**: Anna Koob, "What Does Candid's Grants Data Say About Funding for Racial Equity in the United States?," *Candid* (blog), July 24, 2020, blog.candid.org/post /what-does-candids-grants-data-say-about-funding-for-racial-equity-in-the-united -states/?utm.

106 **channeled donor dollars**: See, for example, Sean Campbell, "Black Lives Matter Secretly Bought a $6 Million House," *Intelligencer*, April 4, 2022, nymag.com/intelligencer /2022/04/black-lives-matter-6-million-dollar-house.html. See also Ailsa Chang, Jason Fuller, and Kathryn Fox, "Secret $6 Million Home Has Allies and Critics Skeptical of BLM Foundation's Finances," NPR, April 7, 2022, https://www.npr.org/2022/04/07 /1091487910/blm-leaders-face-questions-after-allegedly-buying-a-mansion-with -donation-money. See further William Bredderman, "Inside Shaun King's Shadowy $6.7 Million Nonprofit," *Daily Beast*, Sept. 21, 2022, www.thedailybeast.com/inside-shaun -kings-shadowy-dollar67-million-nonprofit-grassroots-law-project-formed-after-george -floyds-death.

106 **extreme political causes**: Thomas B. Edsall, "The Law of Unintended Political Consequences Strikes Again," *New York Times*, Jan. 5, 2022, www.nytimes.com/2022/01/05 /opinion/progressive-philanthropy-critics.html. A ballot measure to abolish the Minneapolis Police Department, for example, received major funding from the Open Society Policy Center; ironically, a majority of voters in some affluent and predominantly white parts of the city supported the measure, while a clear majority of those in less affluent and predominantly Black parts of the city voted it down. As the journalist Jonathan Chait has argued in *New York* magazine, the strong support that major foundations have given to identity-based activists groups had a major influence on the left's ideological makeup. "In recent years, a host of new slogans and plans—the Green New Deal, 'Defund the police,' 'Abolish ICE,' and so on—have leaped from the world of nonprofit activism onto the chyrons of MSNBC and Fox News." Jonathan Chait, "Joe Biden's Big Squeeze," *Intelligencer*, Nov. 22, 2021, nymag.com/intelligencer/2021/11/joe-biden-agenda.html.

107 **"To help foster conversation"**: "Employee Enrichment for Inclusivity," Coca-Cola Company, accessed Jan. 12, 2023, www.coca-colacompany.com/social-impact/diversity -and-inclusion/racial-equity/internal-action/employee-enrichment.

107 **"try to be less white"**: Dan MacGuill, "Did Coca-Cola's Diversity Training Tell Workers 'Try to Be Less White'?," Snopes, Feb. 23, 2021, www.snopes.com/fact-check/coca-cola -training-less-white/.

107 **broader training program**: A statement from Coca-Cola read, "The video in question was accessible on a third-party platform and was not part of the company's curriculum, so it was not required." While the material was part of a course offered by LinkedIn, and not Coca-Cola directly, employees claimed that Coca-Cola's statement was inaccurate, and the course was in fact mandatory. Paul Bond, "LinkedIn Removes Diversity Lesson Telling Employees to 'Be Less White,'" *Newsweek*, Feb. 23, 2021, www.newsweek.com /linkedin-removes-diversity-lesson-less-white-1571205.

107 **dozens of major corporations**: Daniel Bergner, "'White Fragility' Is Everywhere. But Does Antiracism Training Work?," *New York Times*, Aug. 6, 2021, www.nytimes.com/2020 /07/15/magazine/white-fragility-robin-diangelo.html.

108 **"The term 'psychological safety'"**: Raafi-Karim Alidina, "Diversity and Inclusion: How

to Foster Interfaith Understanding in the Workplace," HRZone, Feb. 14, 2020, www
.hrzone.com/lead/culture/diversity-and-inclusion-how-to-foster-interfaith
-understanding-in-the-workplace.

108 **Google, for example:** Arooj Ahmed, "The List of Top Ten US Colleges That Apple,
Facebook, and Google Hire From," Digital Information World, June 24, 2020, www
.digitalinformationworld.com/2020/06/the-list-of-top-ten-us-colleges-that-apple
-facebook-and-google-hire-from.html.

108 **graduates from Ivy League:** Weng Cheong, "The Hiring Policy at McKinsey, One of the
World's Most Elite Management Consultancies, Is Defined by One Thing: Harvard,"
Business Insider, Dec. 22, 2020, www.businessinsider.com/mckinsey-hiring-policy-2013-9.

108 **Goldman Sachs branches out:** Jeff Schmitt, "The Top Feeder Schools to Google,
Goldman Sachs, and More," Poets & Quants for Undergrads, Jan. 7, 2015, poetsandquants
forundergrads.com/rankings/the-top-feeder-schools-to-google-goldman-sachs-and
-more/2/.

108 **a significant share:** For an overview of academic work studying "insider activism," see
Forrest Briscoe and Abhinav Gupta, "Social Activism in and Around Organizations,"
Academy of Management Annals 10, no. 1 (2016): 671–727, doi.org/10.5465/19416520
.2016.1153261 as well as Tom C. W. Lin, "Incorporating Social Activism," *Boston University Law Review* 98, no. 6 (2018): 1535–606.

109 **"The voice of the workforce":** *Future of Work: Adapting to the Democratised Workplace*,
Herbert Smith Freehills, accessed Mar. 19, 2023, 4, www.herbertsmithfreehills.com
/latest-thinking/the-new-world-of-work-report-warns-of-an-unprecedented-rise
-in-workplace-activism-v2.

109 **four hundred C-suite executives:** *Future of Work*, 8.

109 **"In the first half of 2015":** Adrian Ma, "'Social Movements Are Contagious': Protests
Within Mass. Companies Are Part of a Growing Trend," WBUR News, Aug. 4, 2020,
www.wbur.org/news/2020/08/04/company-protests-black-lives-matter-whole-foods.
This pressure from the inside was often complemented by strategic interventions from
outside interest groups. The Human Rights Campaign, a major LGBT activist group, for
example, has developed an index to measure to what extent major corporations comply
with its preferences—and incentivize them to do better. As Apoorva Ghosh argues, the
so-called Corporate Equality Index serves as a "'certifier' of diversity achievement," incentivizing "Fortune 500 corporations that wish to retain and attract talented employees
and to portray a diversity-inclusive image to their customers and markets [to] chase high
scores on this index to demonstrate their diversity credentials." This mechanism was especially powerful at tech companies, consulting firms, and investment banks. All of these
ferociously compete for the top talent in each graduating class, in part by promising
would-be employees that a company's culture would match their values, allowing them
to "do good" while "doing well." In fact, Ghosh finds that the inclusion of new criteria
on the index had a very rapid and significant effect, with major companies scrambling to
offer expanded health coverage to their transgender employees to maintain a high rating
on the Corporate Equality Index. As Ghosh writes in the context of LGBT activism,
"Insider activists make the business case by advocating how these policy changes and
practices would help their employer in retaining (as well as attracting) talented LGBT
employees." See Apoorva Ghosh, "The Politics of Alignment and the 'Quiet Transgender
Revolution' in Fortune 500 Corporations, 2008 to 2017," *Socio-economic Review* 19, no.
3 (2021): 1095–125.

109 **"All it takes is one particularly vocal":** *Future of Work*, 10.

109 **process of "isomorphic diffusion":** In addition to Ghosh, see Forrest Briscoe and Sean
Safford, "The Nixon-in-China Effect: Activism, Imitation, and the Institutionalization
of Contentious Practices," *Administrative Science Quarterly* 53, no. 3 (2008): 460–91,
doi.org/10.2189/asqu.53.3.460.

109 **"highlight the adoption":** Ghosh, "Politics of Alignment," 1099.

109 **leaders of its industry:** Gabriel Rossman, "Why Woke Organizations All Sound the Same," *City Journal*, Autumn 2021, www.city-journal.org/why-woke-organizations-all -sound-the-same.

110 **kinds of training programs:** "To decide whether an institution had discriminated against a protected group, courts and regulators would often use a 'best practices' approach, meaning that if your competitors adopted the latest fad coming out of academia or the HR world, you felt the need to do the same" (Richard Hanania, "Woke Institutions Is Just Civil Rights Law," *Richard Hanania's Newsletter*, June 1, 2021, richardhanania .substack.com/p/woke-institutions-is-just-civil-rights). Similarly, a 2019 *Harvard Business Review* article found that discrimination lawsuits resulted in increased diversity and inclusion efforts and measurable gains in managerial diversity. There are multiple mechanisms behind this effect but one is likely the impression that diversity efforts safeguard against further discrimination lawsuits. Elizabeth Hirsch, "Do Lawsuits Improve Gender and Racial Equality at Work?," *Harvard Business Review*, Nov. 14, 2019, hbr.org/2019 /11/do-lawsuits-improve-gender-and-racial-equality-at-work.

110 **"Suppose that you're a manager":** Rossman, "Why Woke Organizations All Sound the Same."

Chapter 7: Dissent Discouraged

113 **The reasons for concern:** Jessica Taylor, "Trump Calls for 'Total and Complete Shutdown of Muslims Entering' U.S.," NPR, Dec. 7, 2015, www.npr.org/2015/12/07 /458836388/trump-calls-for-total-and-complete-shutdown-of-muslims-entering-u-s; Mark Berman, "Trump Tells Police Not to Worry About Injuring Suspects During Arrests," *Washington Post*, July 7, 2017, www.washingtonpost.com/news/post-nation/wp /2017/07/28/trump-tells-police-not-to-worry-about-injuring-suspects-during-arrests/; Jeremy Diamond, "Trump on 'Lock Her Up' Chant: 'I'm Starting to Agree,'" CNN, July 29, 2016, www.cnn.com/2016/07/29/politics/donald-trump-lock-her-up/index.html; Alan Rappeport, "Donald Trump Wavers on Disavowing David Duke," *New York Times*, Feb. 28, 2016, archive.nytimes.com/www.nytimes.com/politics/first-draft/2016/02 /28/donald-trump-declines-to-disavow-david-duke/; Jeremy Diamond, "Donald Trump: 'I Will Totally Accept' Election Results 'If I Win,'" CNN, Oct. 20, 2016, www.cnn.com /2016/10/20/politics/donald-trump-i-will-totally-accept-election-results-if-i-win/index .html.

113 **fears turned into reality:** Michael D. Shear and Helene Cooper, "Trump Bars Refugees and Citizens of 7 Muslim Countries," *New York Times*, Jan. 27, 2017, www.nytimes .com/2017/01/27/us/politics/trump-syrian-refugees.html; Joshua Block, Chase Strangio, and James Esseks, "Breaking Down Trump's Trans Military Ban: News & Commentary," American Civil Liberties Union, March 30, 2018, www.aclu.org/news/lgbtq -rights/breaking-down-trumps-trans-military-ban; Michael Shear and Matt Apuzzo, "F.B.I. Director James Comey Is Fired by Trump," *New York Times*, May 9, 2017, www .nytimes.com/2017/05/09/us/politics/james-comey-fired-fbi.html; Steve Inskeep, "Timeline: What Trump Told Supporters for Months Before They Attacked," NPR, Feb. 8, 2021, www.npr.org/2021/02/08/965342252/timeline-what-trump-told-supporters-for -months-before-they-attacked.

114 **huge outpouring of protest:** Perry Stein, Steve Hendrix, and Abigail Hauslohner, "Women's Marches: More Than One Million Protesters Vow to Resist President Trump," *Washington Post*, Jan. 22, 2017, www.washingtonpost.com/local/womens-march-on -washington-a-sea-of-pink-hatted-protesters-vow-to-resist-donald-trump/2017/01/21 /ae4def62-dfdf-11e6-acdf-14da832ae861_story.html.

114 **executive order on immigration:** Lauren Gambino et al., "Thousands Protest Against Trump Travel Ban in Cities and Airports Nationwide," *Guardian*, Jan. 29, 2017, www .theguardian.com/us-news/2017/jan/29/protest-trump-travel-ban-muslims-airports.

114 **small-donor donations:** Joanna Walters, "Progressive Causes See 'Unprecedented' Upswing in Donations After US Election," *Guardian*, Dec. 25, 2016, www.theguardian .com/us-news/2016/dec/25/progressive-donations-us-election-planned-parenthood -aclu.

114 **mobilized its members:** Ezra Levin, Leah Greenberg, and Angel Padilla, "To Stop Trump, Democrats Can Learn from the Tea Party," *New York Times*, Jan. 2, 2017, www .nytimes.com/2017/01/02/opinion/to-stop-trump-democrats-can-learn-from-the-tea -party.html.

114 **never held political office:** In the 2018 midterms, of 125 House districts that were competitive or occupied by a retiring incumbent Democrat, 73 Democratic nominees had never run for office before. Elena Schneider, "'Something Has Actually Changed': Women, Minorities, First-Time Candidates Drive Democratic House Hopes," *Politico*, Sept. 11, 2018, www.politico.com/story/2018/09/11/white-men-democratic-house-candidates -813717.

114 **"faithless electors" in the Electoral College:** Ed Pilkington, "'Faithless Electors' Explain Their Last-Ditch Attempt to Stop Donald Trump," *Guardian*, Dec. 19, 2016, www .theguardian.com/us-news/2016/dec/19/electoral-college-faithless-electors-donald -trump.

114 **breathless predictions on cable news:** At one point in the early stages of Trump's presidency, even betting markets gave Trump about a one-in-two chance of leaving office before the end of his term. See Gwynn Guilford, "Betting Markets Put the Odds of a Trump Impeachment or Resignation at around 48%," *Quartz*, February 12, 2017, https://qz.com/908600/will-donald-trump-be-impeached-or-resign-betting-markets -put-the-odds-at-around-48-percent.

114 **impeach the president:** Mitt Romney was the only senator not to agree with his caucus, voting to impeach Trump on charges relating to an "abuse of power" (while voting to acquit Trump on charges relating to obstruction of Congress). Richard Cowan, "Breaking with Republicans, Romney Votes 'Guilty' in Trump Impeachment Trial," Reuters, Feb. 5, 2020, www.reuters.com/article/us-usa-trump-impeachment-romney/breaking-with -republicans-romney-votes-guilty-in-trump-impeachment-trial-idUSKBN1ZZ2Q6.

115 **last women's march:** The organizers of the march claimed that twenty-five thousand people participated, but this is likely to be an overestimate. Austa Somvichian-Clausen, "After Low Attendance, Is the Women's March Still Relevant?," *Hill*, Jan. 22, 2020, thehill .com/changing-america/respect/equality/479358-after-low-attendance-is-the-womens -march-still-relevant/.

115 **"Maybe I can't end racism":** Ryan Grim, "Meltdowns Have Brought Progressive Advocacy Groups to a Standstill at a Critical Moment in World History," *Intercept*, June 13, 2022, theintercept.com/2022/06/13/progressive-organizing-infighting-callout-culture/.

116 **Donald McNeil, the first print journalist:** See, for example, Joe Pompeo, "'It's Chaos': Behind the Scenes of Donald McNeil's New York Times Exit," *Vanity Fair*, Feb. 10, 2021, www.vanityfair.com/news/2021/02/behind-the-scenes-of-donald-mcneils-new -york-times-exit; Maxwell Tani and Lachlan Cartwright, "Star NY Times Reporter Accused of Using 'N-Word,' Making Other Racist Comments," *Daily Beast*, Jan. 28, 2021, www.thedailybeast.com/star-new-york-times-reporter-donald-mcneil-accused -of-using-n-word-making-other-racist-comments.

116 **lost his position:** Matthew Yglesias, "The Real Stakes in the David Shor Saga," *Vox*, July 29, 2020, www.vox.com/2020/7/29/21340308/david-shor-omar-wasow-speech.

116 **misinterpreted a hand gesture:** Yascha Mounk, "Stop Firing the Innocent," *Atlantic*, June 27, 2020, www.theatlantic.com/ideas/archive/2020/06/stop-firing-innocent/613615. These are three examples that happened to make major headlines. But as a recent collection of similar incidents shows, there are hundreds or thousands of similar stories all across the country. See Philip K. Fry (@SoOppressed), "Since so many claim that cancel culture doesn't exist, I propose a challenge: For every additional 1,000 followers I get,

I will present 10 examples of cancel culture," Twitter, July 12, 2020, 4:01 p.m., twitter.com /sooppressed/status/1282404647160942598.

117 **"It's hard to find":** Grim, "Meltdowns."

117 **A lot of movement insiders:** As the Working Families Party director Maurice Mitchell warns, many activists complain that "our spaces are 'toxic' or 'problematic,' often sharing compelling and troubling personal anecdotes as evidence of this. People in leadership are finding their roles untenable, claiming it is 'impossible' to execute campaigns or saying they are in organizations that are 'stuck.'" Maurice Mitchell, "Building Resilient Organizations: Toward Joy and Durable Power in a Time of Crisis," *Nonprofit Quarterly*, Nov. 29, 2022, nonprofitquarterly.org/building-resilient-organizations-toward-joy-and-durable -power-in-a-time-of-crisis/. (I say more about Mitchell in the conclusion.)

117 **"So much energy has been devoted":** Grim, "Meltdowns."

117 **"We used to want to make":** Grim, "Meltdowns."

117 **"Isn't it odd that the true enemy":** Roy D'Andrade, "Moral Models in Anthropology," *Current Anthropology* 36, no. 3 (June 1995): 408, www.jstor.org/stable/2744050.

117 **In the spring of 1915:** David Stout, "Solomon Asch Is Dead at 88; A Leading Social Psychologist," *New York Times*, Feb. 29, 1996, www.nytimes.com/1996/02/29/us/solomon -asch-is-dead-at-88-a-leading-social-psychologist.html.

118 **prone to conformity:** Solomon Asch, "Effects of Group Pressure upon the Modification and Distortion of Judgments," in *Groups, Leadership, and Men: Research in Human Relations*, ed. Harold Steere Guetzkow (New York: Carnegie Press, 1951), 177–90. As Asch put it, "It can be of decisive importance whether or not a group will, under certain conditions, submit to existing pressures" (Asch, "Effects of Group Pressure," 177). Other psychologists have confirmed its main findings across a variety of different cultures. Rod Bond and Peter B. Smith, "Culture and Conformity: A Meta-analysis of Studies Using Asch's (1952b, 1956) Line Judgment Task," *Psychological Bulletin* 119, no. 1 (1996): 111–37, doi.org/10.1037/0033-2909.119.1.111.

118 **replicated by psychologists:** Bond and Smith, "Culture and Conformity."

119 **In the experiments:** Cass R. Sunstein, David Schkade, and Daniel Kahneman, "Are Juries Less Erratic Than Individuals? Deliberation, Polarization, and Punitive Damages" (John M. Olin Program in Law and Economics Working Paper No. 81, 1999).

119 **groups deliberating on damages:** Sunstein found that across a variety of mock damages cases, the average median compensation by an individual was $385,000, while the average median compensation determined by a group was $1,510,000. Sunstein, Schkade, and Kahneman, "Are Juries Less Erratic Than Individuals?"

119 **"the law of group polarization":** Cass R. Sunstein, "The Law of Group Polarization" (John M. Olin Program in Law and Economics Working Paper No. 91, 1999).

120 **"Internal criticism and dissent":** Levi Adelman and Nilanjana Dasgupta, "Effect of Threat and Social Identity on Reactions to Ingroup Criticism: Defensiveness, Openness, and a Remedy," *Personality and Social Psychology Bulletin* 45, no. 5 (2018): 740, doi.org /10.1177/0146167218796785. The tremendous influence that a few dissenters can have on moving the opinion of the whole group was even evident in the experiment by Solomon that helped to shape the whole field. When all of the other group members claimed that the wrong line matched the length of the original one, the students in his experiment also gave the wrong answer 36.8 percent of the time (compared with 1 percent when left alone). But if one other member of the group gave the right answer, they were much more likely to defy the majority: in those cases the number of incorrect answers dropped to a quarter of the ordinary error rate.

120 **Many groups are tolerant:** "Contrary to the assumed wisdom that dissenters face personal censure, there is a growing body of work showing that groups can be surprisingly accepting of dissenters within their ranks." Jolanda Jetten and Matthew J. Hornsey, "Deviance and Dissent in Groups," *Annual Review of Psychology* 65 (2014): 473, doi.org /10.1146/annurev-psych-010213-115151.

120 **perceived as loyal members:** "[Studies] consistently show that in-group members criticizing the group are downgraded less strongly than outsiders who make exactly the same comments." Jetten and Hornsey, "Deviance and Dissent in Groups," 473. See, for example, Aimée A. Kane, Linda Argote, and John M. Levine, "Knowledge Transfer Between Groups via Personnel Rotation: Effects of Social Identity and Knowledge Quality," *Organizational Behavior and Human Decision Processes* 96, no. 1 (2005): 56–71, doi.org /10.1016/j.obhdp.2004.09.002.

120 **And research also suggests:** The idea of reputational cascades is introduced by Timur Kuran and Cass Sunstein to refer to the phenomenon by which, "if a particular perception of an event somehow appears to have become the social norm, people seeking to build or protect their reputations will begin endorsing it through their words and deeds, regardless of their actual thoughts." Timur Kuran and Cass R. Sunstein, "Availability Cascades and Risk Regulation," *Stanford Law Review* 51, no. 4 (1999): 687, doi.org/10.2307/1229439.

121 **high moral stakes:** "Moral rebellion represents a threat to group members on three fronts: (*a*) The rebel's moral stance is seen as an implicit criticism of those who did not take the stance, so group members anticipate condemnation from the rebel; (*b*) the actions of the rebel make you question your own assumptions and attitudes, leading to a dissonance-like state; and (*c*) the rebel strips those of us who conspire in immoral acts from the rationalization that we had no choice." Jetten and Hornsey, "Deviance and Dissent in Groups," 470.

121 **making its members feel:** "The ingroup advantage related to openness to criticism is erased when perceivers feel their group is under threat. The results further suggest that the psychological mechanism underlying defensive responses to criticism is attributional— Threat elicits greater suspicion of ingroup critics' motives, which eliminates the ingroup critic's advantage relative to outgroup critics." Adelman and Dasgupta, "Effect of Threat and Social Identity on Reactions to Ingroup Criticism," 740.

121 **"Intergroup conflict increases enforcement":** Adelman and Dasgupta, "Effect of Threat and Social Identity on Reactions to Ingroup Criticism," 741. Notably, the preference for in-group over out-group critics disappears in such circumstances: "While people respond better to criticism of their group when it comes from a fellow ingroup member in the absence of conflict, that preference is diminished or eliminated when conflict is salient." Adelman and Dasgupta, "Effect of Threat and Social Identity on Reactions to Ingroup Criticism," 741.

121 **"criticism from ingroup members":** Adelman and Dasgupta, "Effect of Threat and Social Identity on Reactions to Ingroup Criticism," 742.

122 **open form of dissent:** This idea, that any criticism is in the service of right-wing extremism, is a core component of the critiques levied against those who worry about illiberal currents on the left. For instance, in a Twitter thread critiquing myself and others, the historian Thomas Zimmer asserted, "They will double down: Keep ridiculing the left-wing critique as 'alarmism,' keep downplaying the threat from the Right and all the warnings about fascistic extremism as hysterical, keep playing up the threat of 'woke' radicalism and the 'illiberal Left.'" The fact that I (and the other writers listed) have spoken extensively about the dangers of right-wing extremism does not matter; in-group criticism is sufficient evidence of betrayal. Thomas Zimmer (@tzimmer_history), Twitter, Nov. 26, 2022, 2:06 p.m., twitter.com/tzimmer_history/status/1596581239036805120.

122 **Bush's Manichaean claim:** "Address to a Joint Session of Congress and the American People," Sept. 20, 2001, National Archives and Records Administration, georgewbush -whitehouse.archives.gov/news/releases/2001/09/20010920-8.html. For criticisms of Bush's speech, see, for example, Michael Kinsley, "Lying in Style," *Washington Post*, April 19, 2002, https://www.washingtonpost.com/archive/opinions/2002/04/19/lying-in-style /e99ef2a5-daf4-4d21-a5be-d52cd97a1123/, as well as (more amusingly) Dan Skinner, "Calling Bush's Views Manichean Is an Insult to the Manicheans," History News Network, http://hnn.us/articles/7202.html, last accessed 24 March 2023.

122 **"In writing *How to Be an Antiracist*"**: Ibram X. Kendi, "Racist or Antiracist," UUA .org, Aug. 4, 2020, www.uua.org/worship/words/reading/racist-or-antiracist.

123 **gap in income:** The lack of clarity about which dimension of racial disparity should be reduced is one of many problems with Kendi's theory. As Amartya Sen has argued in his classic work, *Equality of What?*, reducing inequality along one dimension (such as overall income) is only possible at the price of increasing inequality along another dimension (such as hourly wage). Similarly, in many contexts, an action that reduces racial disparity along one dimension (such as the racial disparity in grades at the high school level) may increase racial disparity along another dimension (such as the racial disparity in college graduation rates). Without a clear set of criteria about *what kind* of racial disparity an antiracist policy would need to reduce, many policies will therefore turn out to be simultaneously racist (in aggravating one racial disparity) and antiracist (in alleviating another racial disparity).

123 **between white and Black:** As Kendi puts it, "A racist policy is any measure that produces or sustains racial inequity between racial groups." Ibram X. Kendi, *How to Be an Antiracist* (New York: Random House Large Print, 2020), 19. As one article by a scholar at the Brookings Institution points out, this view amounts to a denial that "policies can have disparate racial outcomes without being racist." Universal health care, for example, would lead to disparate racial outcomes, and thus be considered racist so long as "Black communities had fewer or lower quality health care providers and facilities or if Black patients were reluctant to take advantage of universal health care for any reason, such as past mistreatment and discrimination." William G. Gale, "Reflections on What Makes a Policy Racist," Brookings Institution, Nov. 4, 2021, www.brookings.edu/wp-content /uploads/2021/11/Reflections-on-What-Makes-a-Policy-Racist-1.pdf.

123 **racial disparities are racist:** "Standardized tests have become the most effective racist weapon ever devised to objectively degrade Black and Brown minds and legally exclude their bodies from prestigious schools" ("Read Ibram X. Kendi's Testimony in Support of the Working Group Recommendation to #Suspendthetest," Boston Coalition for Education Equity, Oct. 21, 2020, www.bosedequity.org/blog/read-ibram-x-kendis-testimony -in-support-of-the-working-group-recommendation-to-suspendthetest). "Historically capitalism + racism are interlinked, which is why I call them the conjoined twins + historians like me call them 'racial capitalism' in the singular. But some self-described forms of 'antiracism' are not anti-capitalist, which in my book means they're not antiracism" (Ibram X. Kendi [@DrIbram], Twitter, Sept. 6, 2020, 5:44 p.m., twitter.com/dribram /status/1302724276412387334?lang=en).

123 **"Americans who self-identity as not racist":** Othering & Belonging Institute, "Ibram X. Kendi on How to Be an Antiracist, at UC Berkeley | #400Years," YouTube, video, 2:04:24, Sept. 18, 2019, www.youtube.com/watch?v=mxa43H8m034.

123 **Robin DiAngelo has a message for you:** Sandee LaMotte, "Robin DiAngelo: How 'White Fragility' Supports Racism and How Whites Can Stop It," CNN, June 7, 2020, https:// edition.cnn.com/2020/06/07/health/white-fragility-robin-diangelo-wellness/index.html.

124 **"If you object to any":** John McWhorter, "The Dehumanizing Condescension of 'White Fragility,'" *Atlantic*, July 15, 2020, www.theatlantic.com/ideas/archive/2020 /07/dehumanizing-condescension-white-fragility/614146/.

124 **most sold books:** Stephanie Merry and Ron Charles, "Books About Race and Racism Are Dominating Bestseller Lists," *Washington Post*, June 4, 2020, www.washingtonpost .com/entertainment/books/books-about-race-and-racism-are-dominating-bestseller -lists/2020/06/04/e6efdab6-a69b-11ea-bb20-ebf0921f3bbd_story.html; Jemima McEvoy, "Books About Racism Dominate Best-Seller Lists amid Protests," *Forbes*, June 11, 2020, www.forbes.com/sites/jemimamcevoy/2020/06/11/black-lives-matter-dominates -best-seller-lists-amid-protests/.

124 **spawning a franchise:** Merry and Charles, "Books About Race and Racism."

124 **"Babies are taught":** Ibram X. Kendi and Ashley Lukashevsky, *Antiracist Baby* (New York: Kokila, 2020).

124 **major television programs:** Donovan X. Ramsey, "Being Antiracist Is Work, Even for Ibram X. Kendi," *Wall Street Journal*, July 6, 2020, www.wsj.com/articles/being-antiracist -is-work-even-for-ibram-x-kendi-11594039803.

124 **antiracist reading lists:** See, for example, Diana Shi, "Reading List: Books for Building an Anti-racist Workplace," *Fast Company*, June 4, 2020, www.fastcompany.com/90512400 /7-important-books-for-building-an-anti-racist-workplace.

PART III: THE FLAWS OF THE IDENTITY SYNTHESIS

129 **For white students to wear:** Personal communication with a student at the school.

130 **progressives have drawn:** Given the number of claims that writers and activists rooted in the popularized version of the identity synthesis have made about a vast array of topics with great practical importance, I could easily have included a discussion of other contro-versial topics, like the nature of gender or the merits of meritocracy. (I do briefly have something to say about both in chapter 13.) Conversely, it is clear that many academics who embrace core tenets of the identity synthesis would not endorse all of these ideas; indeed, many intellectual progenitors of identitarianism, from Kimberlé Crenshaw to Michel Foucault, likely would have incisive criticisms about many of them.

   And yet there is a real logic to the topics discussed in this part of the book. All five are advocated by writers and activists who trace their position back to the language and the values of the popularized form of the identity synthesis; concern issues of great practical importance; have quickly come to have real influence in the world; and stand in direct or indirect conflict with the liberal-universalist norms they are designed to supplant. In assessing them, we can test whether the popularized form of the identity synthesis can help us overcome the injustices that persist in contemporary democracies—or whether it is likely to lead us astray, ultimately running the risk of aggravating existing injustices.

Chapter 8: How to Understand Each Other

133 **"I got there just during the rehearsal":** Joseph Stein, "Fiddler on the Roof and Me," *Guardian*, May 18, 2007, www.theguardian.com/stage/theatreblog/2007/may/18 /fiddlerontheroofandme.

133 **into something "universal":** Stein, "Fiddler on the Roof and Me."

134 **"I am human":** Terence, *Heauton Timorumenos*, act 1, scene 1, line 77.

134 **this humanist tradition:** Even early postcolonial scholars and activists still held on to this hope, as when Frantz Fanon argued that "an individual must endeavor to assume the universalism inherent in the human condition." Frantz Fanon, *Black Skin, White Masks* (New York: Grove Press, 2008), xiv.

134 **"We Are the World":** Michael Jackson, "We Are the World" (Columbia Records, 1985).

134 **ingrained racism and implicit bias:** See chapter 5.

134 **advise aspiring novelists:** As the author Jared Marcel Pollen recounted, "The long-used adage of writing workshops—'write what you know'—a thing often meant to guide a person's creativity to the aliveness of their own experience, is now becoming a kind of injunction, delivered in the same menacing tone as 'check your privilege' or 'stay in your lane.'" Jared Marcel Pollen, "Truth, Social Justice, and the American Writer," *Smart Set*, April 6, 2020, www.thesmartset.com/truth-social-justice-and-the-american-writer/.

134 **apologized for portraying characters:** Scottie Andrew, "Tom Hanks Says 'Philadelphia' Wouldn't Get Made Today with a Straight Actor in a Gay Role," CNN, June 16, 2022, www.cnn.com/2022/06/16/entertainment/tom-hanks-gay-character-philadelphia -cec/index.html; Hannah Sparks, "Eddie Redmayne Says Trans Role in 'The Danish Girl' Was 'a Mistake,'" *New York Post*, Nov. 22, 2021, nypost.com/2021/11/22/why -eddie-redmayne-regrets-trans-role-in-the-danish-girl/; Eric Deggans, "Jenny Slate and Kristen Bell Will Stop Playing Biracial Cartoon Characters," NPR, June 25, 2020, www

.npr.org/sections/live-updates-protests-for-racial-justice/2020/06/25/883622069
/jenny-slate-and-kristen-bell-will-stop-playing-biracial-cartoon-characters.

134 **voicing an Asian American:** Jordan Moreau, "'BoJack Horseman' Star Alison Brie Apologizes for Voicing Vietnamese American Character," Decider, June 28, 2020, decider.com/2020/06/28/bojack-horseman-star-alison-brie-apologizes-for-voicing -vietnamese-american-character/.

134 **"Don't come to me":** "8 Lessons from 'The Future of Solidarity: How White People Can Support the Movement for Black Lives,'" Catalyst Project, April 18, 2016, uucsj.org /wp-content/uploads/2016/05/How-White-People-Can-Support-the-Movement-for -Black-Lives.pdf.

134 **"Even if they can hear you":** Reni Eddo-Lodge, *Why I'm No Longer Talking to White People About Race* (New York: Bloomsbury, 2019), x.

136 **a hallucination induced:** René Descartes, *Discourse on Method* (1637), pts. 4 and 5.

136 **philosophers debate such questions:** The traditional "tripartite" understanding of "knowledge" adds a third condition beyond true belief: the believer must be "justified" in believing that the proposition is true. For instance, if I believe a coin flip will land heads, and the coin happens to land heads, my belief was correct, but I didn't "know" it would land heads. See Jonathan Jenkins Ichikawa and Matthias Steup, "The Analysis of Knowledge," in *Stanford Encyclopedia of Philosophy*, March 7, 2017, plato.stanford.edu /entries/knowledge-analysis/#KnowJustTrueBeli.

136 **depends on the identity group:** Donna Haraway, "Situated Knowledges: The Science Question in Feminism and the Privilege of Partial Perspective," *Feminist Studies* 14, no. 3 (1988), doi.org/10.2307/3178066.

136 **"standpoint epistemology":** Early proponents of standpoint epistemology criticized traditional ways to acquire knowledge about the world as positing an unrealistic "view from nowhere." Traditional scientific research, they pointed out, is written from the perspective of humanity in general: "The subject of knowledge claims was to be an idealized agent who performed the 'God trick' of speaking authoritatively about everything in the world from no particular location or human perspective at all" (Sandra G. Harding, *The Feminist Standpoint Theory Reader: Intellectual and Political Controversies* [London: Routledge, 2009], 4). But in practice, they claimed, this simply amounted to ascribing a neutral authority to the perspective of the white men who carried out most scientific research. This blind spot could only be addressed by recognizing that a researcher's standpoint can actually enhance (or constrain) their ability to gain key insights.

136 **"The social location of women":** Harding, *Feminist Standpoint Theory Reader*, 4.

136 **"race, ethnicity-based, anti-imperial":** Harding, *Feminist Standpoint Theory Reader*, 3.

137 **impossibility of mutual comprehension:** Harding, *Feminist Standpoint Theory Reader*, 3.

137 **"In everyday conversation":** Lidal Dror, "Is There an Epistemic Advantage to Being Oppressed?," *Noûs*, June 23, 2022, 2, doi.org/10.1111/nous.12424.

138 **the group special insight:** As Lidal Dror expresses this point in a critical appraisal, what he calls the inversion thesis holds that "socially marginalized people, by virtue of their social location, have a superior epistemic position than non-oppressed people when it comes to knowing things about the workings of social marginalization that concern them." Dror, "Epistemic Advantage," 2.

138 **special perspective of women:** In this view, women's integral role in reproduction and as the caretaker of the household gives them an epistemic advantage in understanding the ways patriarchy fails to meet people's needs. For a discussion of this point, see Elizabeth Anderson, "Feminist Epistemology and Philosophy of Science," in *Stanford Encyclopedia of Philosophy*, Feb. 13, 2020, plato.stanford.edu/entries/feminism-epistemology/.

138 **other feminist philosophers:** For one classic argument against the idea that women have an essential core, whether based on the experience of child rearing or of being sexually objectified, see Elizabeth V. Spelman, *Inessential Woman: Problems of Exclusion in Feminist Thought* (Boston: Beacon Press, 1988).

138 **burden of caregiving:** Members of privileged groups can also make choices—such as joining a social movement that fights on behalf of the downtrodden—that enhance their level of insight into the experiences of less fortunate groups. Charles Mills, for example, has argued that the experience of the picket line gives working-class people experiential knowledge of class oppression, but a labor activist from a middle-class family will come to have the same experience, and may well draw the same insights from it. Charles Mills, *Blackness Visible* (Ithaca, N.Y.: Cornell University Press, 1998), 31–32. See also the discussion of this point in Dror, "Epistemic Advantage," 4.

138 **"You're going to have to abandon":** Rachel Fraser, interview by Yascha Mounk, *Persuasion*, Sept. 11, 2021, podcast, www.persuasion.community/p/-you-just-wont-understand #details. Interestingly, past attempts by the people who have had the most influence on the identity synthesis to define women by some common feature have, especially from the perspective of today's progressive activists, aged badly. When first floating the idea of "strategic essentialism" in an interview, for example, Spivak advocated defining women by the fact that they have a clitoris, an assumption that most advocates of the tradition would now strongly reject. See the section "The Embrace of Strategic Essentialism" in chapter 2.

139 **knowledge that are inaccessible:** As Dror points out, this is especially important because some injustices are not readily apparent from the perspective of one person; structural inequities, in particular, are only evident by comparing how different people are treated in similar situations. As Dror writes, "Because much oppression and injustice is structural, and thus simply incapable of being appreciated except by seeing how institutions treat whole classes of persons, some privileged people, with superior access to information that is costly to acquire and process, will have an epistemically privileged position. Even if marginalized people have good local evidence, they aren't always in the position of some privileged people to access the general information required for certain judgements about the workings of social marginalization." Dror, "Epistemic Advantage," 7.

139 **"Though an exploited factory worker":** Dror, "Epistemic Advantage," 5. Anyone who thinks this point is purely abstract should read the work of Friedrich Engels, the scion of a family that owned textile factories in both Germany and England. See Friedrich Engels, *The Condition of the Working Class in England* (Leipzig: Otto Wigand, 1845).

139 **impossible to know:** There is even a limit to the extent to which I can come to have the same feelings by *choosing* to put myself in a position that will give me some of the same experiences. For, as Jarvis Cocker recognized in "Common People," a rich person who chooses to live in poverty (or to join a picket line) will always have a crucial lifeline:

> Rent a flat above a shop
> Cut your hair and get a job
> Smoke some fags and play some pool
> Pretend you never went to school
> But still you'll never get it right
> 'Cause when you're laid in bed at night
> Watching roaches climb the wall
> If you called your dad he could stop it all.

> (Pulp, "Common People")

139 **real limits to the extent:** As Uma Narayan argues, "Unlike concerned 'outsiders' whose knowledge of the experience of oppression is always more or less abstract and theoretical, the knowledge of 'insiders' is enriched by the emotional reactions/responses that the lived experience of oppression confers" (Uma Narayan, "Working Together Across Difference: Some Considerations on Emotions and Political Practice," *Hypatia* 3, no. 2 [1988]: 31–47, doi.org/10.1111/j.1527-2001.1988.tb00067.x). But as Dror points out, in

many contemporary debates "the purported epistemic advantage is not limited to experiential knowledge of what it feels like to be oppressed. Rather, the oppressed are supposed to also have an epistemic position superior to that of non-marginalized people when it comes to knowing descriptive and normative facts concerning social relations, social institutions, social thought, the functioning of systems of power, and what is oppressive, with respect to the systems that leave them socially marginalized" (Dror, "Epistemic Advantage," 2).

139 **what philosophers call "propositional" knowledge:** Dror, "Epistemic Advantage," 15.

140 **legal for sex workers:** Fraser, interview by Mounk.

140 **strong arguments against:** Molly Smith and Juno Mac, *Revolting Prostitutes: The Fight for Sex Workers' Rights* (London: Verso, 2018). Note that I am not taking a position on whether the Nordic model is, all things considered, a good policy.

140 **"The role of experience in politics":** Fraser, interview by Mounk.

140 **"While the oppressed may often have":** Dror, "Epistemic Advantage," 3.

141 **"often want to say that the fruits":** Fraser, interview by Mounk.

141 **"If you're not prepared":** Ian Schwartz, "Rep. Ayanna Pressley: 'We Don't Need Any More Brown Faces That Don't . . . ,'" Real Clear Politics, July 14, 2019, www.realclearpolitics .com/video/2019/07/14/rep_ayanna_pressley_we_dont_need_any_more_brown _faces_that_dont_want_to_be_a_brown_voice.html.

142 **does or does not represent:** Pressley is not alone in making these claims. As Lidal Dror has pointed out, academics have often tried to draw a similar distinction between someone who "merely happens to be black" and someone who expresses a "truly black" perspective: "Many standpoint theorists distinguish between the 'mere' *perspective* of a marginalized group of people (say, women) and the *standpoint* of a marginalized people (say, the feminist standpoint), where the standpoint denotes a collectively achieved, ideologically committed way of looking that is open to people inside and outside of the group. Often, then, these theorists claim that epistemic advantage accrues to those who possess the *standpoint*, as opposed to those who merely have the relevant *perspective*." Dror, "Epistemic Advantage," 4.

142 **a legitimate spokesperson:** Let us assume that we have, despite these difficulties, somehow managed to appoint a spokesperson for each disadvantaged group. We have identified the legitimate "queer voice." We have also identified the legitimate "Muslim voice." But as it happens, the representatives of these two groups have a fundamental disagreement about an important question of public policy. This gives rise to a second problem: Whose preferences should now take precedence?

It might seem as though there were an obvious answer to this. People would need to listen carefully to the experiences and arguments of both groups. Then they would decide which demand to support in accordance with their own views and values. But according to standpoint theory, this is wrong. We are, after all, incapable of truly understanding the experiences of more oppressed groups, and should abstain from evaluating the justice of their demands for ourselves. But how, then, is anybody who is neither Muslim nor queer supposed to decide between the rival claims of these two groups?

In the real world, the answer is simple. Even though they claim that it is impossible to understand or evaluate the causes of more oppressed groups, virtually all adherents of standpoint theory will think themselves perfectly capable of relating to the experience of others enough to know, say, that disabled Black women are more oppressed than gay white men. But this only serves to show that they do not practice what they preach: faced with the problem of adjudication, they listen to the demands and experiences of both groups and then make a reasoned decision about the extent to which each justifies redress.

142 **dean of the Harvard Kennedy School:** Douglas Elmendorf, "Updates on Diversity, Inclusion, and Belonging at HKS," Oct. 20, 2022, www.hks.harvard.edu/announcements /updates-diversity-inclusion-and-belonging-hks.

142 **president of the United States:** Soo Kim, "Joe Biden Saying 'Latinx' Sparks Widespread Mockery, Wave of Jokes," *Newsweek*, June 25, 2021, www.newsweek.com/joe-biden -saying-latinx-sparks-widespread-mockery-wave-jokes-1604032.

142 **prefer the new locution:** Marc Caputo and Sabrina Rodriguez, "Democrats Fall Flat with 'Latinx' Language," *Politico*, Dec. 6, 2021, www.politico.com/news/2021/12/06 /hispanic-voters-latinx-term-523776. See also comments by Ruben Gallego, a Latino member of the House of Representatives who is currently running for the Democratic nomination in Arizona's 2024 election for the U.S. Senate: "First start by not using the term Latinx. Second we have to be in front of them year round not just election years. That is what we did in AZ." Ruben Gallego (@RubenGallego), Twitter, Nov. 4, 2020, 2:28 p.m., twitter.com/rubengallego/status/1324071039085670401.

143 **powerful members within:** That might seem like an abstract concern. But in practice, the determination of who is a legitimate representative is almost always fraught with bias and opportunism.

Take the case of Sharice Davids, a former mixed martial arts professional who entered Congress in 2018 alongside members of "the Squad" like Alexandria Ocasio-Cortez and Ilhan Omar. As a young, lesbian Native American with a fascinating life story and great charisma, Davids should be a shooting star in a party that celebrates youth and diversity. But while Pressley, Omar, and especially Ocasio-Cortez have often been on the front pages of glossy magazines, Davids is little known outside her own district. Why?

Here's one explanation. The members of the Squad all hail from deep blue districts and have views that place them on the far left of the Democratic Party. Davids, who represents Kansas's Third District, comes from a much more politically heterogeneous part of the country. She ran on a moderate platform, is a member of the centrist New Democrat Coalition, and secured her nomination in a tough primary contest against a candidate endorsed by Bernie Sanders.

Part of the explanation for why the members of the Squad have become the face of the Democratic congressional delegation, while most Americans have never heard of Davids, is that their views are more similar to those of editors, producers, anchors, and opinion writers at the country's most influential left-of-center news outlets. After all, it has long been the strange fate of American socialism to be much more popular among the kinds of graduates of elite colleges who go on to work for *The New York Times* or MSNBC than it is among maids, welders, or fast-food workers.

But there is also something deeper going on. In the United States, journalists, think tankers, and philanthropists tend to associate nonwhite voters and politicians with far-left policies. When they listen to Pressley or Ocasio-Cortez, they take the opinions they put forward to be typical of a rising generation of nonwhite voters. When they listen to Davids, they take her to be an outlier—somebody who may happen to be Native American but is not, as Pressley might say, a "Native American voice."

The bitter irony, of course, is that this is a misperception. Far from being more radical than white Democrats, for example, Black and brown Democrats are actually significantly more likely to consider themselves moderate or conservative. Even on issues where African Americans *do* tend to be more progressive than other Democrats, like racial justice and police reform, their opinions are far more mainstream than those of the voices that supposedly represent them. While AOC and other members of the Squad have embraced the slogan "Defund the Police," for example, polls show that most African Americans oppose cuts to police budgets and would like to have more cops patrolling their neighborhoods. (Kim Parker and Kiley Hurst, "Growing Share of Americans Say They Want More Spending on Police in Their Area," Pew Research Center, Oct. 26, 2021, www.pewresearch.org/fact-tank/2021/10/26/growing-share-of-americans-say-they -want-more-spending-on-police-in-their-area/.)

These distortions are, sadly, closer to being the rule than the exception. The desire to have a "Black voice" or a "brown voice" at the table is understandable. But is it really a surprise that a political conception that boils more than forty million African Americans and more than sixty million Latinos down to such simplistic shorthand will often fail to capture the actual views of the people in whose name it purports to speak? This endnote draws on Yascha Mounk, "Lessons of the 2020 Election: What Democrats and Republicans Must Now Do to Win," *Wall Street Journal*, Nov. 20, 2020, www.wsj.com/articles/lessons-of-the-2020-election-what-democrats-and-republicans-must-now-do-to-win-11605887801.

143 **"The notion of the undifferentiated":** Bayard Rustin, "The Failure of Black Separatism," *Harper's Magazine*, Jan. 1970, 27.

143 **defer to an oppressed group:** This way of building political coalitions also risks perpetuating a deep inequality of status. Instead of being rooted in the recognition of shared values or interests, the willingness to pursue a common political goal is merely a function of one party recognizing that the other party belongs to a group that is more oppressed. Meant to overcome deep forms of status inequality, standpoint theory makes its putative beneficiaries forever conscious of being the recipients of a kind of political charity—one rooted in the mutual recognition of their social inferiority. For a similar point in a different context, see Elizabeth S. Anderson, "What Is the Point of Equality?," *Ethics* 109, no. 2 (1999): 287–337.

Chapter 9: The Joys of Mutual Influence

148 **a self-portrait:** Cao Fei, *Plant Contest*, Hood Museum of Art, accessed Jan. 30, 2023, hoodmuseum.dartmouth.edu/objects/2018.37.32.

148 **an extra string:** For a canonical mention of Therpandrus in the history of political thought, see Benjamin Constant, *The Liberty of Ancients Compared with That of Moderns* (1819). ("Among the Spartans, Therpandrus could not add a string to his lyre without causing offense to the ephors.")

148 **fears about the cultural changes:** For broader context on the end of Chinese seafaring, see, for example, Sue Gronewald: "The Ming Voyages," Asia for Educators, Columbia University, afe.easia.columbia.edu/special/china_1000ce_mingvoyages.htm#, accessed Mar. 24, 2023.

148 **spoil the authenticity:** *Encyclopædia Britannica*, s.v. "Wagner's Anti-Semitism," accessed Mar. 24, 2023, www.britannica.com/biography/Richard-Wagner-German-composer/Wagners-anti-Semitism.

149 **danger of the moment:** See, for example, Ben Zimmer, "The Origins of the 'Globalist' Slur," *Atlantic*, March 14, 2018, www.theatlantic.com/politics/archive/2018/03/the-origins-of-the-globalist-slur/555479/.

149 **defenders of traditional mores:** Matina Stevis-Gridneff, "'Protecting Our European Way of Life'? Outrage Follows New E.U. Role," *New York Times*, Sept. 12, 2019, www.nytimes.com/2019/09/12/world/europe/eu-ursula-von-der-leyen-migration.html.

149 **cultures of others:** "There is a way of appreciating a culture that respects that it's off limits." Nadia Khamsi, "Respecting the Lodge," Indigenous Land, Urban Stories, accessed Jan. 24, 2023, indigenouslandurbanstories.ca/portfolio-item/sweat-lodge/.

149 **"Birmingham School of Cultural Studies":** Sean Johnson Andrews, "The Birmingham School of Cultural Studies," in *Oxford Research Encyclopedia of Communication*, Oct. 27, 2020, doi.org/10.1093/acrefore/9780190228613.013.44.

150 **"Who represents whom":** Sabine Wilms, "Orientalism, Cultural Appropriation, and Critical Thinking (Part One)," Happy Goat Productions, Jan. 22, 2017, www.happygoatproductions.com/blog/2017/1/22/orientalism-cultural-appropriation-and-critical-thinking-part-one; Vinay Lal, "History of British India [LEC 02]," YouTube, Jan. 26, 2014, www.youtube.com/watch?v=q3eiZjzhRGg. (Starts at 46:18.)

150 **"in every cultural appropriation":** Robert S. Nelson and Richard Shiff, *Critical Terms for Art History*, 2nd ed. (Chicago: University of Chicago Press, 2003), 172.

150 **book contracts canceled:** See, for example, Andrew R. Chow, "Lucky Lee's Restaurant Sparks Cultural Appropriation Debate," *Time*, April 10, 2019, time.com/5567450/lucky -lees-chinese-food-appropriation/; and Alexandra Alter, "Y.A. Author Pulls Her Debut After Pre-publication Accusations of Racism," *New York Times*, Jan. 31, 2019, www.nytimes .com/2019/01/31/books/amelie-wen-zhao-blood-heir-ya-author-pulls-debut-accusations -racism.html.

150 **allowing a Gentile writer:** Shiryn Ghermezian, "Bon Appetit Magazine Edits Haman-taschen Article to 'Better Convey' Purim Holiday and Jewish Culture," Algemeiner .com, Feb. 12, 2021, www.algemeiner.com/2021/02/12/bon-appetit-magazine-edits -hamantaschen-article-to-better-convey-purim-holiday-and-jewish-culture/.

150 **traditional Jewish head covering:** Armin Langer, "Lasst die Kippa uns Juden!," *Spiegel Online*, April 25, 2018, www.spiegel.de/kultur/gesellschaft/berlin-deutsche-sollten-keine -kippa-tragen-a-1204689.html.

150 **And in the U.K.:** Eromo Egbejule, "World Jollof Day: Jamie Oliver's #Ricegate and Other Scandals," *Guardian*, Aug. 22, 2016, www.theguardian.com/world/2016/aug/22/world -jollof-day-jamies-oliver-rice-scandals; Frances Perraudin, "Gordon Ramsay Defends New Restaurant in Cultural Appropriation Row," *Guardian*, April 14, 2019, www.theguardian .com/food/2019/apr/14/gordon-ramsay-defends-lucky-cat; "Adele Accused of Cultural Appropriation over Instagram Picture," *Guardian*, Sept. 1, 2020, www.theguardian.com /music/2020/sep/01/adele-accused-of-cultural-appropriation-over-instagram-picture.

151 **steal the songs:** Brian Ward, "Champion or Copycat? Elvis Presley's Ambiguous Relation-ship with Black America," *Conversation*, Aug. 14, 2017, theconversation.com/champion -or-copycat-elvis-presleys-ambiguous-relationship-with-black-america-82293.

151 **"Cinco de Drinko":** Samantha Schmidt, "Baylor Frat Holds 'Cinco de Drinko' Party. Students Reportedly Dressed as Maids, Construction Workers," *Washington Post*, May 3, 2017, www.washingtonpost.com/news/morning-mix/wp/2017/05/03/baylor-frat-holds -drinko-de-mayo-party-dressed-as-maids-construction-workers-students-say/.

151 **"My dad is a painter":** Schmidt, "Baylor Frat."

152 **rightful intellectual property:** See the discussion of such claims, and a critique of them, in Kristen A. Carpenter, Sonia K. Katyal, and Angela R. Riley, "In Defense of Property," *Yale Law Journal* 118, no. 6 (April 2009): 1022–255, www.yalelawjournal.org/article /in-defense-of-property.

152 **form of oppression:** Erich Hatala Matthes, "Cultural Appropriation and Oppression," *Philosophical Studies* 176, no. 4 (2018): 1003–13, doi.org/10.1007/s11098-018-1224-2.

152 **impinges on the "intimacy":** C. Thi Nguyen and Matthew Strohl, "Cultural Appro-priation and the Intimacy of Groups," *Philosophical Studies* 176, no. 4 (Jan. 2019): 981–1002, doi.org/10.1007/s11098-018-1223-3.

152 **"mixes his labor":** John Locke, *Second Treatise of Government*, ed. C. B. Macpherson (Indianapolis: Hackett, 1980), 11–12.

153 **raked over the coals:** See, for example, Conor Friedersdorf, "Oberlin College's Food Fight," *Atlantic*, Dec. 21, 2015, www.theatlantic.com/politics/archive/2015/12/the-food -fight-at-oberlin-college/421401/. For another case involving two women running a burrito truck, see Tim Carman, "Should White Chefs Sell Burritos? A Portland Food Cart's Revealing Controversy," *Washington Post*, May 26, 2017, www.washingtonpost.com /news/food/wp/2017/05/26/should-white-chefs-sell-burritos-a-portland-restaurants -revealing-controversy/.

154 **"Trying to find some primordially authentic":** Kwame Anthony Appiah, "The Case for Contamination," *New York Times*, Jan. 1, 2006, www.nytimes.com/2006/01/01/magazine /the-case-for-contamination.html.

155 **first created the rebozo:** "Deciphering the various threads of the rebozo's history is com-plex. The multitude of influences was global—Chinese silk and scarves, Southeast Asian *ikate*, shawls that arrived with the Manila galleon, pre-Hispanic woven garments, and Spanish and Moorish designs." Marion Oettinger and Lee Boltin, *Folk Treasures of Mex-*

ico: The Nelson A. Rockefeller Collection in the San Antonio Museum of Art and the Mexican Museum, San Francisco (Houston, Tex.: Arte Público Press, 2010).

155 **inappropriate for white women:** See, for example, Montse Olmos and Mayte Acolt, "The Rebozo & Beyond: Cultural Appropriation & Birth," *Your Birth Partners*, May 3, 2021, podcast, yourbirthpartners.org/rebozo-appropriation/; and "The Rebozo Craze and Non-Latinx Birth Workers: Bini Birth," Bini Birth | Childbirth Education & Doula Training, Jan. 13, 2020, binibirth.com/the-rebozo-craze-and-non-latinx-birth-workers/.

155 **the collective "owners":** Indeed, some do argue this position: Sammitha Sreevathsa, "Classical Dance and Appropriation: How to Think About a Field Whose Foundations Rest on Cultural Violence," *Firstpost*, Dec. 1, 2019, www.firstpost.com/living/classical-dance-and-appropriation-how-to-think-about-a-field-whose-foundations-rest-on-cultural-violence-7708381.html.

156 **hail from Spain:** "Cochinita Pibil," DishRoots, July 30, 2018, www.dishroots.com/post/cochinita-pibil.

157 **The Toronto Star:** "a white owned trendy spot on ossington is selling bone broth across from golden turtle pho. also sexualizing 'jerk' sauce and pho hot sauce and making 'superfood dumplings' for profit? y'all im sick" (Evy Kwong [@EVYSTADIUM], Twitter, Nov. 18, 2020, 12:15 p.m., twitter.com/EVYSTADIUM/status/1329110893133783040). See also "UPDATE: Permission, the store that shared space the that *spot* is immediately ending the partnership" (Evy Kwong [@EVYSTADIUM], Twitter, Nov. 19, 2020, 1:45 p.m., twitter.com/EVYSTADIUM/status/1329496148353101826).

157 **from Black musicians:** Matthew Swayne, "How the 1950s Racism Helped Make Pat Boone a Rock Star," InnerSelf.com, accessed Mar. 24, 2023, innerself.com/social/culture-wars/14776-how-the-1950s-racism-helped-make-pat-boone-a-rock-star.html.

158 **enjoying the rightful fruits:** Michael Harriot, "The 10 Biggest Cultural Thefts in Black History," *Root*, May 30, 2019, www.theroot.com/the-10-biggest-cultural-thefts-in-black-history-1835106474. Similarly, the term "cultural appropriation" does not adequately capture what is unjust about the fact that key artworks from former British colonies like India and Kenya are owned by the British Museum. The problem is not that it is inherently inappropriate for art from one country to be owned by or displayed in the cultural institutions of another country; it is that many of these artworks were acquired under deeply unjust circumstances. The problems at stake include property theft and the broader ills of colonial domination, a stark reality that talk about "cultural appropriation" does more to cloak than to reveal.

158 **Traditional Polish culture:** The largest religion in Poland is Roman Catholicism, the country uses the Arabic numerical system, letters that are based (with small alterations) on Latin script, and its cuisine makes heavy use of potatoes.

158 **was cultural hybridity:** "[Eighth- and ninth-century] Baghdad enjoyed a pluralistic, cosmopolitan, and multi-confessional atmosphere with multi-cultural ethnic and religious gatherings of Muslims, Christians, Jews, Zoroastrians, pagans, Arabs, Persians, as well as various Asian populations." Reuven Snir, "'The Eye's Delight': Baghdad in Arabic Poetry," *Orientalia Suecana* 70 (2021): 12–52, doi.org/10.33063/diva-437598.

Chapter 10: Speak Freely

161 **in Central Europe:** Yascha Mounk, *The Populist Curtain*, BBC Radio 4, www.bbc.co.uk/programmes/m00048p9.

162 **people of Bangkok:** For more on the state of free speech internationally, see annual reports by the nonprofit Freedom House. The 2022 Freedom House report, for instance, gave Turkey a score of 5/16 in the category "Freedom of Expression and Belief." Under President Erdoğan, "media outlets are often censored, fined, or shut down, and journalists are detained regularly," and the government "monitors more than 45 million social media accounts," arbitrarily punishing those that criticize the state. "Turkey: Freedom in

the World 2022 Country Report," Freedom House, accessed Jan. 5, 2023, freedomhouse
.org/country/turkey/freedom-world/2022.

162 **restrict how public employees:** On recent efforts to ban certain forms of content in
public education, see David French, "Free Speech for Me but Not for Thee," *Atlantic*,
April 11, 2022, newsletters.theatlantic.com/the-third-rail/email/1eff62d6-d95e-49f2
-8e85-5a8ac4333206. On restrictions of free speech relating to abortion, see Yascha
Mounk, "Why Freedom of Speech Is the Next Abortion Fight," *Atlantic*, Sept. 1, 2022,
www.theatlantic.com/ideas/archive/2022/08/freedom-speech-mississippi-abortion
-rights/671202/.

162 **speech they prohibit:** See, for example, Adam Steinbaugh, "Why Florida's Betrayal of
the First Amendment to 'Stop Woke' Should Concern Everyone, Including Conservatives,"
Foundation for Individual Rights and Expression, Nov. 29, 2022, www.thefire.org
/news/why-floridas-betrayal-first-amendment-stop-woke-should-concern-everyone;
Conor Friedersdorf, "Ron DeSantis's Speech Policing Could Hurt the Right Too," *Atlantic*,
Nov. 22, 2022, www.theatlantic.com/ideas/archive/2022/11/ron-desantis-individual
-freedom-act-free-speech/672211; and Yascha Mounk, "How to Save Academic Freedom
from Ron DeSantis," *Atlantic*, March 7, 2023, https://www.theatlantic.com/ideas/archive
/2023/03/ron-desantis-book-illiberal-policies-florida-education/673297/.

162 **prohibited any teaching materials:** "Tennessee SB0623: 2021–2022: 112th General
Assembly," LegiScan, 2021, legiscan.com/TN/text/SB0623/id/2409134.

162 **state of Florida:** Ian Millhiser, "The Constitutional Problem with Florida's 'Don't Say
Gay' Bill," *Vox*, March 15, 2022, www.vox.com/2022/3/15/22976868/dont-say-gay
-florida-unconstitutional-ron-desantis-supreme-court-first-amendment-schools-parents.

162 **constitutions of all fifty states:** See David Schultz, "State Constitutional Provisions on
Expressive Rights," *The First Amendment Encyclopedia*, Sept. 2017, www.mtsu.edu/first
-amendment/article/874/state-constitutional-provisions-on-expressive-rights.

163 **BEING OFFENSIVE IS AN OFFENSE:** Yascha Mounk (@Yascha_Mounk), Twitter, Feb. 21,
2021, 8:51 p.m., twitter.com/Yascha_Mounk/status/1363667618608087042. According
to English law, being offensive is not in fact a criminal offense. But the fact that a police
force produced and publicly displayed billboards stating as much shows just how fuzzy
the boundaries of what can be said have become and how easily unfortunate citizens
could become subjects of a police investigation over behavior that is not in fact illegal.
And while the exact phrasing of the billboard displayed by Merseyside police is errone-
ous, many British citizens have in fact been punished for a wide variety of speech, often
under very concerning circumstances. See, for example, Kenan Malik, "The 'Nazi Pug':
Giving Offence Is Inevitable and Often Necessary in a Plural Society," *Guardian*, March
25, 2018, theguardian.com/commentisfree/2018/mar/25/being-offensive-should-not-be
-illegal-in-society-that-defends-free-speech; and Scott Shackford, "She Posted Rap Lyr-
ics to Remember a Dead Teen, so the U.K. Prosecuted Her for Hate Speech," *Reason*,
April 23, 2018, reason.com/2018/04/23/she-posted-rap-lyrics-to-remember-a-dead/.

163 **antifascist merchandise:** Derek Scally, "Man Faces Court for Anti-Nazi Use of Swastika,"
Irish Times, Sept. 27, 2006, www.irishtimes.com/news/man-faces-court-for-anti-nazi
-use-of-swastika-1.1007969. While a judge ultimately ruled that the stickers did not violate Germany's anti-swastika laws, the ambiguity of this sort of law continues to have a
chilling effect. See also DW Staff, "Anti-Nazi Images," *DW*, March 15, 2007, www.dw
.com/en/germany-allows-anti-nazi-swastikas/a-2385967.

163 **investigated the publishers:** "Queer.de: Darf Benedikt XVI. posthum als homophober
Hetzer bezeichnet werden?," *Der Spiegel*, Jan. 9, 2023, www.spiegel.de/panorama/darf
-benedikt-xvi-posthum-als-homophober-hetzer-bezeichnet-werden-a-8815a43d-2956
-4cd4-b2e5-458ff63a0ee0.

163 **government minister criticized:** Adam Satariano and Christopher F. Schuetze, "Where
Online Hate Speech Can Bring the Police to Your Door," *New York Times*, Sept. 23, 2022,
www.nytimes.com/2022/09/23/technology/germany-internet-speech-arrest.html.

163 **vowed to ban:** For instance, Mark Zuckerberg testified in Congress that Facebook has made "fighting misinformation and providing people with authoritative information a priority for the company." Danielle Abril, "What Big Tech CEOs Will Tell an Angry Congress about Policing Misinformation and Extremism," *Fortune*, March 24, 2021, https://fortune.com/2021/03/24/facebook-alphabet-twitter-ceos-congressional -hearing-testimony-misinformation-extrimism-online-big-tech-congress/.

163 **they consider "misinformation":** For a statement of some of the problems with the concept of "misinformation," which ultimately argued that the concept could be made useful if it were to be applied more rigorously, see Conor Friedersdorf, "How 'Big Disinformation' Can Overcome Its Skeptics," *Atlantic*, April 21 2022, https://www.theatlantic .com/ideas/archive/2022/04/anti-disinformation-laws-social-media/629612/. Also note that the general public isn't very cleare on what constitutes "misinformation" or "fake news." According to a 2017 survey by Gallup and the Knight Foundation, 48 percent believe that "people knowingly portraying false information as if it were true" is "always" fake news, and another 46 percent believe it is "sometimes" fake news. More surprisingly, 28 percent of those surveyed said that "accurate stories casting a politician or political group in a negative light" are always fake news, and another 50 percent said they sometimes are. "Unsurprisingly, It's Hard to Define 'Fake News,'" News Literacy Project, accessed Mar. 24, 2023, newslit.org/tips-tools/did-you-know-negative-light/.

163 **artificially limited discussion:** Cristiano Lima, "Facebook No Longer Treating 'Man-Made' Covid as a Crackpot Idea," *Politico*, May 26, 2021, www.politico.com/news/2021 /05/26/facebook-ban-covid-man-made-491053.

163 **scandals surrounding the son:** Elizabeth Dwoskin, "Facebook and Twitter Take Unusual Steps to Limit Spread of New York Post Story," *Washington Post*, Oct. 15, 2020, www.washingtonpost.com/technology/2020/10/15/facebook-twitter-hunter-biden/. It is reasonable to disagree about how important the original story about Hunter Biden in the *New York Post* was. But major social media networks took the highly unusual step of suspending the account of a long-standing news outlet with the justification that the core claim, that information recovered from Hunter Biden's laptop was authentic, was false. As later reporting by *The New York Times* and other media outlets confirmed, that was not the case. See, for example, Katie Brenner, Kenneth P. Vogel, and Michael S. Schmidt, "Hunter Biden Paid Tax Bill, but Broad Federal Investigation Continues," *New York Times*, March 16, 2022, www.nytimes.com/2022/03/16/us/politics/hunter-biden-tax -bill-investigation.html.

163 **removed episodes of shows:** To name but a few examples, in August 2021, Comedy Central removed *The Office* episode "Diversity Day," which satirizes the hollowness of corporate diversity and inclusion efforts, from its rotation (Carly Mayberry, "Comedy Central Caves to Cancel Culture, Removes Episode from 'The Office' Line-Up," *Newsweek*, Aug. 30, 2021, www.newsweek.com/comedy-central-caves-cancel-culture-removes -episode-office-line-1623873). In June 2020, HBO Max acquired *South Park*, but didn't allow streaming of five of the more controversial episodes (Randall Colburn, "South Park Is Now on HBO Max—with Five Episodes Missing," The A.V. Club, June 25, 2020, https://www.avclub.com/hbo-max-removes-all-south-park-episodes-referencing-the -1844162728). Finally, a number of episodes of *30 Rock* have been taken out of syndication and taken off-line on streaming services, including Hulu and Amazon Prime, because they feature a satirical portrayal of a character using blackface (Ryan Reed, "'30 Rock' Episodes Featuring Blackface Removed from Streaming, Syndication," *Rolling Stone*, June 22, 2020, rollingstone.com/tv-movies/tv-movie-news/30-rock-blackface -episodes-pulled-1019167/).

163 **canceled the release:** The author Kosoko Jackson canceled the publication of *A Place for Wolves*, a young adult novel that had received extensive advance praise, after the public outcry that followed a Goodreads review criticizing the book's portrayal of Muslims. Katy Waldman, "In Y.A., Where Is the Line Between Criticism and Cancel Culture?,"

New Yorker, March 21, 2019, www.newyorker.com/books/under-review/in-ya-where-is
-the-line-between-criticism-and-cancel-culture.

163 **canceled shows by comedians:** For instance, a performance by Dave Chappelle at the
First Avenue in Minneapolis was canceled after employees of the venue objected to his
show. Derek Saul, "Minnesota Venue Cancels Dave Chappelle Show as Transphobia
Controversy Boils Over," *Forbes*, July 22, 2022, www.forbes.com/sites/dereksaul/2022
/07/21/minnesota-venue-cancels-dave-chappelle-show-as-transphobia-controversy
-boils-over/?sh=6a4dcbc52c1d.

163 **Universities disinvited speakers:** See the disinvitation of the geophysicist Dorian Abbot
from a lecture at MIT because of his opposition to affirmative action. Michael Powell,
"M.I.T.'s Choice of Lecturer Ignited Criticism. So Did Its Decision to Cancel," *New York
Times*, Oct. 20, 2021, www.nytimes.com/2021/10/20/us/dorian-abbot-mit.html; and
Yascha Mounk, "Why the Latest Campus Cancellation Is Different," *Atlantic*, Oct. 10, 2021,
www.theatlantic.com/ideas/archive/2021/10/why-latest-campus-cancellation
-different/620352/.

163 **summarily fired from their jobs:** For example, the data analyst David Shor was fired
after tweeting a summary of a study showing the electoral effects of violent protest, and
Emmanuel Cafferty, a Latino electrical worker, was fired after an activist took a picture
of his hand in the OK symbol, a niche white power symbol. See Yascha Mounk, "Stop
Firing the Innocent," *Atlantic*, June 27, 2020, www.theatlantic.com/ideas/archive/2020
/06/stop-firing-innocent/613615.

164 **abstain from expressing:** Emily Ekins, "Poll: 62% of Americans Say They Have Political
Views They're Afraid to Share," Cato Institute, July 22, 2020, www.cato.org/publications
/survey-reports/poll-62-americans-say-they-have-political-views-theyre-afraid-share.

164 **having self-censored:** "Largest Ever Free Speech Survey of College Students Ranks Top
Campuses for Expression," Foundation for Individual Rights and Expression, Sept.
29, 2020, www.thefire.org/largest-ever-free-speech-survey-of-college-students-ranks-top
-campuses-for-expression/.

164 **paper's own employees:** The full results of the internal survey have not been released.
But according to media reports, only 51 percent of respondents to the survey agreed with
the statement "there is free exchange of views in this company; people are not afraid to
say what they really think." See Jon Levine, "Half of New York Times Employees Feel
They Can't Speak Freely: Survey," *New York Post*, Feb. 13, 2021, nypost.com/2021/02
/13/new-york-times-employees-feel-they-cant-speak-freely-survey/.

164 **"practices a social tyranny":** John Stuart Mill, *On Liberty* (London: Broadview Press,
1859), 9.

165 **right to lambaste slavery:** See, most famously, Frederick Douglass, "A Plea for Free Speech
in Boston (1860)," National Constitution Center, accessed Jan. 21, 2023, constitutioncenter
.org/the-constitution/historic-document-library/detail/frederick-douglass-a-plea-for
-free-speech-in-boston-1860.

165 **opposing the war:** See the landmark case *Tinker v. Des Moines*, where the Supreme
Court upheld the right of students to protest the Vietnam War in schools. *Tinker v. Des
Moines Independent Community School District*, 393 U.S. 503 (1969).

165 **left has long championed:** Martin Luther King Jr. spoke movingly about the attack on
free speech during the Vietnam War: "A fifth casualty of the war in Viet Nam is the principle of dissent. An ugly repressive sentiment to silence peace-seekers depicts . . . persons
who call for a cessation of bombings in the north as quasi-traitors, fools or venal enemies
of our soldiers and institutions. Free speech and the privilege of dissent and discussion
are rights being shot down by bombers in Viet Nam. When those who stand for peace are
so vilified it is time to consider where we are going and whether free speech has not become one of the major casualties of the war." Martin Luther King Jr., "Martin Luther King
Jr. on the Vietnam War" (speech, Beverly Hills, Calif., Feb. 25, 1967), *Atlantic*, www
.theatlantic.com/magazine/archive/2018/02/martin-luther-king-jr-vietnam/552521/.

165 **"Liberty is meaningless"**: Douglass, "Plea for Free Speech in Boston (1860)."

165 **"merely a service"**: Alexandra Ocasio-Cortez (@AOC), Twitter, March 18, 2022, 5:50 p.m., twitter.com/aoc/status/1504938290386030598.

165 **"the right to say bigoted"**: Owen Jones (@OwenJones84), Twitter, Sept. 11, 2022, 1:11 p.m., twitter.com/OwenJones84/status/1569010714420838401.

165 **"At the end of the day"**: Ellen Pao (@ekp), Twitter, April 5, 2022, 7:31 p.m., twitter.com/ekp/status/1511486807451463680.

166 **in "Repressive Tolerance"**: Herbert Marcuse, "Repressive Tolerance," in *A Critique of Pure Tolerance*, ed. Robert Paul Wolff and Barrington Moore, 5th ed. (Boston: Beacon Press, 1969), 81–123.

166 **defined by class domination**: Contemporary society, Marcuse wrote, was characterized by "the toleration of the systematic moronization of children and adults alike by publicity and propaganda." Marcuse, "Repressive Tolerance," 83.

166 **"freedom (of opinion, of assembly, of speech)"**: Marcuse, "Repressive Tolerance," 83.

166 **"toleration of speech and assembly"**: A radical reform of the educational system, Marcuse claimed, would also be extremely important: there should be "new and rigid restrictions on teachings and practices in the educational institutions which, by their very methods and concepts, serve to enclose the mind within the established universe of discourse and behavior." Marcuse, "Repressive Tolerance," 100–101.

166 **an intellectual vanguard**: Marcuse doubled down on this view in a postscript to his essay published in 1968: "Tolerance would be restricted with respect to movements of a demonstrably aggressive or destructive character (destructive of the prospects for peace, justice, and freedom for all). Such discrimination would also be applied to movements opposing the extension of social legislation to the poor, weak, disabled. As against the virulent denunciations that such a policy would do away with the sacred liberalistic principle of equality for 'the other side,' I maintain that there are issues where either there is no 'other side' in any more than a formalistic sense, or where 'the other side' is demonstrably 'regressive' and impedes possible improvement of the human condition." Marcuse, "Repressive Tolerance," 120.

166 **"the democratic educational dictatorship"**: Marcuse, "Repressive Tolerance," 108.

166 **highly influential rejection**: Stanley Fish, *There Is No Such Thing as Free Speech: And It's a Good Thing Too* (New York: Oxford University Press, 1994).

166 **"abstract concepts like free speech"**: Fish, *No Such Thing*, 102.

166 **impossible to draw a principled boundary**: The upshot of this conclusion seems to be that we should abandon talk of "free speech." However, Fish himself has, at least at times, come to a less radical conclusion: "The moral is not that First Amendment talk should be abandoned, for even if the standard First Amendment formulas do not and could not perform the function expected of them (the elimination of political considerations in decisions about speech), they still serve a function that is not at all negligible: they slow down outcomes in an area in which the fear of overhasty outcomes is justified by a long record of abuses of power. It is often said that history shows (itself a formula) that even a minimal restriction on the right of expression too easily leads to ever-larger restrictions; and to the extent that this is an empirical fact (and it is a question one could debate), there is some comfort and protection to be found in a procedure that requires you to jump through hoops—do a lot of argumentative work—before a speech regulation will be allowed to stand." Fish, *No Such Thing*, 113–14.

167 **"provoke the average person"**: "The trouble with this definition is that it distinguishes not between fighting words and words that remain safely and merely expressive but between words that are provocative to one group (the group that falls under the rubric 'average person') and words that might be provocative to other groups, groups of persons not now considered average. And if you ask what words are likely to be provocative to those nonaverage groups, what are likely to be *their* fighting words, the answer is anything and everything, for as Justice Holmes said long ago (in *Gitlow v. New York*), every idea is an

incitement to somebody, and since ideas come packaged in sentences, in words, every sentence is potentially, in some situation that might occur tomorrow, a fighting word and therefore a candidate for regulation." Fish, *No Such Thing*, 106.

167 **the boundary between:** Fish also mounted a second attack on free speech, which is subtly distinct. According to this line of argument, institutions that claim to do so never actually treat free speech as an absolute value; when the exercise of free speech conflicts with the broader goals of an institution, the institution will set limits on what can be said. In John Milton's famous defense of free speech in the *Areopagitica*, for example, the seventeenth-century poet introduces a major caveat: "popery and open superstition" should, according to Milton, be beyond the scope of free speech. This kind of move, Fish claims, is a feature rather than a bug. "When the pinch comes (and sooner or later it always will come) and the institution (be it church, state, or university) is confronted by behavior subversive of its core rationale, it will respond by declaring 'of course we mean not tolerated ———, that we extirpate'" (Fish, *No Such Thing*, 104). This, according to Fish, is a kind of invariable rule: "I want to say that all affirmations of freedom of expression are like Milton's, dependent for their force on an exception that literally carves out the space in which expression can then emerge." Fish, *No Such Thing*, 103.

167 **"Free speech," Fish concludes:** Fish, *No Such Thing*, 102. The objection according to which limits of free speech are completely arbitrary sounds appealing, but on closer examination it does not hold water.

As one of the oldest philosophical paradoxes points out, it is extremely hard to know where the line between a bald man and a non-bald man falls. If you took a man with a full head of luscious hair, and removed one follicle at a time, it would always seem irrational to declare that the removal of a single hair had suddenly made him bald. Does this mean that a man who has had all of his hair removed shouldn't be considered bald? But though this paradox points to the existence of hard cases, whose correct description is a matter of judgment, and can even be a little arbitrary, it clearly doesn't demonstrate that Zac Efron is bald or that Bruce Willis has a full head of hair. (In philosophy, the logical puzzles introduced by vague terms are often referred to by reference to the famous sorites paradox. See Dominic Hyde and Diana Raffman, "Sorites Paradox," in *Stanford Encyclopedia of Philosophy*, March 26, 2018, plato.stanford.edu/entries/sorites-paradox/.)

The same is true for free speech. There are many hard cases in which it is a genuine question of judgment whether some form of expression should qualify for the protections offered by the First Amendment. Imagine someone who is enraged by the policy adopted by a local school and calls up the principal, telling her, "You will pay for what you did." Is this simply a strong form of legitimate criticism? Or does it amount to a concrete threat that goes beyond the expression of dissent? This judgment call is genuinely hard. Reasonable people can come to different conclusions about it, and critics like Fish are undoubtedly right that power relations will help to determine the exact boundaries of free speech. But none of this means that it is impossible to distinguish between a parent publicly criticizing the policy of the school (a clear exercise of free speech) and someone calling in a bomb threat (a disruptive threat that would rightly be considered illegal).

167 **"We must not fetishize 'debate'":** Nadia Whittome (@NadiaWhittomeMP), Twitter, July 23, 2020, 1:47 p.m., twitter.com/nadiawhittomemp/status/1286357272025796608?lang=en.

167 **"racist ideas are both false":** Twitter Together (@TwitterTogether), Twitter, June 11, 2020, 7:29 p.m., twitter.com/TwitterTogether/status/1271223142493507584.

167 **"When is the free speech":** Francesca Truitt, "Black Lives Matter Protests American Civil Liberties Union," *Flat Hat News*, Oct. 2, 2017, flathatnews.com/2017/10/02/black-lives-matter-protests-american-civil-liberties-union/. An academic article published in the journal of the American Association of University Professors is even more explicit in its dismissal of free speech: "In the end the issue is less about free speech and more about what we value. We must ask ourselves these fundamental questions: Do we

value free speech that seeks to promote racism, homophobia, transphobia, bigotry, misogyny, rape culture, violence against women, and a disregard for disabled individuals on our campus?" Reshmi Dutt-Ballerstadt, "When Free Speech Disrupts Diversity Initiatives: What We Value and What We Do Not," *AAUP Journal of Academic Freedom* 9 (2018): 18.

168 **formal or informal restrictions:** See, for example, "A More Specific Letter on Justice and Open Debate," Objective, July 10, 2020, objectivejournalism.org/2020/07/a-more-specific-letter-on-justice-and-open-debate/.

168 **"'Consequence culture' is needed":** Dana Brownlee, "Is 'Cancel Culture' Really Just Long Overdue Accountability for the Privileged?," *Forbes*, July 1, 2021, www.forbes.com/sites/danabrownlee/2021/07/01/is-cancel-culture-really-just-long-overdue-accountability-for-the-privileged/?sh=7f03df33a22b. The writer and academic Roxane Gay agreed, opining that "cancel culture is this boogeyman that people have come up with to explain away bad behavior and when their faves experience consequences." Molly Schwartz, "Roxane Gay Says Cancel Culture Does Not Exist," *Mother Jones*, March 5, 2021, www.motherjones.com/media/2021/03/roxane-gay-says-cancel-culture-does-not-exist/.

168 **case for free speech:** Mill, *On Liberty*. Recent attacks on free speech have also inspired some important defenses of the tradition. See, for example, Timothy Garton Ash, *Free Speech: Ten Principles for a Connected World* (New Haven, Conn.: Yale University Press, 2017); and Jacob Mchangama, *Free Speech: A History from Socrates to Social Media* (New York: Basic Books, 2022). For a recent philosophical treatment, see David Braddon-Mitchell and Caroline West, "What Is Free Speech?," *Journal of Political Philosophy* 12, no. 4 (2004).

168 **Two arguments are especially common:** In the next two paragraphs, I am following John Stuart Mill's classic account in *On Liberty*. There is also a third classic argument in favor of free speech, which tends to be favored by "deontological" rather than "consequentialist" liberals. This argument emphasizes that the government does not have a right to side with the moral or religious convictions of some citizens over those of others. Giving authorities the right to censor supposedly noxious speech would, in this view, violate the moral autonomy of ordinary citizens.

This idea goes back to a long-standing debate about what justifies the coercive power wielded by modern states. Some political philosophers, like Thomas Hobbes, believe that the state is needed to protect us from each other. Others, like John Locke, believe that it is needed to adjudicate conflicts because nobody is dispassionate when it comes to their own interests. Others still, including those worried about what we would today call "state failure," believe that the state is needed to provide key public goods, like food and shelter for the most vulnerable.

But what virtually all philosophically liberal theories of the state have in common is a conviction that we are all born equal and that this limits what the state can rightfully do to us. The purpose of our institutions is neither to determine the truth about weighty issues of morality and theology nor to tell us how to lead our lives. Though citizens of a liberal democracy agree to be bound by a set of laws, they reserve the right to decide questions of good or evil, and heaven or hell, for themselves.

This fundamental moral freedom to think for ourselves would be intolerably undermined if the state had the right to censor what its citizens can and cannot say. Autonomous citizens who are free to determine the weightiest questions of morality for themselves need to preserve the right to decide on their own what to say, and whose words to heed. Any state that claims the right to determine which words are too dangerous for its own citizens is therefore overstepping the bounds of its rightful authority. Rather than facilitating the conditions that allow each of us to lead our lives in peace and prosperity, it unjustly claims for itself the role of an educator instructing its wayward children.

169 **"Truth, thus held":** Mill, *On Liberty*, 34. Living truths are capable of withstanding

attack and motivating our actions. But once they become sacrosanct, and any expression of disagreement is censored, they turn into empty formulas to which we merely pay lip service. When changed circumstances allow those who disagree with the idea to make their case against it, a "few phrases retained by rote" are unlikely to fend off the challenge. Because taboos rarely last forever, the price for protecting an idea today may be to weaken it tomorrow.

We might want to add that it becomes easy to misunderstand both the nature and the implications of a view that is rarely or never challenged. Take an example from the last chapter: if we accept that cultural appropriation is bad without thinking about why that is supposed to be the case, we will end up needlessly "problematizing" some forms of mutual influence that are actually completely harmless—all the while missing what makes other practices, which happen not to fall under the rubric of "cultural appropriation," deeply unjust.

169 **Having such weak foundations:** This is why, according to Mill, those who are strongly committed to a particular belief should welcome disagreement even if their idea really is true. "If opponents of all important truths do not exist," Mill suggested, "it is indispensable to imagine them, and supply them with the strongest arguments which the most skillful devil's advocate can conjure up." Mill, *On Liberty*, 36.

169 **change their minds:** In 1996, 27 percent of Americans supported legal recognition of gay marriage. By 2021, support had risen to a record high of 70 percent. Justin McCarthy, "Record-High 70% in U.S. Support Same-Sex Marriage," Gallup, June 8, 2021, news .gallup.com/poll/350486/record-high-support-same-sex-marriage.aspx.

169 **resist pernicious ideas:** The third argument that philosophical defenders of free speech have traditionally made also retains relevance today. I too worry that states that don't respect the limits on their rightful authority run the danger of violating the moral autonomy of their citizens. Modern states legitimately play a huge variety of ambitious roles, from the maintenance of law and order to the provision of a welfare state. But for a government official to determine what I can or cannot read is for him to misunderstand his role, which is to serve me and my compatriots, not to sit in judgment of our views.

170 **seem to clash:** In the United States, Abraham Lincoln's administration significantly restricted free speech and the free press during the Civil War. Similarly, in the U.K., Winston Churchill restricted free expression during World War II. But while some narrow limits on free expression, such as information about troop movements or bomb shelters that would present a clear threat to national security, may be justified in genuine emergencies, broad limits on free speech do have serious drawbacks, even in wartime. In fact, democracies often outperform autocracies in battle in part because public attention to military failures can help these countries overcome weaknesses. See, for example, David Runciman, *The Confidence Trap: A History of Democracy in Crisis from World War I to the Present* (Princeton, N.J.: Princeton University Press, 2013). See also George Orwell, "The Freedom of the Press," *Times Literary Supplement*, Sept. 15, 1972, www.orwellfoundation .com/the-orwell-foundation/orwell/essays-and-other-works/the-freedom-of-the-press/; and George Orwell, "Poetry and the Microphone," *New Saxon Pamphlet*, no. 3 (March 1945), www.orwellfoundation.com/the-orwell-foundation/orwell/essays-and-other-works /poetry-and-the-microphone/.

170 **allow the truth:** Note that this possibility does not contradict Mill's argument, rightly understood. He was well aware that even in a society with free speech falsehoods can often persist for many decades or centuries. What he maintained is that a lack of censorship will preserve a fighting chance for the truth to emerge over a long period of time, something that would be less likely if certain views could be barred from consideration altogether. The nature of this claim is still essentially empirical, and some people will no doubt dispute its accuracy, but it is much more subtle and sophisticated than easy dismissals of the "marketplace of ideas" would suggest.

171 **political scientists and organizational sociologists:** This point is made most famously by the sociologist Robert Michels in the form of what he calls "goal displacement": "There

is a process of 'goal displacement' by which the original often radical or idealistic goals of the organization are replaced by the lesser goals needed to maintain the organization and keep the leadership in power" (Martin Slattery, "The Iron Law of Oligarchy," in *Key Ideas in Sociology* [Cheltenham, U.K.: Nelson Thornes, 2003], 52–55). While Michels's broader conclusions are controversial, the phenomenon of goal displacement "has been demonstrated in widely varying organizational settings." Kees Huizinga and Martin de Bree, "Exploring the Risk of Goal Displacement in Regulatory Enforcement Agencies: A Goal-Ambiguity Approach," *Public Performance and Management Review* 44, no. 4 (2021): 868–98, doi.org/10.1080/15309576.2021.1881801.

171 **influential social institutions:** The impulse to consolidate power was recognized by the Founding Fathers centuries ago. This is why, in Federalist Paper No. 51, James Madison insisted that "ambition must be made to counteract ambition. The interest of the man must be connected with the constitutional rights of the place. It may be a reflection on human nature, that such devices should be necessary to control the abuses of government." James Madison, Federalist Paper No. 51 (1788), Bill of Rights Institute, billofrightsinstitute .org/primary-sources/federalist-no-51.

172 **censoring unpopular viewpoints:** What Fish and Marcuse share is a conviction that speech codes are likely to be written by people whose moral and political judgment is superior to that of the people who are bound by them. Fish, for example, argues, "To the student reporter who complains that in the wake of the promulgation of a speech code at the University of Wisconsin there is now something in the back of his mind as he writes, one could reply: 'There was always something in the back of your mind, and perhaps it might be better to have this code in the back of your mind than whatever was in there before'" (Fish, *No Such Thing*, 111). But this confidence in the superiority of the censor's judgment turns on the implicit assumption that it is people like Fish and Marcuse who will get to write the rules, something that would be unlikely to happen if their rejection of free speech were to be adopted more broadly.

The same remains true today. Many progressive opponents of free speech simultaneously endorse two positions. Building on the pessimism that is a core part of the identity synthesis, they portray their societies as fundamentally rotten, racist, or white supremacist. At the same time, they favor the creation of bureaucratic authorities, whether on campus or in Silicon Valley, that would restrict what people can say. But they never seem to reflect seriously on how the first proposition undermines support for the second. If the United States is deeply racist, sexist, transphobic, and white supremacist, then why should they trust the most powerful people in the country to make good or well-intentioned decisions about what kind of speech to ban?

The answer to that question is sociological rather than philosophical. Progressive groups usually start to advocate severe restrictions on free speech within spaces and institutions in which they enjoy a lot of power, like university campuses. They then apply those same preferences to society as a whole, seemingly without realizing that a principle that might serve their political goals within an institution in which they are effectively in charge is likely to have very different consequences within a big and varied country in which their political views are highly unpopular.

172 **danger of (attempted) coups:** On the corrosive influence of partisan polarization on democratic stability, see Jennifer McCoy et al., "Reducing Pernicious Polarization: A Comparative Historical Analysis of Depolarization," Carnegie Endowment for International Peace, May 5, 2022, carnegieendowment.org/2022/05/05/reducing-pernicious -polarization-comparative-historical-analysis-of-depolarization-pub-87034; and Yascha Mounk, "The Doom Spiral of Pernicious Polarization," *Atlantic*, May 21, 2022, www .theatlantic.com/ideas/archive/2022/05/us-democrat-republican-partisan-polarization /629925/.

173 **persuade your compatriots:** The basic idea that political elites are less willing to accept democratic elections as a mechanism for who should rule when a loss at the ballot box

would incur big costs on them has long been accepted by social scientists. According to Daron Acemoglu and James A. Robinson, for example, economic elites in dictatorships are much more likely to accept a democratic transition when wealth and income are distributed comparatively equally, because democratic rule under such circumstances is less likely to lead to strongly redistributive public policies. See Daron Acemoglu and James A. Robinson, "A Theory of Political Transitions," *American Economic Review* 91, no. 4 (2001): 938–63. See also Carles Boix, *Democracy and Redistribution* (Cambridge: Cambridge University Press, 2003).

One kind of cost from losing elections is economic. But by simple extension, the expected costs of being ruled by a different political faction in terms of noneconomic factors like being able to speak freely or not having to fear going to jail should also govern the willingness of losers to accept the outcome of political elections. The empirical literature on transitional justice, for example, suggests that certain forms of amnesty for those responsible for political crimes in a previous nondemocratic regime can contribute to the stability of subsequent democratic systems because it reduces their incentive to militate against the new institutions. As one recent meta-analysis finds, "prosecutions increase physical integrity protections, while amnesties increase the protection of civil and political rights." Geoff Dancy et al., "Behind Bars and Bargains: New Findings on Transitional Justice in Emerging Democracies," *International Studies Quarterly* 63, no. 1 (March 2019): 99–110, doi.org/10.1093/isq/sqy053.

173 **reason to go to any length:** This account also makes clear how to respond to one of the most common objections to maintaining absolute rights to free speech in certain spheres. According to one such objection, the stakes of political competition are too serious to allow bad actors free rein. At a time when extremist politicians are on the rise and liberal democracies are threatened on every continent, it can seem especially dangerous to allow the enemies of liberty to have their say. But this argument cuts both ways. For the fact that the next government may be actively hostile to the political institutions that guarantee our freedom, or to the rights of marginalized groups, is also the reason why it is so dangerous to mainstream restrictions on free speech.

An important feature of this argument is that it applies both to formal and to informal restrictions on free speech. The stakes of elections are raised in an especially egregious way if someone has good reason to fear that a victory by their opponent could lead to them getting arrested or jailed for criticizing the new government (as is often the case in "competitive authoritarian regimes," like Thailand and Pakistan). But less formal ways to stifle speech also increase the incentive to stay in power by illicit means. If a politician and his supporters fear that losing power will result in them getting locked out of opportunities to make their case on major social media platforms, effectively ending their ability to communicate with a mass audience, they may also come to doubt that they will have another chance of winning back power at the next election.

173 **construction of new homes:** "The policies that regulate land use and housing production make it extremely difficult to add more homes in desirable locations." Jenny Schuetz, "Dysfunctional Policies Have Broken America's Housing Supply Chain," Brookings, Feb. 22, 2022, www.brookings.edu/blog/the-avenue/2022/02/22/dysfunctional-policies-have-broken-americas-housing-supply-chain/.

174 **family had perished:** The exhibition was first shown in Hamburg in the spring of 1995 and elicited a heated debate because it punctured a popular myth according to which ordinary soldiers had not taken part in the Holocaust. For a good English-language overview of the exhibition and the debate about it, see Michael Z. Wise, "Bitterness Stalks Show on Role of the Wehrmacht," *New York Times*, Nov. 6, 1999, www.nytimes.com/1999/11/06/arts/bitterness-stalks-show-on-role-of-the-wehrmacht.html.

175 **extremely vague rules:** For instance, Joseph Kelly was convicted for violating the 2003 Communications Act in the U.K. after he tweeted, "The only good Brit soldier is a deed

one, burn auld fella, buuuuurn." David Meikle, "Scot Posted 'Only Good Brit Soldier Is a Deed One' After Captain Tom Death," *Daily Record*, Jan. 31, 2022, www.dailyrecord .co.uk/news/scottish-news/scot-posted-only-good-brit-26099298.

175 **vague categories of speech:** Yascha Mounk, "Is Germany Overstepping with Its Online Hate Speech Law?," *New Republic*, April 3, 2018, newrepublic.com/article/147364/verboten -germany-law-stopping-hate-speech-facebook-twitter.

176 **expressing their hateful views:** According to an influential argument against the First Amendment, absolute restrictions on the regulation of free speech make institutions complicit in the worst forms of expression they license. When states allow their citizens to deny the Holocaust, or universities give bigoted speakers a platform, the argument goes, they end up granting these views a form of legitimacy. But there are ways for governments and institutions to disavow the content of noxious speech without going so far as to ban it outright. It would, for example, violate the First Amendment for government officials to punish citizens for expressing especially noxious views, but as the political theorist Corey Brettschneider has argued, it would not undermine the state's obligation to uphold free expression for them to disavow such views in an official capacity. Similarly, I believe that university presidents must ensure that controversial speakers who are invited to campus by academic departments or student groups are able to have their say, but when especially noxious speakers come to campus, nothing stops them from being first in line to protest the content of their views in a peaceful manner that does not disrupt the event. See Corey Lang Brettschneider, *When the State Speaks, What Should It Say? How Democracies Can Protect Expression and Promote Equality* (Princeton, N.J.: Princeton University Press, 2016); and Yascha Mounk, "Corey Brettschneider on Free Speech," *The Good Fight*, July 23, 2022, podcast, www.persuasion.community/p/brettschneider #details.

176 **adopt strong protections:** The so-called Chicago Statement drafted by the University of Chicago (and adopted by a number of other universities) is a good place to start. The statement pledges that "the University's fundamental commitment is to the principle that debate or deliberation may not be suppressed because the ideas put forth are thought by some or even by most members of the University community to be offensive, unwise, immoral, or wrong-headed." "Report of the Committee on Freedom of Expression," University of Chicago, accessed Jan. 22, 2023, provost.uchicago.edu/sites/default/files /documents/reports/FOECommitteeReport.pdf.

176 **doubt a popular consensus:** Fish might respond that this stance is incoherent. In his view, universities can only adopt norms of free speech in service of some larger social goal. And as soon as they clarify that larger social goal, there will be times when certain forms of speech conflict with them. But this fails to distinguish between particular instances of speech and the rules that would be necessary to be able to suppress them. There are undoubtedly many forms of expression in which professors engage that do not favor the traditional purpose of the university, which is to produce knowledge. But allowing university presidents to fire professors for "wrong"—which, practically speaking, is to say unpopular—speech would undermine that purpose much more. In other words, the right question is what policies institutions like universities should adopt. And, contrary to what Fish suggests, the best policy for universities to adopt if they are to serve their core goals is to maintain academic freedom.

177 **political views of employees:** In D.C., "political affiliation" is a protected class according to the Human Rights Act of 1977. See "Protected Traits in DC," D.C. Office of Human Rights, accessed Jan. 25, 2023, ohr.dc.gov/protectedtraits. In Seattle, political ideology—defined as "any idea or belief, or coordinated body of ideas or beliefs, relating to the purpose, conduct, organization, function or basis of government and related institutions and activities, whether or not characteristic of any political party or group"—is protected. Title 14—Human Rights, Chapter 14.06: Unfair Public Accommodations

Practices, Seattle Municipal Code, accessed Jan. 25, 2023, library.municode.com/wa
/seattle/codes/municipal_code?nodeId=TIT14HURI_CH14.06UNPUACPR
&showChanges=true.

177 **confidence to express themselves:** For a defense of this position, see Zaid Jilani, "A Better Remedy for Cancel Culture," *Persuasion*, July 6, 2020, www.persuasion.community
/p/a-better-remedy-for-cancel-culture.

177 **barred from using these services:** For a discussion of this issue, see Todd Zywicki, "Cancel Culture Comes to Banking," *Newsweek*, Jan. 13, 2022, www.newsweek.com/cancel
-culture-comes-banking-opinion-1668200.

177 **like other public utilities:** The laws governing public utilities vary on a state-by-state
basis. In New York, for instance, gas, electric, and steam utilities can refuse (timely) service only for reasons related to safety, labor strikes, physical problems such as weather
conditions, failure to pay fees, or failure to comply with building requirements. Department of Public Service, "Consumer Guide: Your Rights as a Residential Gas, Electric, or
Steam Customer Under HEFPA," accessed Jan. 23, 2023, dps.ny.gov/consumer-guide
-your-rights-residential-gas-electric-or-steam-customer-under-hefpa.

178 **an inadvertent leak:** Lima, "Facebook No Longer Treating 'Man-Made' Covid as a
Crackpot Idea."

178 **seriously at the highest echelons:** Julian E. Barnes, "Intelligence Review Yields No Firm
Conclusion on Origins of Coronavirus," *New York Times*, Aug. 27, 2021, www.nytimes
.com/2021/08/27/us/politics/covid-origin-lab-leak.html.

178 **Musk bought the company:** The hypocrisy is also clear in the actions of Musk himself,
who suspended the accounts of several journalists for allegedly putting him in danger by
sharing his location, despite there being no evidence that any of them did so. Paul Farhi,
"Musk Suspends Journalists from Twitter, Claims 'Assassination' Danger," *Washington
Post*, Dec. 15, 2022, www.washingtonpost.com/media/2022/12/15/twitter-journalists
-suspended-musk/.

178 **voluntarily adopt stringent restrictions:** For a strong statement of this position, see
David French: "The 'Twitter Files' Show It's Time to Reimagine Free Speech Online,"
Persuasion, Dec. 12, 2022, www.persuasion.community/p/the-twitter-files-show-its-time
-to. It's perfectly fine for social media platforms to concentrate on particular forms of
content, branding themselves as politically progressive or conservative. But in that case
the analogy to traditional publishers is even clearer. So social media platforms with an
explicit political lean should be able to delete content they do not like, but precisely for
that reason they should, like other publishers, not enjoy Section 230 protections.

178 **illegal, extreme, or uncivil behavior:** For a discussion of how social media platforms
could continue to censor forms of expression, like libel or child pornography, that are
actually illegal without having to act as ideological censors, see David French, "A Better
Way to Ban Alex Jones," *New York Times*, Aug. 7, 2018, www.nytimes.com/2018/08/07
/opinion/alex-jones-infowars-facebook.html.

179 **content-neutral criterion:** Similar legislative action can also help to limit the extent to
which other powerful social actors can undermine a culture of free speech. Virtually
every major university in the United States, for example, receives significant public funding. The federal government already requires universities to follow extensive rules about
many things—from the sports teams they maintain to the way they investigate alleged
sexual misconduct—if they want to keep getting taxpayer dollars. One of these rules
should ensure that universities maintain a genuine culture of academic freedom, barring
them from discriminating against their students, staff, or faculty on the basis of their
political views.

179 **"the tendency of society":** Mill, *On Liberty*, 9.

180 **four warning signs:** Jonathan Rauch, "The Cancel Culture Checklist," *Persuasion*, Aug.
6, 2020, www.persuasion.community/p/the-cancel-culture-checklist-c63. Rauch's full
list includes two additional criteria: moral grandstanding ("the display of moral outrage

to impress one's peer group, dominate others, or both") and truthiness (a lack of concern for whether an accusation is truthful).

180 **"is about shaping the information battlefield"**: Rauch, "Cancel Culture Checklist."

Chapter 11: The Case for Integration

183 **"the intermingling in the school"**: John Dewey, *Democracy and Education: An Introduction to the Philosophy of Education* (New York: Free Press, 1916), 21–22.

183 **"our goal is to have a country"**: Larry King, "Interview with Barack Obama," *Larry King Live*, CNN, Oct. 19, 2006, edition.cnn.com/TRANSCRIPTS/0610/19/lkl.01.html.

183 **"when children learn and play"**: Barack Obama, "Presidential Proclamation—60th Anniversary of Brown v. Board of Education," National Archives and Records Administration, May 15, 2014, obamawhitehouse.archives.gov/the-press-office/2014/05/15/presidential-proclamation-60th-anniversary-brown-v-board-education.

184 **Posey experienced in Atlanta:** See introduction.

184 **universities are building dorms:** See Dion J. Pierre, "Demands for Segregated Housing at Williams College Are Not News," *National Review*, May 8, 2019, www.nationalreview.com/2019/05/american-colleges-segregated-housing-graduation-ceremonies/.

184 **hosting separate graduation ceremonies:** Meimei Xu, "Black, Latinx, BGTLQ, and First-Gen Graduates Celebrate in University-Wide Affinity Ceremonies," *Harvard Crimson*, May 27, 2022, www.thecrimson.com/article/2022/5/27/affinity-graduations-2022/. (While the events were officially organized by students, the university's administration provided funding and administrative support for them.)

184 **physical education classes:** Adam Barnes, "Controversy Erupts after Ivy League University Excludes White People from New Class," *The Hill*, May 5, 2021, https://thehill.com/changing-america/respect/equality/551951-controversy-erupts-after-ivy-league-university-excludes/.

184 **performance of Aleshea Harris's:** After a public backlash, a spokeswoman for the National Arts Centre did reassure the public that "there will be no checkpoints for Black Out Night ticket holders" to assess that they have the requisite racial credentials. David Millward, "Theatres Spark Outrage with Black-Only Audience Policy," *Telegraph*, Jan. 29, 2023, www.telegraph.co.uk/world-news/2023/01/29/theatres-spark-outrage-black-only-audience-policy/.

184 **state-funded faith schools:** For a discussion of multiculturalism and Britain's publicly funded faith schools, see Yascha Mounk, *The Great Experiment: Why Diverse Democracies Fall Apart and How They Can Endure* (London: Penguin Press, 2022), 158–59.

184 **"engage in racial identity work":** Cheryl E. Matias and Janiece Mackey, "Breakin' Down Whiteness in Antiracist Teaching: Introducing Critical Whiteness Pedagogy," *Urban Review* 48, no. 1 (2015): 48, doi.org/10.1007/s11256-015-0344-7.

185 **freedom of association:** Miller McPherson, Lynn Smith-Lovin, and James M. Cook, "Birds of a Feather: Homophily in Social Networks," *Annual Review of Sociology* 27 (Aug. 2001): 415–44, doi.org/10.1146/annurev.soc.27.1.415.

185 **"Race is the child of racism":** Ta-Nehisi Coates, *Between the World and Me* (New York: Spiegel & Grau, 2014), 7.

185 **"we consider natural":** Kimberlé Crenshaw, "Mapping the Margins: Intersectionality, Identity Politics, and Violence Against Women of Color," *Stanford Law Review* 43, no. 6 (1991), 1296.

186 **what they call "racecraft":** Karen E. Fields and Barbara Jeanne Fields, Racecraft: *The Soul of Inequality in American Life* (London: Verso, 2022), 74.

186 **"I will no longer enter into":** Thomas Chatterton Williams, *Self-Portrait in Black and White: Unlearning Race* (New York: W. W. Norton, 2020), 49. See also Conor Friedersdorf, "Unraveling Race," *Atlantic*, Nov. 16, 2019, www.theatlantic.com/ideas/archive/2019/11/thomas-chatterton-williams-self-portrait-black-white/601408/.

186 **"There are not fundamentally"**: Isaac Chotiner, "Thomas Chatterton Williams on Race, Identity, and 'Cancel Culture,'" *New Yorker*, July 22, 2020, www.newyorker.com /news/q-and-a/thomas-chatterton-williams-on-race-identity-and-cancel-culture.

186 **Following the lead:** For more on Spivak and the role that the concept of "strategic essentialism" played in the formation of the identity synthesis, see chapter 2.

186 **embrace socially constructed categories:** Crenshaw, "Mapping the Margins," 1296– 98. These ideas have now become the conventional wisdom in the organizations that facilitate workshops on race and identity in America's most elite schools. Take the training materials used by Pollyanna, a nonprofit that has worked with schools from Harvard-Westlake to Horace Mann and Vermont Academy, to introduce its "Racial Literacy Curriculum." The presentation starts with the rejection of race as a biological category. As the biological anthropologist Alan Goodman has argued, "Race is not based on biology, but race is rather an idea we have ascribed to biology." But it then quickly pivots to the importance of affirming, not denying, the social construct of race: "Even if biologically/genetically untrue, race is one of the most powerful social constructions of the last 400+ years." For that reason, the organization encourages its students to embrace a "both/and" approach: though race was "created as a tool of discrimination," students should regard it as "a meaningful source of one's identity." All quotations are from Monique Vogelsang, "Middle School Parent/Guardian Event: Overview of Racial Literacy Curriculum," Pollyanna, bbk12e1-cdn.myschoolcdn.com/ftpimages/98/misc/misc_238556.pdf. List of schools for which Pollyanna works drawn from Charles Fain Lehman, "NYC Prep School Adopts Questionable Anti-racism Curriculum," *City Journal*, March 15, 2021, www .city-journal.org/nyc-prep-school-admins-adopt-questionable-anti-racism-curriculum.

186 **importance of these categories:** This ambivalence toward the role of identity is also evident in the work of scholars like Tommie Shelby who seek to combine a sympathetic account of Black nationalism with a defense of liberal principles. See Tommie Shelby, *We Who Are Dark: The Philosophical Foundations of Black Solidarity* (Cambridge, Mass.: Belknap Press of Harvard University Press, 2007). Shelby argues for a solidarity grounded in a common experience of oppression, in contrast to the position that "collective black identity is essential for an effective black solidarity." Tommie Shelby, "Foundations of Black Solidarity: Collective Identity or Common Oppression?," *Ethics* 112, no. 2 (2002): 233, doi.org/10.1086/340276.

187 **ethnic identity recedes:** This belief is intertwined with the deep pessimism espoused by Derrick Bell, who asserted that "black people will never gain full equality in this country." Derrick Bell, "Racism Is Here to Stay: Now What?," *Howard Law Journal* 35, no. 1 (Fall 1991): 79. See also chapter 3 of this book.

187 **Harm required a physical injury:** In an academic context, the philosophical idea of harm has come under considerable scrutiny, with some contending the concept is incoherent. See, for instance, Ben Bradley, "Doing Away with Harm," *Philosophy and Phenomenological Research* 85, no. 2 (2012): 390–412, doi.org/10.1111/j.1933-1592.2012.00615.x.

187 **prejudice could consist of implicit biases:** The concept of implicit bias has been embraced by mainstream figures like Barack Obama and Hillary Clinton. But there is little evidence for any strong connection between implicit bias and discriminatory behavior, or for the promise that reductions in implicit bias might diminish such behavior. See, for example, Jesse Singal, *The Quick Fix: Why Fad Psychology Can't Cure Our Social Ills* (New York: Farrar, Straus and Giroux, 2021), chap. 6; Heather Mac Donald, "The False 'Science' of Implicit Bias," *Wall Street Journal*, Oct. 9, 2017, www.wsj.com/articles/the-false -science-of-implicit-bias-1507590908; and Patrick S. Forscher et al., "A Meta-analysis of Procedures to Change Implicit Measures," *Journal of Personality and Social Psychology* 117, no. 3 (2019): 522–59, doi.org/10.1037/pspa0000160.

187 **paradigmatic examples of "microaggression":** See, for example, Derald Wing Sue et al., "Racial Microaggressions in Everyday Life: Implications for Clinical Practice," *American*

Psychologist 62, no. 4 (2007), as well as examples of the application of this idea such as "Tool: Recognizing Microaggressions and the Messages They Send."

187 **suffering serious harm:** For more on this, see Greg Lukianoff and Jonathan Haidt, *The Coddling of the American Mind: How Good Intentions and Bad Ideas Are Setting Up a Generation for Failure* (New York: Penguin Press, 2019).

187 **increasingly pervasive form:** Lukianoff and Haidt, *Coddling of the American Mind*, 6.

187 **Campuses of elite universities:** In 2015, racial minorities made up 43 percent of incoming students at Ivy League colleges, a much larger percentage than a few decades earlier. "Ivy League Schools Brace for Scrutiny over Race in Admissions," NBCNews.com, Aug. 7, 2017, www.nbcnews.com/news/nbcblk/ivy-league-schools-brace-scrutiny-over-race -admissions-n790276.

188 **the corporate world:** According to a recent report, for example, 46 percent of newly appointed members of boards of directors for S&P 500 companies came from historically underrepresented racial or ethnic groups in 2022. See Hope King, "Gender Representation on S&P 500 Boards Reach New Milestone," *Axios*, Nov. 2, 2022, www.axios.com /2022/11/02/board-diversity-sp-500-spencer-stuart. However, the overall composition of the top leadership of corporate America continues to be markedly less diverse than the country's demographic makeup.

188 **institutions remained inhospitable:** One of the first sexual harassment cases in the United States (*Miller v. Bank of America*, 1976) involved Margaret Miller, a young African American woman working at the Bank of America. Miller's supervisor appeared at her house unprompted, telling her, "I've never felt this way about a black chick before," and promising her a better job if she was sexually "cooperative." After she rebuffed his advances, her supervisor had her fired. While there is less data on racial harassment, it is clear that sexual harassment was quite common as women entered the workforce. A survey at the Coal Employment Project's 1980 conference found that 54 percent of female miners had been propositioned by a boss, 76 percent propositioned by a co-worker, and 17 percent had been "physically attacked." Carrie N. Baker, "Race, Class, and Sexual Harassment in the 1970s," *Feminist Studies* 30, no. 1 (Spring 2004): 10, 16, www.jstor .org/stable/3178552.

188 **universities, foundations, and corporations:** Beginning in the 1960s, diversity training was centered on the antidiscrimination legislation (most prominently the 1963 Equal Pay Act and Title VII of the Civil Rights Act of 1964) passed that decade. In the 1980s, the goal of diversity efforts started to become a little more ambitious, attempting to foster cooperation and respect in the workplace. Bridget Read, "Inside the Booming Diversity-Equity-and-Inclusion Industrial Complex," *Cut*, May 26, 2021, www.thecut.com/article /diversity-equity-inclusion-industrial-companies.html. Also see Frank Dobbin and Alexandra Kalev, "Why Doesn't Diversity Training Work? The Challenge for Industry and Academia," *Anthropology Now* 10, no. 2 (April 2018): 48–55, doi.org/10.1080/19428200 .2018.1493182.

188 **group at Williams College:** Coalition Against, "An Open Letter to the Trustees of Williams," *Williams Record*, April 17, 2019, williamsrecord.com/73648/opinions/an-open -letter-to-the-trustees-of-williams/.

188 **"race-based caucusing":** Matt Markovich, "Segregated Diversity Training at Seattle City Hall Stirs Controversy," KOMO, July 9, 2020, komonews.com/news/local/segregated -diversity-training-seattle-city-hall-stirs-controversy.

188 **embraced separatist trends:** Daniel Patrick Moynihan, *Miles to Go: A Personal History of Social Policy* (Cambridge, Mass.: Harvard University Press, 1996).

189 **"We want to racialize whites":** John Yemma, "'Whiteness Studies' an Attempt at Healing," *Boston Globe*, Dec. 21, 1997, A1. Reassuringly, Flint faced pushback at the time. Noel Ignatiev, a fellow at Harvard's W. E. B. Du Bois Institute, commented in the same article that "to concede any validity to whiteness as a category is to perpetuate injustice."

189 **As she writes in *White Fragility*:** Robin J. DiAngelo, *White Fragility: Why It's So Hard to Talk to White People About Racism* (Boston: Beacon Press, 2018), xiv.

189 **world of progressive pedagogy:** Paul Sperry, "Elite K–8 School Teaches White Students They're Born Racist," *New York Post*, July 1, 2016, nypost.com/2016/07/01/elite-k-8-school -teaches-white-students-theyre-born-racist/.

190 **my last book:** See Mounk, *Great Experiment*, especially chap. 3.

190 **41 percent of undergraduates:** "Johns Hopkins University Diversity: An In-Depth Look," *CollegeVine* (blog), Jan. 1, 2021, blog.collegevine.com/johns-hopkins-university -diversity-statistics/.

191 **favor the in-group:** For an introduction to this aspect of group psychology, see Jonathan Haidt, *The Righteous Mind: Why Good People Are Divided by Politics and Religion* (New York: Penguin Press, 2013), chaps. 9 and 10. See also Mounk, *Great Experiment*, chap. 1.

191 **groups that are peaceful:** For some relevant social science literature on these questions, see Muzafer Sherif, B. Jack White, and O. J. Harvey, "Status in Experimentally Produced Groups," *American Journal of Sociology* 60, no. 4 (1955): 370–79, doi.org/10.1086 /221569; Orlando Patterson, "Context and Choice in Ethnic Allegiance: A Theoretical Framework and Caribbean Case Study," in *Ethnicity: Theory and Experience*, ed. Nathan Glazer and Daniel Patrick Moynihan (Cambridge, Mass.: Harvard University Press, 1975), 305; Yan Chen and Sherry Xin Li, "Group Identity and Social Preferences," *American Economic Review* 99, no. 1 (Jan. 2009): 431–57, doi.org/10.1257/aer.99.1.431; Rogers Brubaker and Frederick Cooper, "Beyond 'Identity,'" *Theory and Sociology* 29, no. 1 (Feb. 2000): 1–47; Daniel N. Posner, "The Political Salience of Cultural Difference: Why Chewas and Tumbukas Are Allies in Zambia and Adversaries in Malawi," *American Political Science Review* 98, no. 4 (2004): 529–45, doi.org/10.1017/s0003055404041334.

192 **help other people overcome:** Gordon W. Allport *The Nature of Prejudice* (Boston: Addison-Wesley, 1954).

192 **social psychologists painstakingly demonstrated:** Thomas Pettigrew and Linda Tropp's 2006 meta-analysis of 515 studies in intergroup contact theory found that contact generally reduces intergroup prejudice, particularly when Allport's four key conditions were met. Thomas F. Pettigrew and Linda R. Tropp, "A Meta-analytic Test of Intergroup Contact Theory," *Journal of Personality and Social Psychology* 90, no. 5 (May 2006): 751–83, doi.org/10.1037/0022-3514.90.5.751.

192 **more positive views:** "The more frequent and intense the contacts with older German civilians, the more favorable were the opinions towards the German people." Samuel A. Stouffer, *The American Soldier: Combat and Its Aftermath* (New York: John Wiley and Sons, 1949), 570.

192 **integrated housing projects:** Morton Deutsch and Mary Evans Collins, *Interracial Housing: A Psychological Evaluation of a Social Experiment* (Minneapolis: University of Minnesota Press, 1951). For a similar case, see also Daniel M. Wilner, Rosabelle Price Walkley, and Stuart W. Cook, *Human Relations in Interracial Housing* (Minneapolis: University of Minnesota Press, 1955).

192 **in Northern Ireland:** Fiona A. White et al., "Improving Intergroup Relations Between Catholics and Protestants in Northern Ireland via E-contact," *European Journal of Social Psychology* 49, no. 2 (2019): 429–38, doi.org/10.1002/ejsp.2515.

192 **with Black colleagues:** Allport, *Nature of Prejudice*, 274.

193 **ensure that intergroup contact:** It is important to note that while these conditions help to secure and maximize the positive effect of intergroup contact, contact generally has a positive effect even if these conditions are not fully met. As Pettigrew and Tropp put it, "They are facilitating conditions that enhance the tendency for positive contact outcomes to emerge." Pettigrew and Tropp, "Meta-analytic Test," 766.

193 **the relevant authorities:** This formulation of the four conditions under which intergroup contact theory works well draws on Allport, *The Nature of Prejudice*, and further work by Thomas Pettigrew, especially Thomas F. Pettigrew, "Intergroup Contact Theory," *An-*

nual Review of Psychology 49 (Feb. 1998): 65–85, doi.org/10.1146/annurev.psych.49.1.65. For more details on intergroup contact theory, see Mounk, *Great Experiment*, 87–92.

194 **leaders of sports teams:** Unsurprisingly, there is ample evidence that team sports act to reduce intergroup prejudice. See Kendrick T. Brown et al., "Teammates on and off the Field? Contact with Black Teammates and the Racial Attitudes of White Student Athletes," *Journal of Applied Social Psychology* 33, no. 7 (2003): 1379–403, doi.org/10.1111 /j.1559-1816.2003.tb01954.x.

194 **"jigsaw pedagogy":** Elliot Aronson and Shelley Patnoe, *Cooperation in the Classroom: The Jigsaw Method* (London: Pinter & Martin, 2011).

195 **sweeping social conflicts:** As one influential model puts it, asserting that "we are all Americans" amounts to "denial of the racial experiences of people of color" and "denial of the necessity to take action against racism." Derald Wing Sue, *Microaggressions in Everyday Life* (Hoboken, N.J.: John Wiley & Sons, 2020), 38.

196 **subtle signs of prejudice:** For instance, one microaggressions guide from the University of California, Santa Cruz, states that asking, "How did you get so good at math?" communicates that "people of color are generally not as intelligent as Whites." "Tool: Recognizing Microaggressions and the Messages They Send."

196 **report their classmates:** Ashe Schow, "University Introduces Website to Report Microaggressions," *Washington Examiner*, Feb. 24, 2016, https://www.washingtonexaminer .com/university-introduces-website-to-report-microaggressions.

197 **the central distinction:** Michael Lind, *The Next American Nation: The New Nationalism and the Fourth American Revolution* (New York: Free Press, 1995).

197 **86 percent of Americans:** "Historical Census Statistics on Population Totals by Race, 1790 to 1990, and by Hispanic Origin, 1970 to 1990, for the United States, Regions, Divisions, and States," Census.gov.

197 **markers of self-identification:** According to some scholars, this began to change in the interwar years. Ronald Bayor, for example, describes the orthodox view that though many white people still associated with their ethnic group, "between World Wars I and II, or at the latest in the 1950s, these mainly southern and eastern European immigrant groups (also Germans, and earlier the Irish) basically saw their identity based on nationality fade, and as a result of tensions with African Americans, coalesced into a white identity group." Ronald H. Bayor, "Another Look at 'Whiteness': The Persistence of Ethnicity in American Life," *Journal of American Ethnic History* 29, no. 1 (Jan. 2009): 13–30, doi.org/10.2307/40543562.

197 **corporate diversity trainings:** Advocates of the identity synthesis are likely to respond that this is naive: that Americans of European descent already do think of themselves, primarily, as whites. But this answer is hardly convincing. After all, many of the prescriptions of progressive separatism are grounded in the presupposition that enlightened educators need to *encourage* people to "embrace race" and "own their European heritage." But, to state the obvious, such encouragement of self-defining as (first, and most important) white would not be necessary if people already did so. Whatever the precise extent to which some Americans already think of their primary self-identification as white, the question is whether the better course of action is to lessen or to intensify the extent to which this is the case.

197 **to define membership:** Many conflicts throughout history pitted diverse, multiethnic groups against one another, and had little to do with our modern understanding of race. For example, "Scholars generally concur that Greek and Roman cultures did not think in terms of race and ethnicity: the ancients may have thought more in terms of borders, conquests and alliances, language, and communication." Rebecca Stuhr and Cheyenne Riehl, "Diversity in the Stacks: Ethnicity in the Ancient World," Penn Libraries, Sept. 2, 2020, www.library.upenn.edu/blogs/libraries-news/diversity-stacks-ethnicity-ancient-world.

198 **most salient group:** "Minimal in-group bias has been found in young children—even as young as age three—highlighting the deeply ingrained nature of this bias among

humans." Scott Barry Kaufman, "In-Group Favoritism Is Difficult to Change, Even When the Social Groups Are Meaningless," *Scientific American* (blog), June 7, 2019, blogs .scientificamerican.com/beautiful-minds/in-group-favoritism-is-difficult-to-change-even -when-the-social-groups-are-meaningless/.

198 **identify as white:** While I have made this point with reference to the United States, similar misgivings about encouraging people to "own" their identity as whites hold even more strongly for the U.K. As the British Nigerian writer Tomiwa Owolade has pointed out, when British people discuss race, "we now talk with an American accent." (Tomiwa Owolade, "Please Stop Imposing American Views About Race on Us," *Persuasion*, Oct. 1, 2020, www.persuasion.community/p/please-stop-imposing-american-views.)

But in truth, Britain's history is very different. In America, many working-class people defined themselves as white to emphasize the social gulf that separated them from slaves and (later) nonwhite immigrants. But Britain was, until fairly recently, much more ethnically homogeneous. Lacking a clear foil within their own country, its residents thus had less reason to define themselves as white. This suggests that attempts to weaken white self-identification may prove more successful in Britain than in the United States, and attempts to strengthen it turn out to be even more counterproductive.

198 **"I am not certain":** Bayard Rustin, "The Failure of Black Separatism," *Harper's Magazine*, Jan. 1970, 31.

199 **destructive interethnic competition:** For a more extensive version of this argument, see Mounk, *Great Experiment*, chap. 9.

199 **In much of Europe:** Between 1990 and 2015 alone, the percentage of immigrants in the EU almost doubled, growing from 5.6 percent to 10.4 percent ("European Union Immigration Statistics 1960–2023," MacroTrends, accessed Jan. 23, 2023, www.macrotrends .net/countries/EUU/european-union/immigration-statistics). The growth in the immigrant population is even more striking when you compare numbers from the immediate postwar period with 2022.

199 **once predominantly European:** In 1980, America was almost 80 percent white. As of 2019, it is 60 percent white. William H. Frey, "The Nation Is Diversifying Even Faster Than Predicted, According to New Census Data," Brookings, July 1, 2020, www.brookings .edu/research/new-census-data-shows-the-nation-is-diversifying-even-faster-than -predicted/.

199 **legacy of segregation:** As recently as a decade ago, a majority of Black students in the Northeast attended a school that was 90 to 100 percent Black. In major cities with large Black populations, 89 percent of Black-owned companies had workforces that were at least 75 percent nonwhite, while 58 percent of white-owned companies had entirely white workforces. Elizabeth Anderson, *The Imperative of Integration* (Princeton, N.J.: Princeton University Press, 2013), 26.

199 **message of racial reconciliation:** More than 90 percent of churchgoers attend a church in which at least 80 percent of the congregation shares their race. Anderson, *Imperative of Integration*, 26.

200 **Residential segregation is less:** Elizabeth D. Huttman, *Urban Housing Segregation of Minorities in Western Europe and the United States* (Durham, N.C.: Duke University Press, 1991).

200 **European elites remain:** Mounk, *Great Experiment*, chap. 8.

200 **different ethnic groups:** "European American children attending homogeneous schools displayed racial bias in their interpretations of ambiguous situations as well as in their evaluations of cross-race friendship. Bias was not found, however, in the interpretations and evaluations of European American or African American children from heterogeneous schools." Heidi McGlothlin and Melanie Killen, "How Social Experience Is Related to Children's Intergroup Attitudes," *European Journal of Social Psychology* 40, no. 4 (2010): 625–34, doi.org/10.1002/ejsp.733.

200 **likely to lack resources:** For instance, "Residence in segregated black neighborhoods is

associated with poor health outcomes. Mortality rates are higher, the higher the percentage of blacks in a neighborhood, for black and white residents alike, after controlling for socioeconomic status." Anderson, *Imperative of Integration*, 30. See sections 2.2–2.4 of *The Imperative of Integration* more broadly.

200 **"If a firm is overwhelmingly white":** Anderson, *Imperative of Integration*, 34.

200 **access to elite institutions:** For example, the reaction to coeducation at Dartmouth in the early 1970s was vicious in many cases. One sports team circulated a list titled "Why Beer Is Better Than Women" that included items like "When your beer goes flat you can toss it" and "Beer doesn't demand equality." "Why Beer Is Better Than Women," accessed Mar. 24, 2023, "Women of Dartmouth" Vertical File, Rauner Special Collections Library, Dartmouth College, exhibits.library.dartmouth.edu/s/coeducation/item/2721.

200 **most of their time:** There is a crucial balance here. For any one individual, it is legitimate to spend most of their time with members of a subnational group defined by religion, culture, or even shared ethnicity. But if most citizens were to make that choice, it would have serious adverse consequences for the prospects of diverse democracies. For more, see Mounk, *Great Experiment*, esp. chap. 6.

201 **suffered centuries of injustice:** For related reasons, some institutions that predominantly cater to a particular religious or ethnic group can be legitimate. Parents who have strong religious convictions, for example, have a right to educate their children in private schools that emphasize those values. Similarly, historically Black colleges and universities, like Howard and Morehouse, were founded at a time when their students were excluded from most of the country's institutions of higher learning; they now continue to play an important role in offering opportunities for upward social mobility to African American students. For an astute defense of Black nationalism from a liberal perspective, see Shelby, *We Who Are Dark*.

201 **very different backgrounds:** Dalton Conley, "When Roommates Were Random," *New York Times*, Aug. 29, 2011, www.nytimes.com/2011/08/29/opinion/when-roommates -were-random.html.

201 **roommates of like mind:** "Over the last decade, students have started to 'meet'—if only digitally—long before arriving on campus. For most colleges, it is quite common to have a designated Facebook group for incoming classes (generally unaffiliated with the institution). Here, students can chat, plan for their first semester and, in some cases, find a roommate match." Jeremy Bauer-Wolf, "Duke University Blocks Students from Picking Their Roommates Freshman Year," *Inside Higher Ed*, March 2, 2018, www.insidehighered .com/news/2018/03/02/duke-university-blocks-students-picking-their-roommates -freshman-year.

201 **likely to integrate:** By the end of their first semester, first-year undergraduates with randomly assigned different-race roommates reported more positive attitudes toward other racial groups than those with same-race roommates. Natalie J. Shook, Patricia D. Hopkins, and Jasmine M. Koech, "The Effect of Intergroup Contact on Secondary Group Attitudes and Social Dominance Orientation," *Group Processes and Intergroup Relations* 19, no. 3 (June 2015): 328–42, doi.org/10.1177/1368430215572266.

201 **than to separate:** As Ron Daniels, the president of Johns Hopkins University, has argued, around the turn of the twenty-first century many students began "drifting . . . into enclaves of familiarity. And universities have actually abetted these trends by removing policies in areas such as housing, dining, and coursework that had once served to draw students together." Ronald J. Daniels, *What Universities Owe Democracy*, with Grant Shreve and Phillip Spector (Baltimore: Johns Hopkins University Press, 2021), 195.

202 **local public schools:** "The heavy reliance on local funding . . . is at the core of the school finance problems. Extensive research has exposed the challenges associated with this unique American system for funding public schools. Our peer Western nations view public schools as more of a national responsibility and provide resources accordingly." Sylvia Allegretto, Emma García, and Elaine Weiss, "Public Education Funding in the

U.S. Needs an Overhaul: How a Larger Federal Role Would Boost Equity and Shield Children from Disinvestment During Downturns," Economic Policy Institute, July 12, 2022, www.epi.org/publication/public-education-funding-in-the-us-needs-an-overhaul/.

202 **strict zoning laws:** Jerusalem Demsas, "America's Racist Housing Rules Really Can Be Fixed," *Vox*, Feb. 17, 2021, www.vox.com/22252625/america-racist-housing-rules-how-to-fix.

Chapter 12: The Path to Equality

205 **distribution of ventilators:** Lisa Rosenbaum, "Facing Covid-19 in Italy—Ethics, Logistics, and Therapeutics on the Epidemic's Front Line," *New England Journal of Medicine* 382, no. 20 (2020): 1873–75, doi.org/10.1056/nejmp2005492.

205 **Countries from Canada:** "Immunization will begin with the arrival of limited doses, prioritized to high-risk populations, such as the elderly, residents and staff of congregate living arrangements such as long term care facilities, front-line health care workers, and indigenous people in remote and isolated communities." "Canada's COVID-19 Immunization Plan: Saving Lives and Livelihoods," Government of Canada, December 18, 2020, https://www.canada.ca/en/public-health/services/diseases/2019-novel-coronavirus-infection/canadas-reponse/canadas-covid-19-immunization-plan.html.

205 **Italy came up:** Paola D'Errigo et al., "Italy's Vaccination Strategy: Careful Planning and Building Trust," Think Global Health, March 11, 2021, www.thinkglobalhealth.org/article/italys-vaccination-strategy-careful-planning-and-building-trust.

205 **Intensive care units:** Lydia Ramsey Pflanzer, "Hospitals Could Be Overwhelmed with Patients and Run Out of Beds and Ventilators as the Coronavirus Pushes the US Healthcare System to Its Limits," *Business Insider*, March 11, 2020, www.businessinsider.com/coronavirus-intensive-care-unit-shortages-of-ventilators-staff-space-2020-3.

205 **doctors and nurses:** In most places, residents of long-term care facilities were also part of the first priority group because a large share of deaths from COVID-19 occurred in these settings.

205 **likelihood of dying:** "Since the start of the pandemic, people 65 and older have been at greatest risk of hospitalization and death due to COVID-19 compared to other age groups, and represent nearly 80% of all COVID-19 deaths as of September 29, 2021, similar to the rate observed in a July 2020 KFF analysis." Meredith Freed, Juliette Cubanski, and Tricia Neuman, "COVID-19 Deaths Among Older Adults During the Delta Surge Were Higher in States with Lower Vaccination Rates," KFF, Oct. 1, 2021, www.kff.org/policy-watch/covid-19-deaths-among-older-adults-during-the-delta-surge-were-higher-in-states-with-lower-vaccination-rates/.

205 **In its preliminary recommendations:** See, for example, Matthew Yglesias, "Give the Vaccine to the Elderly," *Slow Boring*, Dec. 18, 2020, www.slowboring.com/p/vaccinate-elderly; and Kelsey Piper, "Who Should Get the Vaccine First? The Debate over a CDC Panel's Guidelines, Explained," *Vox*, Dec. 22, 2020, www.vox.com/future-perfect/22193679/who-should-get-covid-19-vaccine-first-debate-explained.

206 **The ethical considerations:** The paragraphs on p. 206 are an edited and expanded version of Yascha Mounk, "Why I'm Losing Trust in the Institutions," *Persuasion*, Dec. 23, 2020, www.persuasion.community/p/why-im-losing-trust-in-the-institutions.

206 **presentation to the Advisory Committee:** Kathleen Dooling, "Phased Allocation of COVID-19 Vaccines," Centers for Disease Control, Nov. 23, 2020, www.cdc.gov/vaccines/acip/meetings/downloads/slides-2020-11/COVID-04-Dooling.pdf.

206 **die from COVID:** In the case of an *infection*-blocking vaccine, prioritizing the elderly would avert 0.5–2.0 percent more deaths compared with plans prioritizing high-risk adults or essential workers. In the case of a *disease*-blocking vaccine, it would avert 2.0–6.5 percent more deaths. Dooling, "Phased Allocation," 20–21.

206 **scientific point of view:** Dooling, "Phased Allocation," 22.

207 **gave both alternatives:** Dooling, "Phased Allocation," 23.

207 **"racial and ethnic minority groups":** Dooling, "Phased Allocation," 31.

207 **three points to essential workers:** Dooling, "Phased Allocation," 32.

207 **ACIP unanimously accepted:** Mounk, "Why I'm Losing Trust in the Institutions."

207 **inscribed racial discrimination:** Ross Douthat, "When You Can't Just 'Trust the Science,'" *New York Times*, Dec. 19, 2020, www.nytimes.com/2020/12/19/opinion/sunday/coronavirus-science.html; Yglesias, "Give the Vaccine to the Elderly."

207 *proportion* **of Latinos:** See also Yglesias, "Give the Vaccine to the Elderly." As it turns out, the practical drawbacks to the plan endorsed by the CDC ended up being most significant. By going down the age ladder in small increments, other countries were able to ensure that most of those who were eligible for the vaccine at any one time were also able to make an appointment. In the United States, by contrast, most states ended up with rules that made a huge swath of the population eligible for the vaccine at the same time. The predictable result was that those with the greatest resources—such as rich social networks that let them know about available appointments and high-speed internet connections that allowed them to click through rapidly—were able to snatch a greater share of the appointments. In the end, the very rule that was supposed to increase equity not only led to avoidable deaths by failing to put the most vulnerable at the front of the line; it might also have contributed to a *more* inequitable distribution of the vaccine across racial groups.

207 **It issued new:** In these new guidelines, essential workers placed in Phase 1b were still prioritized over those sixty-five to seventy-four years old, those sixteen to sixty-four with high-risk conditions, or others placed into Phase 1c. "Categories of Essential Workers: Covid-19 Vaccination," Centers for Disease Control and Prevention, accessed Mar. 24, 2023, www.cdc.gov/vaccines/covid-19/categories-essential-workers.html.

208 **governor of Vermont:** Phil Galewitz, "Vermont to Give Minority Residents Priority for COVID Vaccines," *Scientific American*, April 6, 2021, www.scientificamerican.com/article/vermont-to-give-minority-residents-priority-for-covid-vaccines/.

208 **policy proved controversial:** Jordan Williams, "Vermont Governor Condemns 'Racist' Response to State Prioritizing Vaccinating Minority Communities," *Hill*, April 6, 2021, thehill.com/homenews/state-watch/546672-vermont-governor-condemns-racist-response-to-state-prioritizing/.

208 **businesses owned by women:** "The Small Business Boom Under the Biden-Harris Administration," White House, April 2022, www.whitehouse.gov/wp-content/uploads/2022/04/President-Biden-Small-Biz-Boom-full-report-2022.04.28.pdf.

209 **excluded from full civic rights:** *Encyclopædia Britannica*, s.v. "Slavery in the United States," accessed Mar. 24, 2023, www.britannica.com/topic/African-American/Slavery-in-the-United-States.

209 **immigrants from China:** "Chinese Exclusion Act (1882)," National Archives and Records Administration, accessed Mar. 24, 2023, www.archives.gov/milestone-documents/chinese-exclusion-act.

209 **Americans of Japanese origin:** For an overview of Japanese internment during World War II, see Roger Daniels and Eric Foner, *Prisoners Without Trial: Japanese Americans in World War II* (New York: Hill and Wang, 1995).

209 **fought these injustices:** For instance, Jewish civic leaders and activists were involved from the beginning of the Civil Rights Movement; social worker Henry Moskowitz was one of four Jewish founders of the National Association for the Advancement of Colored People (NAACP) in 1909. "NAACP: A Century in the Fight for Freedom Founding and Early Years," Library of Congress, Feb. 21, 2009, https://www.loc.gov/exhibits/naacp/founding-and-early-years.html.

209 **"The Americans who crossed this bridge":** Barack Obama, "Remarks by the President at the 50th Anniversary of the Selma to Montgomery Marches," March 7, 2015, National Archives and Records Administration, obamawhitehouse.archives.gov/the-press-office/2015/03/07/remarks-president-50th-anniversary-selma-montgomery-marches.

209 **federal judges appointed:** In *Fisher v. University of Texas*, one of the more recent conflicts surrounding race conscious college admissions, Justice Kennedy was the only Republican-appointed judge to side with the majority to uphold the University of Texas's consideration of race in the admissions process. *Fisher v. University of Texas*, 579 U.S. __ (2016).

210 **"racial classifications, however compelling":** *Grutter v. Bollinger*, 539 U.S. 306, 342 (2003).

210 **"25 years from now":** *Grutter*, 539 U.S. at 343.

210 **mounted a radical attack:** See part I.

210 **become taboo to claim:** Maia Niguel Hoskin, "Color-Blindness Perpetuates Structural Racism," *Forbes*, Sept. 28, 2022, www.forbes.com/sites/maiahoskin/2022/09/28/newsflash -color-blindness-perpetuates-structural-racism/?sh=61bd6d11ae91; "What Does Racism Look Like? Colorblindness," Fitchburg State University: Anti-Racism Resources, accessed Mar. 24, 2023, fitchburgstate.libguides.com/c.php?g=1046516&p=7616506.

210 **"racial/cultural beings":** Brendan O'Neill, "College Codes Make 'Color Blindness' a Microaggression," *Reason*, Aug. 5, 2015, reason.com/2015/08/05/speech-codes-and -humanism/.

210 **"The language of color blindness":** Ibram X. Kendi, *How to Be an Antiracist* (New York: Random House Large Print, 2020), 9.

210 **idea of color blindness:** Dani Bostick, "How Colorblindness Is Actually Racist," *Huffington Post*, July 11, 2016, www.huffpost.com/entry/how-colorblindness-is-act_b_10886176.

211 **a Black Marxist:** Yascha Mounk, "Adolph Reed Jr. on Race and Class in America," *Persuasion*, May 21, 2022, www.persuasion.community/p/reed#details.

211 **"I'm proud to stand with":** "Remarks by Vice President Harris at Oakland Generation Fund Event," White House, Aug. 12, 2022, www.whitehouse.gov/briefing-room /speeches-remarks/2022/08/12/remarks-by-vice-president-harris-at-oakland-generation -fund-event/.

211 **"the Federal Government [to] pursue":** "Executive Order on Advancing Racial Equity and Support for Underserved Communities Through the Federal Government," White House, Jan. 20, 2021, www.whitehouse.gov/briefing-room/presidential-actions/2021 /01/20/executive-order-advancing-racial-equity-and-support-for-underserved -communities-through-the-federal-government/.

211 **pursue "race-conscious":** Even when policies are not race conscious, Democrats now often frame them as if they were. See, for example, Marc Novicoff, "Stop Marketing Race-Blind Policies as Racial Equity Initiatives," *Slow Boring*, Feb. 20, 2021, www.slowboring .com/p/race-blind-policies-racial-equity.

211 **exceptions for Sikhs:** The example of Sikhs and helmets has been discussed in great detail by political theorists debating "multiculturalism" in the 1990s. See, for example, Will Kymlicka, *Multicultural Citizenship: A Liberal Theory of Minority Rights* (Oxford: Clarendon Press, 1996), 31.

211 **such policies explicitly:** Both race-sensitive and race-conscious policies aim to further equity. The term "race-sensitive policies" usually refers to those policies that make the way in which the state treats individuals depend on their race. The term "race-conscious policies" usually refers to assessing the effect that a policy has on different demographic groups without explicitly making the treatment of individuals turn on their ascriptive identities. Vermont's decision to make nonwhite residents eligible for a vaccine before white residents is an example of race-sensitive policy; ACIP's recommendation to prioritize essential workers over the elderly because they are more ethnically diverse is an example of race conscious policy.

211 **the strongest predictor:** Through December 6, 2022, mortality rates among Black and Hispanic people were 1.6 and 1.7 times those of white people, while among those sixty-five to seventy-four years old and seventy-five to eighty-four years old, death rates were 60 and 140 times those of eighteen- to twenty-nine-year-olds, respectively. For age, see "Risk

for COVID-19 Infection, Hospitalization, and Death by Age Group," Centers for Disease Control and Prevention, accessed Jan. 24, 2023, www.cdc.gov/coronavirus/2019 -ncov/covid-data/investigations-discovery/hospitalization-death-by-age.html. For race, see "Risk for COVID-19 Infection, Hospitalization, and Death by Race/Ethnicity," Centers for Disease Control and Prevention, accessed Jan. 24, 2023, www.cdc.gov/coronavirus /2019-ncov/covid-data/investigations-discovery/hospitalization-death-by-race -ethnicity.html. For a broader overview of mortality risk factors, see Zelalem G. Dessie and Temesgen Zewotir, "Mortality-Related Risk Factors of COVID-19: A Systematic Review and Meta-analysis of 42 Studies and 423,117 Patients," BioMed Central, Aug. 21, 2021, bmcinfectdis.biomedcentral.com/articles/10.1186/s12879-021-06536-3.

212 **race-neutral policies:** As Heather McGhee states, "Instead of being blind to race, color blindness makes people blind to racism, unwilling to acknowledge where its effects have shaped opportunity." Heather McGhee, "Why Saying 'I Don't See Race at All' Just Makes Racism Worse," Ideas.Ted.Com, March 3, 2021, ideas.ted.com/why-saying-i-dont -see-race-at-all-just-makes-racism-worse/.

212 **boosting the opportunities:** For one of many articles that delves into race-blind policy, see Adia Harvey Wingfield, "The Failure of Race-Blind Economic Policy," *Atlantic*, Feb. 16, 2017, www.theatlantic.com/business/archive/2017/02/race-economic-policy/516966/.

212 **writer Ralph Leonard:** Ralph Leonard (@buffsoldier_96), "The colour blind resolve to treat everyone as citizens, not as bearers of specific 'cultures' or mere representations of 'races' is valuable," Twitter, July 19, 2019, 4:52 p.m., twitter.com/buffsoldier_96/status /1152320415752228867.

213 **are experiencing discrimination:** Leonard, "The colour blind resolve."

213 **"treat everyone equally":** Leonard, "The colour blind resolve."

213 **likely to use crack:** Joseph J. Palamar et al., "Powder Cocaine and Crack Use in the United States: An Examination of Risk for Arrest and Socioeconomic Disparities in Use," *Drug and Alcohol Dependence* 149 (2015): 108–16, doi.org/10.1016/j.drugalcdep.2015.01.029.

214 **aim to alleviate poverty:** Leonard himself uses the term "race-blind" for policies that I would call "race neutral." This is not a deep philosophical difference. But because race blindness is now understood to denote racism blindness, it is likely to lead to precisely the confusion between perception and action I am trying to avoid.

214 **genuine contribution to society:** For a defense of the value of meritocracy, rightly understood, see chapter 13.

215 **nonwhite middle class:** See, for example, Richard V. Reeves and Camille Busette, "The Middle Class Is Becoming Race-Plural, Just Like the Rest of America," Brookings, February 27, 2018, www.brookings.edu/blog/social-mobility-memos/2018/02/27/the-middle-class -is-becoming-race-plural-just-like-the-rest-of-america/.

215 **growing white underclass:** See, for example, Lauren Gurley, "Who's Afraid of Rural Poverty? The Story Behind America's Invisible Poor," *American Journal of Economics and Sociology* 75, no. 3 (May 2016): 589–604, doi.org/10.1111/ajes.12149.

215 **Americans are in poverty:** "Poverty Rate by Race/Ethnicity," KFF, 2021, www.kff.org /other/state-indicator/poverty-rate-by-raceethnicity/.

215 **antipoverty policy:** To get to these numbers, I multiplied the total estimated population of the United States by the percentage of the population that is white (or Black) and the percentage of the white (or Black) population that lives in poverty. For estimates of the total population and America's demographic breakdown, see "Quickfacts: United States," U.S. Census Bureau, www.kff.org/other/state-indicator/poverty-rate-by-raceethnicity/, www.census.gov/quickfacts/fact/table/US/PST045221.

215 **live in deprived neighborhoods:** In 2010, Black people were almost four times as likely as white people to live in neighborhoods with poverty rates greater than 40 percent. Sean F. Reardon, Lindsay Fox, and Joseph Townsend, "Neighborhood Income Composition by Household Race and Income, 1990–2009," *Annals of the American Academy of Political and Social Science* 660, no. 1 (Sept. 2015): 78–97, doi.org/10.1177/0002716215576104.

216 **ancestors were victims:** To be sure, there would be all kinds of practical difficulties in figuring out how such reparations should be apportioned. Perhaps those difficulties are so prohibitive as to vitiate the whole project. Or perhaps they are a reason to target reparations more broadly at communities that contain a lot of descendants of slaves—even though this would mean that some people who do fall into that category would not gain any help, while others who don't are inadvertently included.

But even if we accept the need for such practical compromises and concessions to make reparations workable, the principle that makes the case for reparations plausible is very different from that which supposedly motivates race-sensitive policies; in the language of political philosophy, it concerns the field of "rectificatory" justice. It follows, then, that even those who believe the case for reparations to be compelling should not jump to the conclusion that public policies generally need to be sensitive to immutable characteristics like race.

217 **"The disparitarian ideal":** Adolph Reed Jr. and Walter Benn Michaels, "The Trouble with Disparity," Common Dreams, Aug. 15, 2020, www.commondreams.org/views /2020/08/15/trouble-disparity. As Reed and Michaels go on to say, "Not only will a focus on the effort to eliminate racial disparities not take us in the direction of a more equal society, it isn't even the best way of eliminating racial disparities themselves. . . . It is practically impossible to imagine a serious strategy for winning the kinds of reforms that would actually improve black and brown working people's conditions without winning them for all working people."

217 **The other problem with equity:** For an overview of this objection, see section 6.1, "Kinds of Egalitarianism," in Stefan Gosepath, "Equality," in *Stanford Encyclopedia of Philosophy*, April 26, 2021, plato.stanford.edu/entries/equality/.

218 **Similarly, in India:** Soumya Shankar, "India's Citizenship Law, in Tandem with National Registry, Could Make BJP's Discriminatory Targeting of Muslims Easier," *Intercept*, Jan. 30, 2020, theintercept.com/2020/01/30/india-citizenship-act-caa-nrc-assam/.

219 **state treats citizens:** Another problem is that many of the policies that are designed to help disfavored groups end up harming them in unexpected ways. Competitive opportunities like scholarships and spots at high-ranking universities, for example, are valuable in part because they serve as a signal to future employers. If an applicant has, in the past, won a prestigious honor or gone to a college with highly competitive admissions policies, they must be very talented.

Some economists believe that affirmative action can undermine that signal. If employers know that the average SAT scores of Black students at elite colleges are significantly lower than those of students who belong to different demographic groups, they may discount their success—even when evaluating the application of a candidate who has not in any way benefitted from affirmative action. Policies that help some members of historically disadvantaged groups might simultaneously harm other members of that same group.

See, for example, Bruce Wydick, "Affirmative Action in College Admissions: Examining Labor Market Effects of Four Alternative Policies," *Contemporary Economic Policy* 20, no. 1 (2002): 12–24, doi.org/10.1093/cep/20.1.12; Bruce Wydick, "Do Race-Based Preferences Perpetuate Discrimination Against Marginalized Ethnic Groups?," *Journal of Developing Areas* 42, no. 1 (2008): 165–81, doi.org/10.1353/jda.0.0024; and Terry Eastland, "The Case Against Affirmative Action," *William and Mary Law Review* 1992, no. 34 (1992): 33–52, doi.org/10.3817/0992093145.

219 **for Asian American applicants:** In one study examining admissions data from Fall 1997, Asians who were admitted to elite colleges scored about 140 more points on the SAT than white students who were admitted. See Scott Jaschik, "The Numbers and the Arguments on Asian Admissions," *Inside Higher Ed*, Aug. 7, 2017, www.insidehighered .com/admissions/article/2017/08/07/look-data-and-arguments-about-asian -americans-and-admissions-elite.

219 **on soft criteria:** Jay Caspian Kang, "Where Does Affirmative-Action Leave Asian

-Americans?," *New York Times Magazine*, Aug. 28, 2019, www.nytimes.com/2019/08
/28/magazine/affirmative-action-asian-american-harvard.html. In theory, it is of course
possible to separate these two points. Harvard and Princeton could give Black or brown
students a leg up without at the same time making it artificially difficult for Asian American students to gain admission. But social science also suggests that it is, in practice,
never going to be easy to ensure that race-sensitive policies that favor one minority group
that is underrepresented in positions of power don't have perverse effects on other minority groups that are underrepresented in positions of power—or even come to run directly
counter to their original intentions.

219 **have a stake:** It is, for example, suggestive that the same policies receive more support
with a class-based framing then a race-based framing. See Micah English and Joshua
Kalla, "Racial Equality Frames and Public Policy Support: Survey Experimental Evidence," OSF Preprints, April 23, 2021, doi:10.31219/osf.io/tdkf3.

219 **"Do you want a society":** Quoted in Carol M. Allen, *Ending Racial Preferences: The
Michigan Story* (Lanham, Md.: Lexington Books, 2009), 2.

220 **Save Our State:** "California Proposition 187," Ballotpedia, accessed Mar. 24, 2023,
ballotpedia.org/California_Proposition_187,_Prohibit_Persons_in_Violation_of
_Immigration_Law_from_Using_Public_Healthcare,_Schools,_and_Social_Services
Initiative(1994).

220 **majority of Californians:** "California Proposition 209, Affirmative Action Initiative
(1996)," Ballotpedia, accessed Mar. 24, 2023, ballotpedia.org/California_Proposition
_209,_Affirmative_Action_Initiative_(1996).

220 **majority of its population:** Hans Johnson, Eric McGhee, and Marisol Cuellar Mejia,
"California's Population," Public Policy Institute of California, Jan. 2022, www.ppic
.org/publication/californias-population/; Eric McGhee, "California's Political Geography 2020," Public Policy Institute of California, Feb. 2020, www.ppic.org/publication
/californias-political-geography/.

220 **the exception of:** List of California Governors, California State Library, accessed Mar.
24, 2023, governors.library.ca.gov/list.html.

220 **key institutional players:** Endorsers included Twitter, Wells Fargo, and Reddit. For a
full list, see "California Proposition 16, Repeal Proposition 209 Affirmative Action
Amendment (2020)," Ballotpedia, accessed Jan. 25, 2023, ballotpedia.org/California
_Proposition_16,_Repeal_Proposition_209_Affirmative_Action_Amendment
_(2020).

220 **they outspent opponents:** Supporters garnered more than $25 million compared with
approximately $1.75 million for opponents. "California Proposition 16, Repeal Proposi-
tion 209 Affirmative Action Amendment (2020)."

220 **maintain the ban:** "Live Election Results: 2020 California Results," *Politico*, accessed
Mar. 24, 2023, www.politico.com/2020-election/results/california/.

221 **tackling the deep:** See, for example, Sherif Girgis, "Dobbs's History and the Future of
Abortion and Privacy Law," *SCOTUSblog*, June 28, 2022, www.scotusblog.com/2022
/06/dobbss-history-and-the-future-of-abortion-and-privacy-law/.

221 **a greater understanding:** For an influential version of this statement, see Jeremy Wal-
dron, "The Core of the Case Against Judicial Review," *Yale Law Journal* 115 (2005):
1346–406.

221 **set of criteria:** *Adarand Constructors Inc. v. Peña*, 515 U.S. 200 (1995).

221 **"Government may treat people":** *Adarand Constructors Inc.*, 515 U.S. at 227.

221 **serve a "compelling interest":** *Adarand Constructors Inc.*, 515 U.S. at 227.

221 **be "narrowly tailored":** *Adarand Constructors Inc.*, 515 U.S. at 227.

222 **"We apply strict scrutiny":** *City of Richmond v. J. A. Croson Co.*, 488 U.S. 469 (1989).

222 **much stricter limits:** Adam Liptak, "Supreme Court Seems Ready to Throw Out Race-
Based College Admissions," *New York Times*, Oct. 31, 2022, www.nytimes.com/2022
/10/31/us/supreme-court-harvard-unc-affirmative-action.html.

222 **likely to be announced:** *Students for Fair Admissions v. President and Fellows of Harvard College*, citation pending.

Chapter 13: On Structural Racism, Gender, and Meritocracy

226 **add a new concept:** Structural racism is often viewed as similar or synonymous to institutional racism. The term "institutional racism" traces back to Stokely Carmichael and Charles V. Hamilton's *Black Power*: "[Institutional racism] is less overt, far more subtle, less identifiable in terms of *specific* individuals committing the acts. But it is no less destructive of human life. [It] originates in the operation of established and respected forces in the society, and thus receives far less public condemnation than the first type. When . . . five hundred black babies die each year because of the lack of proper food, shelter and medical facilities, and thousands more are destroyed and maimed physically, emotionally and intellectually because of conditions of poverty and discrimination in the black community, that is a function of institutional racism." Stokely Carmichael and Charles V. Hamilton, *Black Power: The Politics of Liberation in America* (New York: Random House, 1992), 1.

226 **"policies and practices that exist":** *Cambridge Dictionary*, s.v. "systemic racism," accessed Mar. 24, 2023, dictionary.cambridge.org/dictionary/english/systemic-racism.

227 **"Racism," one online guide:** "Dismantling Racism Works Web Workbook," dRworks-Book, accessed Mar. 24, 2023, www.dismantlingracism.org/. See also Yascha Mounk, "The Political Inconvenience of the Jersey City Shooting," *Atlantic*, Dec. 12, 2019, www.theatlantic.com/ideas/archive/2019/12/political-inconvenience-jersey-city-shooting/603472/.

227 **"It is literally impossible":** Manisha Krishnan, "Dear White People, Please Stop Pretending Reverse Racism Is Real," *Vice*, Oct. 2, 2016, www.vice.com/en/article/kwzjvz/dear-white-people-please-stop-pretending-reverse-racism-is-real.

227 **"Jews, as white people":** Farah Stockman, "Women's March Roiled by Accusations of Anti-Semitism," *New York Times*, Dec. 23, 2018, www.nytimes.com/2018/12/23/us/womens-march-anti-semitism.html.

228 **even more "white adjacent":** Ari Blaff, "Whitewashing Success," *Tablet*, Nov. 15, 2021, www.tabletmag.com/sections/news/articles/whitewashing-asian-americans.

228 **wave of hate crimes:** See, for example, Masood Farivar, "Anti-Asian Hate Crime Crosses Racial and Ethnic Lines," VOA, March 24, 2021, www.voanews.com/a/usa_anti-asian-hate-crime-crosses-racial-and-ethnic-lines/6203679.html. For an explanation of how the same mechanism can also encourage the media to downplay attacks on Jews, see Mounk, "Political Inconvenience of the Jersey City Shooting."

228 **subverting traditional gender norms:** See, for example, Judith Butler, *Gender Trouble: Feminism and the Subversion of Identity*, 2nd ed. (New York: Routledge, 1999).

228 **are profoundly unhappy:** This profound unhappiness is obvious reading the accounts of transgender participants in a 2022 Pew focus group. "As a small child, like around kindergarten [or] first grade . . . I just was [fascinated] by how some people were small girls, and some people were small boys, and it was on my mind constantly. And I started to feel very uncomfortable, just existing as a young girl" (Trans man, early thirties). "I've known ever since I was little. I'm not really sure the age, but I just always knew when I put on boy clothes, I just felt so uncomfortable" (Trans woman, late thirties). See Travis Mitchell, "The Experiences, Challenges, and Hopes of Transgender and Nonbinary U.S. Adults," Pew Research Center's Social & Demographic Trends Project, June 7, 2022, www.pewresearch.org/social-trends/2022/06/07/the-experiences-challenges-and-hopes-of-transgender-and-nonbinary-u-s-adults/.

229 **"A simple binary view":** Agustín Fuentes, "Biological Science Rejects the Sex Binary, and That's Good for Humanity," *Scientist*, May 12, 2022, www.the-scientist.com/news-opinion/biological-science-rejects-the-sex-binary-and-that-s-good-for-humanity-70008.

229 **a key determinant:** Vera Regitz-Zagrosek, "Sex and Gender Differences in Health," *EMBO Reports* 13, no. 7 (2012): 596–603, doi.org/10.1038/embor.2012.87.

229 **an intersex condition:** See, for example, Leonard Sax, "How Common Is Intersex? A Response to Anne Fausto-Sterling," *Journal of Sex Research* 39, no. 3 (Jan. 2002): 174–78, doi.org/10.1080/00224490209552139. A determination of the exact percentage is complicated because it depends on the precise definition of "intersex." However, according to most experts, "a child is born so noticeably atypical in terms of genitalia that a specialist in sex differentiation is called in in between 1 in 1500 to 1 in 2000 births." "How Common Is Intersex?," Intersex Society of North America, accessed Jan. 18, 2023, isna.org/faq /frequency/.

230 **"History! Dr. Rachel Levine":** GLAAD (@glaad), Twitter, March 24, 2021, twitter .com/glaad/status/1374840653704728578.

230 **demands of sex:** I am not responding to a straw man here. See, for example, this article in a prominent medical journal recommending that "questions about sex assigned at birth [in a medical context] are abandoned": Ash B. Alpert, Roman Ruddick, and Charlie Manzano, "Rethinking Sex-Assigned-at-Birth Questions," *British Medical Journal* 373, no. 8294 (2021), doi.org/10.1136/bmj.n1261.

230 **significant physical advantages:** Stephanie Burnett, "Do Trans Athletes Have an Unfair Advantage?," *DW*, July 24, 2021, www.dw.com/en/fact-check-do-trans-athletes -have-an-advantage-in-elite-sport/a-58583988.

231 **the American dream:** This element of the American dream is present from its inception. When the historian James Truslow Adams first coined the term, he wrote that it is the "dream of a land in which life should be better and richer and fuller for everyone, with opportunity for each according to ability or achievement. It is a difficult dream for the European upper classes to interpret adequately, and too many of us ourselves have grown weary and mistrustful of it. It is not a dream of motor cars and high wages merely, but a dream of social order in which each man and each woman shall be able to attain to the fullest stature of which they are innately capable, and be recognized by others for what they are, regardless of the fortuitous circumstances of birth or position." James Truslow Adams, *The Epic of America* (Boston: Little, Brown, 1931), 404.

231 **incomes of most Americans:** Drew DeSilver, "For Most U.S. Workers, Real Wages Have Barely Budged in Decades," Pew Research Center, Aug. 7, 2018, www.pewresearch org /fact-tank/2018/08/07/for-most-us-workers-real-wages-have-barely-budged-for-decades/.

231 **Meanwhile, the costs:** "The Cost of Living in America: Helping Families Move Ahead," White House, Aug. 11, 2021, www.whitehouse.gov/cea/written-materials/2021/08/11 /the-cost-of-living-in-america-helping-families-move-ahead/.

231 **a decent standard of living:** See, for example, Ben S. Bernanke and Peter Olson, "Are Americans Better Off Than They Were a Decade or Two Ago?," Brookings, Oct. 19, 2016, www.brookings.edu/blog/ben-bernanke/2016/10/19/are-americans-better-off-than -they-were-a-decade-or-two-ago/; and Devon Haynie, "A Global Anomaly, the U.S. Declines in Annual Quality of Life Report," *U.S. News & World Report*, Sept. 11, 2020, www.usnews.com/news/best-countries/articles/2020-09-11/a-global-anomaly-the-us -declines-in-annual-quality-of-life-report.

231 **a viral interview:** Sean Illing, "How Meritocracy Harms Everyone—Even the Winners," *Vox*, Oct. 21, 2019, www.vox.com/identities/2019/10/21/20897021/meritocracy-economic -mobility-daniel-markovits.

231 **Michael Sandel argues:** Michael J. Sandel, *The Tyranny of Merit* (New York: Farrar, Straus and Giroux, 2020), 14.

231 **"Objective truth, like merit":** Richard Delgado and Jean Stefancic, *Critical Race Theory: An Introduction*, 2nd ed. (New York: New York University Press, 2012), 104.

232 **"the promise of equality":** Naa Oyo Kwate and Ilan H. Meyer, "The Myth of Meritocracy and African American Health," *American Journal of Public Health* 100, no. 10 (2010): 1831–34, doi.org/10.2105/ajph.2009.186445.

232 **one business consultant:** Tim Enwall, "Open Letter to My White CEO, VC Colleagues: 'Meritocracy' Is Likely a Racist Belief," *Medium*, June 14, 2020, tenwall.medium
.com/open-letter-to-my-white-ceo-vc-colleagues-meritocracy-is-likely-a-racist-belief
-ad7a72dbee92.

232 **a big leg up:** Sandel, *Tyranny of Merit*.

232 **study or strive:** The negative effects of non-meritocratic systems on economic development and good governance are widely observed. For instance, political scientists have explained Greece's economic struggles in part by pointing to its lack of a meritocratic bureaucracy. See, for example, Francis Fukuyama, *Political Order and Political Decay: From the Industrial Revolution to the Globalization of Democracy* (New York: Farrar, Straus and Giroux, 2015), 76–77.

233 **legitimate aspirations of millions:** For the best statement of this position, see Adrian Wooldridge, *The Aristocracy of Talent: How Meritocracy Made the Modern World* (New York: Skyhorse, 2021).

PART IV: IN DEFENSE OF UNIVERSALISM

239 **the best guide:** For a canonical history of liberalism, see Edmund Fawcett, *Liberalism: The Life of an Idea* (Princeton, N.J.: Princeton University Press, 2018). For an intellectual history more focused on the permutations of the word's meaning, see Helena Rosenblatt, *The Lost History of Liberalism: From Ancient Rome to the Twenty-first Century* (Princeton, N.J.: Princeton University Press, 2018). For classic texts in the liberal tradition, see, for example, Benjamin Constant, *The Liberty of Ancients Compared with That of Moderns* (1819); and John Rawls, *Political Liberalism* (New York: Columbia University Press, 1993). For recent defenses from a philosophical perspective, see Francis Fukuyama, *Liberalism and Its Discontents* (New York: Farrar, Straus and Giroux, 2022); and from an empirical perspective, Deirdre McCloskey, *Why Liberalism Works: How True Liberal Values Produce a Freer, More Equal, Prosperous World for All* (New Haven, Conn.: Yale University Press, 2019).

240 **tends to be right-wing:** John Lichfield, "Call Emmanuel Macron Any Name You Like—but Not 'Liberal,'" *Politico*, Feb. 5, 2019, www.politico.eu/article/call-emmanuel-macron
-any-name-you-like-but-not-liberal-lef-right-division-politics/.

240 **In the United Kingdom:** Michael Goldfarb, "Liberal? Are We Talking About the Same Thing?," *BBC News*, July 20, 2010, www.bbc.com/news/world-10658070.

240 **frequently labeled "liberals":** For a version of this argument, see David Greenberg, "Stop Calling Bernie Sanders and Alexandria Ocasio-Cortez Liberals," *Washington Post*, Sept. 12, 2019, www.washingtonpost.com/outlook/2019/09/12/stop-calling-bernie-sanders
-alexandria-ocasio-cortez-liberals/.

Chapter 14: A Response to the Identity Synthesis

241 **The movement, Richard Delgado:** Richard Delgado and Jean Stefancic, *Critical Race Theory: An Introduction*, 3rd ed. (New York: New York University Press, 2017), 25.

241 **so consistently focused:** "Looking to Enlightenment liberals for progress on race is like looking to Jim Crow segregationists for progress on race." Ibram X. Kendi (@DrIbram), Twitter, July 20, 2020, 9:11 a.m., twitter.com/dribram/status/1281576823256743936.

242 **"rational reconstruction of an entity":** Hannes Leitgeb and André Carus, "Rudolf Carnap—Methodology," in *Stanford Encyclopedia of Philosophy* (Fall 2022 ed.), ed. Edward N. Zalta and Uri Nodelman, plato.stanford.edu/entries/carnap/methodology
.html#RatiReco. Such a rational reconstruction, Carnap admitted, could never hope to capture the full complexity of the original. Indeed, the same body of thought may even be subject to different reconstructions. As the *Stanford Encyclopedia of Philosophy* notes,

"The output of a rational reconstruction differs from the input or *reconstruendum* ('This viewpoint allows and even requires deviations of the construction from the actual process of cognition,' §143), and it is consistent with a 'multiplicity of possibilities' (§92) regarding the procedure for carrying out the rational reconstruction" (Leitgeb and Carus, "Carnap"). But this does not mean the produced reconstruction is arbitrary; "new definitions should be superior to the old in clarity and exactness, and, above all, should fit into a systematic structure of concepts." Rudolf Carnap, *The Logical Structure of the World; and, Pseudoproblems in Philosophy*, trans. Rolf A. George (Chicago: Open Court, 2003), 5.

242 **assess its core claims:** Hannes Leitgeb and André Carus, "The Reconstruction of Scientific Theories," in *Stanford Encyclopedia of Philosophy*, 2020, plato.stanford.edu/entries/carnap/reconstruct-sci-theories.html.

242 **its underlying logic:** The different focus of each chapter leads me to emphasize different aspects of the ideology. But there is nevertheless some important overlap. For example, the preference for norms, rules, and laws that explicitly distinguish between different people on the basis of their identity is a red thread that reappears in each part of the book: as the "rejection of neutral solutions" in part I; as a rhetorical emphasis on "equity" in part II; as the case for "race-sensitive public policy" in part III; and, in this section, as the need to make how the state treats each citizen depend on their ascriptive identity.

243 **to religious facts:** William R. Downing, ed., "What Is Church History?," in *Notes on Historiography and Early Church History* (Morgan Hill, Calif.: Sovereign Grace Baptist Church of Silicon Valley, 2014), 6; William R. Downing, ed., "The Canon of Scripture," in *Notes on Historiography and Early Church History*, 112–19.

243 **major historical events:** For the canonical defense of Marxist philosophy of history from the perspective of analytical philosophy, see G. A. Cohen, *Karl Marx's Theory of History: A Defence* (New York: Oxford University Press, 1978). For a classic history written with (broadly) Marxist presuppositions, see Eric Hobsbawm, *The Age of Revolution: Europe, 1789–1848* (London: Weidenfeld and Nicolson, 1962); and Eric Hobsbawm, *The Age of Capital: 1848–1875* (London: Weidenfeld and Nicolson, 1975).

243 **a particular prism:** See, for example, the focus on identity in modern archaeology: Stone Age Herbalist, "The Rise of Archaeologists Anonymous," UnHerd, Dec. 3, 2022, unherd.com/2022/12/the-rise-of-archaeologists-anonymous/.

243 **linguists call this:** One influential linguist has distinguished between three kinds of interruptions: (1) non-relational neutral interruptions, which might, for example, serve to clarify what the speaker is saying; (2) relational rapport interruptions, which serve to affirm what the speaker is saying and build a deeper connection; and (3) relational power interruptions, which may serve to assert power over the speaker. While the third type of interruption is indeed common, and may entail a pernicious racial dynamic, effective communication requires occasional interruptions of type 1, and genuine friendship virtually always entails interruptions of type 2. See Julia A. Goldberg et al., "Interrupting the Discourse on Interruptions: An Analysis in Terms of Relationally Neutral, Power-, and Rapport-Oriented Acts," *Journal of Pragmatics* 14, no. 6 (Dec. 1990), www.sciencedirect.com/science/article/pii/037821669090045F.

244 **the whole apparatus:** Jesse Singal, "'White Fragility' Is a Completely Bizarre and Pernicious Book and It's a Terrible Sign That So Many Americans Love It," *Blocked and Reported*, episode 17, June 19, 2020, podcast, www.blockedandreported.org/p/early-access-episode-17-white-fragility-cb8#details. Similarly, most viewers understood Will Smith slapping Chris Rock at the 2022 Oscars ceremony as a straightforward breach of the important norm that you do not respond to a joke you consider rude by resorting to physical violence. But many adherents of the identity synthesis believed that Smith's actions were more justifiable because Rock had made a joke about the hair of his wife, Jada, who is Black; indeed, some members of the left-leaning "Squad" in the House of Representatives initially tweeted in support of Smith's actions. "Reps. Ayanna Pressley, Jamaal Bowman

Tweet, Then Delete, Defense of Will Smith's Oscars Slap," NBCNews.com, March 28, 2022, www.nbcnews.com/politics/politics-news/reps-ayanna-pressley-jamaal-bowman -tweet-delete-defense-will-smiths-os-rcna21787.

244 *neutral rules merely serve:* See chapter 12 for a discussion of identity conscious policy. See chapters 1 and 3 for the intellectual origins of the rejection of universal values and neutral rules.

244 **defended free speech:** See, for example, Harry Blain, "Why the Left Needs to Re-embrace the First Amendment," openDemocracy, May 15, 2017, www.opendemocracy .net/en/transformation/why-left-needs-to-re-embrace-first-amendment/.

244 **they merely cloak:** See part III. Compare also Billie Murray, "The Anti-democratic Con-sequences of the 'More-Speech' System," *Communication and Democracy* 56, no. 2 (2022): 198–204, doi.org/10.1080/27671127.2022.2141720.

245 **This principle helps to justify:** See introduction and chapter 12. To see how these three claims work in concert, it is helpful to revisit the work of Derrick Bell, the founding father of critical race theory. As I described in part I, Bell was a civil rights lawyer who gradually came to believe that many efforts at desegregation in the American South were a serious mistake. This stance may seem deeply counterintuitive at first sight. But a con-sideration of the three key postulates of the identity synthesis helps to explain how he arrived at his conclusion.

Bell began his academic career with a skeptical analysis of the origins of *Brown v. Board of Education*, the Supreme Court ruling that declared racial segregation in public education unconstitutional. At the time, many legal scholars explained the decision as flowing from the deep tension between the universal rules encapsulated in the Constitu-tion as well as the Fourteenth Amendment and the evidently discriminatory practices that persisted in the American South. Meanwhile, many historians and social scientists emphasized the disciplined organizing of the civil rights movement and the social trans-formations brought about by World War II. But Bell believed that such explanations are naive because they do not focus on the way in which identity groups and their interests stand at the center of most important historical developments. Because whites held virtu-ally all power in the America of the 1950s, a landmark decision like *Brown v. Board of Education* must have been in their racial self-interest. The true motivation for desegrega-tion, Bell argued, was to serve the interests of whites by improving America's interna-tional image and making it easier to develop the Sunbelt. (See Derrick A. Bell Jr., "*Brown v. Board of Education* and the Interest-Convergence Dilemma," *Harvard Law Review* 93, no. 3 (Jan. 1980): 524–27.) According to Bell, the key to understanding how one of the most important Supreme Court rulings in American history could have come about con-sisted, as the first postulate of the rational reconstruction of the identity synthesis would imply, in examining the motivation of the justices "through the prism of group identities like race, religion, gender, and sexual orientation."

Bell went on to argue that the conventional interpretation of the effects of *Brown v. Board of Education* was equally naive. Liberals and progressives celebrated the decision as a huge advance. They assumed that a universal rule, which promised to give children ac-cess to the same schools regardless of race, would suffice to treat people fairly. But in real-ity, Bell contended, *Brown v. Board* did virtually nothing to improve the lot of African Americans. Instead, he pointed out, the seemingly neutral rules gave huge advantages to white over Black teachers, required Black students to travel long distances to schools in which they experienced persistent discrimination, and still allowed plenty of white par-ents to send their children to schools that barely enrolled any Black kids. According to Bell, the new neutral rules, as the second postulate of the rational reconstruction of the identity synthesis would imply, "merely served to obscure the ways in which privileged groups dominate those that are marginalized."

These premises led Bell to conclude that the conventional solution to the problem of school segregation is misguided. Because neutral rules merely serve to perpetuate the oppression of disadvantaged identity groups, it would be a mistake to try harder to inte-grate schools, as he himself had once strived to do as an attorney at the NAACP. Instead, activists should all along have focused on creating schools that are separate but truly equal. (Bell, "Interest-Convergence Dilemma," 528–32.) Today, it is high time to remedy that mistake by embracing "race-sensitive" public policies that explicitly aim to remedy op-pression by treating members of different groups differently from each other. Bell came to believe, as the third postulate of the rational reconstruction of the identity synthesis would imply, that "to build a just world, we must adopt norms and laws which explicitly make how the state treats each citizen—and how citizens treat each other—depend on the identity groups to which they belong."

246 **the liberal response:** Note, however, that this response to the identity synthesis does not amount to a rational reconstruction of liberalism itself.

246 **racial or religious groups:** The picture is further complicated by the fact that groups are not the be-all and end-all of human life. While most people are much of the time moti-vated by their allegiance to a group defined by such ethnic, religious, ideological, or cul-tural criteria, others pursue their individual self-interest; believe that justice requires them to serve the interests of a group to which they themselves do not belong; or try to treat all people equally regardless of the groups to which they belong.

246 **makes philosophical liberals:** For one of the best criticisms of such a "monomaniacal" outlook, see Jonathan Haidt, "Monomania Is Illiberal and Stupefying," *Persuasion*, Oct. 1, 2021, www.persuasion.community/p/haidt-monomania-is-illiberal-and.

247 **does help to structure:** See, for example, Dietrich Rueschemeyer, "Why and How Ideas Matter," in *The Oxford Handbook of Contextual Political Analysis*, ed. Robert E. Goodin and Charles Tilly (Oxford: Oxford University Press, 2006), 227–51.

248 **obscure the ways:** See, for example, L. Taylor Phillips, Pamela M. Hong, and Clayton D. Peoples, "How and Why the Wealthy Try to Cover Up Their Privileges," Society for Per-sonality and Social Psychology, April 12, 2021, spsp.org/news-center/character-context -blog/how-and-why-wealthy-try-cover-their-privileges.

248 **historically marginalized communities:** See Becky Pettit and Bruce Western, "Mass Imprisonment and the Life Course: Race and Class Inequality in U.S. Incarcera-tion," *American Sociological Review* 69, no. 2 (2004): 151–69, doi.org/10.1177 /000312240406900201.

248 **commitment to universal values:** See, for example, Dorothy Ross, "Lincoln and the Ethics of Emancipation: Universalism, Nationalism, Exceptionalism," *Journal of Ameri-can History* 96, no. 2 (2009): 379–99, doi.org/10.1093/jahist/96.2.379; and Carlos A. Ball, review of *Essentialism and Universalism in Gay Rights Philosophy: Liberalism Meets Queer Theory*, by Ladelle McWhorter and David A. J. Richards, *Law and Social Inquiry* 26, no. 1 (2001): 271–93, www.jstor.org/stable/829050.

248 **fueled the overthrow:** At the age of twenty-one, in the year 1848, for example, a man named Jyotirao Phule from Pune, India, first encountered Thomas Paine's *Rights of Man*. Paine's effect on Phule was enormous. As a close friend of Phule's put it, unlike many of his contemporaries, "Jotiba and his friends did not become Christians. The reason for this was that they had obtained one or two books from a very great revealer of the truth from America. This man was Thomas Paine." Inspired by Paine's universalism, Phule began to grapple with the deep injustices of India's caste system. Ultimately, he became an influential social reformer taking aim at the caste system and antiquated gender roles, and one of the most important figures in Indian history. Rosalind O'Hanlon, *Caste, Conflict, and Ideology: Mahatma Jotirao Phule and Low Caste Protest in Nineteenth-Century Western India* (Bombay: Orient Longman, 1985).

248 **stirring the conscience:** Even advocacy over issues as dry as the civil service reform of the late nineteenth-century United States was driven by a deep commitment to universalism and fairness. "It is difficult for Americans living in the first quarter of the twenty-first century to understand the emotions which Civil Service Reform aroused in the last quarter

of the nineteenth.... [T]housands, even millions, lined up behind ... three fundamental principles of American democracy: first, that opportunity be made equal to all citizens; second, that the meritorious only be appointed; third, that no public servants should suffer for their political beliefs" (Edmund Morris, *The Rise of Theodore Roosevelt* [New York: Modern Library, 2001], 404–5). For more discussion of the factors influencing civil service reform, see chapter 10 of Francis Fukuyama, *Political Order and Political Decay: From the Industrial Revolution to the Globalization of Democracy* (New York: Farrar, Straus and Giroux, 2015).

249 **intermarriage between members:** Justin McCarthy, "U.S. Approval of Interracial Marriage at New High of 94%," Gallup, Sept. 10, 2021, news.gallup.com/poll/354638 /approval-interracial-marriage-new-high.aspx.

249 **same ethnic stock:** Yascha Mounk, *The Great Experiment: Why Diverse Democracies Fall Apart and How They Can Endure* (London: Penguin Press, 2022), chap. 8.

249 **was deeply immoral:** For the United States, see "LGBT Rights," Gallup, July 13, 2022, news.gallup.com/poll/1651/gay-lesbian-rights.aspx. For the U.K., see Ben Clements and Clieve D. Field, "The Polls—Trends: Public Opinion Toward Homosexuality and Gay Rights in Great Britain," *Public Opinion Quarterly* 78, no. 2 (2014): 523–47, www.jstor .org/stable/24545938.

249 **Today, most citizens:** For the United States, see "LGBT Rights," Gallup. For Western Europe, see "Most Central and Eastern Europeans Oppose Same-Sex Marriage, While Most Western Europeans Favor It," Pew Research Center's Religion & Public Life Project, Oct. 24, 2018, www.pewresearch.org/religion/2018/10/29/eastern-and-western -europeans-differ-on-importance-of-religion-views-of-minorities-and-key-social-issues /pf-10-29-18_east-west_-00-04/.

249 **broadened their conception:** As of 2020, only 31 percent, 32 percent, and 25 percent of British, French, and Germans, respectively, report that it is very/somewhat important to be born in the country to be British/French/German. (Shannon Greenwood, "Views About National Identity Becoming More Inclusive in U.S., Western Europe," Pew Research Center's Global Attitudes Project, May 5, 2021, www.pewresearch.org/global /2021/05/05/views-about-national-identity-becoming-more-inclusive-in-us-western -europe/.) See also Bruce Stokes, "What It Takes to Truly Be 'One of Us'" Pew Research Center, Feb. 1, 2017, and Mounk, *Great Experiment*, chap. 8.

249 **believe that interracial marriage:** McCarthy, "U.S. Approval of Interracial Marriage."

249 **experience upward mobility:** See, for example, Doris Oberdabernig and Alyssa Schnee-baum, "Catching Up? The Educational Mobility of Migrants' and Natives' Children in Europe," *Applied Economics* 49, no. 37 (2017): 3716, doi.org/ 10.1080/ 00036846 .2016.1267843; Cris Beauchemin, "France: Intergenerational Mobility Outcomes of Natives with Immigrant Parents," in *Catching Up? Country Studies on Intergenerational Mobility and Children of Immigrants*, OECD, May 28, 2018, www.oecd-ilibrary.org /sites/9789264301030-en; Tony Sewell et al., *Commission on Race and Ethnic Dispari-ties: The Report*, U.K. Government Commission, March 2021, assets.publishing.service .gov.uk/government/uploads/system/uploads/attachment_data/file/974507 /20210331_-_CRED_Report_-_FINAL_-_Web_Accessible.pdf. Compare also Lucas G. Drouhot and Victor Nee, "Assimilation and the Second Generation in Europe and America: Blending and Segregating Social Dynamics Between Immigrants and Natives," *Annual Review of Sociology* 45, no. 1 (2019): 177–99, doi.org/10.1146/annurev-soc -073117-041335.

249 **experience social mobility:** Ran Abramitzky et al., "Intergenerational Mobility of Im-migrants in the United States over Two Centuries," *American Economic Review* 111, no. 2 (2021): 580–608, doi:10.1257/aer.20191586.

249 **now earn as much:** On Asian American women, see "Usual Weekly Earnings of Wage and Salary Workers: First Quarter 2021," Bureau of Labor Statistics, table 3, accessed Sept. 27, 2021, www.bls.gov/news.release/ pdf/wkyeng.pdf. Compare also the earlier

data in "Asian Women and Men Earned More Than Their White, Black, and Hispanic
Counterparts in 2017," U.S. Bureau of Labor Statistics, accessed Jan. 27, 2023, www.bls
.gov/opub/ted/2018/asian-women-and-men-earned-more-than-their-white-black-and
-hispanic-counterparts-in-2017.htm. For Nigerian Americans, see B. Joseph, "Why Nigerian Immigrants Are One of the Most Successful Ethnic Group in the U.S.," Medium,
July 2, 2018, medium.com/@joecarleton/why-nigerian-immigrants-are-the-most-successful
-ethnic-group-in-the-u-s-23a7ea5a0832. For Indian Americans, see "Indians in US
Wealthier with Average Household Earning of $123,700: Report," *Economic Times*, Aug.
25, 2021, economictimes.indiatimes.com/nri/migrate/indians-in-us-wealthier-with
-average-household-earning-of-123700-report/articleshow/85623601.cms?from=mdr.

250 **earn lower salaries:** See "much less wealth" endnote on p. 313.

250 **in deprived neighborhoods:** See, for example, "Causes and Consequences of Separate
and Unequal Neighborhoods," Urban Institute, accessed Mar. 24, 2023, www.urban
.org/racial-equity-analytics-lab/structural-racism-explainer-collection/causes-and
-consequences-separate-and-unequal-neighborhoods.

250 **large African American middle class:** For a more detailed version of this argument, see
Mounk, *Great Experiment*, chap. 8.

250 **median Black American:** 55.6 percent of African Americans or Black people have
white-collar jobs (sales & office and management, professional, and related). ("Labor
Force Characteristics by Race and Ethnicity, 2020," U.S. Bureau of Labor Statistics, Nov.
1, 2021, www.bls.gov/opub/reports/race-and-ethnicity/2020/home.htm, Chart 3.)
Census data shows 54 percent of Black people live in suburbs, up from 43 percent in
2010. ("Black Population Continues to Grow in Suburbs and Shrink in Cities Across the
U.S.," *Los Angeles Times*, March 14, 2022, www.latimes.com/world-nation/story/2022
-03-14/census-black-population-grows-suburbs-shrinks-cities.) There has been an
inflation-adjusted 30.5 percent increase in hourly wages; a one-third decrease in federal
poverty rates (from 35 to 21 percent); and a sixfold increase in wealth from 1968 to 2016
for Black people. John Schmitt and Valerie Johnson, "African Americans Are Better Off
in Many Ways but Are Still Disadvantaged by Racial Inequality," Economic Policy Institute, Feb. 26, 2018, www.epi.org/publication/50-years-after-the-kerner-commission/.

250 **optimistic about the future:** Carol Graham and Sergio Pinto, "Unequal Hopes and
Lives in the USA: Optimism, Race, Place, and Premature Mortality," *Journal of Population Economics* 32 (2019): 665–733, link.springer.com/article/10.1007/s00148-018
-0687-y. As I have argued in part III, race neutral policies like universal health care and
higher investments in education can make sure that countries like the United States
double down on these first signs of progress, vastly increasing economic opportunities for
historically marginalized groups without pitting them against other ethnic groups in a
zero-sum fight for power and resources.

Chapter 15: A Brief Case for the Liberal Alternative

253 **Most societies in history:** To be sure, historians and anthropologists have uncovered
some interesting societies that seem to have had features we might admire. These cultures, which usually remained very small, were supposedly egalitarian or sexually liberated, racially tolerant, or spiritually open-minded. But even if we take the, at times
tendentiously rosy, descriptions of them at face value, they were small, short-lived, and
very poor. A more unvarnished look reveals that all of them suffered from some combination of a very short life span, high rates of violent crimes, and plenty of other terrible
characteristics that would, if any of us were to think seriously about living in them,
quickly come to outweigh the characteristics we like to celebrate. The Mbuti, for example, are often celebrated for having a society in which "a woman is in no way the social
inferior of a man," but on closer inspection it turns out that they sanctioned a "certain
amount of wife-beating." Holden Karnofsky, "Pre-agriculture Gender Relations Seem

Bad," *Cold Takes*, Oct. 19, 2021, www.cold-takes.com/hunter-gatherer-gender-relations
-seem-bad/.

253 **small group vast powers:** For a good overview, see Daron Acemoglu and James A. Robinson, *The Narrow Corridor: States, Societies, and the Fate of Liberty* (New York: Penguin
Press, 2020). Some evidence suggests that preagricultural societies were comparatively
egalitarian, though they also suffered from very high rates of violence. See, for example,
D. W. Harding, "Hierarchical or Egalitarian?," in *Rewriting History: Changing Perceptions of the Past* (Oxford: Oxford University Press, 2020).

253 **mired in endemic conflict:** See Steven Pinker, *The Better Angels of Our Nature: Why
Violence Has Declined* (New York: Viking, 2011).

253 **norms of the community:** See the idea of the "cage of norms" introduced by Acemoglu
and Robinson in *The Narrow Corridor*.

253 **Christian crusaders converted:** See Christopher Tyerman, *God's War: A New History of
the Crusades* (Cambridge, Mass.: Belknap Press of Harvard University Press, 2008), 159.

253 **campaigns of eradication:** Benjamin Madley, *An American Genocide: The United States
and the California Indian Catastrophe, 1846–1873* (New Haven, Conn.: Yale University
Press, 2017).

253 **rigid caste system:** Susan Bayly, *Caste, Society, and Politics in India from the Eighteenth
Century to the Modern Age* (Cambridge: Cambridge University Press, 1999).

253 **vast construction projects:** "Great Wall of China," History.com, Aug. 24, 2010, www
.history.com/topics/ancient-china/great-wall-of-china.

253 **waged endemic war:** Richard Reid, "Warfare in Pre-colonial Africa," in *The Encyclopedia
of War*, ed. Gordon Martel (Malden, Mass.: Wiley-Blackwell, 2011), doi.org/10.1002
/9781444338232.wbeow687.

253 **Slaves have existed:** See, for example, *Encyclopædia Britannica*, s.v. "The Law of Slavery,"
accessed Mar. 24, 2023, www.britannica.com/topic/slavery-sociology/The-law-of-slavery.

254 **continues to exist:** Alexis Okeowo, "Freedom Fighter," *New Yorker*, Sept. 1, 2014, www
.newyorker.com/magazine/2014/09/08/freedom-fighter.

254 **failed to deliver:** See, for example, Karlsson Klas-Göran and Michael Schoenhals,
Crimes Against Humanity Under Communist Regimes: Research Review (Stockholm:
Living History Forum, 2008); and Stéphane Courtois et al., *The Black Book of Commu-
nism: Crimes, Terror, Repression* (Cambridge, Mass.: Harvard University Press, 1999).

255 **one set of institutions:** For an overview of some good recent defenses of liberalism, see
"the best guide" endnote in part IV, p. 370.

255 **live in fear:** Daron Acemoglu and James A. Robinson, *Why Nations Fail: The Origins of
Power, Prosperity, and Poverty* (New York: Crown, 2012).

255 **fundamental problem of politics:** Another crucial question, of course, is about who is
included in the "people," the group that is thought of as part of those who shall be ruled.
Indeed, the deepest injustices in the history of liberal democracy often stemmed not from
how they treated those whom they thought of as part of the people but rather from how
they treated those, like metics in ancient Greece or African Americans in the early
United States, whom they did not consider a part of the people. This is a problem that all
political traditions, including liberalism, face. For more on this topic in the context of
liberalism, see Michael J. Sandel, *Liberalism and the Limits of Justice* (Cambridge: Cambridge University Press, 2010); Michael J. Sandel, "Moral Argument and Liberal Toleration: Abortion and Homosexuality," *California Law Review* 77, no. 3 (1989): 521, doi
.org/10.2307/3480558; and Michael Walzer, *Spheres of Justice: A Defense of Pluralism
and Equality* (New York: Basic Books, 2010).

255 **resolve this tension:** The great historical contribution of Thomas Hobbes consists in
recognizing this set of fundamental insights. Grappling with the implications of the English Civil War and the historical failure of Italian city-states, he thought that self-
governing republics could not solve the problem of political stability; hence his preference
for a monarchy over a parliamentary system. But though Hobbes favored political abso-

lutism, he paved the way for subsequent thinkers, who grew more optimistic about the ability of self-governing republics to maintain political stability, to make a case for something that looks recognizably like liberal democracy. In that sense, Hobbes was, in some ways despite himself, a key founder of the liberal tradition. For a compelling interpretation of Hobbes in this vein, see Richard Tuck's introduction to *Leviathan*: Thomas Hobbes, *Leviathan*, ed. Richard Tuck (Cambridge,: Cambridge University Press, 1996).

256 **a powerful argument:** On the surface, this may sound as though it were expressing skepticism toward claims to scientific truths. But this is a fundamental misunderstanding of the nature of the scientific enterprise. Obviously, there are many circumstances in which laypeople have good reason to defer to the judgment of trained experts. But the reason why science has historically made such great strides, and deserves deference within reasonable limits, is that the scientific method—with mechanisms like peer review and its radical skepticism toward received wisdom—is based on a notion of equality. For an excellent explanation of the scientific method, see Jonathan Rauch, *The Constitution of Knowledge: A Defense of Truth* (Washington, D.C.: Brookings Institution Press, 2021).

257 **commitment to political equality:** The detractors of liberalism have often claimed that this commitment to individual rights elides the importance that religious beliefs and personal ties play in the lives of most people. But this is to misunderstand the nature of the tradition. Liberals realize that many people give fundamental importance to the demands of their faith or the dictates of their conscience. They are also well aware that few people completely reinvent themselves when they turn eighteen as though they were not embedded in networks of deep affection and kinship with the communities in which they grew up. Indeed, this is precisely why liberals are so insistent on the right to free speech and free worship, of association and assembly. The alternative would require us to put groups at the very heart of government, giving them the power to rule over their members. But this would blatantly violate the principle of equality, because it would reimport the principle of natural hierarchy that supposedly allows a priest to rule over his flock or the leader of a cultural group to tell its members how to live. (For a more detailed version of this argument, see chapter 4 of my last book, *The Great Experiment: Why Diverse Democracies Fall Apart and How They Can Endure* (London: Penguin Press, 2022).

257 **government that refrains:** This is not to say that liberals are unable to acknowledge the need for some accommodations toward religious minorities, such as the reasonable exemptions that Sikhs should enjoy from requirements to wear helmets when riding a motorbike. For a much deeper explanation of the liberal view on such group-specific policies, see chapter 12.

258 **an incentive to deliver:** See, for example, Francis Fukuyama, *Political Order and Political Decay: From the Industrial Revolution to the Globalization of Democracy* (New York: Farrar, Straus and Giroux, 2015), chaps. 1 and 8–13; and Joseph A. Schumpeter, *Capitalism, Socialism, and Democracy* (London: Routledge, 1976), particularly "Another Theory of Democracy."

258 **to collective self-determination:** Amartya Sen, *Poverty and Famines: An Essay on Entitlement and Deprivation* (Oxford: Oxford University Press, 1982).

259 **forms of government partiality:** See, for example, Johan Brosché, "Conflict over the Commons: Government Bias and Communal Conflicts in Darfur and Eastern Sudan," *Ethnopolitics*, Jan. 19, 2022, 1–23, doi.org/10.1080/17449057.2021.2018221.

259 **sustain key public goods:** Acemoglu and Robinson, *Why Nations Fail*; and Acemoglu and Robinson, *Narrow Corridor*.

259 **different in some salient way:** If citizens view themselves as members of disparate and competing groups, society is prone to conflict. This is why, as one study found, "advancing national status" and "cultivating common attributes" are "important for avoiding internal conflict." Nicholas Sambanis and Moses Shayo, "Social Identification and Ethnic Conflict," *SSRN Electronic Journal* 107, no. 2 (May 2013): 319, doi.org/10.2139/ssrn.1955111.

259 **that is already affluent:** For an argument that democracy has exogenous causes, implying

that affluence is more likely to lead to stable democracy than democracy is to lead to affluence, see Adam Przeworski and Fernando Limongi, "Modernization: Theories and Facts," *World Politics* 49, no. 2 (1997): 155–83; and Adam Przeworski, Fernando Limongi, and Salvador Giner, "Political Regimes and Economic Growth," in *Democracy and Development: Proceedings of the IEA Conference Held in Barcelona, Spain* (London: Palgrave Macmillan, 1995), 3–27. For a response, see Carles Boix and Susan C. Stokes, "Endogenous Democratization," *World Politics* 55, no. 4 (2003): 517–49.

260 **avoid the terrible suffering:** For a strong recent statement of this position, see Martin Wolf, *The Crisis of Democratic Capitalism* (New York: Penguin Press, 2023).

260 **the dream destinations:** A Gallup survey conducted between 2013 and 2016 asking potential migrants what country they would like to move to found that 21 percent chose the United States, 6 percent Germany, and 5 percent each Canada, France, and the U.K. Less than 10 percent chose countries other than liberal democracies. Neli Esipova, Julie Ray, and Anita Pugliese, "Number of Potential Migrants Worldwide Tops 700 Million," Gallup, June 8, 2017, news.gallup.com/poll/211883/number-potential-migrants-worldwide-tops-700-million.aspx?g_source=World&g_medium=newsfeed&g_campaign=tiles.

260 **Out of the thirty countries:** The exceptions are Singapore (ranked twelfth) and the United Arab Emirates (ranked twenty-sixth). "Statistical Annex: Human Development Index and Its Components," in *Human Development Report 2021/2022: Uncertain Times, Unsettled Lives: Shaping Our Future in a Transforming World* (New York: UNDP, 2022), 272.

261 **longest life expectancy:** Only China charts, ranking at twenty-nine. "Life Expectancy at Birth" (indicator), OECD (2023), accessed Jan. 29, 2023, doi:10.1787/27e0fc9d-en.

261 **highest GDP per capita:** Malta, Iceland, Macau, San Marino, Brunei, and Luxembourg all have populations below four million. See GDP per capita by country 2023, accessed Jan. 29, 2023, worldpopulationreview.com/country-rankings/gdp-per-capita-by-country. (Data aggregated from World Economic Outlook, Oct. 2022.)

261 **resources they need:** For related arguments, see John Rawls on "primary goods" in John Rawls, *A Theory of Justice* (Cambridge, Mass.: Harvard University Press, 1971); as well as Amartya Sen and Martha Nussbaum on capabilities: Amartya Sen, "Human Rights and Capabilities," *Journal of Human Development* 6, no. 2 (2005): 151–66; and Martha C. Nussbaum, "Capabilities as Fundamental Entitlements: Sen and Social Justice," in *Capabilities Equality*, ed. Alexander Kaufman (New York: Routledge, 2006), 54–80.

Conclusion: How to Escape the Identity Trap

265 **upper-middle-class life:** Patel describes his experience with the identity synthesis in Eboo Patel, "What I Want My Kids to Learn About American Racism," *New York Times*, May 10, 2022, www.nytimes.com/2022/05/10/opinion/race-teaching-school.html; pages 265–67, including quotes from Patel, are based on this article. See also his latest book: Eboo Patel, *We Need to Build: Field Notes for Diverse Democracy* (Boston: Beacon Press, 2022), and his interview with the author: "What an Overly Pessimistic View of America Gets Wrong," *Persuasion*, July 30, 2022, podcast, www.persuasion.community/p/patel.

267 **Maurice Mitchell has undergone:** Mitchell describes his experience with the identity synthesis in Maurice Mitchell, "Building Resilient Organizations: Toward Joy and Durable Power in a Time of Crisis," *Nonprofit Quarterly*, Nov. 29, 2022, nonprofitquarterly.org/building-resilient-organizations-toward-joy-and-durable-power-in-a-time-of-crisis/.

267 **"Executives in professional social justice":** Mitchell, "Building Resilient Organizations."

268 **encouraging their students:** Zach Goldberg and Eric Kaufmann, "Yes, Critical Race Theory Is Being Taught in Schools," *City Journal*, Oct. 20, 2022, www.city-journal.org/yes-critical-race-theory-is-being-taught-in-schools.

268 **forms of cultural appropriation:** For one example, see Julia Halperin, "How the Dana

Schutz Controversy—and a Year of Reckoning—Have Changed Museums Forever," *Artnet News*, March 6, 2018, news.artnet.com/art-world/dana-schutz-controversy-recent -protests-changed-museums-forever-1236020.

268 **diversity, equity, and inclusion trainings:** Christopher F. Rufo, "The DEI Regime," *City Journal*, July 13, 2022, www.city-journal.org/the-diversity-equity-and-inclusion -regime.

268 **identity-sensitive public policies:** The Biden administration has explicitly focused on equity since day one. See, for example, "Advancing Equity and Racial Justice Through the Federal Government," White House, accessed Mar. 24, 2023, www.whitehouse.gov/equity/. Similarly, the Democratic National Committee has recently avowed that "race-neutral policies are not sufficient to rectify race-based disparities." See "Healing the Soul of America," Democratic National Committee, accessed Mar. 24, 2023, democrats.org /where-we-stand/party-platform/healing-the-soul-of-america/.

268 **staged ceremonial burnings:** Thomas Gerbet, "Des écoles détruisent 5000 livres jugés néfastes aux Autochtones, dont Tintin et Astérix," Radio-Canada, Sept. 7, 2021, ici .radio-canada.ca/nouvelle/1817537/livres-autochtones-bibliotheques-ecoles-tintin -asterix-ontario-canada. Suzy Kies, who was co-chair of the Indigenous peoples' commission in the Liberal Party of Canada in 2019, advised a Catholic school board to burn, recycle, or bury more than forty-seven hundred books. After no record of Kies's Indigenous ancestry could be found, the Liberal Party condemned her actions and she resigned shortly thereafter. Kevin J. Jones, "Indigenous 'Expert' Advised Book Burnings at Catholic Schools," Catholic News Agency, Oct. 6, 2021, www.catholicnewsagency.com /news/249209/indigenous-expert-who-advised-book-burnings-at-catholic-schools -in-canada-draws-scrutiny.

268 **resign her teaching post:** Richard Adams, "Sussex Professor Resigns After Transgender Rights Row," *Guardian*, Oct. 28, 2021, www.theguardian.com/world/2021/oct/28/sussex -professor-kathleen-stock-resigns-after-transgender-rights-row.

268 **rock band was canceled:** "Zurich Bar Cancels Concert by Musicians—Because of Rastas," *Switzerland Times*, Aug. 17, 2022, switzerlandtimes.ch/local/zurich-bar-cancels-concert -by-musicians-because-of-rastas/.

268 **white man to translate:** Nicole Daniels, "Should White Writers Translate a Black Author's Work?," *New York Times*, March 31, 2021, www.nytimes.com/2021/03/31/learning /should-white-writers-translate-a-black-authors-work.html.

269 **"We all live on campus":** Andrew Sullivan, "We All Live on Campus Now," *Intelligencer*, Feb. 9, 2018, nymag.com/intelligencer/2018/02/we-all-live-on-campus-now.html.

269 **reluctant to express:** An article by Ryan Grim in *The Intercept* went viral because it featured so many quotations from leaders of progressive organizations who described the destructive effects of the identity synthesis on their organizations, giving voice to a diffuse feeling many had had for a long time. Ryan Grim, "Meltdowns Have Brought Progressive Advocacy Groups to a Standstill at a Critical Moment in World History," *Intercept*, June 13, 2022, theintercept.com/2022/06/13/progressive-organizing-infighting -callout-culture/. See also chapter 7.

269 **moral panics on social media:** Institutional leaders are also growing more cognizant of the risks of callout culture during the hiring process. One remarked, "I'm now at a point where the first thing I wonder about a job applicant is, 'How likely is this person to blow up my organization from the inside?'" Grim, "Meltdowns."

269 **compel state employees:** See, for example, Anemona Hartocollis, "After a Legal Fight, Oberlin Says It Will Pay $36.59 Million to a Local Bakery," *New York Times*, Sept. 8, 2022, www.nytimes.com/2022/09/08/us/oberlin-bakery-lawsuit.html; Pacific Legal Foundation, "Lawsuit Filed Against City of Seattle for Hostile Workplace Caused by Pervasive 'Racial Equity Training,'" Nov. 16, 2022, pacificlegal.org/press-release/lawsuit -filed-against-city-of-seattle-for-hostile-workplace-caused-by-pervasive-racial-equity -training/; and Michael Paulson, "New 42 Worker Files Bias Lawsuit over Diversity

Training," *New York Times*, June 9, 2022, www.nytimes.com/2022/06/09/theater/new-42-diversity-lawsuit.html.

269 **contrast to the "woke" ethos:** See, for example, Helen Holmes, "How Dimes Square Became the NYC Nabe We Love to Hate," *Daily Beast*, Aug. 11, 2022, www.thedailybeast.com/how-dimes-square-became-the-new-york-neighborhood-we-love-to-hate; Ben Smith, "They Had a Fun Pandemic. You Can Read About It in Print," *New York Times*, March 7, 2021, www.nytimes.com/2021/03/07/business/media/the-drunken-canal-media-nyc.html; Aidan Walker, "Dimes Square," Know Your Meme, Aug. 17, 2022, knowyourmeme.com/memes/subcultures/dimes-square.

270 **way into mainstream:** See, for example, Megan Twohey and Christina Jewett, "They Paused Puberty, but Is There a Cost?," *New York Times*, Nov. 14, 2022, www.nytimes.com/2022/11/14/health/puberty-blockers-transgender.html; Katie J. M. Baker, "When Students Change Gender Identity, and Parents Don't Know," *New York Times*, Jan. 22, 2023, www.nytimes.com/2022/11/14/health/puberty-blockers-transgender.html; John McWhorter, "Wokeness Is Oversimplifying the American Creed," *New York Times*, Oct. 26, 2021, www.nytimes.com/2021/10/26/opinion/wokeness-america.html; and Editorial Board, "America Has a Free Speech Problem," *New York Times*, March 18, 2022, www.nytimes.com/2022/03/18/opinion/cancel-culture-free-speech-poll.html.

270 **"sometimes people just want":** "Obama's Advice for Democrats," *Pod Save America*, Oct. 15, 2022, crooked.com/podcast/obamas-advice-for-democrats/.

270 **"In the 1960s, left-wing radicals":** David Brooks, "This Is How Wokeness Ends," *New York Times*, May 13, 2021, www.nytimes.com/2021/05/13/opinion/this-is-how-wokeness-ends.html.

270 **entrenched in the ideology:** The political scientist Ruy Teixeira takes a similar stance: Ruy Teixeira, "Ruy Teixeira Asks Whether America Has Reached 'Peak Woke,'" *Economist*, Oct. 19, 2022, www.economist.com/by-invitation/2022/10/19/ruy-teixeira-asks-whether-america-has-reached-peak-woke.

270 **Other illiberal norms:** For example, congressional Democrats quickly abandoned a special loan assistance program for racial minorities after it faced legal challenges. Maeve Sheehey, "Democrats Abandon Race-Based Loan Relief After White Farmers Sue," Bloomberg Law, Aug. 22, 2022, news.bloomberglaw.com/social-justice/democrats-pivot-on-race-based-loan-relief-as-white-farmers-sue.

271 **from local schools:** Hannah Natanson and Moriah Balingit, "Caught in the Culture Wars, Teachers Are Being Forced from Their Jobs," *Washington Post*, June 16, 2022, www.washingtonpost.com/education/2022/06/16/teacher-resignations-firings-culture-wars/.

272 **to yoga studios:** Kat Rosenfield, "The Cruel World of Yoga," UnHerd, May 12, 2022, unherd.com/2022/05/the-cruel-world-of-yoga/.

272 **communities built around gaming:** Lewis Pennock, "Video Game Firm Fires Woman After Trans Activist Publicly Branded Her a 'Transphobe' for Following Conservative Accounts and 'Voicing Excitement over Harry Potter Game,'" *Daily Mail*, Jan. 25, 2023, www.dailymail.co.uk/news/article-11675683/Video-game-company-fires-employee-follows-conservative-Twitter-accounts.html.

272 **focused on sewing:** Calla Wahlquist, "Stitch-Up: Online Sewing Community at War over Cultural Appropriation," *Guardian*, June 1, 2019, www.theguardian.com/lifeandstyle/2019/jun/01/stitch-up-online-sewing-community-at-war-over-cultural-appropriation.

272 **Latino electrician who was fired:** Yascha Mounk, "Stop Firing the Innocent," *Atlantic*, June 27, 2020, www.theatlantic.com/ideas/archive/2020/06/stop-firing-innocent/613615. See also Anne Applebaum, "The New Puritans," *Atlantic*, Aug. 31, 2021, theatlantic.com/magazine/archive/2021/10/new-puritans-mob-justice-canceled/619818/.

274 **issues have transformed radically:** For instance, as recently as 2008, neither Barack Obama nor Hillary Clinton supported gay marriage. "Factbox: Presidential Candidates' Views on Gay Marriage," Reuters, May 15, 2008, www.reuters.com/article/us-usa-politics-gaymarriage/factbox-presidential-candidates-views-on-gay-marriage-idUKN1534301220080516.

275 **normal forms of persuasion are futile:** John McWhorter, *Woke Racism: How a New Religion Has Betrayed Black America* (New York: Portfolio, 2021). According to McWhorter, "We are witnessing the birth of a new religion, just as Romans witnessed the birth of Christianity" (McWhorter, *Woke Racism*, 23–24). This claim, he emphasizes, is not hyperbolic: "I do not mean that [this] ideology is 'like' a religion. . . . I mean that it actually is a religion" (McWhorter, *Woke Racism*, 23). "Superstition, clergy, sinfulness, a proselytizing impulse, a revulsion against the impure—it's all there," McWhorter writes in his characteristically sharp prose. "They think of it all as logic incarnate. But so, as he lustily led the Spanish Inquisition, did Torquemada" (McWhorter, *Woke Racism*, 26). Just as it is futile to argue with people who hold strong religious beliefs, McWhorter concludes, it is a mistake to try convincing advocates of (what I would call) the identity synthesis through the power of argument.

275 **changed their mind:** Taylor Orth, "Which Political Issues Do Americans Change Their Minds on and Why?," YouGovAmerica, Aug. 16, 2022, today.yougov.com/topics/politics /articles-reports/2022/08/16/how-often-and-why-do-americans-change-their-minds.

275 **tendency to downplay:** Diane Lowenthal and George Loewenstein, "Can Voters Predict Changes in Their Own Attitudes?," *Political Psychology* 22, no. 1 (March 2001): 65–87, doi.org/10.1111/0162-895x.00226; Jordi Quoidbach, Daniel T. Gilbert, and Timothy D. Wilson, "The End of History Illusion," *Science* 339, no. 6115 (2013): 96–98, doi.org /10.1126/science.1229294; Gregory B. Markus, "Stability and Change in Political Attitudes: Observed, Recalled, and 'Explained,'" *Political Behavior* 8, no. 1 (1986): 21–44, doi.org/10.1007/bf00987591.

275 **drift to the right:** See, for example, Benny Geys, Tom-Reiel Heggedal, and Rune J. Sørensen, "Age and Vote Choice: Is There a Conservative Shift Among Older Voters?," *Electoral Studies* 78 (2022): 102485; and Joe Chrisp and Nick Pearce, "Grey Power: Towards a Political Economy of Older Voters in the UK," *Political Quarterly* 90, no. 4 (2019): 743–56. Note that there is some evidence that millennials in the United Kingdom and the United States may be breaking the trend by becoming more conservative as they age at a much slower pace. See, for example, John Burn-Murdoch, "Millennials Are Shattering the Oldest Rule in Politics," *Financial Times*, Dec. 30, 2022, www.ft.com/content /c361e372-769e-45cd-a063-f5c0a7767cf4.

275 **According to one recent study:** Stephen Hawkins et al., "Defusing the History Wars: Finding Common Ground in Teaching America's National Story," More in Common, accessed Mar. 24, 2023, www.historyperceptiongap.us/.

277 **to counteract polarization:** Stephen Hawkins et al., "Hidden Tribes: A Study of America's Polarized Landscape," More in Common, 2018, hiddentribes.us/media/qfpekz4g /hidden_tribes_report.pdf.

277 **skeptical of long-standing norms:** The description of progressive activists in the report is very similar, though of course not identical, to what I would call advocates of the identity synthesis. Progressive activists, it says, "are skeptical of traditional authority and norms. They see those values as being established by socially dominant groups such as straight white men, for their own benefit. Progressive Activists seek to correct the historical marginalization of groups based on their race, gender, sexuality, wealth and other forms of privilege." Hawkins et al., "Hidden Tribes," 10.

277 **less likely than whites to share:** Compared with the average American, progressive activists were "eleven percent more likely to be white" and "twice as likely to have completed college" (Hawkins et al., "Hidden Tribes," 30). Meanwhile, other polls have shown robust majorities of Americans from all demographic groups opposing race-sensitive public policies or worrying that the policing of language has gone too far. Far from pitting whites against so-called people of color, the fight over the identity trap may be better understood as a cultural civil war between different factions of America's predominantly white elite. See Vianney Gómez, "U.S. Public Continues to View Grades, Test Scores as Top Factors in College Admissions," Pew Research Center, April 26, 2022, www.pewresearch.org

/fact-tank/2022/04/26/u-s-public-continues-to-view-grades-test-scores-as-top-factors
-in-college-admissions/; Scott Jaschik, "Poll Finds the Public Doesn't Favor Affirmative
Action," *Inside Higher Ed*, May 2, 2022, www.insidehighered.com/admissions/article
/2022/05/02/poll-finds-public-doesnt-favor-affirmative-action; and Yascha Mounk,
"Americans Strongly Dislike PC Culture," *Atlantic*, Oct. 10, 2018, www.theatlantic.com
/ideas/archive/2018/10/large-majorities-dislike-political-correctness/572581/.

277 **"silent majority"**: See, for example, Matthew D. Lassiter, *The Silent Majority: Suburban
Politics in the Sunbelt South* (Princeton, N.J.: Princeton University Press, 2007).

278 **Some Marxist thinkers:** For example, Marcuse is key to understanding the identity synthesis's opposition to free speech. See chapter 10. Similarly, Freire is often invoked by
defenders of progressive separatism; see chapter 11 and appendix.

278 **why Marxist writers:** See Olúfẹ́mi O. Táíwò, *Elite Capture: How the Powerful Took Over
Identity Politics (and Everything Else)* (Chicago: Haymarket Books, 2022); as well as Yascha Mounk, "Do the Politics of Class and Race Stand in Tension?," *The Good Fight*, June
25, 2022, podcast, 56:41, www.persuasion.community/p/taiwo#details.

278 **"The disposition to catalog":** Adolph L. Reed, Introduction to *Class Notes: Posing as
Politics and Other Thoughts on the American Scene* (New York: New Press, 2000), 19.

278 **Some conservatives fall:** This is particularly true of the right in Europe. See, for instance, "How 'Identitarian' Politics Is Changing Europe," *Economist*, March 28, 2018,
www.economist.com/europe/2018/03/28/how-identitarian-politics-is-changing
-europe; and Thomas Chatterton Williams; "The French Origins of 'You Will Not Re-
place Us,'" *New Yorker*, Nov. 27, 2017, www.newyorker.com/magazine/2017/12/04/the
-french-origins-of-you-will-not-replace-us. A version of this argument is also made by
Eric Kaufmann. Though a critic of the identity synthesis who is himself mixed race,
Kaufmann ultimately embraces the need for white ethnic groups to adopt a form of strategic essentialism in their own right. See Eric Kaufmann: *Whiteshift: Populism, Immigration, and the Future of White Majorities* (New York: Abrams Press, 2019).

278 **classic conservative principles:** Blake Smith, "Conservatives Need Multiculturalism,"
UnHerd, Sept. 14, 2021, unherd.com/2021/09/conservatives-need-multiculturalism/.

279 **such conservatives skeptical:** For an excellent overview of the debate between the post-
liberal and the liberal right, see Benjamin Wallace-Wells, "David French, Sohrab Ahmari, and the Battle for the Future of Conservatism," *New Yorker*, Sept. 12, 2019, www
.newyorker.com/news/the-political-scene/david-french-sohrab-ahmari-and-the-battle
-for-the-future-of-conservatism. For a critique of Vermeule's idea of "common-good constitutionalism," see Garrett Epps, "Common-Good Constitutionalism Is an Idea as Dangerous as They Come," *Atlantic*, April 3, 2020, www.theatlantic.com/ideas/archive
/2020/04/common-good-constitutionalism-dangerous-idea/609385/. Also see James
Chappel, "Nudging Toward Theocracy: Adrian Vermeule's War on Liberalism," *Dissent*,
Spring 2020, www.dissentmagazine.org/article/nudging-towards-theocracy. On Curtis
Yarvin, see Damon Linker, "The Red-Pill Pusher," *Persuasion*, Jan. 23, 2023, www
.persuasion.community/p/the-red-pill-pusher.

279 **"post-liberal right":** David French, "A Christian Defense of American Classical Liberalism," *Dispatch*, Oct. 31, 2021, thedispatch.com/newsletter/frenchpress/a-christian-defense
-of-american-classical/.

279 **emphasized the irrelevance:** See, for example, Donald S. Lutz, "The Relative Influence
of European Writers on Late Eighteenth-Century American Political Thought," *American Political Science Review* 78, no. 1 (1984): 189–97, doi.org/10.2307/1961257. For a
canonical use of this idea in the Jewish tradition, see Abraham Joshua Heschel, "Religion
and Race" (speech, Chicago, Jan. 14, 1963), Voices of Democracy, voicesofdemocracy
.umd.edu/heschel-religion-and-race-speech-text/.

279 **"there is neither Jew":** Galatians 3:28. Similar points are repeated throughout the Scrip-
tures, including in Ephesians 6:8 ("Knowing that whatsoever good thing any man doeth,
the same shall he receive of the Lord, whether he be bond or free") and Corinthians 12:13

("For by one Spirit are we all baptized into one body, whether we be Jews or Gentiles, whether we be bond or free; and have been all made to drink into one Spirit").

279 **Islam to Buddhism:** For instance, in a 1998 lecture, the fourteenth Dalai Lama said that "at the heart of Buddhism lies the idea that the potential for awakening and perfection is present in every human being and that realizing this potential is a matter of personal effort. The Buddha proclaimed that each individual is a master of his or her own destiny, highlighting the capacity that each person has to attain enlightenment. In this sense, the Buddhist world view recognizes the fundamental sameness of all human beings." Dalai Lama XIV Bstan-dzin-rgya mtsho, "Buddhism, Asian Values, and Democracy," *Journal of Democracy* 10, no. 1 (1999): 3–7, doi:10.1353/jod.1999.0005.

279 **"the principle of the oneness":** Abdu'l-Bahá, "Abdu'l-Bahá on Divine Philosophy," Bahá'í Library Online, 1998, 176, bahai-library.com/abdul-baha_divine_philosophy. Electronic version of the English translation by Elizabeth Fraser Chamberlain, published in 1918.

280 **"Is not the same sun":** Abdu'l-Bahá, "Abdu'l-Bahá on Divine Philosophy."

280 **consensus among critics:** John Rawls has used the idea of an "overlapping consensus" as a term of art in his defense of political liberalism. See John Rawls, *Political Liberalism* (New York: Columbia University Press, 1993), as well as John Rawls, "The Idea of an Overlapping Consensus," *Oxford Journal of Legal Studies* 7, no. 1 (1987): 1–25. My use of the term here is more colloquial.

280 **deformed their scholarship:** Private communication.

281 **I once called 180ism:** Yascha Mounk, "The Perils of 180ism," *Persuasion*, June 25, 2021, www.persuasion.community/p/mounk-the-perils-of-180ism.

282 **adopt free speech principles:** See, for example, the "Chicago Statement," in the endnote for "adopt strong protections," page 355.

282 **one big nonprofit organization:** Personal communication.

283 **intimidate their colleagues:** See, for example, Grim, "Meltdowns"; Joe Pompeo, "'It's Chaos': Behind the Scenes of Donald McNeil's New York Times Exit," *Vanity Fair*, Feb. 10, 2021, www.vanityfair.com/news/2021/02/behind-the-scenes-of-donald-mcneils-new-york-times-exit; and Katie Robertson and Benjamin Mullin, "Infighting Overshadows Big Plans at the Washington Post," *New York Times*, June 17, 2022, www.nytimes.com /2022/06/17/business/media/sally-buzbee-washington-post.html.

283 **social media guidelines:** Often the guidelines that do exist are vague and broadly interpretable. See "Recommendations for Social Media Use on the National Desk," from National social media committee to Steven Ginsberg (national editor) and Lori Montgomery (deputy national editor), April 20, 2020, www.documentcloud.org/documents/21582916 -washington-post-social-media-guidelines (from Karl Bode, "New York Times Editors Still Don't Understand How Twitter or the Internet Work," *Techdirt*, April 13, 2022, www.techdirt.com/2022/04/13/new-york-times-editors-still-dont-understand-how -twitter-or-the-internet-work/).

Index

Abbot, Dorian, 346n
Abdu'l-Bahá, 280
abortion, 221, 317n
academia, *see* universities
Acemoglu, Daron, 352n
activists, 67, 71, 114–17, 125, 272, 277,
    282, 381n
actors, 134
Adams, James Truslow, 369n
Adarand Constructors Inc. v. Peña, 221
Adele, 150
Adelman, Levi, 120, 121
Advisory Committee on Immunization
    Practices (ACIP), 206–8, 364n
advocacy groups, 3, 189, 198
affinity groups, 2, 3, 184, 197, 201, 203
affirmative action, 187, 209, 220, 221, 222,
    316n, 366–67n
Africa, 253, 254
African Americans, *see* Black Americans
African American Studies, 64
Ahmari, Sohrab, 279
Alcoff, Linda Martin, 318n
Alidina, Raafi-Karim, 108
allies, 192
    former adversaries becoming, 274–76
    of members of marginalized groups,
        134, 135, 143, 145
Allport, Gordon, 192–94, 196
Althusser, Louis, 28, 30, 304n
Amazon, 107n, 108, 345n

American Association of University
    Professors, 348–49n
American Civil Liberties Union (ACLU),
    80, 101–5, 111, 114, 117, 167, 328n
American College of Physicians, 7
American dream, 231, 369n
American Express, 107
American Journal of Public Health, 232
American Medical Association, 7
American Public Health Association, 7
American Rescue Plan, 299n
anarcho-syndicalism, 35, 36
Anderson, Elizabeth, 200
anorexia, 85
anthropology, 310–11n
antiracism, 122–26, 270
Antiracist Baby (Kendi and Lukashevsky), 124
anti-Semitism, 30, 227
apologizing, 283
Appiah, Kwame Anthony, 154
Arab Spring, 84
Arafat, Yasser, 42
Areopagitica (Milton), 348
Aronson, Elliot, 194, 195
art, 151, 343n
Asch, Solomon, 117–19, 333n
Asian Americans, 2, 134, 148, 155–56, 208,
    209, 219, 228, 249, 367n
Atlanta Black Star, 1
Atlantic, 102
authoritarianism, 16, 169, 260, 352n

Baha'i faith, 279–80
Baldwin, James, 175
Bank of America, 357n
Bank Street School for Children, 3, 189, 198
Baylor University, Cinco de Drinko party at,
      151–52, 156–57
Bayor, Ronald, 359n
Bazelon, Lara, 102
BBC, 161, 172
Beauvoir, Simone de, 28, 305n
Belarus, 322n
Bell, Derrick, 19, 51–57, 60–62, 65, 69, 76,
      210, 241, 316n, 318n, 356n, 372–73n
Bell, Kristen, 134
Bell, Melissa, 90
Bentham, Jeremy, 31
Between the World and Me (Coates), 185
biases, implicit, 12, 134, 187, 245, 356n
Biden, Hunter, 163, 345n
Biden, Joe, 70, 105, 208, 211, 220
Birmingham School of Cultural Studies, 149
Black Americans, 10, 49–51, 55, 75, 95, 209,
      216, 276, 316n, 376n
   affirmative action and, *see* affirmative
      action
   "authentic" voices for, 142, 143, 340n
   civil rights movement and, 19, 49–58,
      61–62, 70, 209, 248, 363n, 372n
   and contact with white people,
      192–93
   health care and, 5–6, 207–8, 211–12
   elected to high offices, 50, 312n
   income of, 50, 123, 215, 216, 250,
      313n, 335n
   middle class, 10, 215, 250
   musicians, 157–59
   pessimism about progress of, 69
   political views among, 340–41n
   racism and, *see* racism
   recent immigrants, 216, 249–50
   voters, 49
   wealth and, 217
   women, 58–60, 62, 71, 312n, 316n
Black colleges and universities, 361n
Black Lives Matter, 329n
Black Power (Carmichael and Hamilton),
      301n, 368n
Black Power movement, 300–301n
blasphemy, 175
blogs, 88
Bojack Horseman, 134
Bon Appétit, 150
Boone, Pat, 157

Bordo, Susan, 311n
Bostick, Dani, 210
Boston Consulting Group, 108
Bourguiba, Habib, 40
Branch, Denise, 168
Brennan, Timothy, 310n
Brettschneider, Corey, 353n
Brie, Alison, 134
Brigham and Women's Hospital, 5–6
Briscoe, Sharyn, 1, 3, 4
Britain, 7, 11, 39, 98, 151, 162–63, 175, 176,
      184, 231–33, 240, 249, 260, 268,
      276–78, 344n, 360n
British East India Company, 308n
British Museum, 343n
Brooks, David, 270
Brown, Michael, 94n
Brown v. Board of Education, 2, 52–54,
      56, 372n
Bruce, Lori, 6
Buddhists, 278, 279, 281, 383n
Bush, George W., 122
Butler, Judith, 68, 318n, 319n

Cafferty, Emmanuel, 116, 302n, 346n
California, 219–20
Canada, 7, 11, 98, 158, 199, 231, 260, 268
cancel culture, 7, 15, 168, 175, 180–82,
      299n, 332n, 349n
Candid, 106
Cao Fei, 147–48, 155–56
capitalism, 25, 27, 28, 270, 287, 309n
   racism and, 123, 335n
cardiology, 5–6, 297n
Carmichael, Stokely, 301n, 368n
Carnap, Rudolf, 242
Cedillo, Gil, 299–300n
censorship, 164, 165, 181
   of political debate, 176–79
   powerful empowered by, 170–72, 181
   on social media, 163, 168, 176–79, 345n
   see also dissent, discouragement of; free
      speech
Centers for Disease Control (CDC), 6–7,
      205–6, 211, 218, 223, 363n
Chait, Jonathan, 329n
Chappelle, Dave, 346n
Charlottesville, Va., Unite the Right rally
      in, 94n, 103, 104
chefs, 150, 153
Chicago Statement, 353n
China, 63, 84, 166, 209, 253, 254, 260
Chomsky, Noam, 35–36, 43

Christians, 218, 243, 253, 278, 279, 281

Churchill, Winston, 350n

Cinco de Drinko party, 151–52, 156–57

Civil Rights Act of 1964, 58, 219, 357n

civil rights movement, 19, 49–58, 61–62, 70, 209, 248, 363n, 372n

civil service reform, 373–74n

Civil War, 350n

class, 63–64, 149, 243, 246, 247, 278, 280, 289, 338n

Clinton, Hillary Rodham, 113, 356n, 380n

cloth, 154

Clyburn, Jim, 142

Coal Employment Project, 357n

Coaston, Jane, 75

Coates, Ta-Nehisi, 69, 185

Coca-Cola, 106–7, 110, 111, 123, 189, 329n

cocaine, 213–14

Cocker, Jarvis, 338n

cohesion, fostering, 190–93

Collins, Francis Joseph, 102

Collins, Patricia Hill, 72

colonialism, 39–40, 43, 308n, 309n
    art and, 151
    Marx's view of, 309n
    Mill's view of, 308–9n
    postcolonialism, 9, 40, 41, 44–45, 47, 55, 61, 65, 76, 99, 149

colorblindness, 3, 66, 210
    racism blindness versus, 212–14, 365n

Color of Change, 117

Combahee River Collective, 316n

comedians, 163, 346n

Comedy Central, 345n

"Common People," 338n

communism, 25, 26, 27, 28, 30, 56, 63, 161, 254, 280, 288, 304–5n, 309n

conformity and peer pressure, 117–21, 125, 333n

consequence culture, 130, 168, 181
    cancel culture, 7, 15, 168, 175, 180–82, 299n, 332n, 349n

Conservative Party, 142, 240

conservatives, 100–101, 142, 178, 209, 222, 224, 240, 275, 278–79

Considerations on Representative Government (Mill), 308–9n

Constitution, U.S., 55–56, 123, 210, 222, 279, 314n, 315n, 372n
    First Amendment to, 102, 104, 162, 165, 167, 176, 178, 225, 347n, 348n, 353n
    Fourteenth Amendment to, 2, 221, 372n

Corporate Equality Index, 330n

corporations, 106–11, 123, 179, 182, 188, 199, 201, 268, 357n

Counterrevolution and Revolt (Marcuse), 97

COVID pandemic, 4–7, 17, 70, 116, 157, 163, 178, 205–8, 211–12, 228, 245, 296–99n, 362n, 363n

crack and cocaine, 213–14

credit card companies, 175–77

Crenshaw, Kimberlé, 51, 57–62, 65, 71, 75, 76, 79–80, 87, 185, 186, 210, 316n, 321n, 323n, 336n

criminal justice system
    Foucault on, 31–32, 37
    prisons, 10, 31–32, 51, 175, 230, 231, 234, 248
    panopticon, 31–32, 74, 305n

critical legal studies, 55, 58, 166

critical race theory, 9, 58–62, 65, 66, 76, 79, 99, 185, 315n, 321n, 372n

Critical Race Theory (Delgado and Stefancic), 70, 231–32, 241

Cuba, 166

cuisines, 150, 153, 156, 157

cultural appropriation, 20, 67, 89, 125, 129–31, 147–59, 225, 234, 268, 270, 350n
    absurd dilemmas and, 155–56
    and art from colonies, 151, 343n
    collective ownership and, 155, 156, 158, 159
    genuine injustices and offensive behavior, 151–52, 156–59
    left's concern with, 149–51, 158
    problems with concerns about, 151–56
        group membership, 152, 154–56
        original ownership, 152–54

cultural influences, 350n
    anxiety about, 148–49, 151
    celebration of, 131, 134, 151, 158, 159

CVS, 107

Dalai Lama, 383n

Dalton, Russell, 326n

Dalton School, 2–3

damage payments for negligence, 119, 120, 333n

D'Andrade, Roy, 117

Daniels, Byron, 142

Daniels, Ron, 361n

Dartmouth College, 361n

Dasgupta, Nilanjana, 120, 121

Davids, Sharice, 340n

Davies, Norman, 280
death penalty, 221
debate, 167
    censorship of, 176–79
Declaration of Independence, 55, 276, 314n
Dee, Katherine, 85, 86
de Gaulle, Charles, 28
Deleuze, Gilles, 34–35, 45, 305n
Delgado, Richard, 57, 66, 70, 231–32,
        241, 318n
demagogues, 18
democracy(ies), 27, 34, 66, 161, 172, 219,
        222, 232, 239, 241, 246, 248–51,
        256–57, 259–60, 268, 278, 287–88,
        290, 352n, 376n, 377n
    free speech and, 170, 174–76, 181, 349n
    identity groups and, 141–42
    success of, 260–62
Democratic National Convention, 300n
Democratic Party, 11, 80, 210–11, 268, 270,
        276–77, 340n
Demos, 117
Derrida, Jacques, 45, 305n, 311n
Descartes, René, 136
desegregation, see integration
Dewey, John, 183
DiAngelo, Robin, 80, 107, 108, 123–24,
        126, 189, 241, 244, 268
disabilities, 9, 10, 15, 46, 69, 311n,
        319n, 320n
Discipline and Punish (Foucault), 31
discipline and punishment, 31, 73, 74,
        180, 305n
discourses, 33, 36, 37, 40, 42–47, 55, 66
    analysis of, 44, 47, 65–67, 76,
        310–11n, 319n
disparitarianism, 211
dissent, discouragement of, 113–26, 244
    consequence culture, 130
    and intellectual enforcers of the identity
        orthodoxy, 122–26
    powerlessness and, 115, 121
    and rise of identity orthodoxy in
        progressive institutions, 115–17, 122,
        125
    see also censorship; free speech
diversity, 187–88, 201
diversity, equity, and inclusion efforts, 2,
        107–8, 331n
diversity training, 107–8, 110, 122, 123,
        134, 189, 197, 245, 268, 269,
        357n, 359n
Djebar, Assia, 40

Dooling, Kathleen, 206–7
Douglass, Frederick, 54, 69, 165, 300n, 314n
Dror, Lidal, 137, 139–41, 337–39n
drugs
    COVID, 4–7, 17, 70, 206–8, 211–12, 218,
        223, 245, 296–99n, 362n, 363n
    crack and cocaine, 213–14
    unsafe, 173, 174
due process rights, 104
Duke, David, 113
Dutschke, Rudi, 97, 98

Economist, 106
Eddo-Lodge, Reni, 134
Education, Department of, 104
education and schools, 11, 183, 220, 231,
        232, 245, 250, 261, 286, 360n, 373n
    bullying in, 194
    in deprived neighborhoods, 214, 215
    funding for, 202, 226, 361n
    laws on content taught in, 162
    private, 2, 53, 361n
    progressive separatism in, 1–4, 106, 268
    religion and, 361n
    segregation in, 2, 49, 50, 52–54, 56, 184,
        185, 209, 372n
Edward VIII, 41
egalitarianism, 216, 217, 256
Eindhoven University of Technology, 35–36
elections, 256, 351–52n
    free speech and, 165, 170, 172–73,
        181, 352n
    midterm, 270, 332n
    presidential, 80, 113, 114
Electoral College, 114
"embrace race," 2–3, 14, 184, 197–99,
        203–4, 359n
empathy, 135, 225
    fostering, 190–93
    solidarity and, 144–46
employees
    complaints and accusations against, 283
    diversity training for, 107–8, 110, 122,
        123, 134, 189, 197, 245, 268, 269,
        357n, 359n
    free speech and, 162, 163, 168, 177, 180,
        182, 269, 271–72, 282, 346n
    hiring of, 49, 58–59, 232, 379n
    identity synthesis spread to institutions
        by, 97–111
    social media and, 283
    tolerance for different viewpoints
        among, 282

Engels, Friedrich, 287
English Civil War, 376n
Enlightenment, 34
equality, 26, 209–11, 239, 240, 241, 246,
        249, 256–57, 260, 261, 263, 279–81
    equity and, 211–12, 217
    of opportunity, 11, 214
Equality of What? (Sen), 335n
Equal Pay Act, 357n
equity, 57, 70, 211–12, 223, 364n
    appeal of, 216
    diversity, equity, and inclusion efforts, 2,
        107–8, 331n
    equality and, 211–12, 217
    failure as theory, 216–18, 223
    failure in practice, 218–20, 223–24
    racial equity funding, 106
    rise of, 209–12
Erdoğan, Recep Tayyip, 343n
essentialism, strategic, *see* strategic
        essentialism
Ethiopia, 260
ethnicity, *see* race and ethnicity
Europe, 27–28, 39–40, 63, 149, 175, 184,
        249, 280
European Commission, 149
Evanston Township High School, 2
everydayfeminism.com, 89
evolution, convergent, 290

fabrics, 154
Facebook, 7, 74, 80, 84, 90–92, 107,
        163, 170, 171, 178, 179, 324n,
        345n, 361n
fake news, 345n
Fanon, Frantz, 40, 278, 309n, 336n
Farrakhan, Louis, 227
fascism, 27, 334n
FBI, 113
Federalist Paper No. 51, 351n
feedback, 282
feminism, 33, 35, 59–61, 63–64, 68–69, 87,
        89, 136, 228, 307n, 311n, 316n, 317n,
        319n, 323n
    sex work and, 140
    standpoint theory and, 135, 136, 137n,
        138, 145
Feminist Standpoint Theory Reader, The
        (Harding, ed.), 136, 137
Ferguson, Adam, 308n
Fiddler on the Roof, 133
Fields, Barbara and Karen, 186, 290
financial services, 108, 175–77, 182

First Amendment, 102, 104, 162, 165, 167,
        176, 178, 225, 347n, 348n, 353n
Fish, Stanley, 166–67, 169, 347n, 348n,
        351n, 353n
Fisher v. University of Texas, 364n
flash mobs, 322n
Flint, Charley, 189
Florida, 162
Floyd, George, 124
food, 150, 153, 156, 157
Forbes, 168
Ford Foundation, 106
Fortune 500 companies, 11
Foucault, Michel, 19, 29–37, 40, 45, 47,
        55, 65, 66, 73–74, 76, 166, 288,
        304–7n, 311n, 336n
    Chomsky's debate with, 35–36, 43
    on criminal justice system, 31–32, 37
    Deleuze and, 34–35, 45
    on power, 33, 37, 44, 73, 306n
    Said and, 42–44
    on sexuality, 32–33, 37, 306–7n
Founding Fathers, 209, 351n
Fourteenth Amendment, 2, 221, 372n
France, 28, 240, 260, 278
    Communist Party in, 30, 304n
    intellectuals in, 28–29, 40, 43, 45, 288
    Revolution in, 210
Frankfurt School, 149, 166
Fraser, Rachel, 138, 140, 141
freedom, 239, 260, 261, 263, 281
    peace and, 258–59
Freedom House, 343n
freedom of assembly, 102, 377n
freedom of association, 179–80, 185,
        200–201, 225, 377n
free speech, 11, 20, 102, 103, 111, 125, 130,
        131, 161–82, 225, 229, 239, 244,
        248, 279, 282, 284, 286, 287, 377n
    cancel culture, 7, 15, 168, 175, 180–82,
        299n, 332n, 349n
    censorship, 164, 165, 181
        of political debate, 176–79
        powerful empowered by, 170–72, 181
        on social media, 163, 168,
            176–79, 345n
    and conflicts with broader goals, 348n
    consequence culture and, 130
    culture of, 164, 165, 175, 177, 179–82
    dangers of restrictions on, 168–74,
        181, 352n
        closing the safety valve, 170,
            173–74, 181

free speech (*cont.*)
    empowering the powerful,
        170–72, 181
    raising the stakes of elections, 165, 170,
        172–73, 181, 352n
    democracies and, 170, 174–76, 181, 349n
    drawing lines between permissible and
        impermissible speech, 167, 348n
    employees and, 162, 163, 168, 177, 180,
        182, 269, 271–72, 282, 346n
    "fighting words" and, 167, 347–48n
    First Amendment and, 102, 104, 162,
        165, 167, 176, 178, 225, 347n,
        348n, 353n
    freedom of association and, 179–80
    government and, 175–76, 179, 182,
        349n, 350n
    hate speech and, 162, 174–76
    misinformation and, 130, 163, 178, 345n
    offensive language and, 162–63, 344n
    principles of, 174–81
        the government must not have the
            right to lock you up, 175–76,
            179, 182
        there must be limits on censorship of
            political debate, 176–79
    progressive opponents of, two positions
        of, 351n
    publishers and, 163, 168, 179
    racism and, 165, 167, 169, 172, 351n
    right wing and, 165, 168, 174
    roots of the progressive rejection of,
        166–68
    social media and, 163, 168, 176–80, 345n
    television shows and, 163
    traditional arguments for, 168–70,
        181, 349n
    in wartime, 350n
    see also dissent, discouragement of
Freire, Paulo, 278, 287
French, David, 279
French Communist Party, 30, 304n
French Revolution, 210
Friedman, Thomas, 83–84, 321n
Fuentes, Agustín, 229

Gabbard, Christopher, 320n
Galileo, 168
Gandhi, Indira, 40
Gandhi, Mahatma, 40
Gastañaga, Claire Guthrie, 103
Gates, Henry Louis, Jr., 64
Gay, Roxane, 349n

gay people, 10, 32, 34, 63–64, 69, 169, 243n,
    248, 249, 306n, 350n, 380n
gender, 4, 9, 12–15, 20, 44, 64, 74, 75, 80,
    84, 226, 228–31, 234, 243–44, 278,
    285, 286, 302n
    as one part of understanding the world,
        246–47, 251
    as social construct, 46, 185
    social media and, 85–86
gender dysphoria, 104
General Motors, 58–59
Germany, 27, 67, 148, 163, 175, 176, 192,
    249, 254, 260
    Nazi, 27–29, 166, 174
Ghosh, Apoorva, 109, 330n
Gide, André, 41
Ginsburg, Ruth Bader, 210, 221, 222, 224
GLAAD, 230
Go, Julian, 309n
goal displacement, 350–51n
Goldberg, Zach, 94, 325n
Goldberger, David, 102, 104–5, 327n
Goldman Sachs, 107, 108
Goodman, Alan, 356n
Google, 108, 110
Gordon School, 2
Gornick, Vivian, 304n
government, 255–58, 261
    benefit programs, 7, 219, 220, 223, 224
    collective self-determination and,
        258, 263
    free speech and, 175–76, 179, 182,
        349n, 350n
    neutrality in, 259
    regulation by, 173
    see also public policies
Gramsci, Antonio, 149, 287
grand narratives, 27, 29–31, 34, 36, 40, 43,
    44, 55, 66, 278, 288
Great Awokening, 95
Great Britain, 7, 11, 39, 98, 151, 162–63,
    175, 176, 184, 231–33, 240, 249,
    260, 268, 276–78, 344n, 360n
Great Experiment, The (Mounk), 16, 190
Greece, ancient, 359n, 376n
Greene, Graham, 41
Grim, Ryan, 116–17, 379n
groups
    competition between, 259, 263
    contact between, 192–93
        cooperation and, 193, 195–96, 203
        goals and, 193, 195, 203
        status and, 193–95, 203

and support from authorities and
customs, 193, 196, 203
when it does and doesn't work,
193–96, 203
criticism and, 121, 334n
peer pressure and, 117–21, 125, 333n
people's natural tendency to form,
191–92, 202, 203
polarization of, 119–20
see also identity groups
groupthink, 120
Guardian, 93, 95, 150, 165
Guttmacher Institute, 317n

Haidt, Jonathan, 187
Hall, Stuart, 149
Hamilton, Charles V., 301n, 368n
Hanks, Tom, 134
happiness, 260
Haraway, Donna, 59, 136
Harding, Sandra, 136, 137
harm, expanded conception of, 187
Harper's, 91
Harris, Aleshea, 184
Harris, Kamala, 4, 211, 220
Harvard Business Review, 331n
Harvard University, 57, 58, 64, 108, 172,
219, 222
Hastie, William H., 51–52, 55
hate crimes, 227–28
hate speech, 162, 174–76
HBO Max, 345n
health care, 5, 31, 178, 220, 231, 232, 286
COVID pandemic and, 4–7, 17, 70, 116,
157, 163, 178, 205–8, 211–12, 245,
296–99n, 362n, 363n
mental illness and, 31, 34, 37, 305n
racial minorities and, 4–7, 14, 17, 70, 131,
207–8, 211–12, 218, 223, 245, 290,
296–99n, 335n, 363n
heart failure, 5–6, 297n
Hegel, Georg Wilhelm Friedrich, 30
Here Comes Everybody (Shirky), 322n
heretics, reluctant and defiant, 273
Hispanics and Latinos, 142, 155–57, 159,
207, 211, 212, 341n
Latinx, use of term, 142
historians, 64, 247, 375n
history, 253–55, 262, 274, 286, 375n
Hitler, Adolf, 166
Hobbes, Thomas, 349n, 376–77n
Ho Chi Minh, 308n
Hollywood, 134

Holmes, Oliver Wendell, Jr., 347–48n
Holocaust, 25, 102, 174, 285, 353n
homophily, 185, 201, 202
homosexuality, 10, 32, 34, 63–64, 69, 169,
243n, 248, 249, 306n, 350n, 380n
Honecker, Erich, 254
hot dog/sandwich debate, 190–91
housing, 173, 174, 192, 226, 231
segregation in, 199, 200, 202, 202
How to Be an Antiracist (Kendi),
122–24, 335n
Hulu, 345n
humanism, 134
Human Rights Campaign, 117, 330n
Humphrey, Hubert, 219
Hungary, 161, 304n
Hyppolite, Jean, 30

identity groups, 13, 25–26, 240, 246, 262,
278, 285, 372n, 373n
democracy and, 141–42
dependence of norms and laws upon,
245, 251
as key to understanding the world,
243–44, 251
new categories of, 67
as one part of understanding the world,
246–47, 251
skepticism about, 34–35, 37, 45, 47
political strategy and, 267
perspectives of and understanding
between, see standpoint theory
identity politics, 9
identity-sensitive public policies,
131–32, 205–24, 225, 226, 239, 245,
268, 373n
embrace of, 209–12
equity, see equity
legal framing of, 221–22, 224
race-sensitive, use of term, 364n
identity synthesis, 8–10, 18, 61, 63–76,
124–25, 210, 225–26, 233–35, 239,
241–45, 267, 302n
appeal of, 10–12, 16, 17, 245–46
criticisms of, 15, 19
as aiding the right, 122, 334n
influence of, 15, 19, 125, 268–70
institutions' adoption of, 97–111
liberalism as viewed in, 241–45, 251
liberal response to, 242, 245–52
societies should strive to live up to
universalist aspirations instead of
abandoning them, 249–52

identity synthesis (*cont.*)
  understanding the world depends on
    paying attention to a broad set of
    categories, 246–47, 251
  universal values and neutral rules often
    exclude people in practice but are
    aspirational, 247–48, 251–52
mainstreaming and popularized form of,
  80, 83–96, 124–26, 130, 134,
  240, 336n
main themes of, 65–72, 76
  discourse analysis for political ends, 44,
    47, 65–67, 76
  identity sensitive legislation, 65,
    70–71, 76
  intersectionality, 57–62, 65, 71, 75, 76,
    86, 87, 89, 105, 316n
  pessimism, 65, 69, 76, 262, 351n
  skepticism about objective truth, 26,
    29, 34, 37, 65–66, 73, 76
  standpoint theory, *see* standpoint
    theory
  strategic essentialism, *see* strategic
    essentialism
Marxism and, 19, 26, 278,
  287–90, 307n
misgivings of contributors to, 73–75, 76
new media platforms and, 88–90
as non-falsifiable theory, 124, 126
orthodoxy of, 115–17, 122, 125
  intellectual enforcers of, 122–26
pushback against, 269–70
rational reconstruction of, 242–45,
  251, 288
  citizens must be treated according to
    their identity groups, 245, 251, 288,
    289, 373n
  group identities are the key to
    understanding the world, 243–44,
    251, 288
  universal values and neutral rules
    obscure domination by privileged
    groups, 244, 251, 288
Thought Catalog and, 88, 93, 96
Tumblr and, 84–88, 93, 96, 322n, 323n
identity trap, 12–16, 262
  dangers of, 284–86
  how to argue against, 271–81
    appeal to the reasonable majority,
      276–77
    claim the moral high ground, 272–74
    don't become a reactionary, 280–81
    don't vilify those who disagree, 274

    make common cause with other
      opponents, 277–80
    remember that adversaries can become
      allies, 274–76
  importance of discussing, 16–18
  personal component of, 14–15
  political component of, 14
  possible futures for, 268–71
  right-wing populism and, 16–18
identity trap, how to escape from, 18–21,
  234, 265–86
  in organizations, 281–84
    adopt procedures for dealing with
      complaints, 283
    cultivate tolerance and diversity, 282
    don't issue insincere apologies, 283
    solicit real feedback, 282
    stop bullying on social media, 283
Ignatiev, Noel, 357n
implicit biases, 12, 134, 187, 245, 356n
immigrants, 44, 149, 199, 200, 209, 216,
  220, 226, 231, 249–50, 276, 360n
Imperative of Integration,
  The (Anderson), 200
income, 231, 249–50
  of Black Americans, 50, 123, 215, 216,
    250, 313n, 335n
  guaranteed, 7, 70
India, 41, 45, 218, 249, 309n, 311n,
  343n, 373n
Instagram, 68, 84, 88, 99, 180
Institute for Social Research (Frankfurt
  School), 149, 166
institutions, 80–81, 95–96, 97–111, 130,
  183, 246, 267–69
  conflict invited in, 196
  corporations, 106–11, 123, 179, 182, 188,
    199, 201, 268, 357n
  escaping from identity trap in, 281–84
    adopt procedures for dealing with
      complaints, 283
    cultivate tolerance and diversity, 282
    don't issue insincere apologies, 283
    solicit real feedback, 282
    stop bullying on social media, 283
  identity synthesis spread to, 97–111
  integration and diversification of,
    187–88, 201
  nonprofit, 101–6, 111, 282
  power in, 171, 351n
  progressive, identity orthodoxy in,
    115–17, 122, 125
insults, 162, 175

integration, 19, 50, 62, 131, 183, 185,
        200–202, 204, 219, 225,
        372–73n
    Bell's case against, 51–54, 57
    case for, 199–203
    empathy and cohesion and, 190–93
    and potential of intergroup contact,
        192–93
    intellectuals
    in Europe vs. Asia, 45
    in France, 28–29, 40, 43, 45
Intercept, 116, 379n
intergroup contact, 192–93
    cooperation and, 193, 195–96, 203
    goals and, 193, 195, 203
    status and, 193–95, 203
    and support from authorities and
        customs, 193, 196, 203
    when it does and doesn't work,
        193–96, 203
internet, 83–84, 87, 254, 321n, 322n
    see also social media
interrupting, 243–44, 371n
intersectionality, 57–62, 65, 71, 75, 76, 86,
        87, 89, 105, 316n
intersex condition, 229, 369n
Is God Is (Harris), 184
Islam, Muslims, 113, 114, 184, 243n, 279
isomorphic diffusion, 109
Israel, 317n
Italy, 27, 376n

Jackson, Kosoko, 345n
January 6 Capitol attack, 113, 172
Japan, 133
Japanese Americans, 209
Jaquith, Waldo, 103
Jewish people, 30, 102, 148, 150, 166, 227,
        243n, 284–85, 363n
    Holocaust and, 25, 102, 174, 285, 353n
jigsaw pedagogy, 194, 195
Jinnah, Mohammed Ali, 40
Jobs, Steve, 35
Johns Hopkins University, 190
Johnson, Janetta, 134
Jordan, Jim, 300n
Jones, Owen, 165
journalism, 90–94, 269, 340n
Journal of Medical Ethics, 6
J.P. Morgan, 108
Judt, Tony, 27
judges, 55, 56, 209
Justice Department, 52

Kaminer, Wendy, 328n
Kant, Immanuel, 308n
Karkazis, Katrina, 318n
Karp, David, 85
Kaumann, Eric, 382n
Kellstedt, Paul, 325n
Kelly, Joseph, 352–53n
Kendi, Ibram X., 64, 69, 80, 122–25, 167,
        210, 241, 268, 335n
Kennedy, Anthony, 364n
kente cloth, 154
Kenyatta, Jomo, 40
Khomeini, Ayatollah, 30
Khrushchev, Nikita, 28, 304n
King, Martin Luther, Jr., 9, 50, 51, 54, 55,
        69, 276, 279, 312n, 314–15n, 346n
Klein, Ezra, 90, 91, 324n
knowledge, 135–36, 176, 353n
    experiential versus propositional, 139–40,
        145
    traditional ways of acquiring, 337n
    tripartite understanding of, 337n
Kramer, Larry, 69
Krishnan, Manisha, 227
Kuran, Timur, 334n
Kuwait, 261

Labour Party, 240
Lafontaine, Oskar, 326n
Lal, Vinay, 150
language, 67
Late Show with Stephen Colbert, The, 124
Latinos and Hispanics, 142, 155–57, 159,
        207, 211, 212, 341n
    Latinx, use of term, 142
Lavergne, Chris, 88
law
    critical legal studies, 55, 58, 166
    grand narratives about, 55
    judges, 55, 56
Lawrence, Charles, 60, 318n
Lebanon, 218
left, the, 8–9, 19, 25–26, 63–64, 75, 81, 101,
        102, 133–34, 210, 240, 244, 279
    cultural appropriation as concern of,
        149–51, 158
    New Left, 166
    nonwhites associated with, 340n
Leonard, Ralph, 212–14
levelling-down objection, 217–18
Levine, Rachel, 230
Lewis, John, 142
Lewis, William, 304n

Lexus and the Olive Tree, The (Friedman), 83–84, 321n
LGBT issues, 330n
    see also sexual orientation; transgender people
liberal democracy, *see* democracy
Liberal Democrats, 240
liberalism, 19, 20, 101, 239–40, 241, 271, 279–81, 290, 377n
    core principles of, 255–57, 263, 287, 288
    core principles of, thriving societies created by, 257–60, 263
        collective self-determination helps to avoid government abuse, 258, 263
        government neutrality averts destructive intergroup competition, 259, 263
        individual freedom helps to keep the peace, 258–59, 263
    identity synthesis's case against, 241–45, 251
        citizens must be treated according to their identity groups, 245, 251, 288, 289, 373n
        group identities are the key to understanding the world, 243–44, 251, 288
        universal values and neutral rules obscure domination by privileged groups, 244, 251, 288
    post-liberalism, 279
    response to identity synthesis, 242, 245–52
        societies should strive to live up to universalist aspirations instead of abandoning them, 249–52
        understanding the world depends on paying attention to a broad set of categories, 246–47, 251
        universal values and neutral rules often exclude people in practice but are aspirational, 247–48, 251–52
    use of term, 240
Liberal Party, 268
liberals, 100–101, 209, 222, 240
    coalition-building and, 277–78
    feelings about race among, 95
life expectancy, 261
Lincoln, Abraham, 276–77, 350n
LinkedIn, 107, 329n
Little Richard, 158
lived experience and first-person content, 91, 93, 135

Locke, John, 33, 152–53, 349n
Lu, Kenny, 86
Lukashenko, Alexander, 322n
Lukianoff, Greg, 187
Lyotard, Jean-François, 29, 34, 288, 305n, 307n

Mac, Juno, 140
MacArthur Foundation, 106
MacFarquhar, Larissa, 61
Mackey, Janiece, 184
Madison, James, 351n
Madness and Civilization (Foucault), 29–31
magazines, 88, 90
Malcolm X, 69
Mallory, Tamika, 227
Marcuse, Herbert, 97, 166, 167, 169, 278, 287, 347n, 351n
marginalized groups, 10–12, 60, 64, 74, 75, 131, 135, 183, 185, 243n, 248, 250, 302n, 338n
    deference to, 130, 135, 138, 141–46, 341n
    insight of, 138, 337n
    perspective versus standpoint of, 339n
    standpoint theory and, 130
        see also standpoint theory
    universal values and neutral rules as obscuring domination of, 244, 251
Markovits, Daniel, 231
marriage, 49, 50, 69, 218, 249, 350n, 380n
Marx, Karl, 30, 43, 149, 287, 309n
Marxism, 19, 25, 27–29, 33–36, 40, 64, 149, 217, 243, 247, 278, 280, 281, 305n, 308n, 309n, 326n
    core claims of, 289
    identity synthesis and, 19, 26, 278, 287–90, 307n
Mary Lin Elementary School, 1, 3
Mastercard, 175, 177
Matias, Cheryl, 184
Matsuda, Mari, 57, 66
Mbuti, 375n
McDonnell, Mae, 109
McGhee, Heather, 365n
McKinsey & Company, 108
McNeil, Donald, 116
McWhorter, John, 124, 275, 276, 381n
media, 44, 80, 90–96, 97, 99, 105, 169–70, 240, 276, 282, 325n
    racial issues as covered in, 93–94, 325
    see also social media
medicine, *see* health care
mental illness, 31, 34, 37, 305n

meritocracy, 226, 231–35
metanarratives, 34, 36
Mexican culture, 151–52, 156–57
Michels, Robert, 350–51n
microaggressions, 12, 94, 100, 108, 187, 196,
    210, 245, 359n
Middle East, 42–43, 259
Mill, John Stuart, 43, 164, 169, 179,
    308–9n, 349n, 350n
Miller, Margaret, 357n
Mills, Charles, 338n
Milton, John, 348
minorities, 10, 11, 44, 149
    far-left policies associated with, 340n
misinformation, 130, 163, 178, 345n
Mitchell, Maurice, 267, 269, 276, 333n
Modi, Narendra, 16
moral high ground, 272–74
morality, 119, 121, 144–45, 169, 257, 349n
    and opposition to racism, 122, 123, 213
    U.S. founding documents and, 220–21
moral rebellion, 334n
More in Common, 277
Morse, Michelle, 5
Moskowitz, Henry, 363n
Movement for Black Lives, 117, 267
Moynihan, Daniel Patrick, 189
Mueller, Robert, 114
musicians, 150, 151, 157–59, 268
Musk, Elon, 178, 354n
Muslims, 113, 114, 184, 243n, 279

Narayan, Uma, 338n
narratives
    grand, 27, 29–31, 34, 36, 40, 43, 44, 55,
        66, 278, 288
    metanarratives, 34, 36
National Arts Centre, 184
National Association for the Advancement
    of Colored People (NAACP), 52,
    114, 363n, 373n
National Association of Independent
    Schools, 2
National Socialist Party of America, 102
    National Socialist Party of America v.
        Village of Skokie, 102, 104,
        105, 327n
Native Americans, 49, 340n
Nazis
    in Germany, 27–29, 166, 174
    Skokie rally of, 102, 104, 105, 327n
Nehru, Jawaharlal, 40
neighborhoods

deprived, 214–15, 250
    segregation in, 199, 200, 202
Nelson, Robert S., 150
Netroots, 141
neutral rules, 12, 20, 51, 67, 239, 245,
    246, 251, 257, 259, 262, 287, 320n,
    372–73n
    as obscuring domination by privileged
        groups, 244, 251
    as often excluding people in practice but
        aspirational, 247–48, 251–52
New Left, 166
newspapers, 88, 90, 325n
Newsweek, 90, 325n
New York, 329n
New York Post, 345n
New York State Department of Health, 6
New York Times, 69, 80, 90, 91, 93–96, 103,
    105, 109, 116, 124, 164, 172, 227,
    270, 279, 325n, 345n
Nixon, Richard, 35
nonprofit organizations, 101–6, 111, 282
North Korea, 63, 254
Nussbaum, Martha, 318n, 319n

Obama, Barack, 54, 69, 79, 94, 183, 209,
    270, 300n, 315n, 356n, 380n
objective truth, 26, 29, 34, 37, 65–66, 72,
    73, 76
Ocasio-Cortez, Alexandria, 165, 340n
O'Connor, Sandra Day, 209–10
Office, The, 345n
Oliver, Jamie, 150
Omar, Ilhan, 340n
180ism, 281
On Grammatology (Derrida), 45
On Liberty (Mill), 169, 349n
optimism, 69, 250
Orbán, Viktor, 161
Order of Things, The (Foucault), 305n
organizations, see institutions
Orientalism (Said), 42–44, 66, 150, 310n
Owolade, Tomiwa, 360n

Pacific Standard, 86
Paine, Thomas, 373n
Palestine, 41–42, 310n, 317n
panopticon, 31–32, 74, 305n
Pao, Ellen K., 165
Parks, Rosa, 276
Parsons, Julie, 2
Patel, Eboo, 265–67, 269, 276, 285
Paxlovid, 4–6, 208, 296n

peace, 258–59, 261, 263
peer pressure, 117–21, 125, 333n
People vs. Democracy, The (Mounk), 16
persuasion, 275
pessimism, 65, 69, 76, 250, 262, 351n
philanthropic foundations, 105–6, 201, 340
Phule, Jyotirao, 373n
Place for Wolves, A (Jackson), 345n
Pod Save America, 270
Poizner, Steve, 220
Poland, 30, 158
police, 10, 51, 60, 94n, 103, 105, 106,
         124, 136–37, 139, 162–63, 175, 176,
         248, 340n
policies, *see* public policies
politics, 64, 67, 71, 119, 278
    Black Americans and, 340–41n
    debate in, 176–79
    elections, 256, 351–52n
        free speech and, 165, 170, 172–73, 181,
            352n
        midterm, 270, 332n
        presidential, 80, 113, 114
    polarization in, 84, 90, 170, 172, 173,
        276–77
    refusal of, 35–36
    role of experience in, 140
    shifting views in, 275–76
    solidarity in, 143–46
    standpoint theory and, 135, 141–43
Pollen, Jared Marcel, 336n
Pollyanna, 356n
populism, 16–18, 84, 169
Posey, Kila, 1, 3–4, 184
postcolonialism, 9, 40, 41, 44–45, 47, 55, 61,
         65, 76, 99, 149
Postmodern Condition, The (Lyotard),
         34, 307n
postmodernism, 9, 19, 34–36, 40, 43–47,
         55, 61, 65, 67, 76, 99, 149, 278, 288
    critical legal studies, 55, 58, 166
    Foucault in, *see* Foucault, Michel
    race and, 55–56
poverty, 212, 214–15, 217, 248, 250
power, 33, 37, 66, 115, 232, 243n, 244, 246,
         248, 253, 256, 319n
    Foucault on, 33, 37, 44, 73, 306n
    government neutrality and, 259
    in institutions, 171, 351n
    struggles for, 258–59
powerlessness, and tolerance of dissent,
         115, 121
prejudice, 200

expanded conception of, 187
intergroup contact and, 192–93
presidential elections, 80, 113, 114
Pressley, Ayanna, 141–42
prisons, 10, 31–32, 51, 175, 230, 231,
         234, 248
    panopticon, 31–32, 74, 305n
progress
    denial of and skepticism about, 32, 34, 36,
         50, 69, 70, 241, 250–51
    false promise of, 29–33
progressives, 8–9, 19
progressive separatism, 4, 20, 131, 183–204,
         225–26
    counterproductive effects of, 194–96
        competition and, 195–96
        goals and, 195
        lack of support and, 196
    and encouraging whites to embrace race,
         184, 197–99, 359n
    rise of, 185–88
    in schools, 1–4, 106, 268
    in universities, 184, 188, 194, 201, 203
    white identity and, 188–90
proletariat, 27, 30, 33, 35, 37, 44, 149, 243,
         288, 289, 304n
property rights, 152–53
Proposition 187, 220
prostitution, 140
public policies, 65, 70–71, 76, 80, 106, 132,
         140, 172, 209, 226
    compelling interest and, 221, 224
    disparate racial outcomes of, 335n
    and free speech as safety valve, 170,
         173–74, 181
    group decisions on, 119
    identity-sensitive, 131–32, 205–24, 225,
         226, 239, 245, 268, 373n
        embrace of, 209–12
        equity, *see* equity
        legal framing of, 221–22, 224
        race-sensitive, use of term, 364n
    and race blindness versus racism
         blindness, 212–14
    race-conscious, use of term, 364n
    race-neutral, 212, 214–16, 219, 223, 224,
         279, 375n
    and representatives of marginalized
         groups, 142–43, 339n
    U.S. founding documents and, 220–21
public utilities, 177, 354n
publishers, 163, 168, 179, 268, 282, 354n
Pulp, 338n

punishment, 31, 73, 74, 180
Putin, Vladimir, 326n

race abolitionism, 186
race and ethnicity, 9, 12–15, 20, 74, 75,
    80, 84, 243–44, 262, 278, 280,
    284–85, 302n
  blindness to, 3, 66, 210
    blindness to racism versus,
      212–14, 365n
  critical race theory and, 58–62, 65, 66,
    76, 79, 99, 185, 315n, 321n, 372n
  health care and, 4–7, 14, 17, 70, 131,
    207–8, 211–12, 218, 223, 245, 290,
    296–99n, 335n, 363n
  mixed-race people, 14
  as one part of understanding the world,
    246–47, 251
  postmodernism applied to questions of,
    55–56
  as social construct, 46, 68, 185–86, 356n
  of white people, 188–90, 197–99, 203–4,
    359n, 360n
race-conscious policies, use of term, 364n
racecraft, 186
race-neutral policies, 212, 214–16, 219, 223,
    224, 279, 375n
race-sensitive policies
  use of term, 364n
  see also identity-sensitive public policies
racial-diversity training, 107–8, 110, 122,
    123, 134, 189, 197, 245, 268, 269,
    357n, 359n
racial equity, 57
  funding for, 106
racial inequality, 94
  race-neutral policies and, 214–16,
    223, 375n
racism, 8, 63–64, 79–80, 110, 115, 134, 209,
    216, 227, 248
  antiracism and, 122–26, 270
  blindness to, 212–14, 223, 365n
  capitalism and, 123, 335n
  civil rights movement and, 19, 49–58,
    61–62, 70, 209, 248, 363n, 372n
  free speech and, 165, 167, 169, 172, 351n
  institutional, 94, 368n
  intersectionality and, see intersectionality
  in marginalized group toward dominant
    group, 227, 234
  media attention to, 93–94
  meritocracy and, 232
  moral duty to oppose, 122, 123, 213
  as permanent condition, 54–57, 62, 69
  segregation, see segregation
  slavery, 49, 55, 56, 123, 162, 165, 209,
    214–16, 223, 253–54, 276, 277,
    314n, 315n
    reparations for, 215–16, 223, 366n
  structural, 80, 94, 226–28, 234, 338n,
    368n
  white allies and, 134, 135
  white people as racist, 123–24, 126
Ramsay, Gordon, 150
Rauch, Jonathan, 180, 181
Rawls, John, 383n
rebozos, 155
Reddit, 88, 165
Redmayne, Eddie, 134
Reed, Adolph, Jr., 211, 216, 217, 278
regulations, 173
relativism, 318n
religion, 8, 9, 14, 15, 25–26, 144, 184, 192,
    197, 218–19, 243n, 246, 247, 257–59,
    278–80, 284–85, 377n
  Buddhists, 278, 279, 281, 383n
  Christians, 218, 243, 253, 278, 279, 281
  Muslims, 113, 114, 184, 243n, 279
  schools and, 361n
reparations, 215–16, 223, 366n
Republican Party, 114, 142, 162, 220,
    276–77, 332n
reputational cascades, 120, 334n
right, the, 13–14, 16–18, 84, 279
  criticism of identity synthesis as aid to,
    122, 334n
  cultural influences and, 149
  drift toward, 275
  free speech and, 165, 168, 174
Rights of Man (Paine), 373n
Robinson, James A., 352n
Robinson, Jean, 317n
Rock, Chris, 371n
Rodriguez, Grace, 151–52, 156–57
Roe v. Wade, 317n
Rome, ancient, 254, 359n
Romney, Mitt, 332n
Rossman, Gabriel, 110
Rowling, J. K., 91
Russia, 84, 114
Rustin, Bayard, 143, 198–99

safety, safetyism, 2, 108, 185, 187, 188,
    194, 203
Said, Edward, 41–44, 47, 65, 66, 74, 76,
    150, 310n

Said, Hilda and Wadie, 41
Salon, 88
Sandel, Michael, 231, 232
Sanders, Bernie, 340n
Sandoval, Chela, 66
San Francisco, Calif., 7
Sarah Lawrence College, 100
Sarsour, Linda, 317n
Sartre, Jean-Paul, 28, 288, 305n
SATs, 123, 366n
Saudia Arabia, 260
Save Our State (SOS), 220
Scalia, Antonin, 221
schools and education, 11, 183, 220, 231,
        232, 245, 250, 261, 286, 360n, 373n
    bullying in, 194
    in deprived neighborhoods, 214, 215
    funding for, 202, 226, 361n
    laws on content taught in, 162
    private, 2, 53, 361n
    progressive separatism in, 1–4, 106, 268
    religion and, 361n
    segregation in, 2, 49, 50, 52–54, 56, 184,
        185, 209, 372n
Schröder, Gerhard, 326n
Schwarzenegger, Arnold, 220
science, 31, 34, 44, 46, 65–66, 169, 181, 254,
        307n, 337n, 377n
Scott, Tim, 142
segregation, 49–52, 123, 199, 202, 214, 248,
        276, 360n
    in housing, 199, 200, 202
    integration, 19, 50, 62, 131, 183, 185,
        200–202, 204, 219, 225, 372–73n
        Bell's case against, 51–54, 57
        case for, 199–203
        empathy and cohesion and, 190–93
        and potential of intergroup contact,
            192–93
    persistent forms of, 199–200
    in schools, 2, 49, 50, 52–54, 56, 184, 185,
        209, 372n
self-determination, 258, 260, 261, 263, 281
Selma to Montgomery march, 209, 315n
Sen, Amartya, 258, 335n
separatism, progressive, 4, 20, 131, 183–204,
        225–26
    counterproductive effects of, 194–96
        competition and, 195–96
        goals and, 195
        lack of support and, 196
    and encouraging whites to embrace race,
        184, 197–99, 359n

rise of, 185–88
    in schools, 1–4, 106, 268
    in universities, 184, 188, 194, 201, 203
    white identity and, 188–90
sex, 226, 228–31, 234
    age of consent and, 30, 305n
    Foucault on, 32–33
    see also gender
sexual misconduct, 104, 108, 110, 357n
sexual orientation, 4, 8, 9, 12–15, 20, 64, 69,
        75, 80, 84, 243–44, 249, 250, 262,
        278, 285, 286, 302n
    Foucault on, 32, 37, 306–7n
    homosexuality, 10, 32, 34, 63–64,
        69, 169, 243n, 248, 249, 306n,
        350n, 380n
    as one part of understanding the world,
        246–47, 251
    social media and, 85–86
sex workers, 140
shame, internalized, 273
Shatz, Adam, 74
Shelby, Tommie, 356n
Shirky, Clay, 322n
Shor, David, 116, 346n
Shrier, Abigail, 104
Sierra Club, 105, 117, 328n
silent majority, 277
Simpson, Wallis, 41
Singapore, 261
skills and talents, 232–33, 235, 261
slavery, 49, 55, 56, 123, 162, 165, 209,
        214–16, 223, 253–54, 276, 277,
        314n, 315n
    reparations for, 215–16, 223, 366n
Smith, Adam, 308n
Smith, Molly, 140
Smith, Will, 371n
social constructs, 46, 68, 185–86, 319n,
        356n
Social Democratic Party, 326n
socialism, 34, 40, 92, 149, 304n, 308n,
        309n, 340n
social media, 7, 15, 19, 51, 74, 80, 83, 84,
        88–93, 95, 96, 99, 101, 105, 109, 110,
        164–65, 170–71, 178–79, 229, 269,
        276, 281, 282, 322n, 354n
    bullying on, 283
    criticism on, 180
    Facebook, 7, 7, 74, 80, 84, 90–92, 107,
        163, 170, 171, 178, 179, 324n,
        345n, 361n
    free speech and, 163, 168, 176–80, 345n

Instagram, 68, 84, 88, 99, 180
as publishers, 354n
TikTok, 67, 84, 88, 170
Tumblr, 84–88, 93, 96, 322n, 323n
Twitter, 7, 74, 80, 84, 88, 90–92, 99, 104,
    109, 116, 163, 165, 170, 175, 178,
    179, 180, 334n
social mobility, 231, 234, 249–50
social science, 190–93
Social Security, 219
sociology, 64, 68
Socrates, 168
Sopron, 161, 162
Sotrovimab, 5
South Park, 345n
Soviet Union, 25, 27–30, 40, 56, 254, 304n
    collapse of, 63–64, 75
Spelman, Elizabeth, 138
Spelman College, 3
Spiegel, 150
Spivak, Gayatri Chakravorty, 19, 45–47, 56,
    65, 68, 75, 76, 186, 321n, 338n
Squad, the, 142, 340n, 371n
SSM Health, 299n
Stalin, Joseph, 28, 30, 304n
standard of living, 231
standpoint theory, 65, 72, 76, 86–87, 89,
    130, 131, 133–46
    claims of, 134, 137–41, 145, 146
    deference to oppressed groups in, 130,
        135, 138, 141–46, 341n
    feminism and, 135, 136, 137n, 138, 145
    "folk" version of, 137
    intuitive appeal of, 136–37, 144
    origins of, 135–38
    perspective versus standpoint in, 339n
    philosophical problems with, 138–41
    political problems with, 135, 141–43
    representation and policy choices in,
        142–43, 146, 339–41n
Stanford University, 67, 108
Stefancic, Jean, 70, 231–32, 241
Stein, Joseph, 133
Stock, Kathleen, 318n
Strangio, Chase, 104
strategic essentialism, 19, 44–47, 56, 65,
    67–69, 75, 76, 185, 290, 321n,
    323n, 338n
    progressive separatism and, 186–89, 102
Stripe, 177
*Students for Fair Admissions v. Harvard
    University*, 222
subjectivism, 318n

Sullivan, Andrew, 269
Sunrise Movement, 117
Sunstein, Cass, 119, 333n, 334n
Supreme Court, 49, 209–10, 222
    Adarand Constructors Inc. v. Peña, 221
    Brown v. Board of Education, 2, 52–54,
        56, 372n
    Fisher v. University of Texas, 364n
    *National Socialist Party of America v.
        Village of Skokie*, 102, 104,
        105, 327n
    Roe v. Wade, 317n
    *Students for Fair Admissions v. Harvard
        University*, 222
surveys, anonymous, 282

Táíwò, Olúfẹ́mi, 278
talents and skills, 232–33, 235, 261
Tatum, Beverly Daniel, 3
Tea Party, 114
television shows, 163, 345n
Tennessee, 162
Terence, 134
terrorism, 122
textiles, 154
Therpandrus, 148
30 Rock, 345n
Thornton, Big Mama, 158
Thought Catalog, 88, 93, 96
TikTok, 67, 84, 88, 170
Time's Up, 117
Tocqueville, Alexis de, 308n
Toronto Star, 157
transgender people, 7, 10, 63–64, 70,
    113, 178, 226, 228–31, 234,
    243n, 368n
Trump, Donald, 17–19, 81, 94n, 103,
    113–17, 121, 122, 125, 162, 220,
    243, 332n
    impeachment of, 300n
    Muslim ban of, 113, 114
truth, objective, 26, 29, 34, 37, 65–66, 72,
    73, 76
Truth, Sojourner, 300n
Tumblr, 84–88, 93, 96, 322n, 323n
Turkey, 343n
Twitter, 7, 74, 80, 84, 88, 90–92, 99, 104,
    109, 116, 163, 165, 170, 175, 178,
    179, 180, 334n
Tyranny of Merit, The (Sandel), 231, 232

UCLA, 210
United Arab Emirates, 261

United Kingdom, 7, 11, 39, 98, 151, 162–63, 175, 176, 184, 231–33, 240, 249, 260, 268, 276–78, 344n, 360n
Unite the Right rally, 94n, 103, 104
universal human being, 311n
universalism and universal values, 8, 11, 20, 26, 51, 62, 66, 70, 74, 131, 183, 184, 216, 233–35, 239, 241, 245–46, 257, 259, 262, 278, 287, 288, 336n, 373n
  as obscuring domination by privileged groups, 244, 251
  as often excluding people in practice but aspirational, 247–48, 251–52
  postmodernism and, 36–37, 46, 47
  rejection of, 12, 44, 189
  striving to live up to, 249–52
universities, 11, 18, 19, 64–65, 75–76, 79–80, 84, 89, 99–100, 150, 176, 199, 317–18n, 351n
  academic freedom in, 176, 268, 282, 353n
  admissions policies at, 209, 219, 220, 222, 366–67n
  conflicts invited at, 196
  controversial speakers at, 163, 284, 346n, 353n
  funding for, 354n
  historically Black, 361n
  housing at, 184, 188, 194, 201, 203, 361n
  integration and diversification of, 187–88, 200–202
  political composition of faculty at, 100–101
  progressive separatism at, 184, 188, 194, 201, 203
  scholarships and other opportunities at, 366n
  sexual misconduct investigations at, 104
  spread of identity synthesis to institutions from, 97–111
  student movements of the 1960s at, 97–98, 111
University of California, 100
University of Chicago, 353n
University of Michigan Law School, 209

VanDerWerff, Emily, 91
Vermeule, Adrian, 279
Vermont, 364n
Vice, 227
Victorian era, 32, 164
Vietnam, 260

Vietnam War, 35, 41, 165, 346n
View, The, 124
Voltaire, 175
von der Leyen, Ursula, 149
Vox, 75, 90–92, 96, 297n, 324n

Wagner, Richard, 148
Washington, George, 276–77
Washington Post, 80, 94, 95, 270, 325n
Waters, Muddy, 158
wealth, 216, 217, 232, 250, 263
"We Are the World," 134
Weber, Max, 11
Weeks, Jeffrey, 306n
welfare benefits, 220, 223, 224
"We Shall Overcome," 56–57
white people
  as allies, 134, 135
  effects of contact with Black Americans, 192–93
  identities among, 197–98
  as percentage of population, 197
  racial identity of, 188–90, 197–99, 203–4, 359n, 360n
  racism toward, 227
  as racist, 123–24, 126
white fragility, 124, 189
White Fragility (DiAngelo), 124, 189
white privilege, 3, 80, 88, 89, 94, 110, 111, 189, 195
white supremacy, 172, 196, 210, 227, 244, 265, 282, 351n
Whittome, Nadia, 167
Why I'm No Longer Talking to White People About Race (Eddo-Lodge), 134
Williams, Thomas Chatterton, 186
Williams College, 188
Wispelwey, Bram, 5
wokeness, 9, 11, 17, 19, 95, 269–71, 277, 281, 287, 325n, 334n
women, 7, 10, 37, 44, 58, 69, 136, 208, 248, 250, 276
  Black, 58–60, 62, 71, 312n, 316n
  child rearing and, 138, 337n
  defining, 46, 338n
  feminism, 33, 35, 59–61, 63–64, 68–69, 87, 89, 136, 228, 307n, 311n, 316n, 317n, 319n, 323n
  sex work and, 140
  standpoint theory and, 135, 136, 137n, 138, 145
  in Mbuti society, 375n

Women's March, 114, 115, 227, 332n
workers, 149, 307n
    see also proletariat
Working Families Party, 117, 267
World War I, 254
World War II, 27–29, 39, 118, 149, 174, 192,
    209, 254, 350n, 372n
Wretched of the Earth, The (Fanon), 309n
Wright, Jeremiah, 315n
Wu, Judy Tzu-Chun, 320n

Yale University, 100
Yarvin, Curtis, 279
Yglesias, Matthew, 90–93, 95, 324n
Yoffe, Emily, 281
YouGov, 275
YouTube, 170, 178

Zimmer, Thomas, 334n
Zionism, 317n
Zuckerberg, Mark, 345n